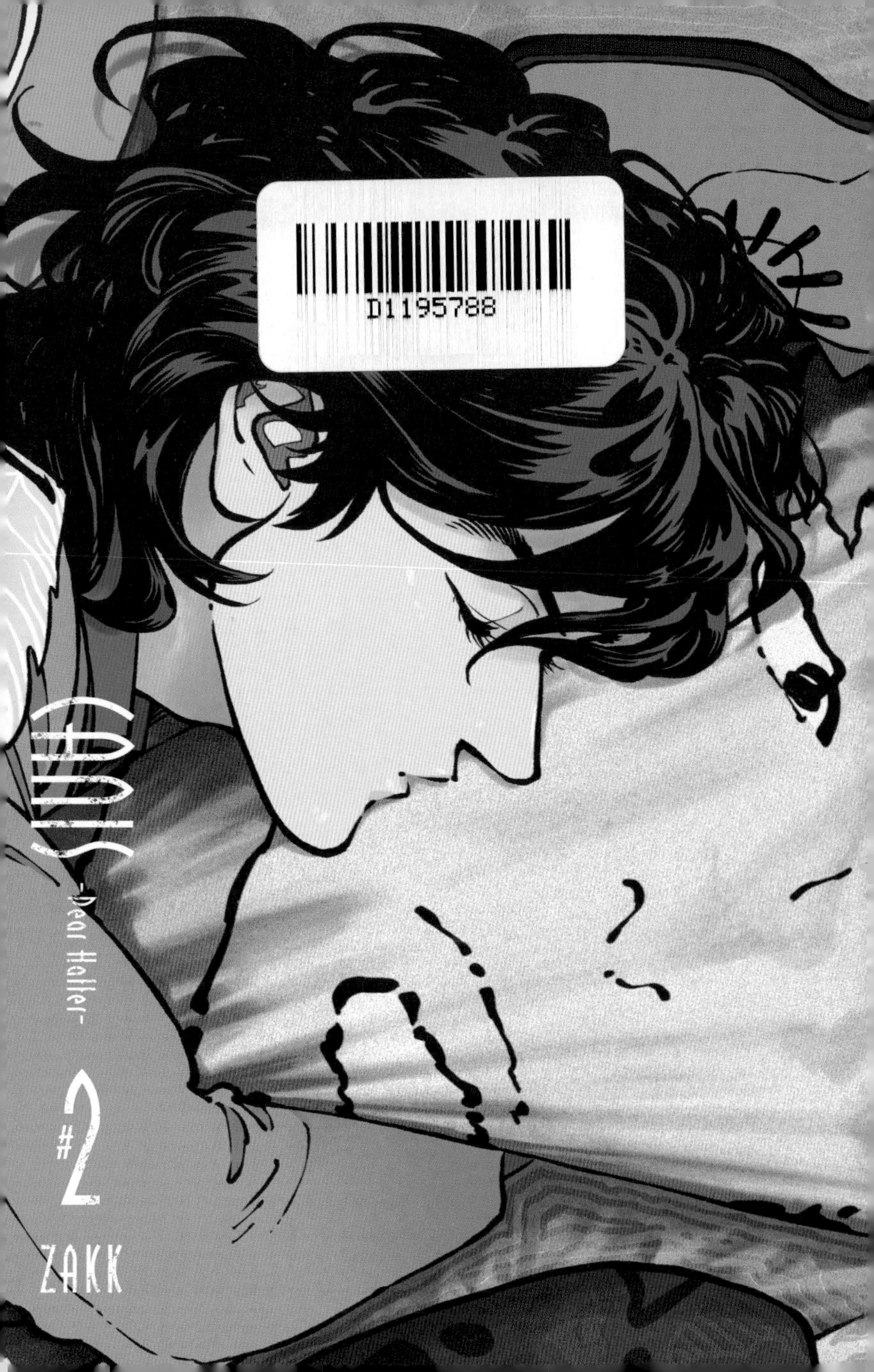
CANIS
-Dear Hatter-
#2
ZAKK

Contents

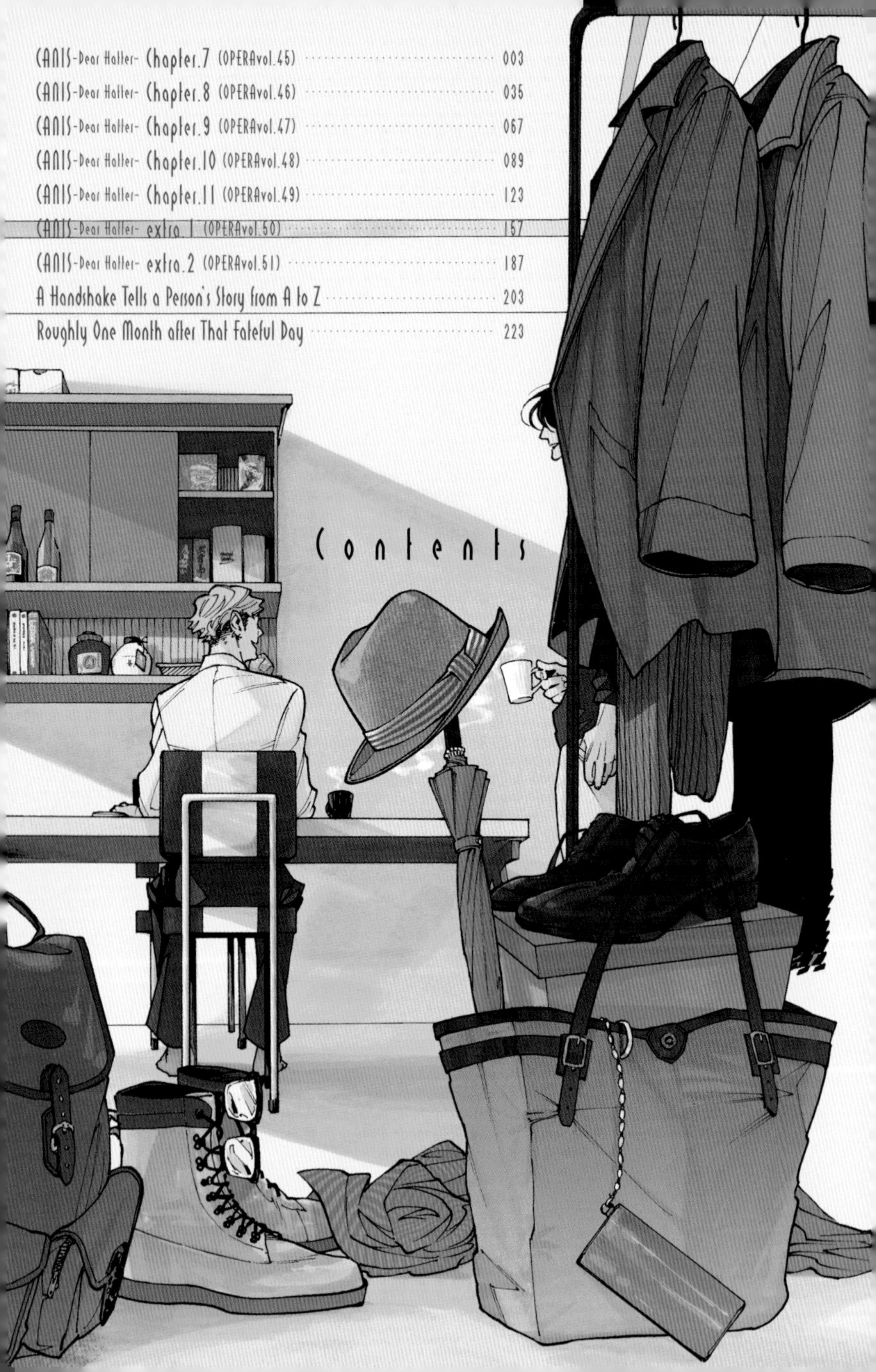

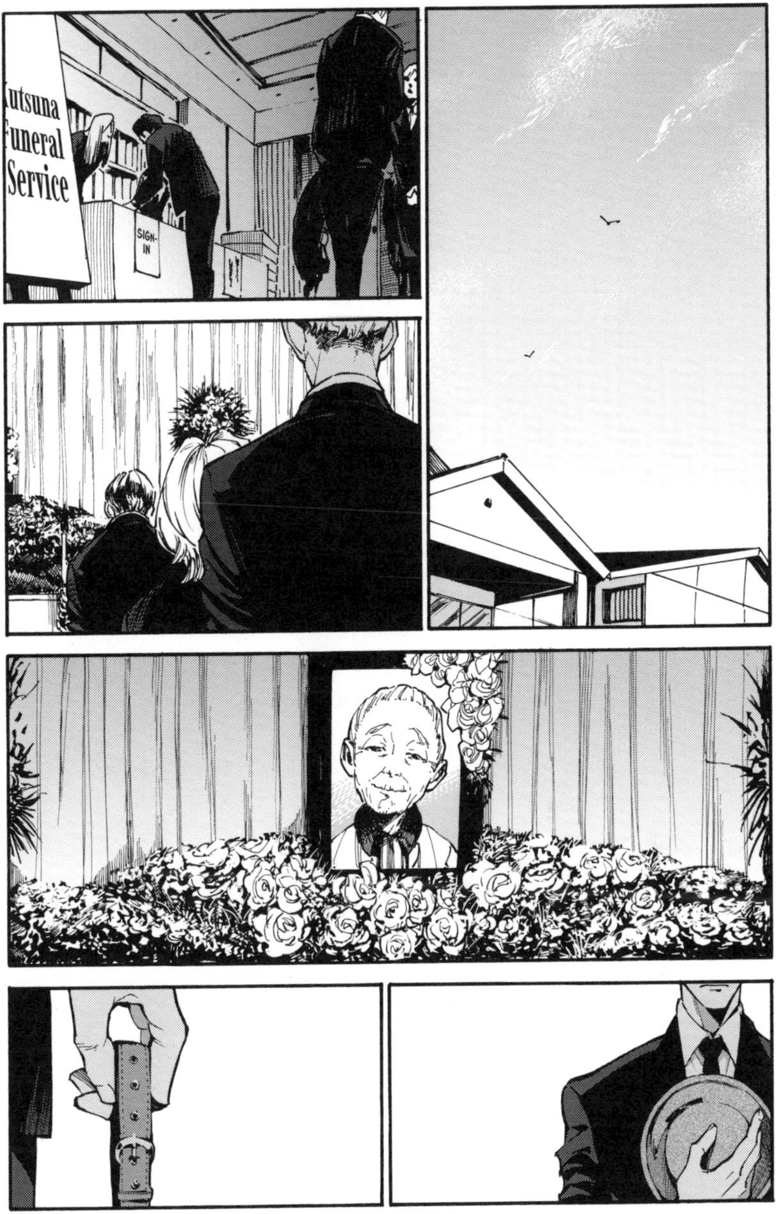
Kutsuna Funeral Service
SIGN-IN

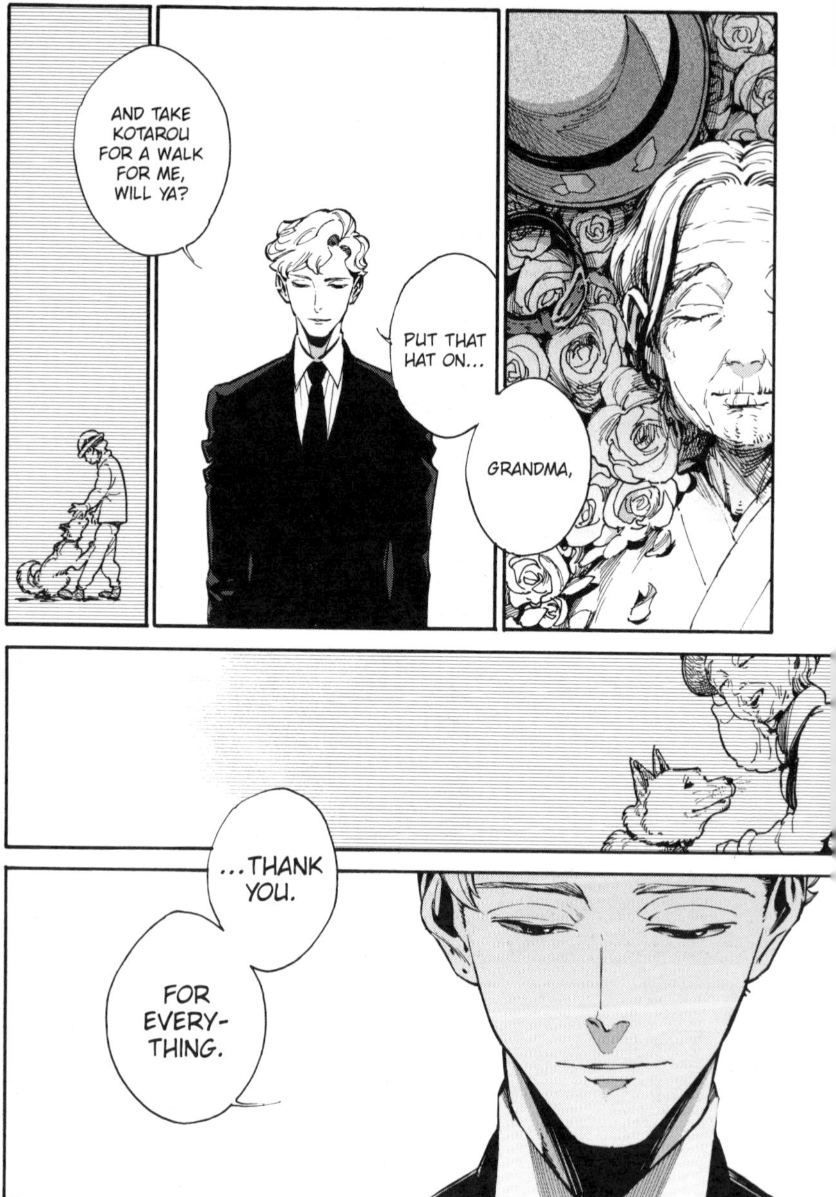
GRANDMA,
PUT THAT HAT ON...
AND TAKE KOTAROU FOR A WALK FOR ME, WILL YA?
...THANK YOU.
FOR EVERY-THING.

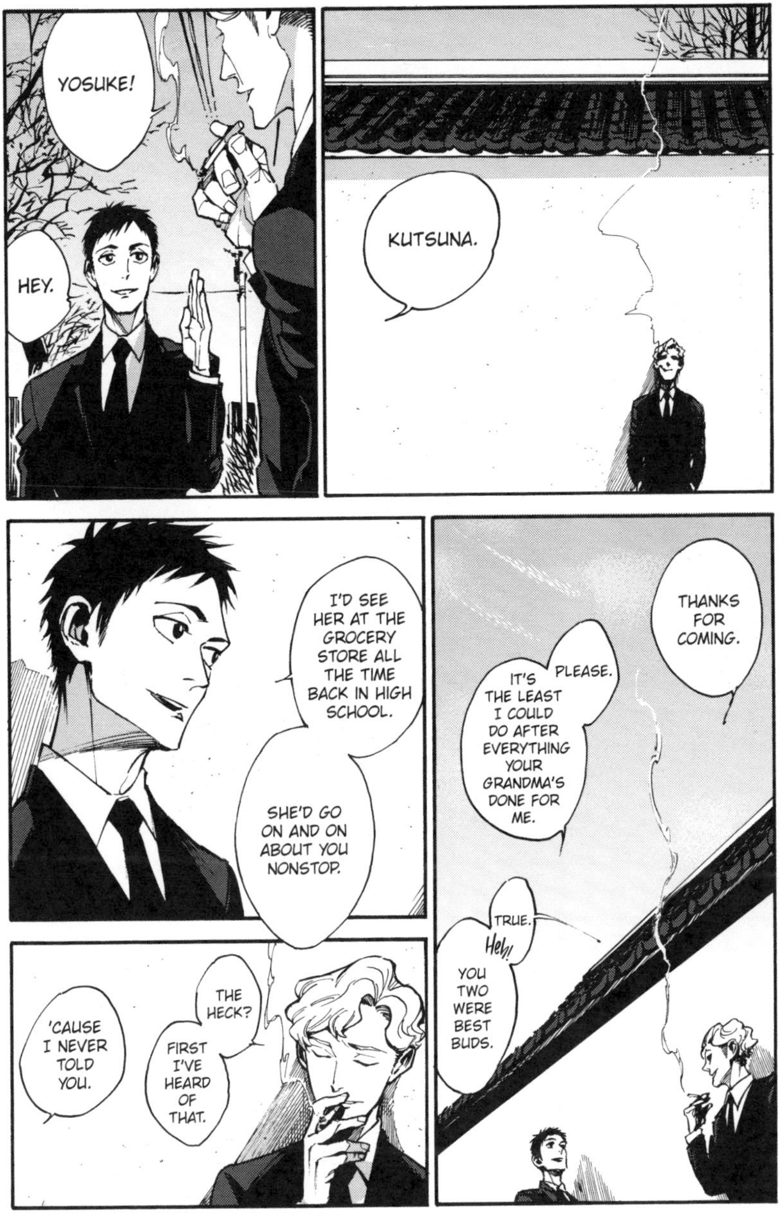
KUTSUNA.
YOSUKE!
HEY.
THANKS FOR COMING.
PLEASE.
IT'S THE LEAST I COULD DO AFTER EVERYTHING YOUR GRANDMA'S DONE FOR ME.
TRUE.
Heh!
YOU TWO WERE BEST BUDS.
I'D SEE HER AT THE GROCERY STORE ALL THE TIME BACK IN HIGH SCHOOL.
SHE'D GO ON AND ON ABOUT YOU NONSTOP.
THE HECK?
FIRST I'VE HEARD OF THAT.
'CAUSE I NEVER TOLD YOU.

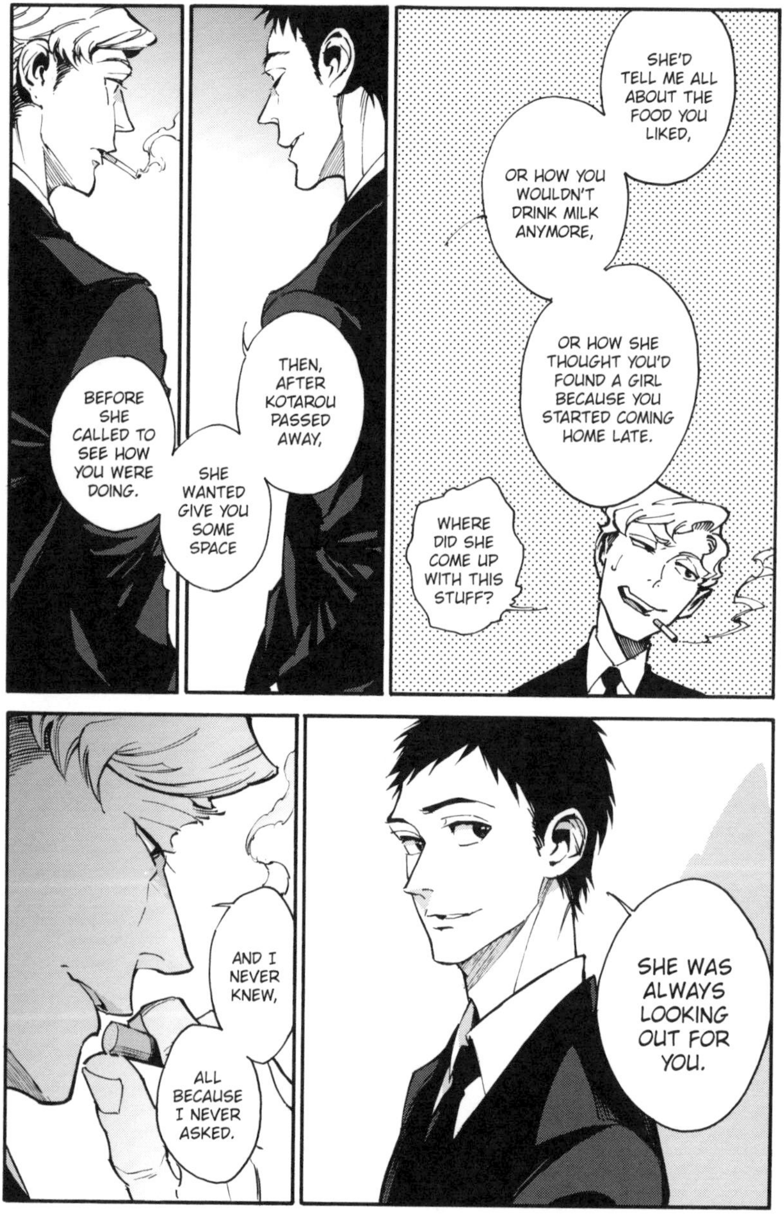
SHE'D TELL ME ALL ABOUT THE FOOD YOU LIKED,
OR HOW YOU WOULDN'T DRINK MILK ANYMORE,
OR HOW SHE THOUGHT YOU'D FOUND A GIRL BECAUSE YOU STARTED COMING HOME LATE.
WHERE DID SHE COME UP WITH THIS STUFF?
THEN, AFTER KOTAROU PASSED AWAY,
SHE WANTED GIVE YOU SOME SPACE
BEFORE SHE CALLED TO SEE HOW YOU WERE DOING.
SHE WAS ALWAYS LOOKING OUT FOR YOU.
AND I NEVER KNEW,
ALL BECAUSE I NEVER ASKED.

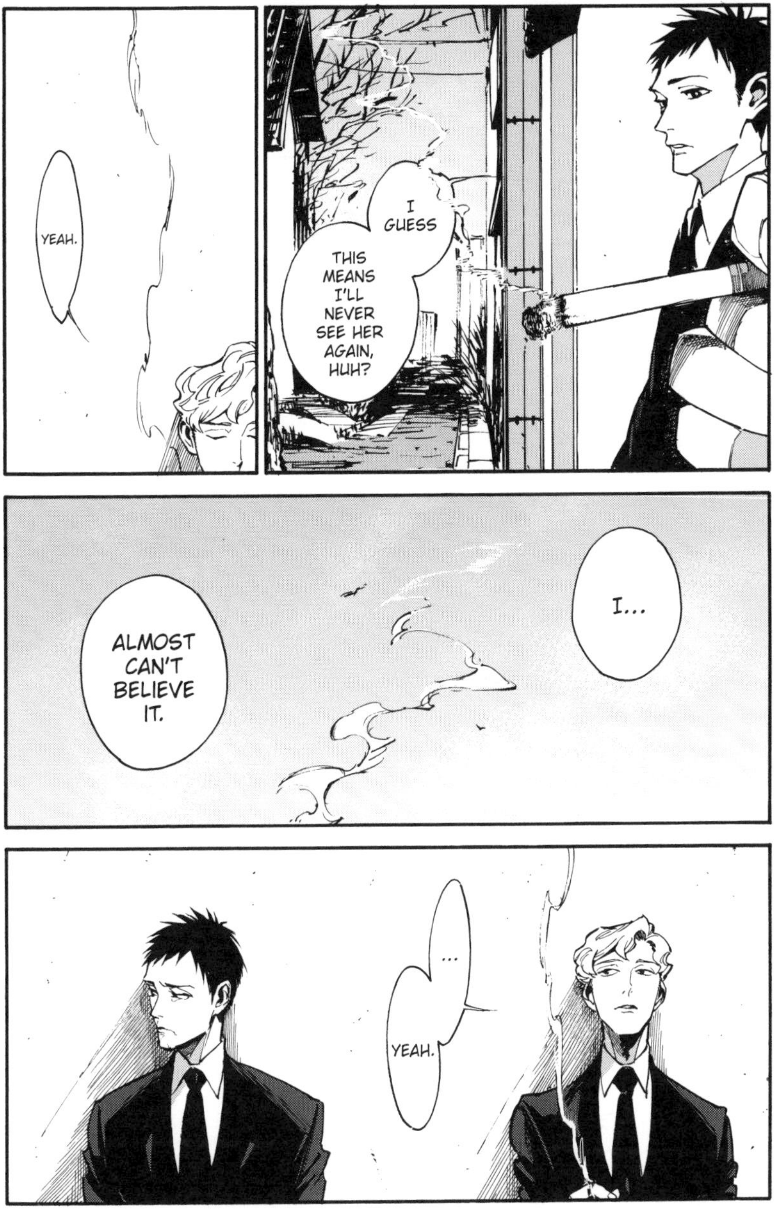
I GUESS
THIS MEANS I'LL NEVER SEE HER AGAIN, HUH?
YEAH.
I...
ALMOST CAN'T BELIEVE IT.
...
YEAH.

ME
NEITHER.

Chapter.7

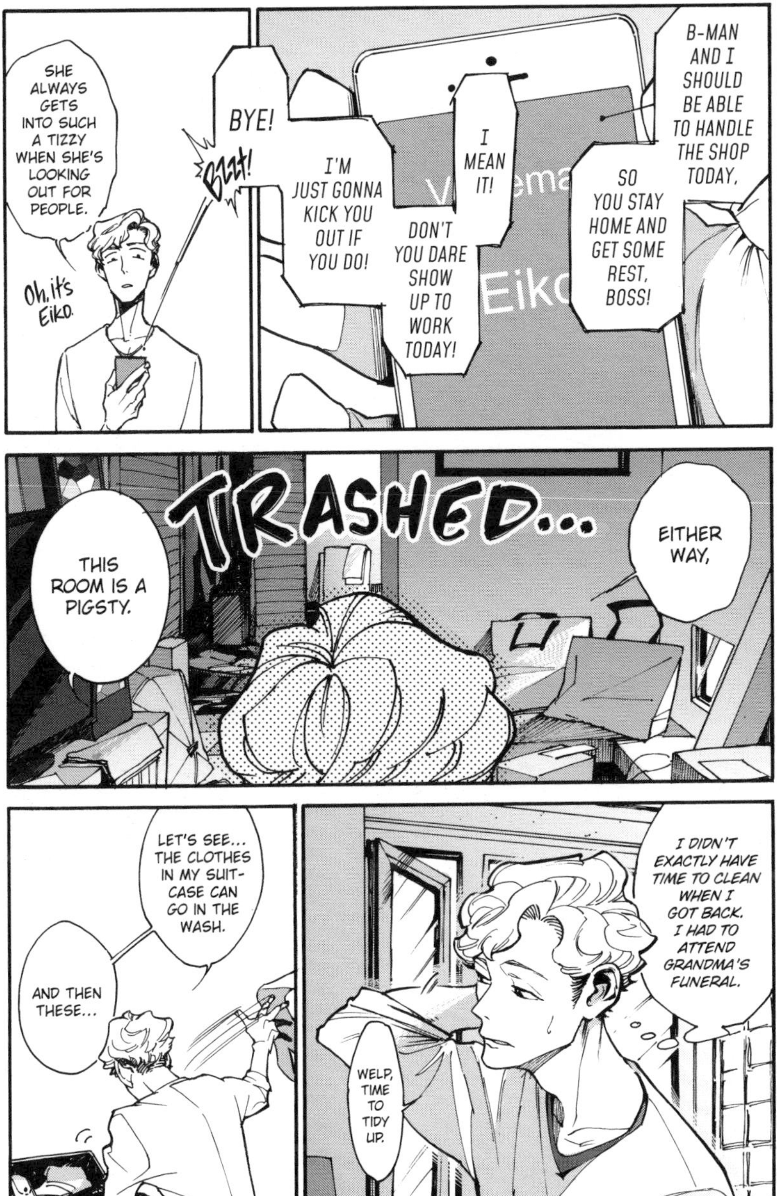
B-MAN AND I SHOULD BE ABLE TO HANDLE THE SHOP TODAY,
SO YOU STAY HOME AND GET SOME REST, BOSS!
I MEAN IT!
DON'T YOU DARE SHOW UP TO WORK TODAY!
I'M JUST GONNA KICK YOU OUT IF YOU DO!
BYE!
BZZT!
SHE ALWAYS GETS INTO SUCH A TIZZY WHEN SHE'S LOOKING OUT FOR PEOPLE.
Oh, it's Eiko.
EITHER WAY,
TRASHED...
THIS ROOM IS A PIGSTY.
I DIDN'T EXACTLY HAVE TIME TO CLEAN WHEN I GOT BACK. I HAD TO ATTEND GRANDMA'S FUNERAL.
WELP, TIME TO TIDY UP.
LET'S SEE... THE CLOTHES IN MY SUIT-CASE CAN GO IN THE WASH.
AND THEN THESE...

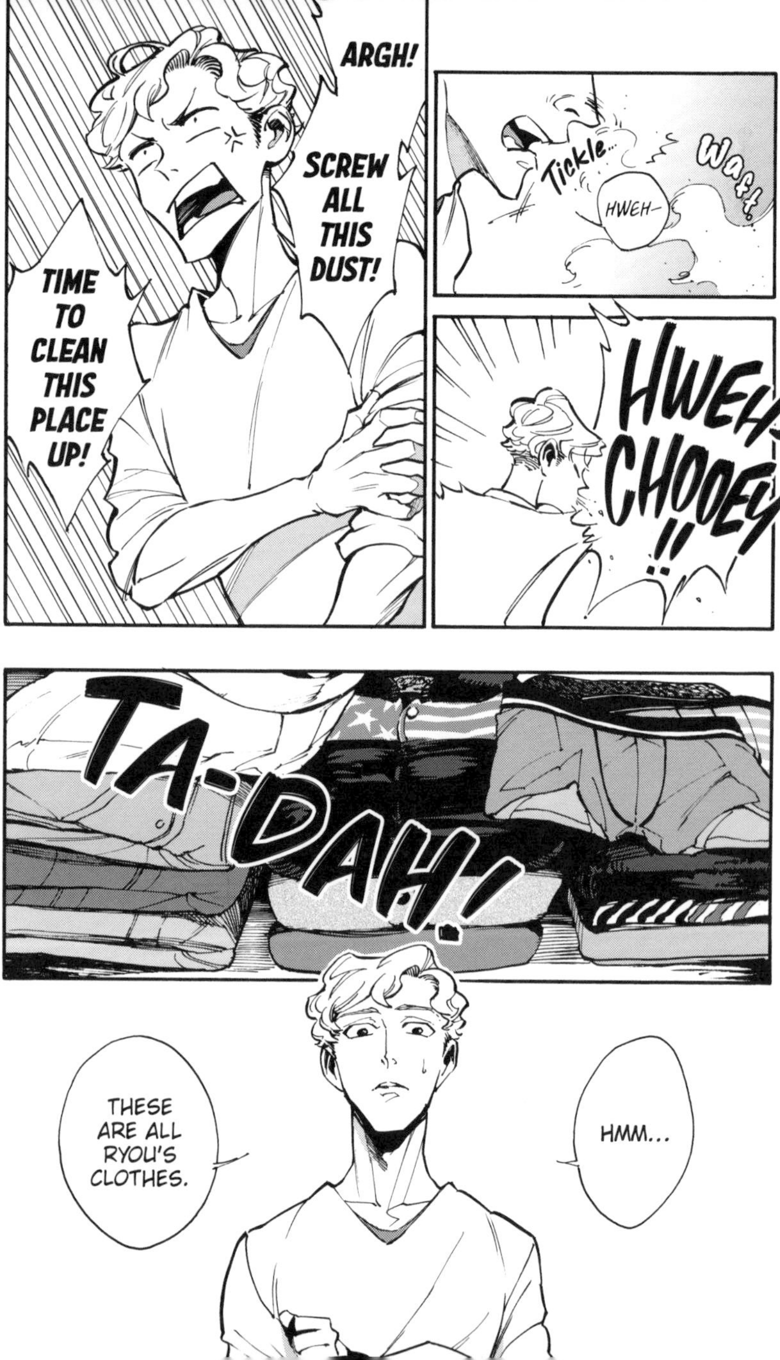

Tickle...
HWEH-
Waft
HWEH-CHOOEY!!
ARGH!
SCREW ALL THIS DUST!
TIME TO CLEAN THIS PLACE UP!
TA-DAH!
HMM...
THESE ARE ALL RYOU'S CLOTHES.

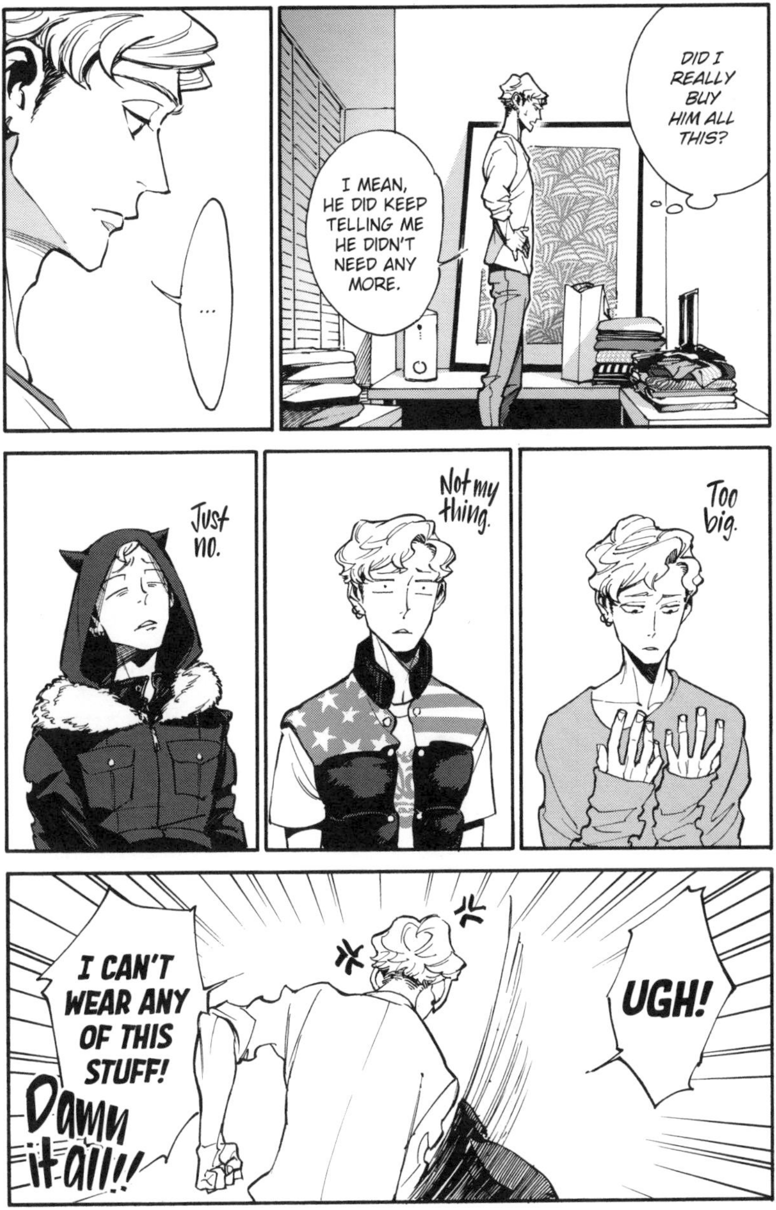
DID I REALLY BUY HIM ALL THIS?
I MEAN, HE DID KEEP TELLING ME HE DIDN'T NEED ANY MORE.
...
Too big.
Not my thing.
Just no.
UGH!
I CAN'T WEAR ANY OF THIS STUFF!
Damn it all!!

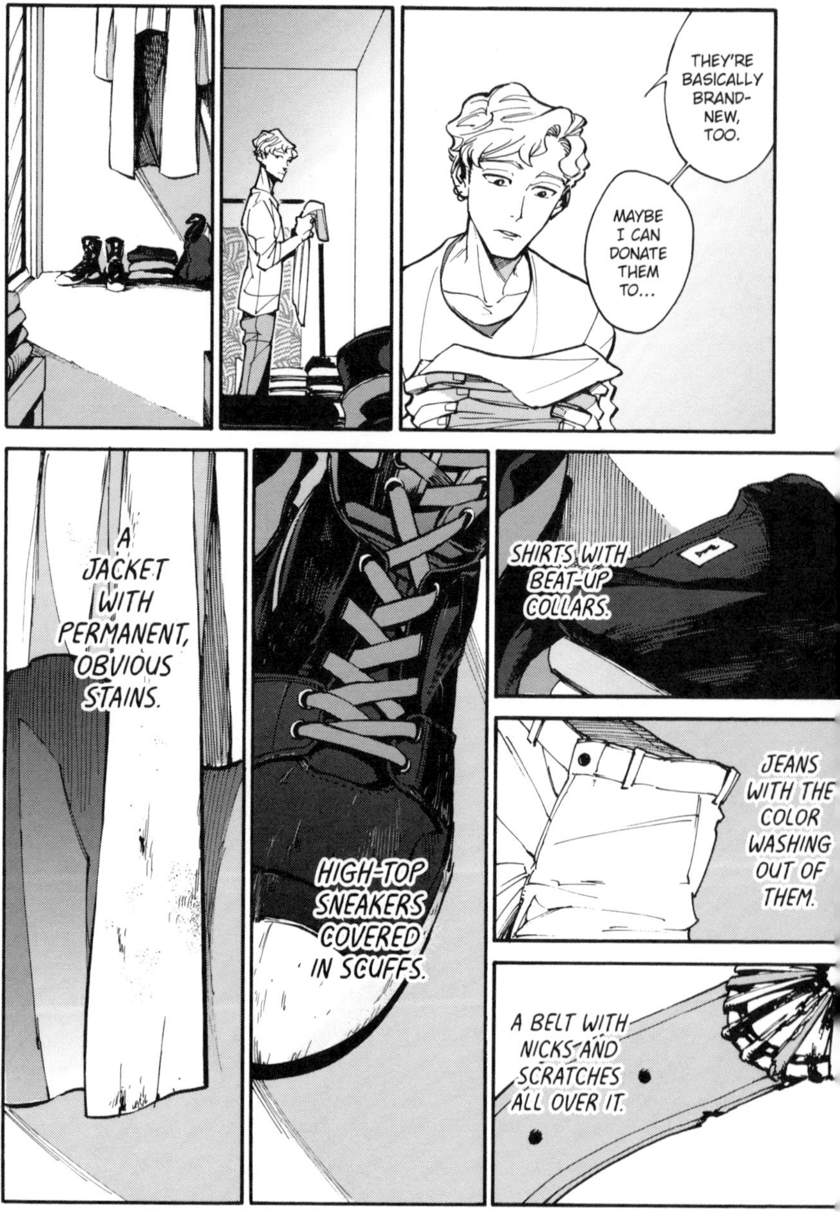
THEY'RE BASICALLY BRAND-NEW, TOO.
MAYBE I CAN DONATE THEM TO...
SHIRTS WITH BEAT-UP COLLARS.
JEANS WITH THE COLOR WASHING OUT OF THEM.
A BELT WITH NICKS AND SCRATCHES ALL OVER IT.
HIGH-TOP SNEAKERS COVERED IN SCUFFS.
A JACKET WITH PERMANENT, OBVIOUS STAINS.

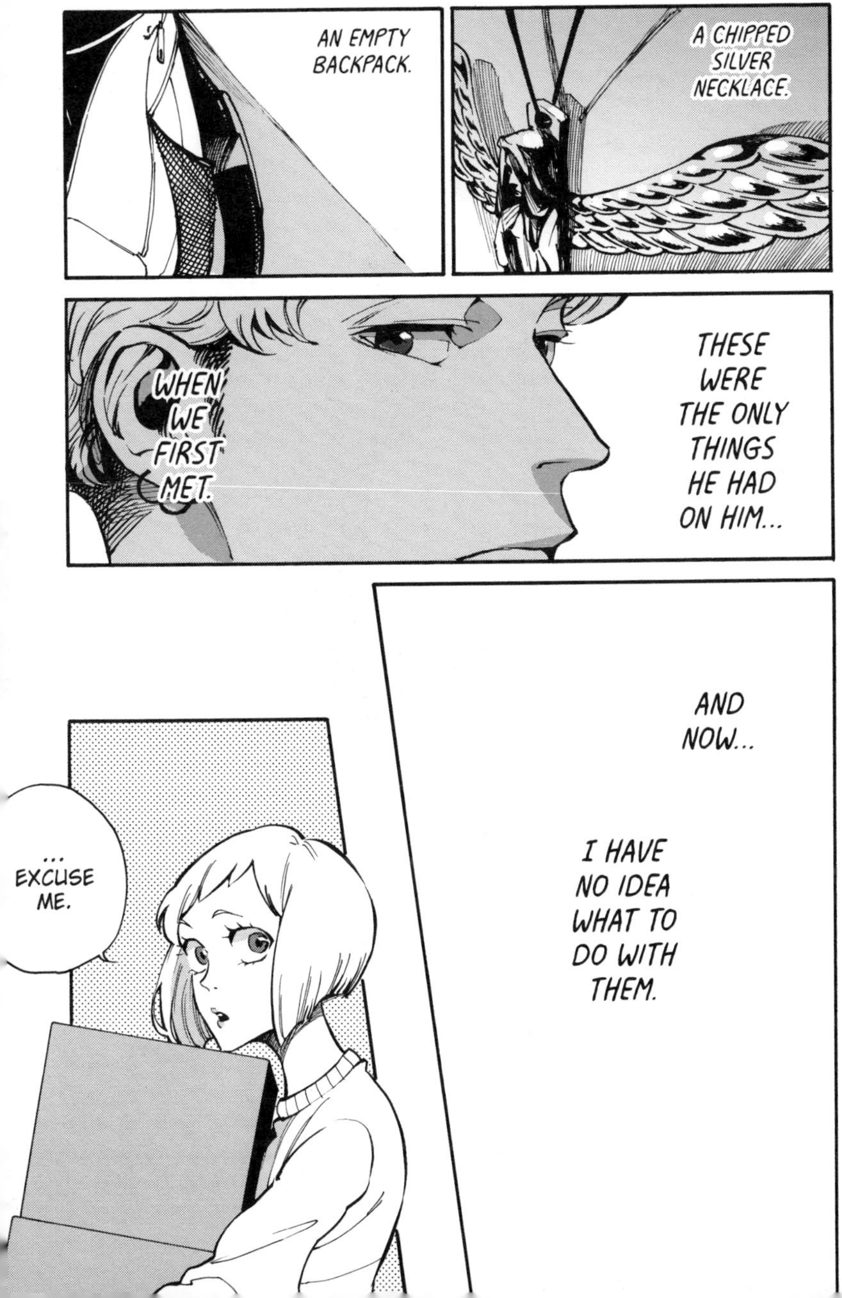
A CHIPPED SILVER NECKLACE.
AN EMPTY BACKPACK.
THESE WERE THE ONLY THINGS HE HAD ON HIM...
WHEN WE FIRST MET.
AND NOW...
I HAVE NO IDEA WHAT TO DO WITH THEM.
...EXCUSE ME.

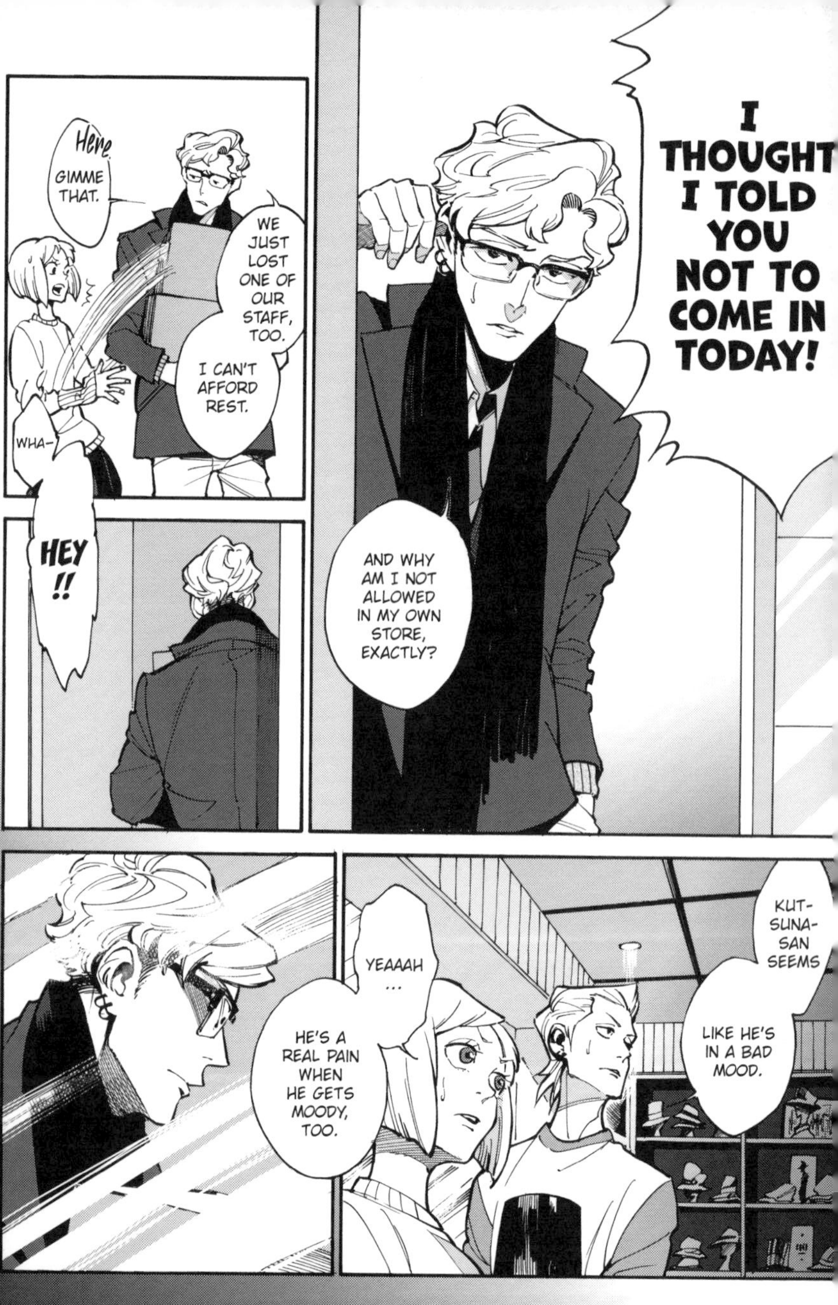
I THOUGHT I TOLD YOU NOT TO COME IN TODAY!
AND WHY AM I NOT ALLOWED IN MY OWN STORE, EXACTLY?
Here. GIMME THAT.
WE JUST LOST ONE OF OUR STAFF, TOO.
I CAN'T AFFORD REST.
WHA-
HEY !!
KUT-SUNA-SAN SEEMS
LIKE HE'S IN A BAD MOOD.
YEAAAH ...
HE'S A REAL PAIN WHEN HE GETS MOODY, TOO.

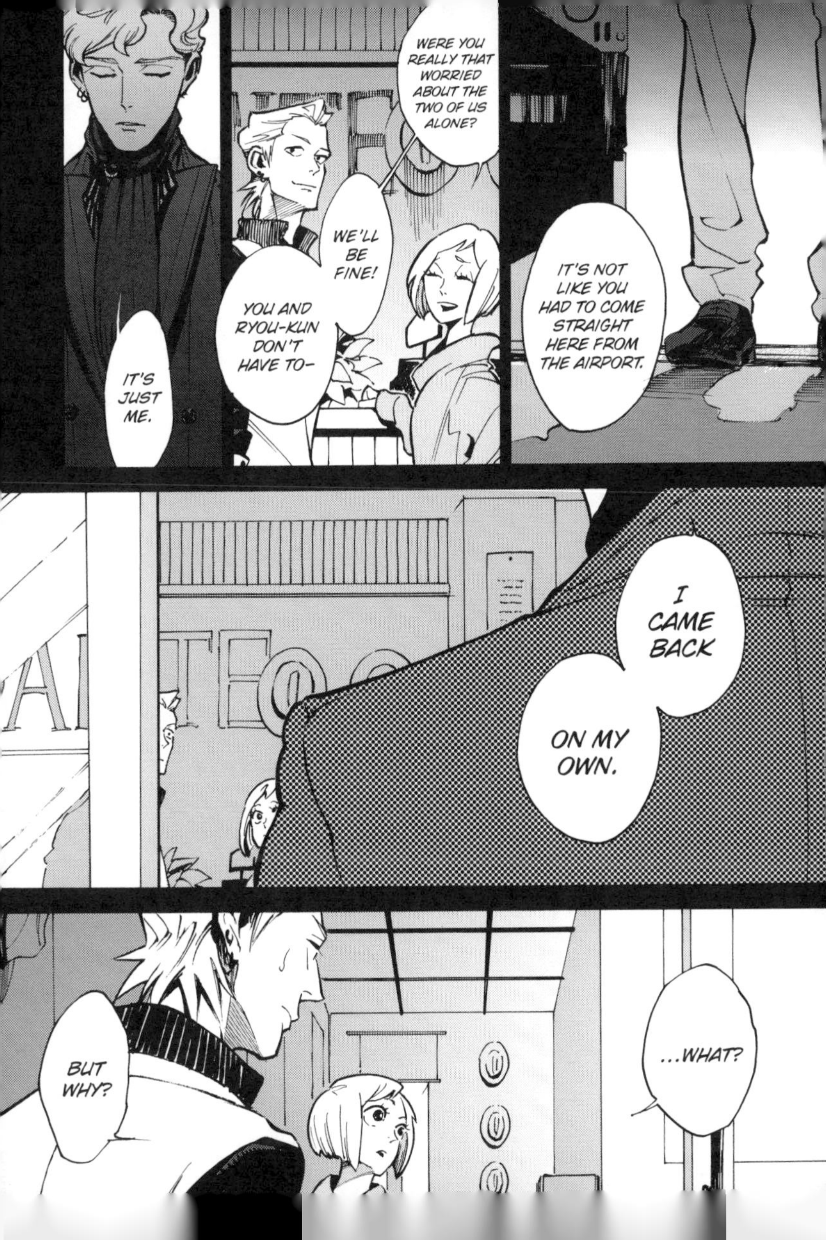
IT'S NOT LIKE YOU HAD TO COME STRAIGHT HERE FROM THE AIRPORT.
WERE YOU REALLY THAT WORRIED ABOUT THE TWO OF US ALONE?
WE'LL BE FINE!
YOU AND RYOU-KUN DON'T HAVE TO-
IT'S JUST ME.
I CAME BACK
ON MY OWN.
...WHAT?
BUT WHY?

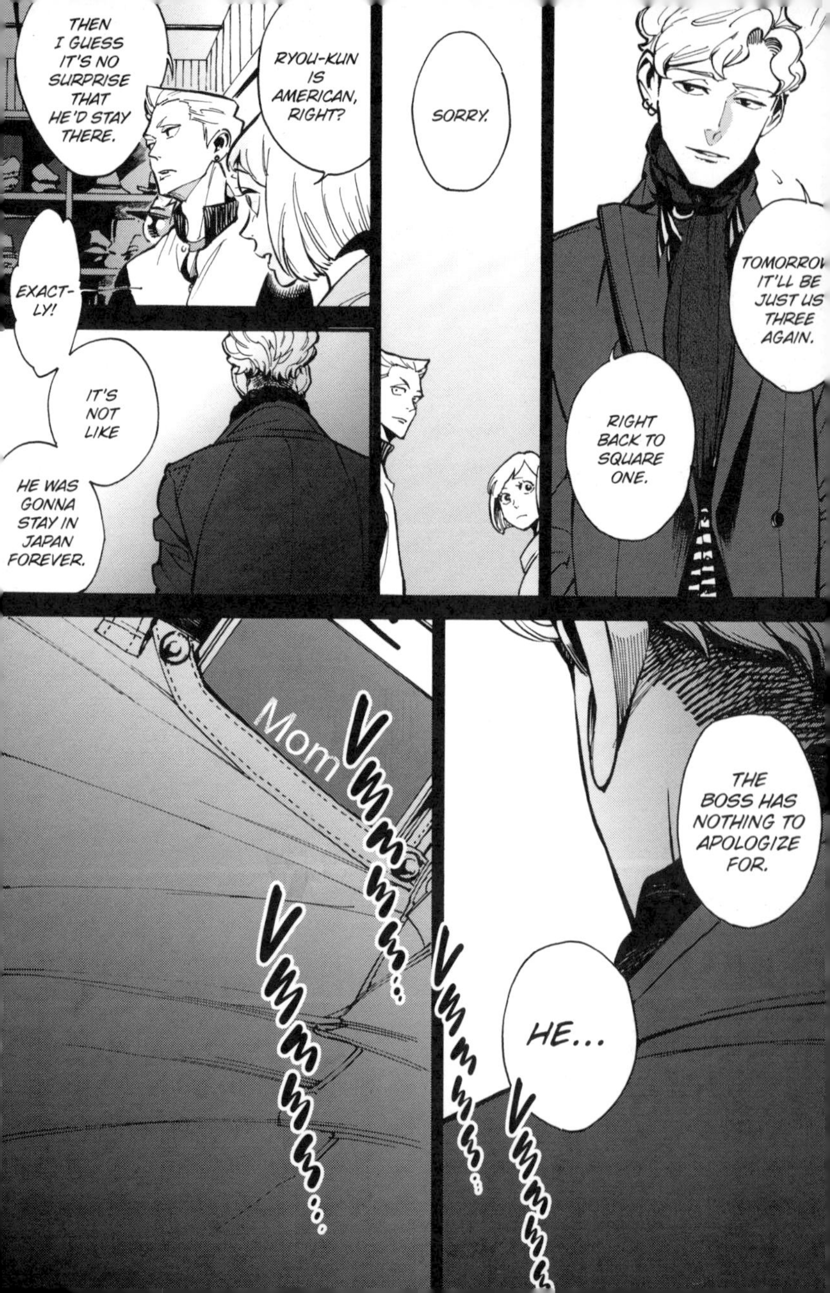
TOMORROW IT'LL BE JUST US THREE AGAIN.
RIGHT BACK TO SQUARE ONE.
SORRY.
RYOU-KUN IS AMERICAN, RIGHT?
THEN I GUESS IT'S NO SURPRISE THAT HE'D STAY THERE.
EXACT-LY!
IT'S NOT LIKE
HE WAS GONNA STAY IN JAPAN FOREVER.
THE BOSS HAS NOTHING TO APOLOGIZE FOR.
HE...
Vmmmm...
Vmmmm...
Mom
Vmmmm...
Vmmmm...

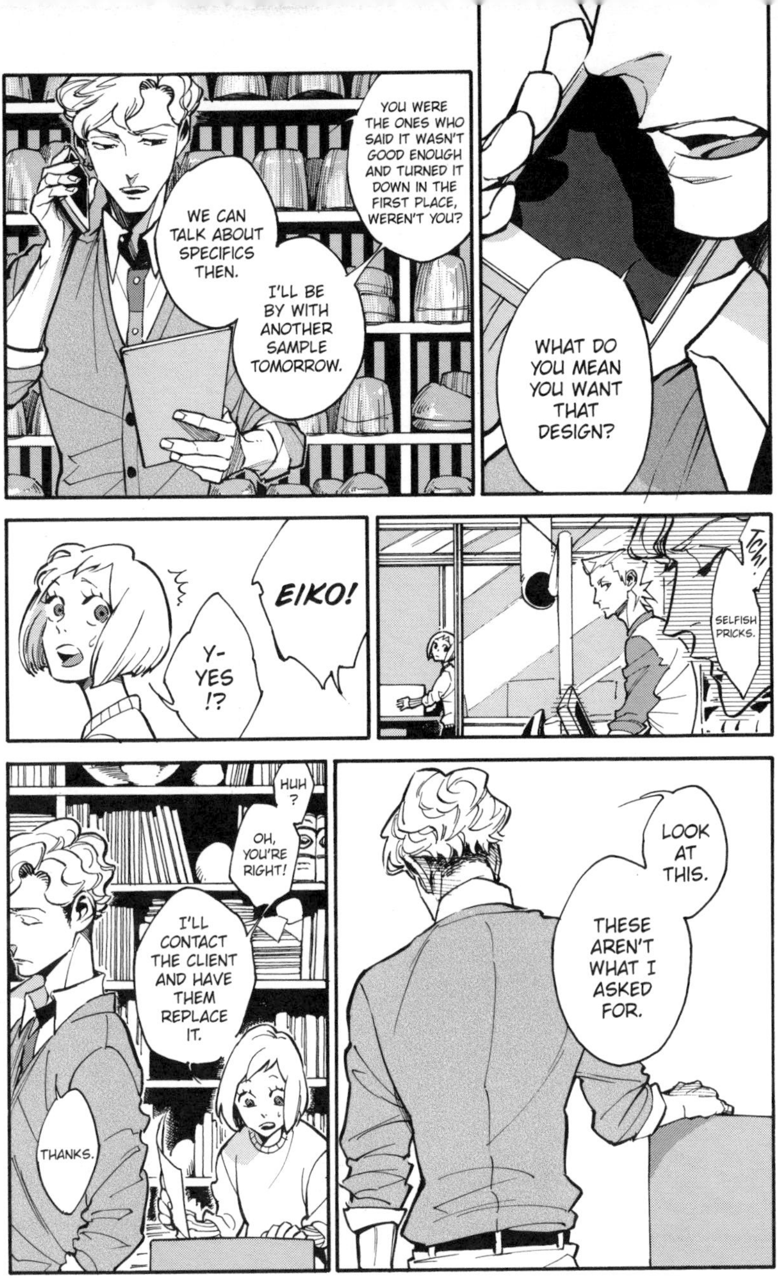
WHAT DO YOU MEAN YOU WANT THAT DESIGN?
YOU WERE THE ONES WHO SAID IT WASN'T GOOD ENOUGH AND TURNED IT DOWN IN THE FIRST PLACE, WEREN'T YOU?
WE CAN TALK ABOUT SPECIFICS THEN.
I'LL BE BY WITH ANOTHER SAMPLE TOMORROW.
TCH!
SELFISH PRICKS.
EIKO!
Y-YES!?
LOOK AT THIS.
THESE AREN'T WHAT I ASKED FOR.
HUH?
OH, YOU'RE RIGHT!
I'LL CONTACT THE CLIENT AND HAVE THEM REPLACE IT.
THANKS.

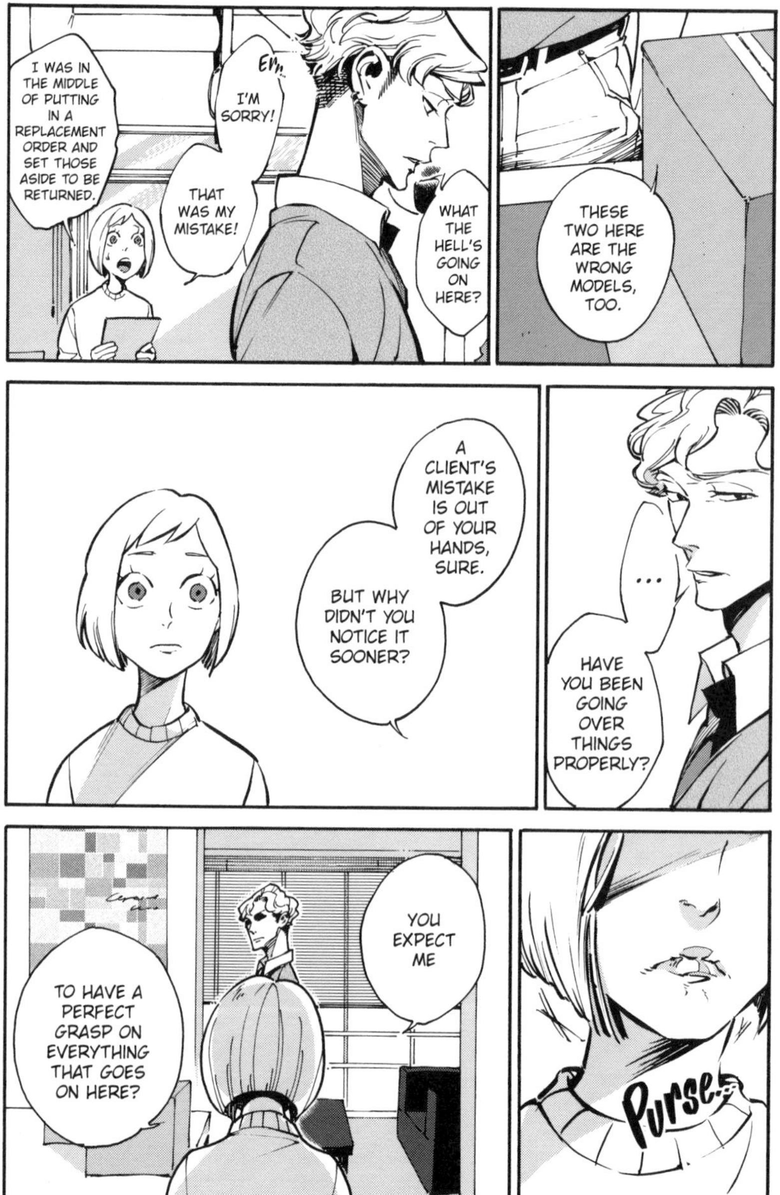
THESE TWO HERE ARE THE WRONG MODELS, TOO.
WHAT THE HELL'S GOING ON HERE?
Em...
I'M SORRY!
THAT WAS MY MISTAKE!
I WAS IN THE MIDDLE OF PUTTING IN A REPLACEMENT ORDER AND SET THOSE ASIDE TO BE RETURNED.
...
HAVE YOU BEEN GOING OVER THINGS PROPERLY?
A CLIENT'S MISTAKE IS OUT OF YOUR HANDS, SURE.
BUT WHY DIDN'T YOU NOTICE IT SOONER?
Purse...
YOU EXPECT ME
TO HAVE A PERFECT GRASP ON EVERYTHING THAT GOES ON HERE?

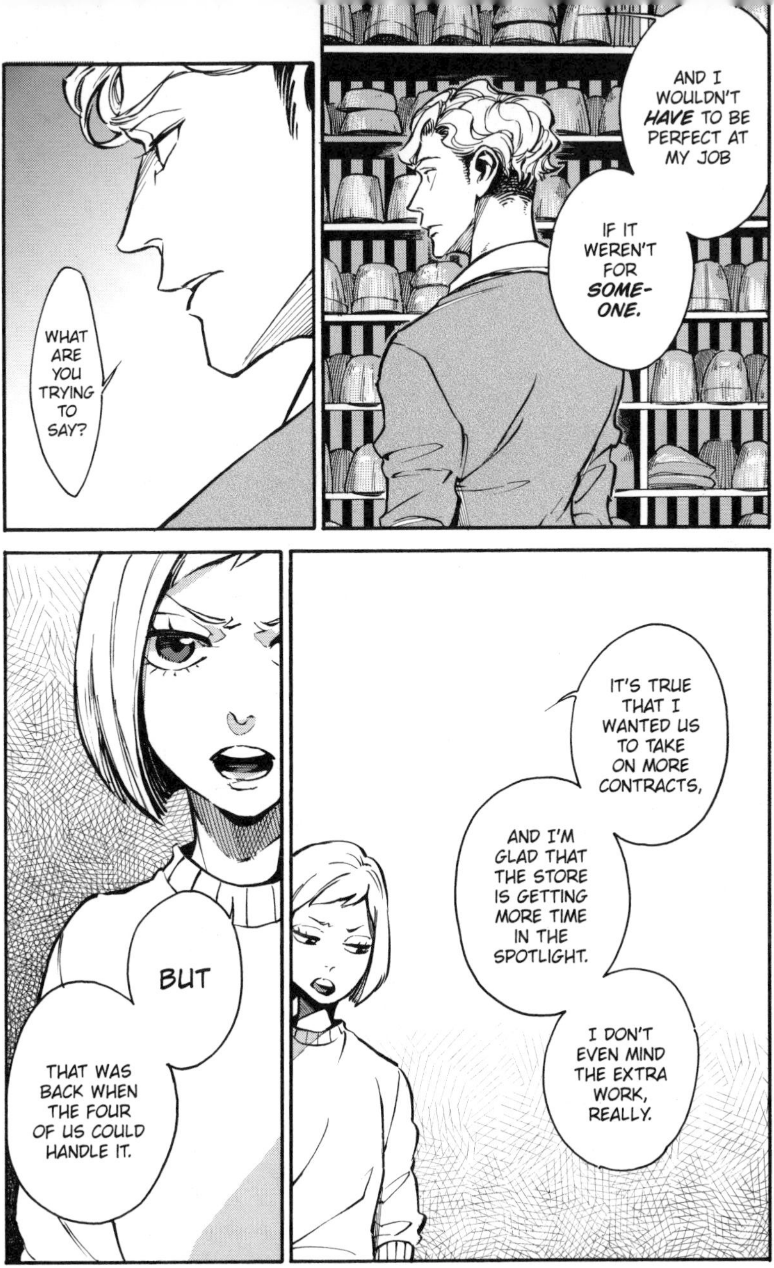
AND I WOULDN'T ***HAVE*** TO BE PERFECT AT MY JOB
IF IT WEREN'T FOR ***SOME-ONE.***
WHAT ARE YOU TRYING TO SAY?
IT'S TRUE THAT I WANTED US TO TAKE ON MORE CONTRACTS,
AND I'M GLAD THAT THE STORE IS GETTING MORE TIME IN THE SPOTLIGHT.
I DON'T EVEN MIND THE EXTRA WORK, REALLY.
BUT
THAT WAS BACK WHEN THE FOUR OF US COULD HANDLE IT.

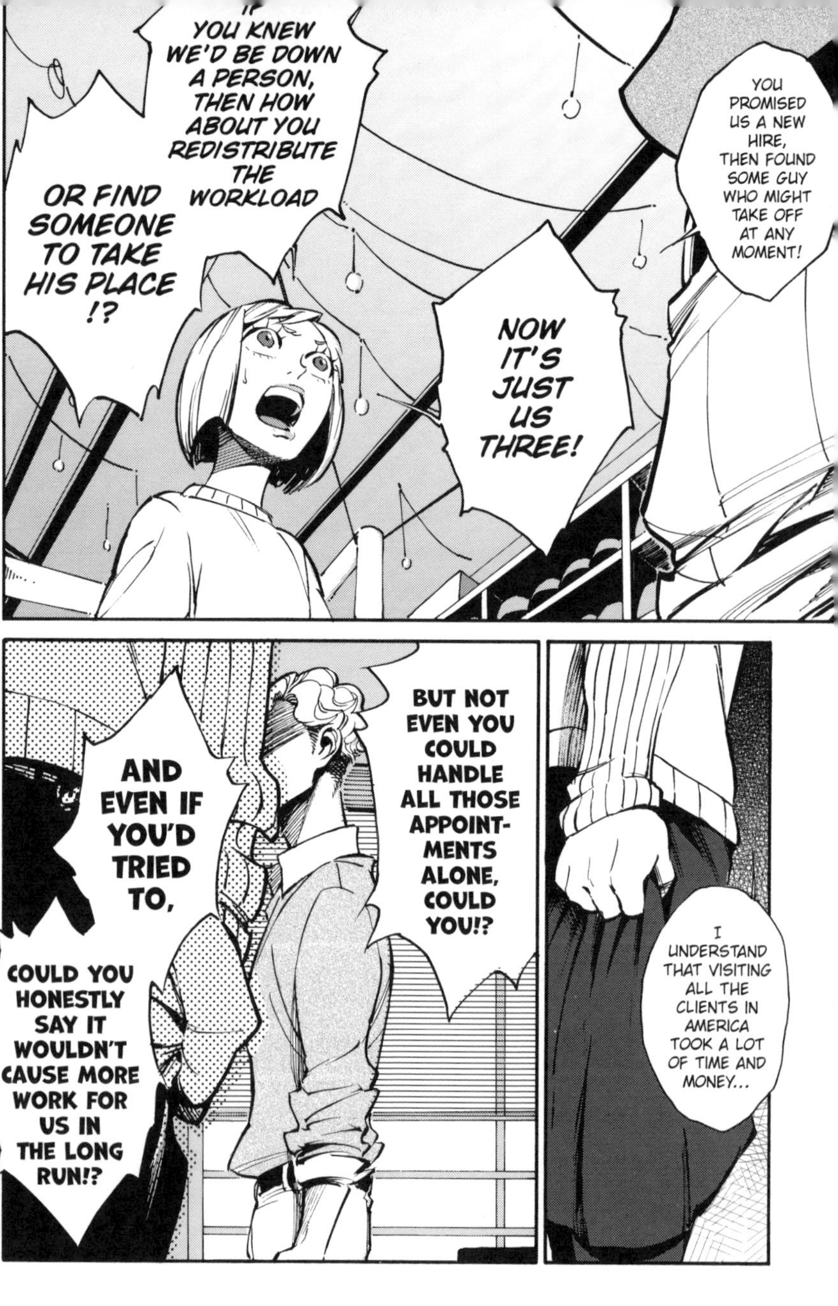
YOU PROMISED US A NEW HIRE, THEN FOUND SOME GUY WHO MIGHT TAKE OFF AT ANY MOMENT!
NOW IT'S JUST US THREE!
IF YOU KNEW WE'D BE DOWN A PERSON, THEN HOW ABOUT YOU REDISTRIBUTE THE WORKLOAD
OR FIND SOMEONE TO TAKE HIS PLACE !?
I UNDERSTAND THAT VISITING ALL THE CLIENTS IN AMERICA TOOK A LOT OF TIME AND MONEY...
BUT NOT EVEN YOU COULD HANDLE ALL THOSE APPOINT-MENTS ALONE, COULD YOU!?
AND EVEN IF YOU'D TRIED TO,
COULD YOU HONESTLY SAY IT WOULDN'T CAUSE MORE WORK FOR US IN THE LONG RUN!?

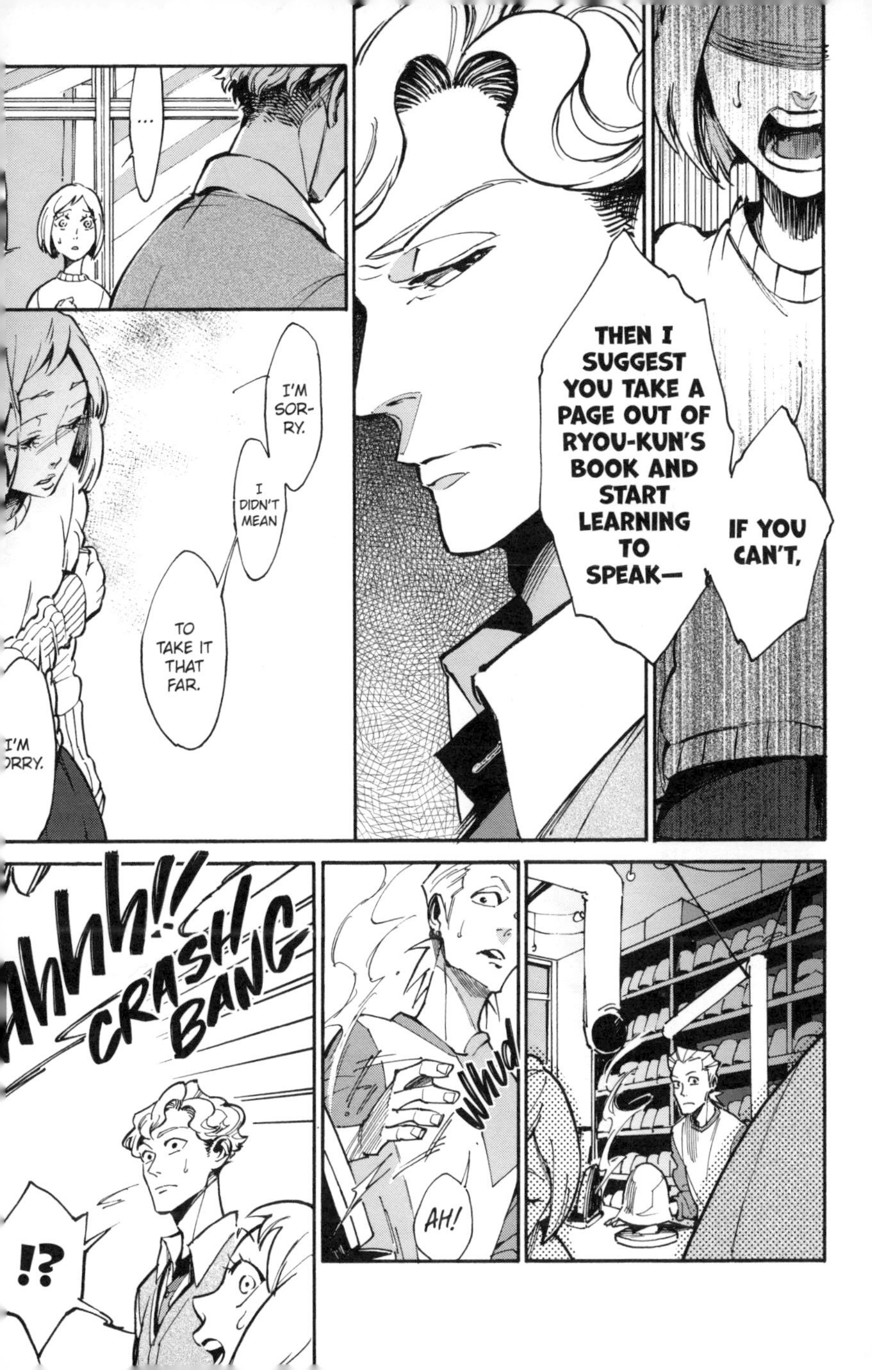

IF YOU CAN'T,
THEN I SUGGEST YOU TAKE A PAGE OUT OF RYOU-KUN'S BOOK AND START LEARNING TO SPEAK—
...
I'M SORRY.
I DIDN'T MEAN
TO TAKE IT THAT FAR.
I'M ORRY.
WHUD
AH!
Ahhh!!
CRASH
BANG
!?

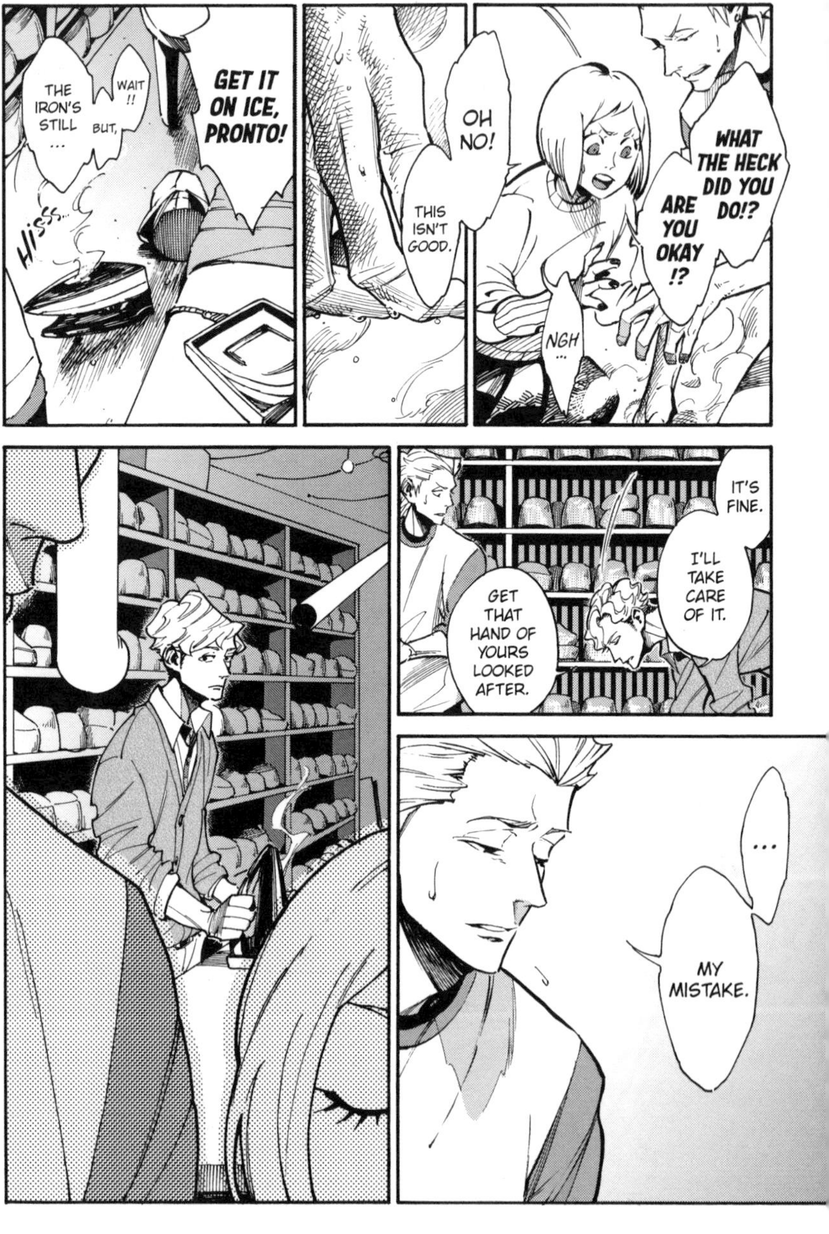
WHAT THE HECK DID YOU DO!?
ARE YOU OKAY !?
NGH ...
OH NO!
THIS ISN'T GOOD.
GET IT ON ICE, PRONTO!
WAIT !! BUT,
THE IRON'S STILL ...
HISSS...
IT'S FINE.
I'LL TAKE CARE OF IT.
GET THAT HAND OF YOURS LOOKED AFTER.
...
MY MISTAKE.

MY MIS-TAKE.

I'M SORRY.

SERI-OUSLY.

WHAT THE HELL AM I DOING?

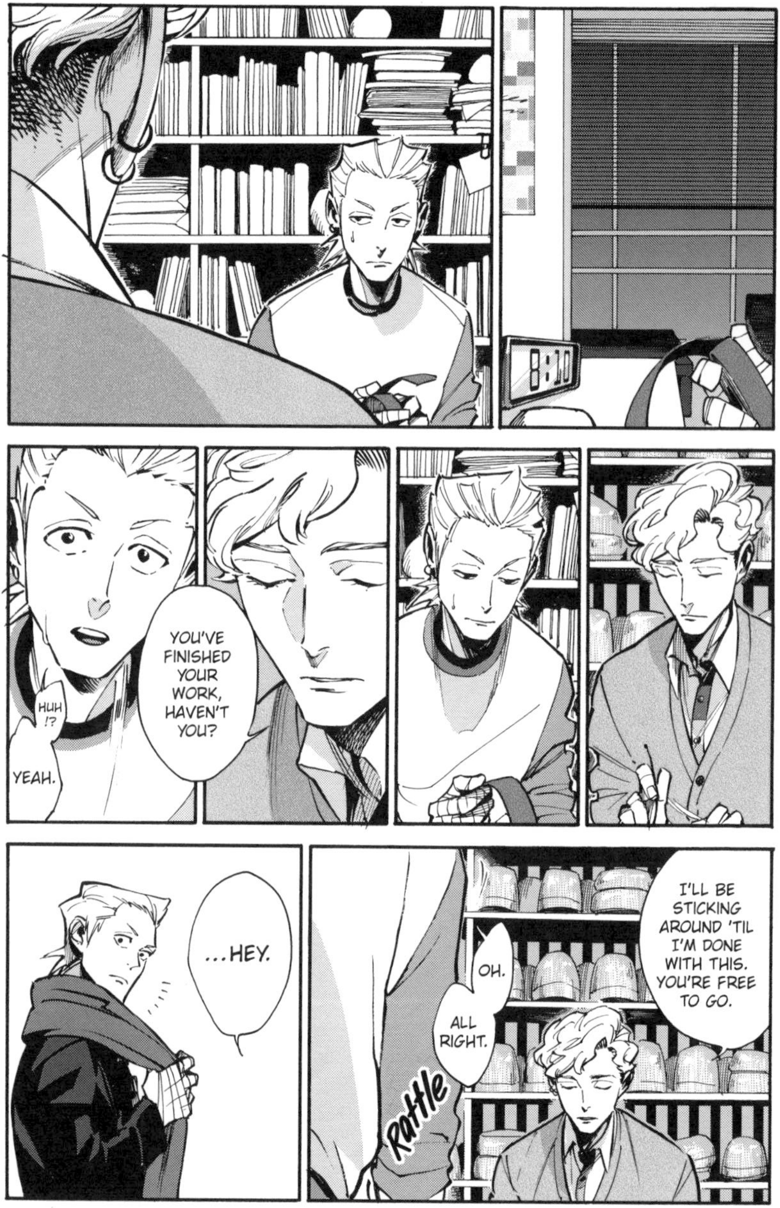
8:10
YOU'VE FINISHED YOUR WORK, HAVEN'T YOU?
HUH !?
YEAH.
I'LL BE STICKING AROUND 'TIL I'M DONE WITH THIS. YOU'RE FREE TO GO.
OH.
ALL RIGHT.
Rattle
...HEY.

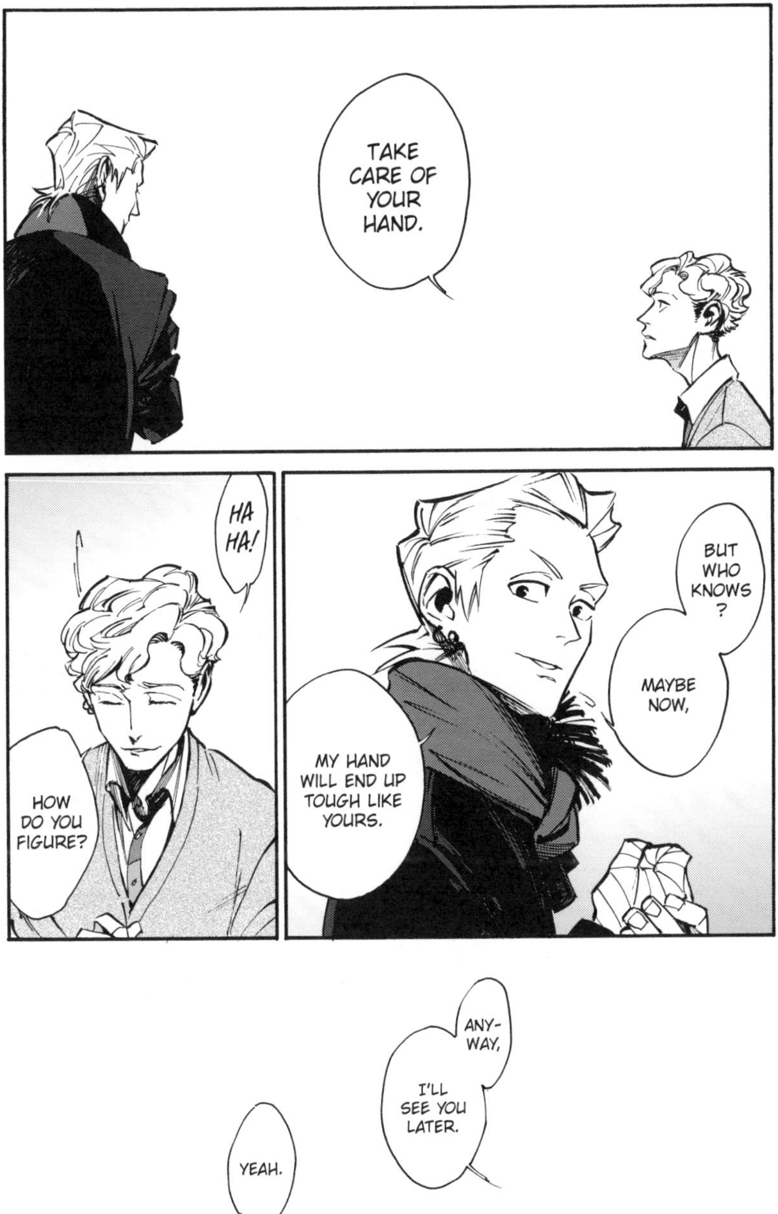
TAKE CARE OF YOUR HAND.
BUT WHO KNOWS?
MAYBE NOW,
MY HAND WILL END UP TOUGH LIKE YOURS.
HA HA!
HOW DO YOU FIGURE?
ANY-WAY,
I'LL SEE YOU LATER.
YEAH.

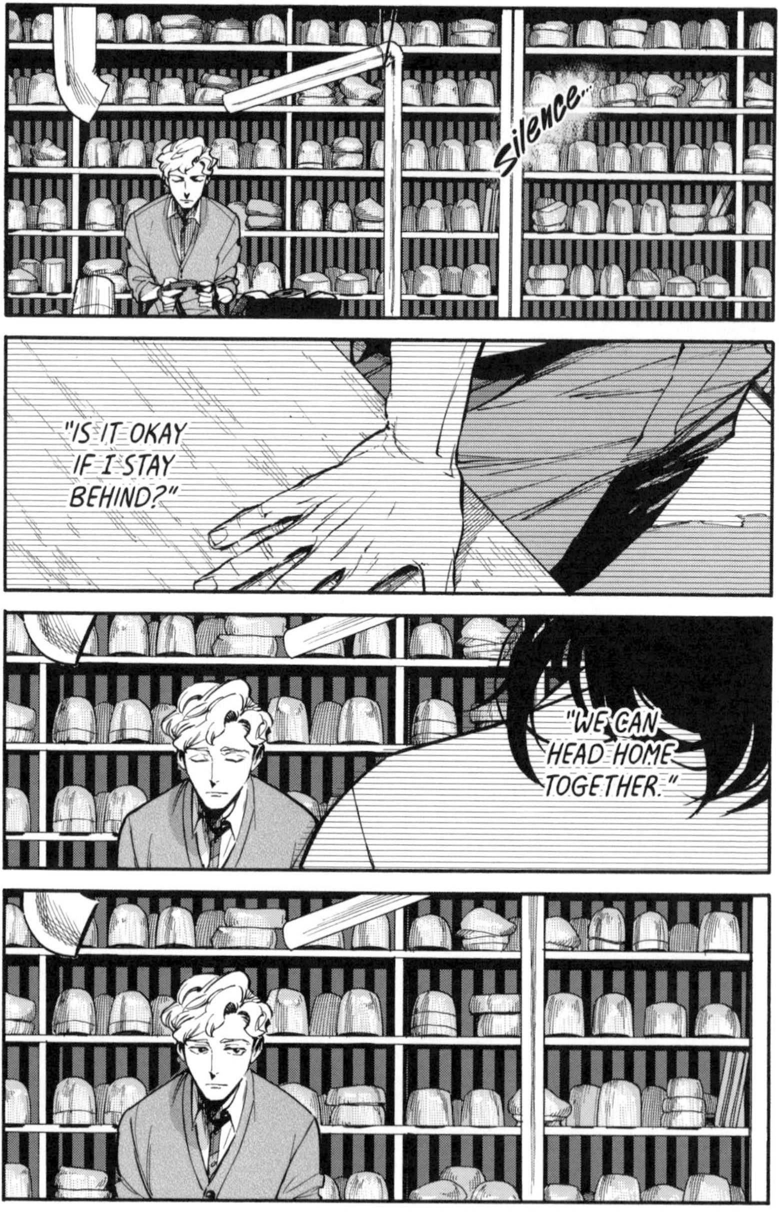
Silence...
"IS IT OKAY IF I STAY BEHIND?"
"WE CAN HEAD HOME TOGETHER."

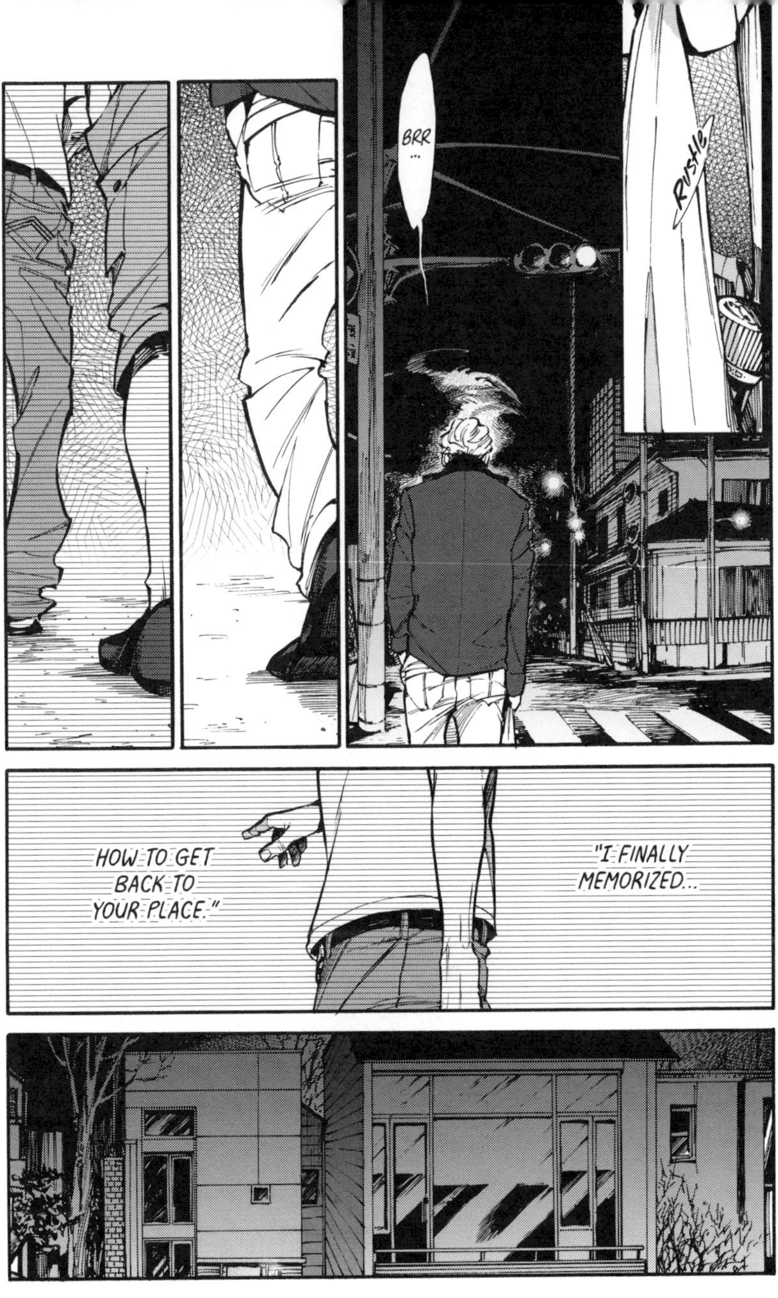
Rustle
BRR...
"I FINALLY MEMORIZED...
HOW TO GET BACK TO YOUR PLACE."

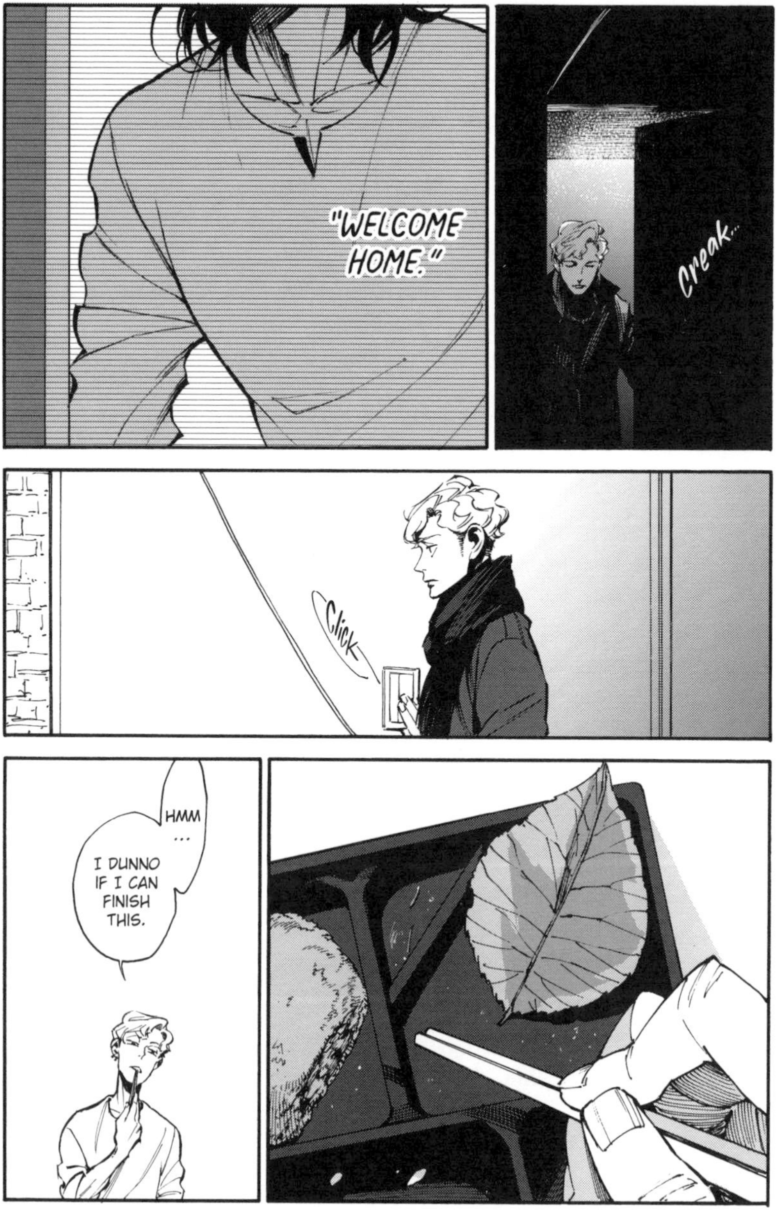
Creak...
"WELCOME HOME."
Click
HMM ...
I DUNNO IF I CAN FINISH THIS.

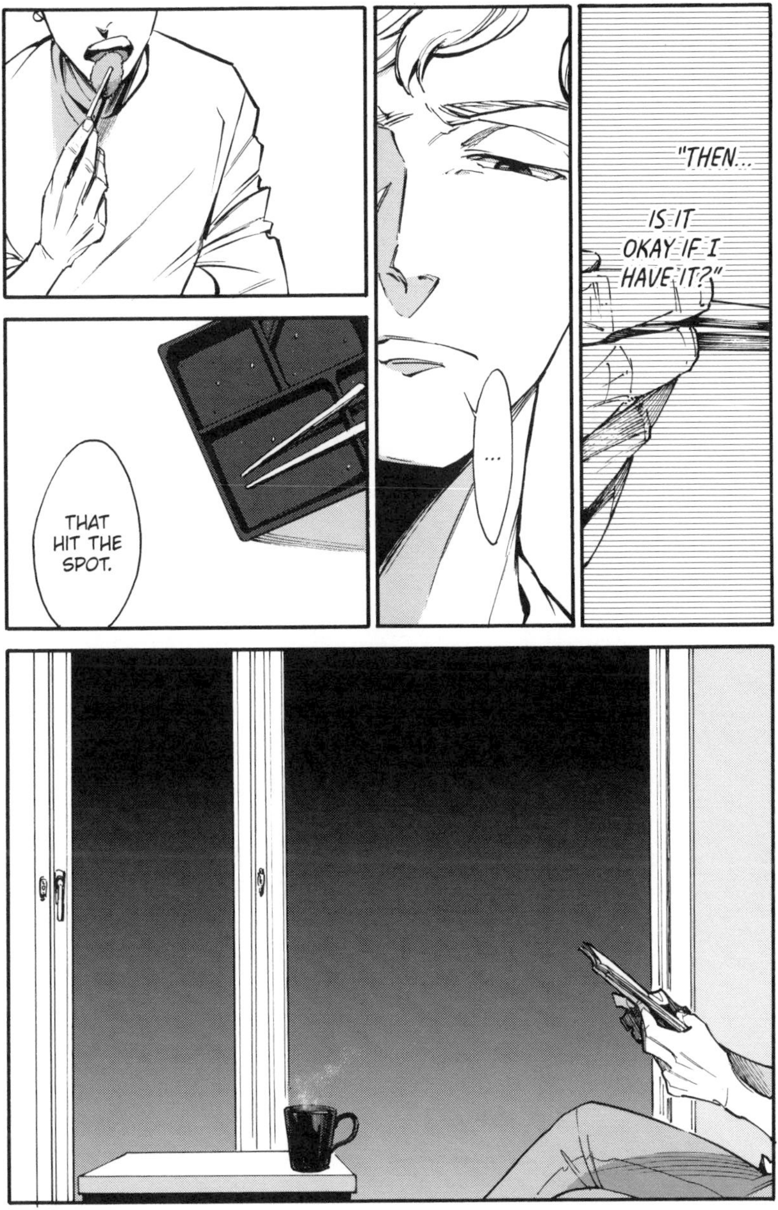
"THEN...
IS IT OKAY IF I HAVE IT?"
...
THAT HIT THE SPOT.

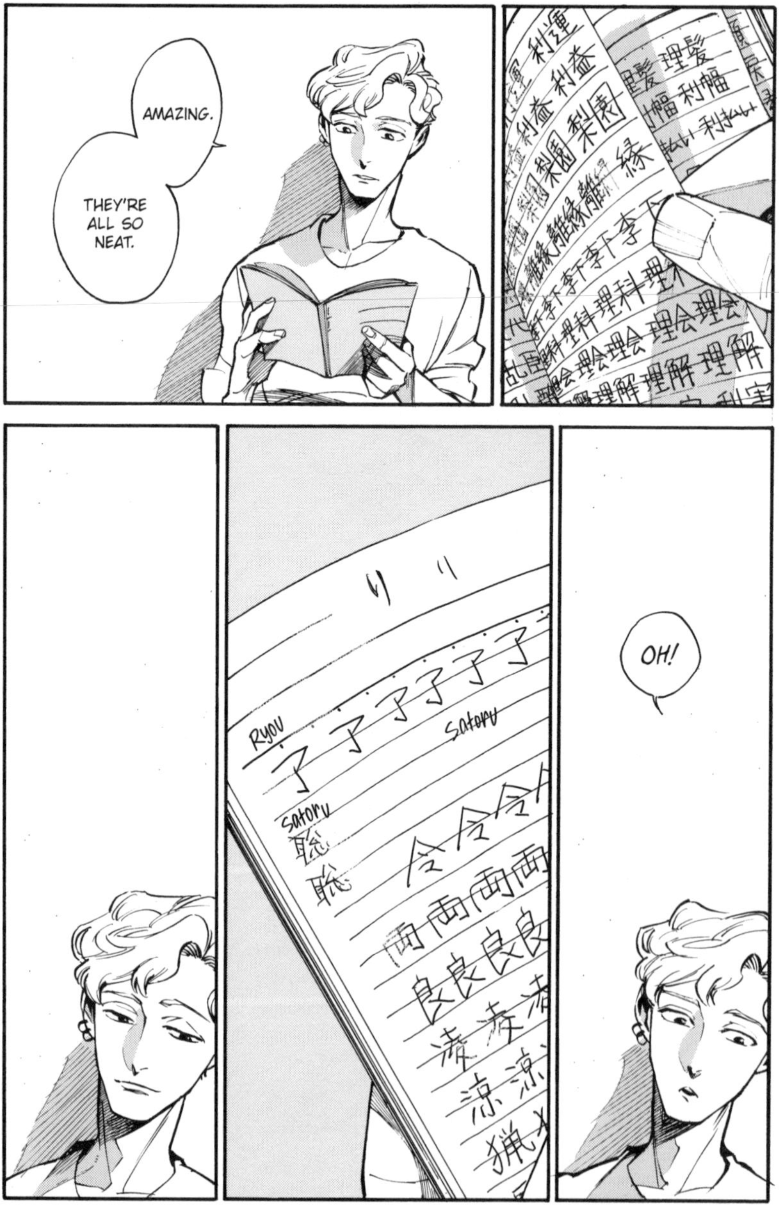
AMAZING.
THEY'RE ALL SO NEAT.
OH!
Ryou
Satoru
Satoru

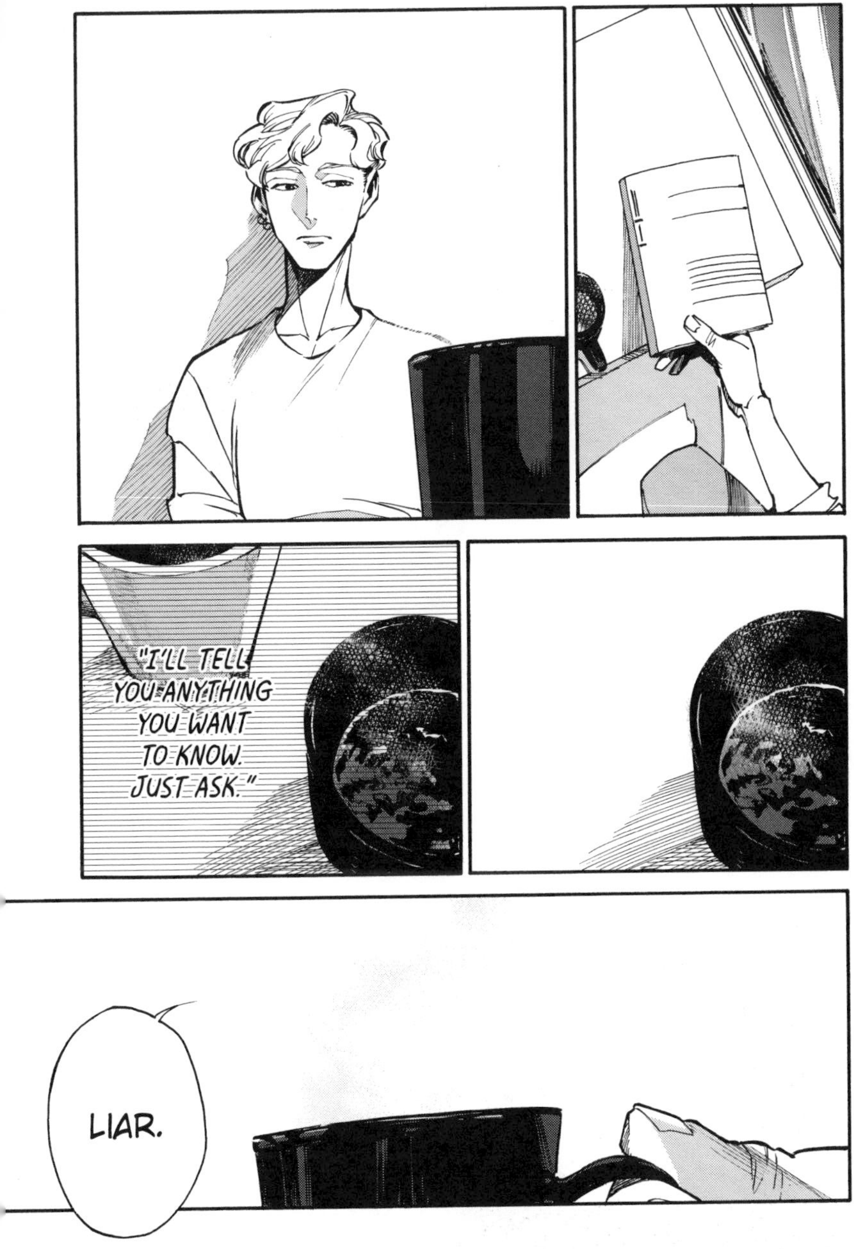
"I'LL TELL YOU ANYTHING YOU WANT TO KNOW. JUST ASK."
LIAR.

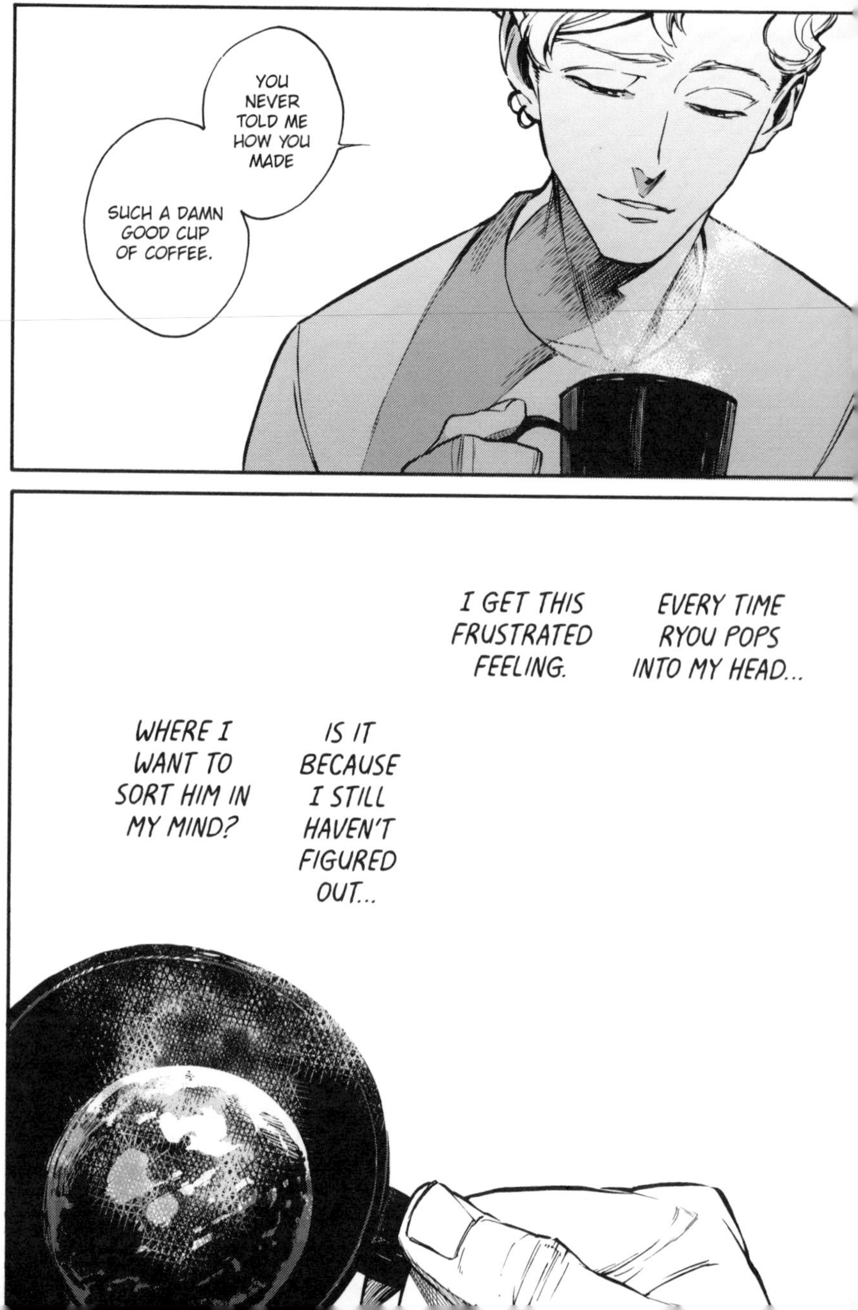
YOU NEVER TOLD ME HOW YOU MADE
SUCH A DAMN GOOD CUP OF COFFEE.
EVERY TIME RYOU POPS INTO MY HEAD...
I GET THIS FRUSTRATED FEELING.
IS IT BECAUSE I STILL HAVEN'T FIGURED OUT...
WHERE I WANT TO SORT HIM IN MY MIND?

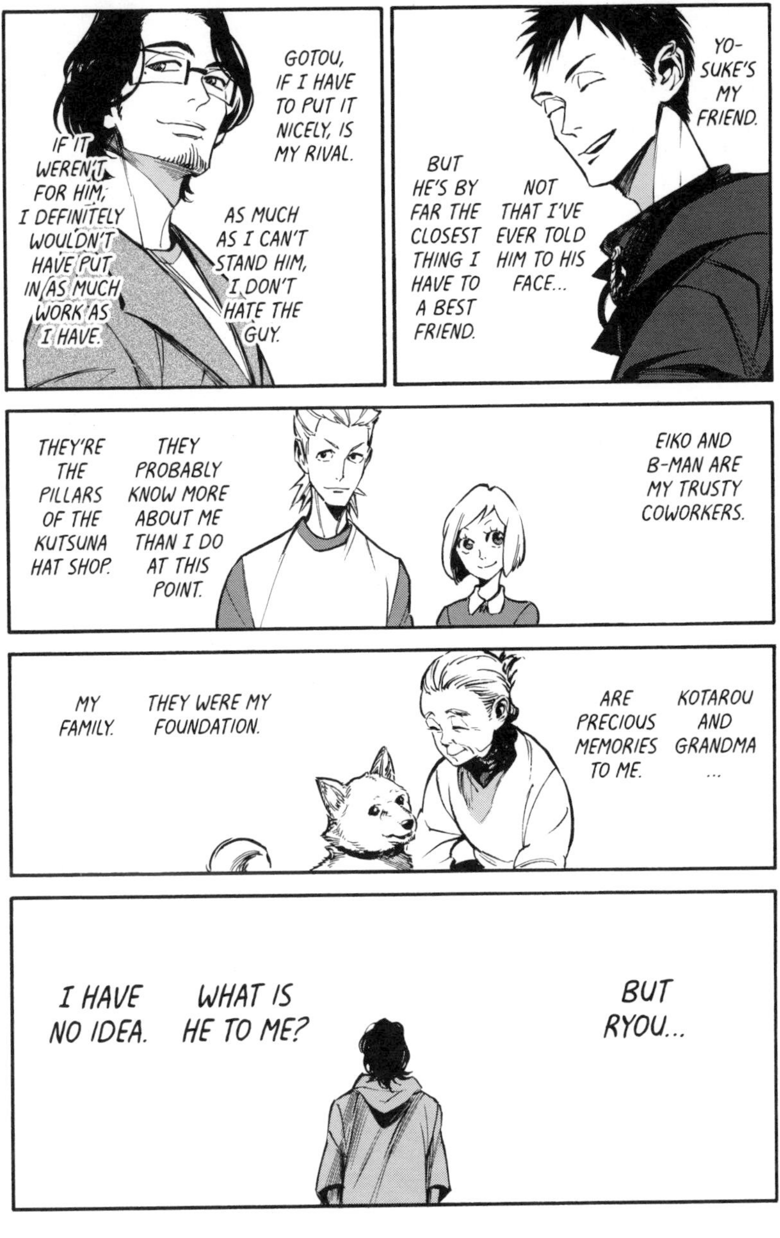
YO-SUKE'S MY FRIEND.
NOT THAT I'VE EVER TOLD HIM TO HIS FACE...
BUT HE'S BY FAR THE CLOSEST THING I HAVE TO A BEST FRIEND.
GOTOU, IF I HAVE TO PUT IT NICELY, IS MY RIVAL.
AS MUCH AS I CAN'T STAND HIM, I DON'T HATE THE GUY.
IF IT WEREN'T FOR HIM, I DEFINITELY WOULDN'T HAVE PUT IN AS MUCH WORK AS I HAVE.
EIKO AND B-MAN ARE MY TRUSTY COWORKERS.
THEY PROBABLY KNOW MORE ABOUT ME THAN I DO AT THIS POINT.
THEY'RE THE PILLARS OF THE KUTSUNA HAT SHOP.
KOTAROU AND GRANDMA...
ARE PRECIOUS MEMORIES TO ME.
THEY WERE MY FOUNDATION.
MY FAMILY.
BUT RYOU...
WHAT IS HE TO ME?
I HAVE NO IDEA.

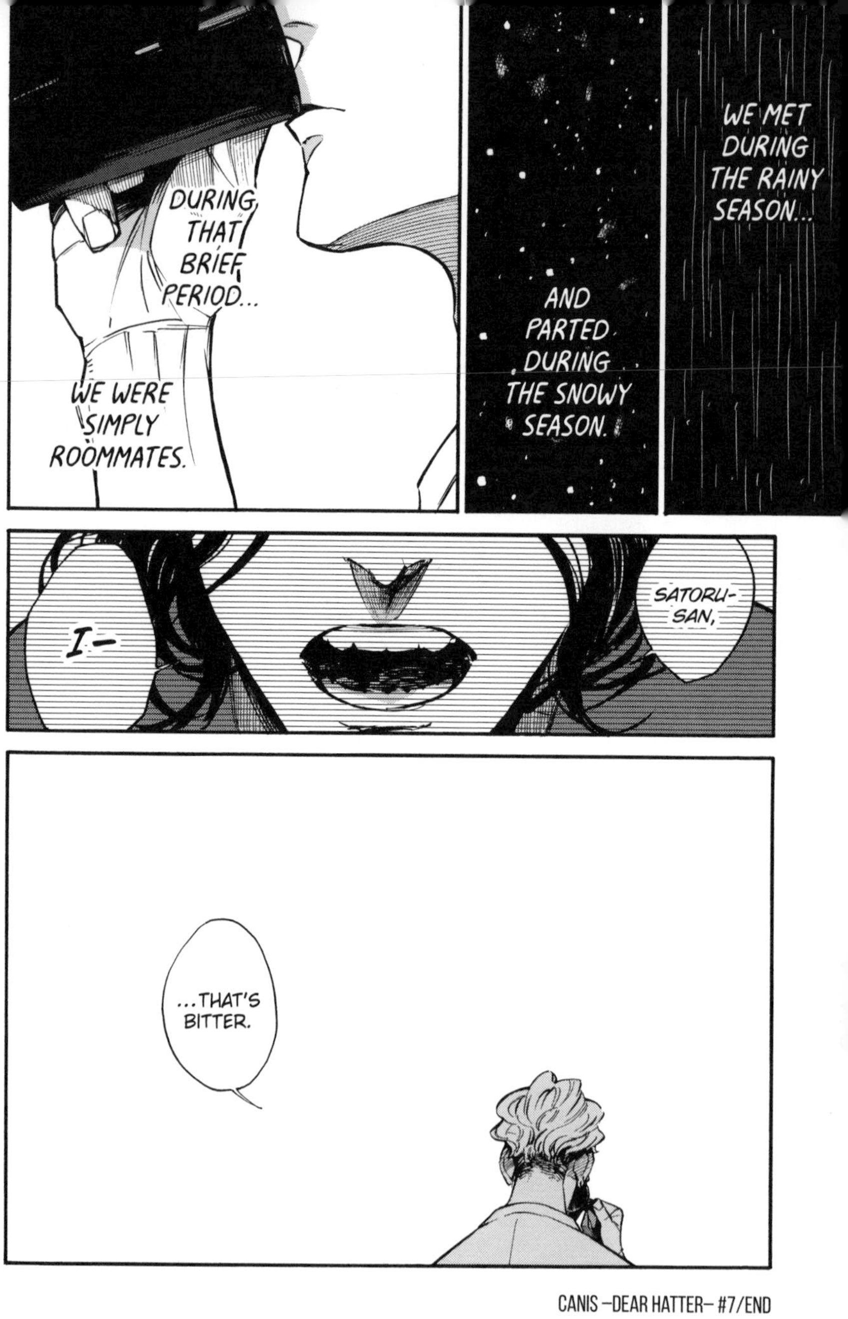
WE MET DURING THE RAINY SEASON...
AND PARTED DURING THE SNOWY SEASON.
DURING THAT BRIEF PERIOD...
WE WERE SIMPLY ROOMMATES.
SATORU-SAN,
I—
...THAT'S BITTER.

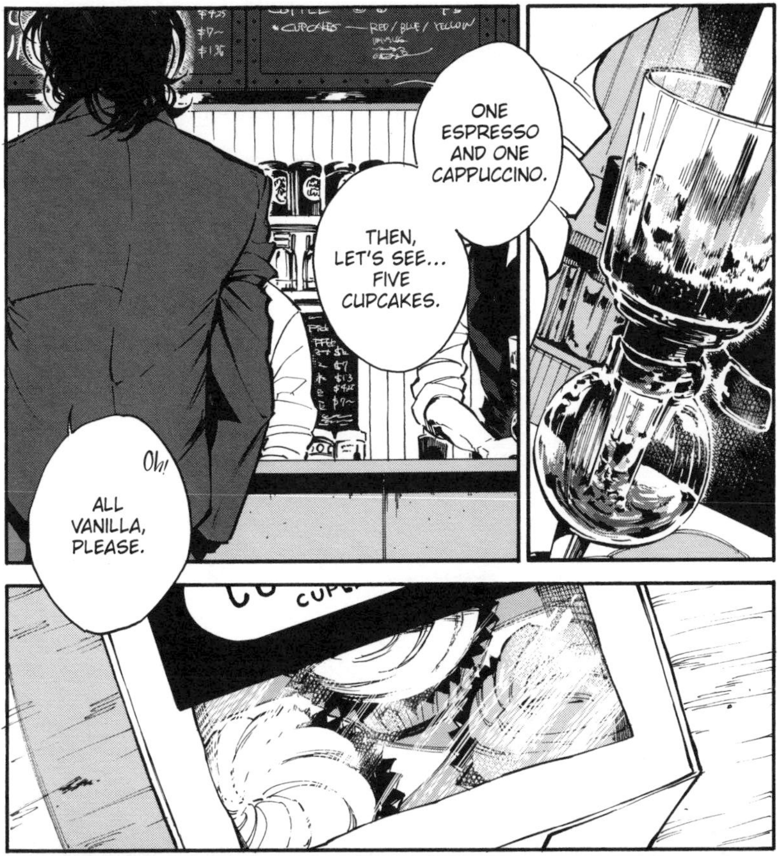
ONE ESPRESSO AND ONE CAPPUCCINO.
CUPCAKES — RED / BLUE / YELLOW
THEN, LET'S SEE... FIVE CUPCAKES.
Oh!
ALL VANILLA, PLEASE.

Chapter. 8

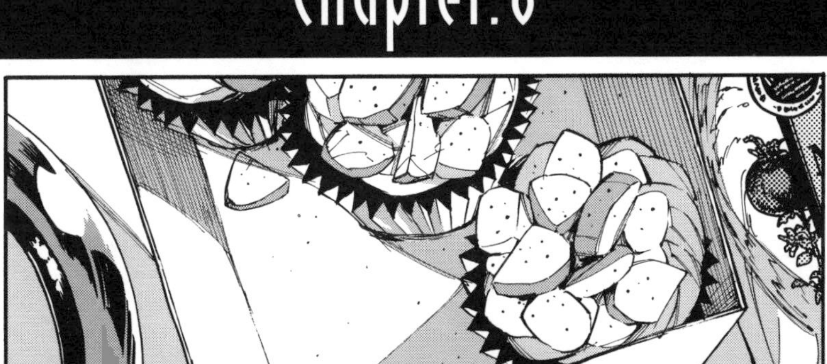

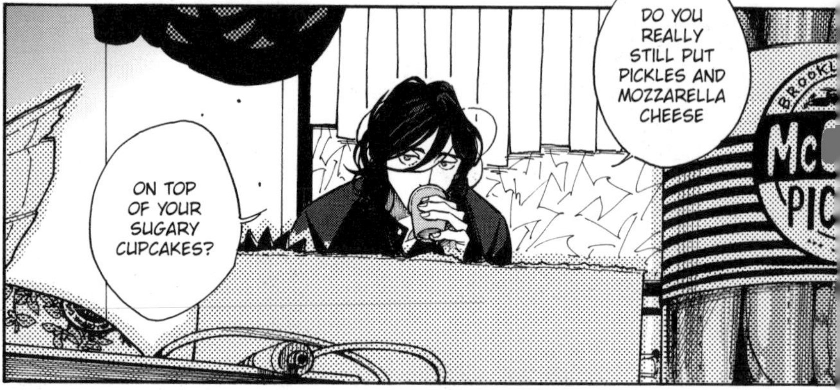
DO YOU REALLY STILL PUT PICKLES AND MOZZARELLA CHEESE
ON TOP OF YOUR SUGARY CUPCAKES?

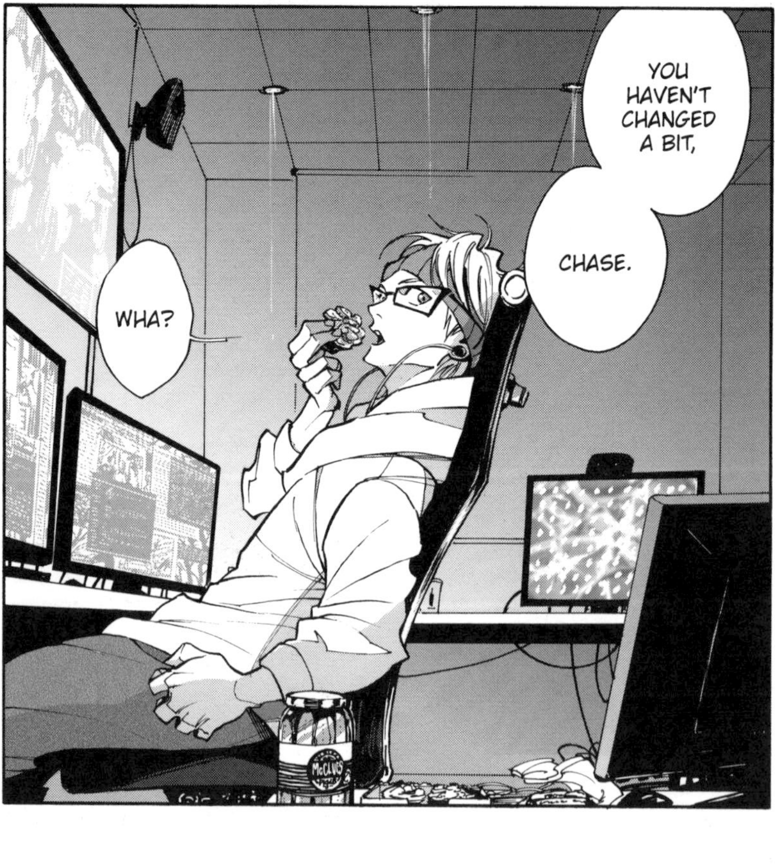
YOU HAVEN'T CHANGED A BIT,
CHASE.
WHA?

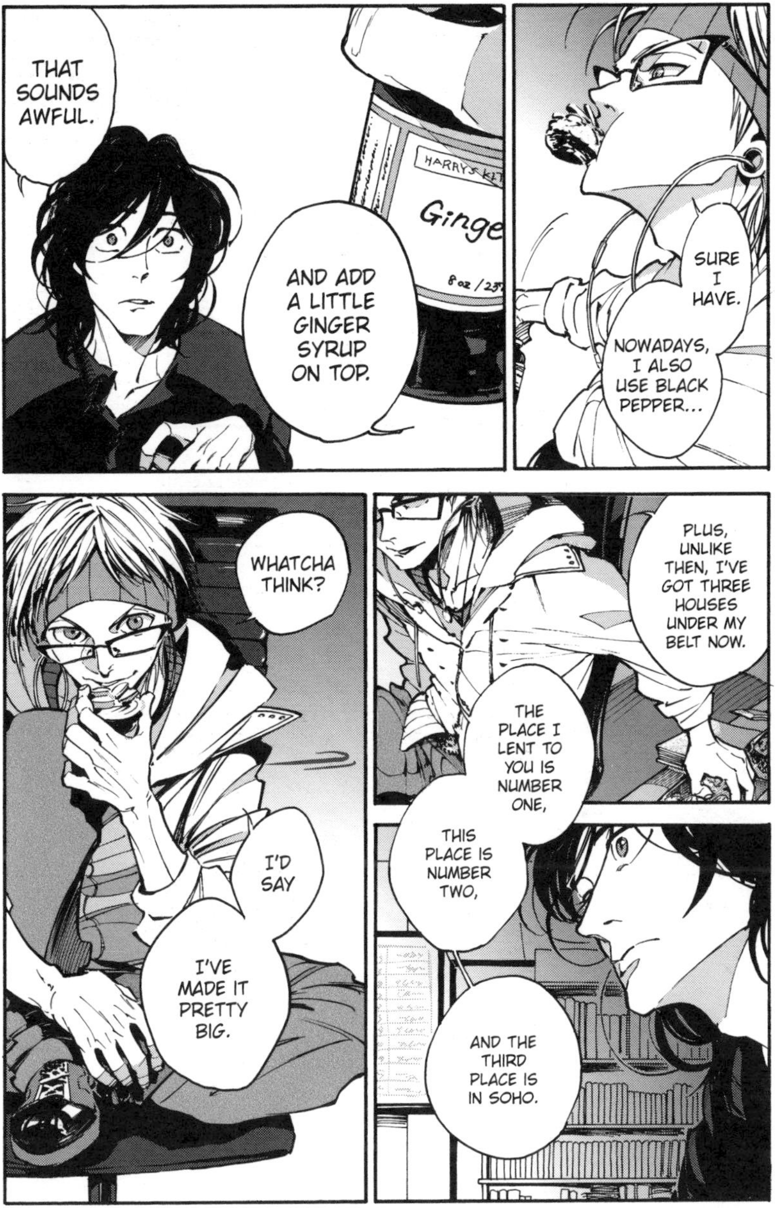
SURE I HAVE.
NOWADAYS, I ALSO USE BLACK PEPPER...
AND ADD A LITTLE GINGER SYRUP ON TOP.
THAT SOUNDS AWFUL.
PLUS, UNLIKE THEN, I'VE GOT THREE HOUSES UNDER MY BELT NOW.
THE PLACE I LENT TO YOU IS NUMBER ONE,
THIS PLACE IS NUMBER TWO,
AND THE THIRD PLACE IS IN SOHO.
WHATCHA THINK?
I'D SAY
I'VE MADE IT PRETTY BIG.

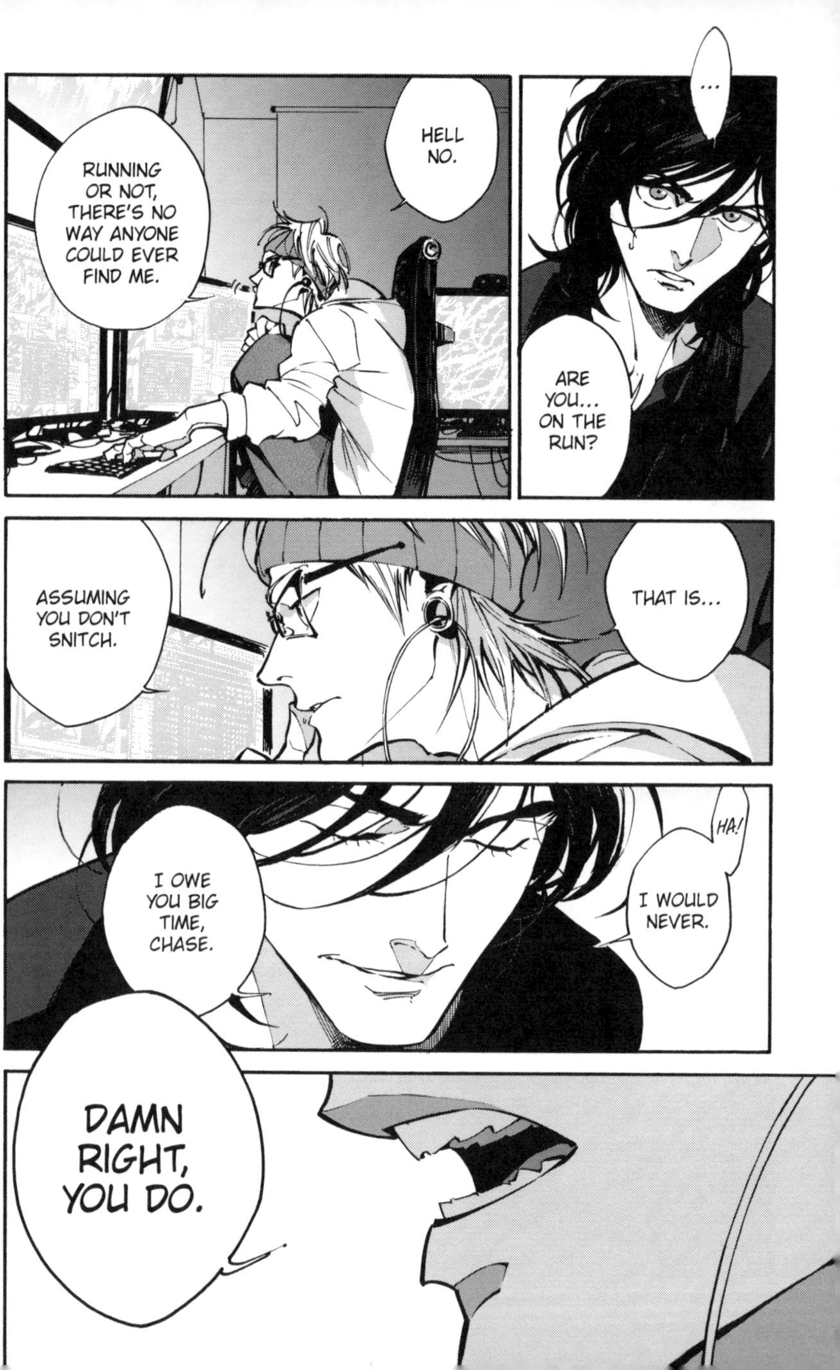
...
ARE YOU... ON THE RUN?
HELL NO.
RUNNING OR NOT, THERE'S NO WAY ANYONE COULD EVER FIND ME.
THAT IS...
ASSUMING YOU DON'T SNITCH.
HA!
I WOULD NEVER.
I OWE YOU BIG TIME, CHASE.
DAMN RIGHT, YOU DO.

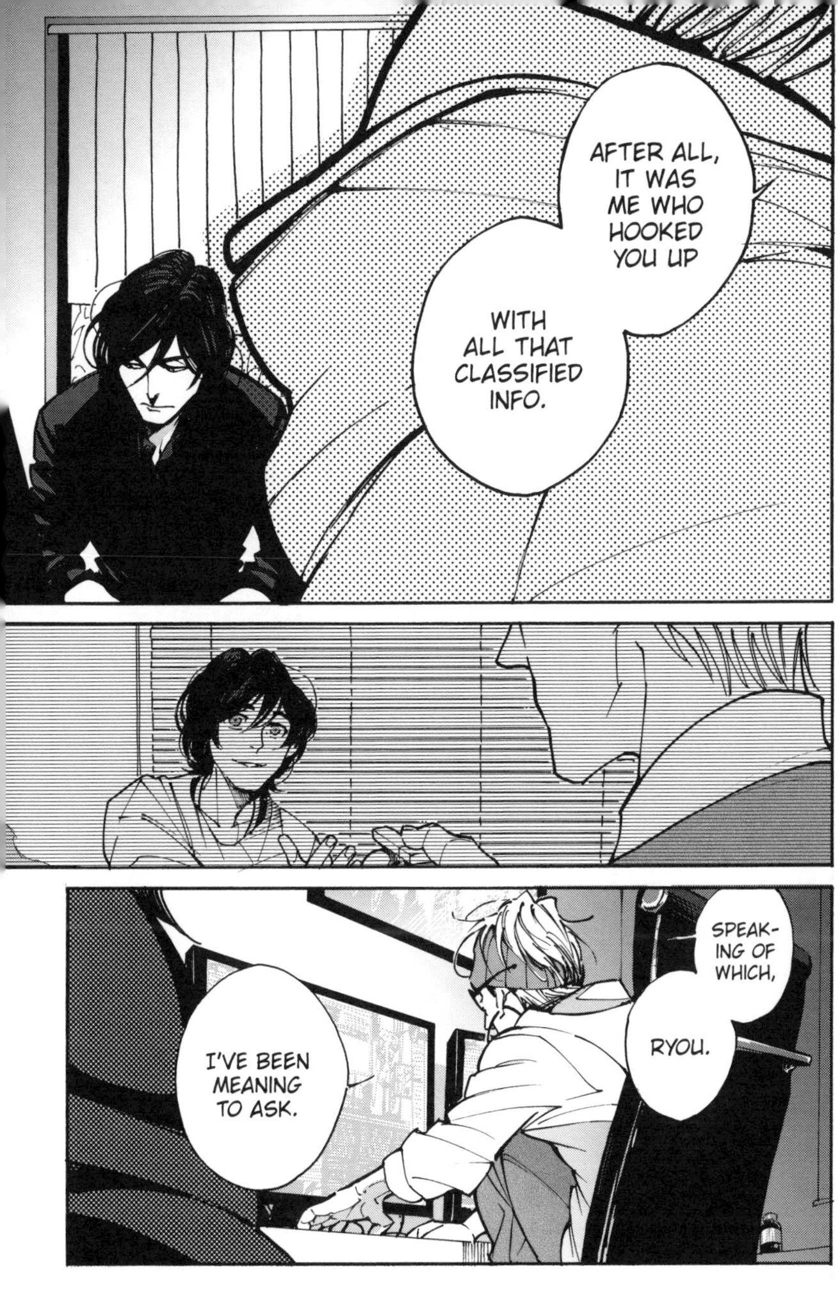
AFTER ALL, IT WAS ME WHO HOOKED YOU UP
WITH ALL THAT CLASSIFIED INFO.
SPEAK-ING OF WHICH,
RYOU.
I'VE BEEN MEANING TO ASK.

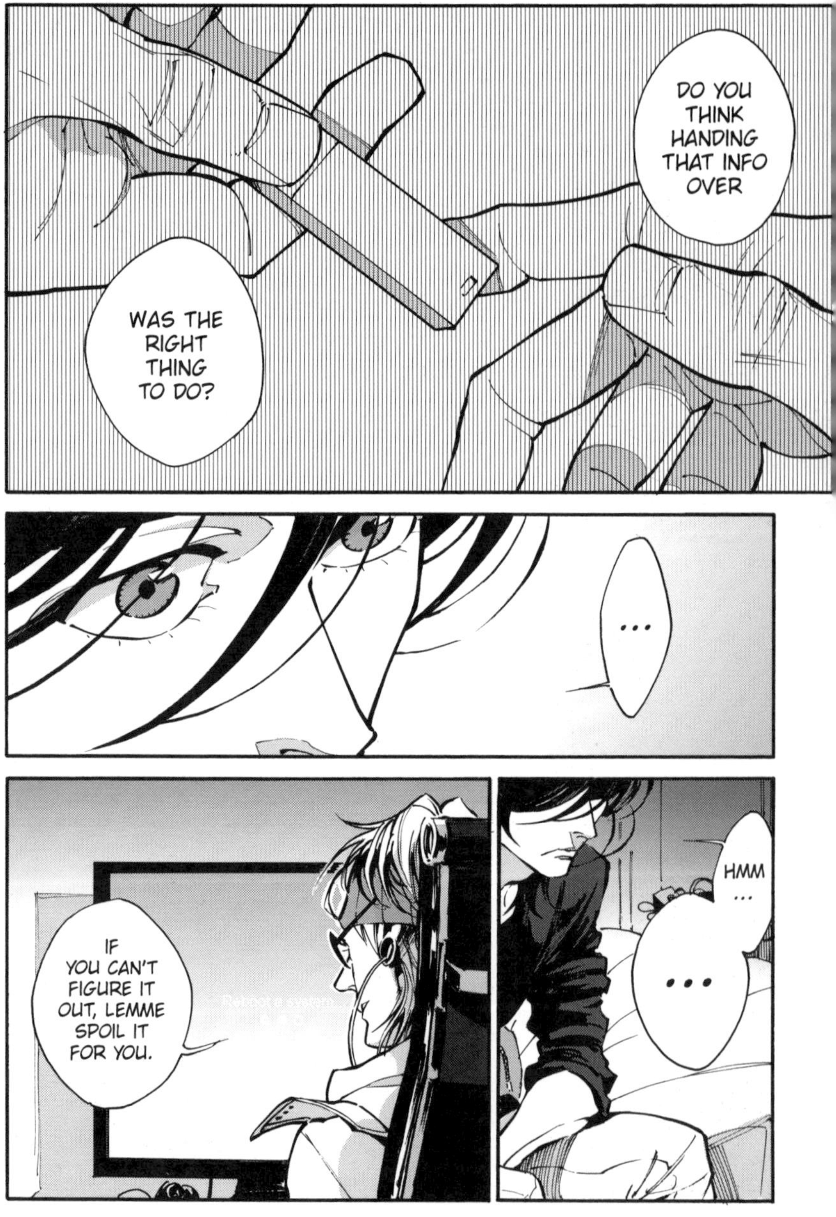
DO YOU THINK HANDING THAT INFO OVER
WAS THE RIGHT THING TO DO?
...
HMM ...
...
IF YOU CAN'T FIGURE IT OUT, LEMME SPOIL IT FOR YOU.

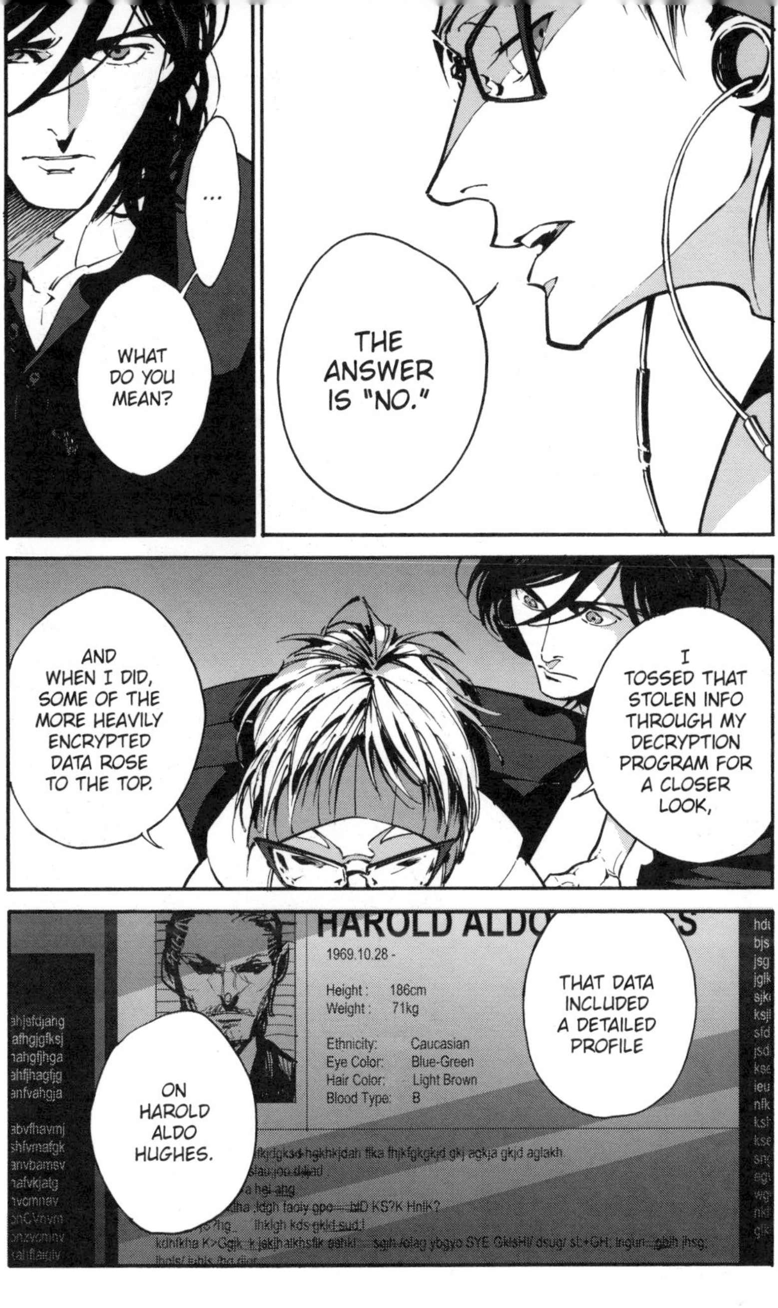
THE ANSWER IS "NO."
...
WHAT DO YOU MEAN?
I TOSSED THAT STOLEN INFO THROUGH MY DECRYPTION PROGRAM FOR A CLOSER LOOK,
AND WHEN I DID, SOME OF THE MORE HEAVILY ENCRYPTED DATA ROSE TO THE TOP.
HAROLD ALDO
1969.10.28 -
Height: 186cm
Weight: 71kg
Ethnicity: Caucasian
Eye Color: Blue-Green
Hair Color: Light Brown
Blood Type: B
THAT DATA INCLUDED A DETAILED PROFILE
ON HAROLD ALDO HUGHES.

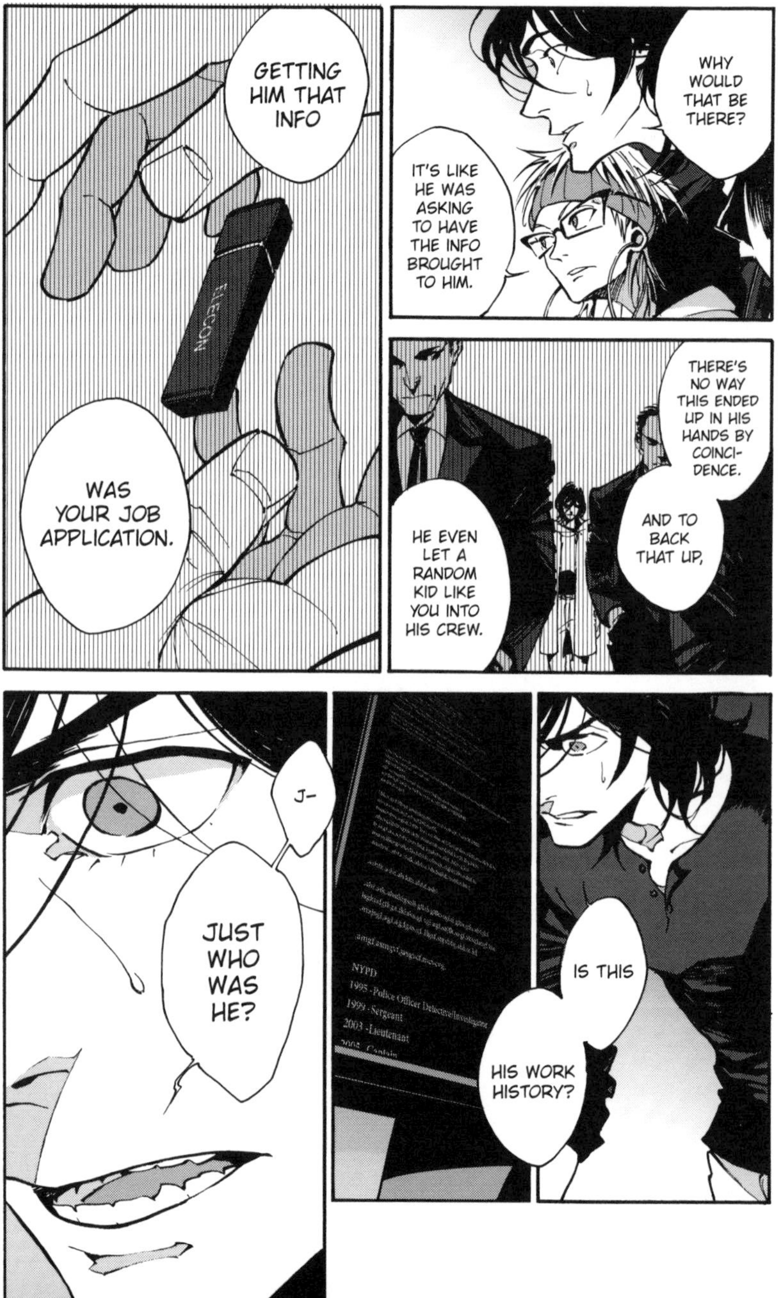
WHY WOULD THAT BE THERE?
IT'S LIKE HE WAS ASKING TO HAVE THE INFO BROUGHT TO HIM.
THERE'S NO WAY THIS ENDED UP IN HIS HANDS BY COINCI-DENCE.
AND TO BACK THAT UP,
HE EVEN LET A RANDOM KID LIKE YOU INTO HIS CREW.
GETTING HIM THAT INFO
ELECON
WAS YOUR JOB APPLICATION.
IS THIS
HIS WORK HISTORY?
NYPD
1999 - Sergeant
2003 - Lieutenant
J-
JUST WHO WAS HE?

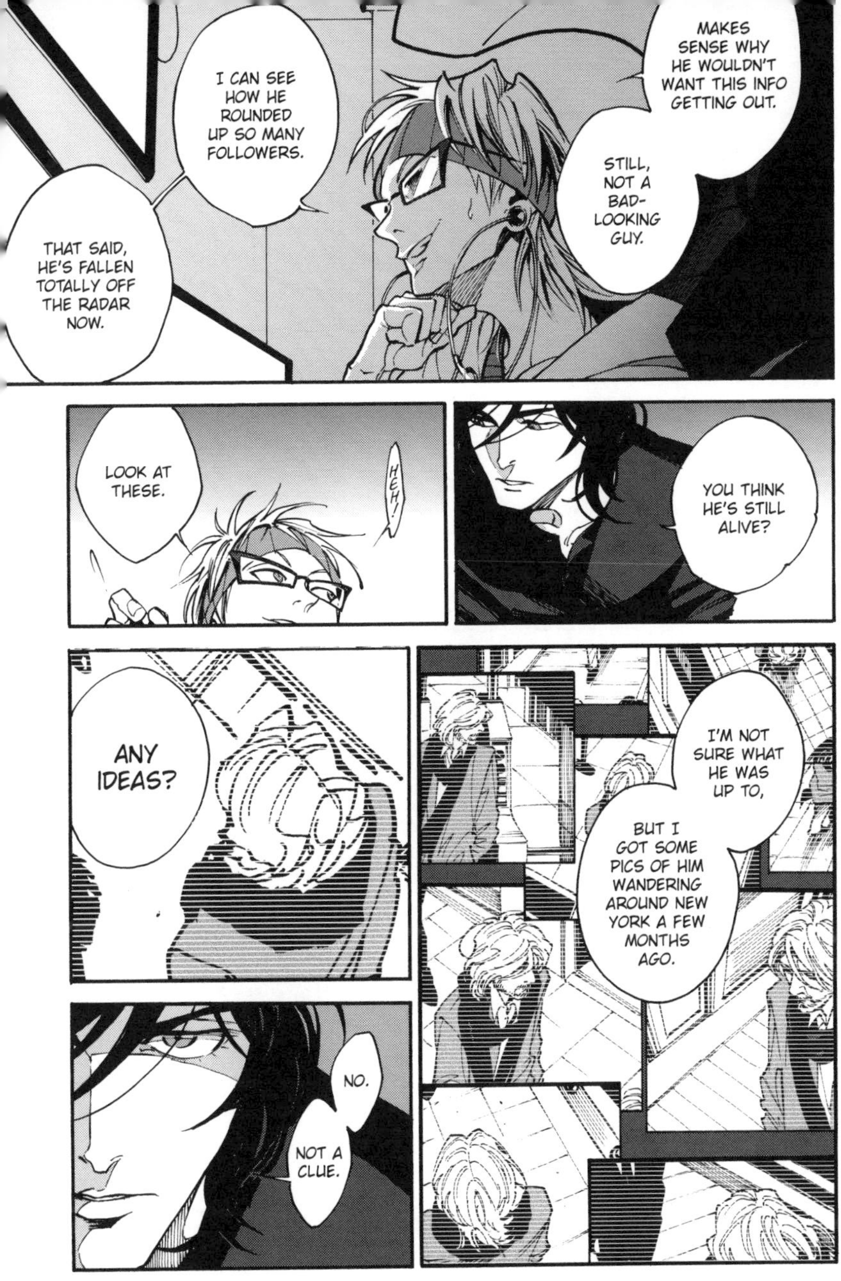
MAKES SENSE WHY HE WOULDN'T WANT THIS INFO GETTING OUT.
STILL, NOT A BAD-LOOKING GUY.
I CAN SEE HOW HE ROUNDED UP SO MANY FOLLOWERS.
THAT SAID, HE'S FALLEN TOTALLY OFF THE RADAR NOW.
YOU THINK HE'S STILL ALIVE?
HEH!
LOOK AT THESE.
I'M NOT SURE WHAT HE WAS UP TO,
BUT I GOT SOME PICS OF HIM WANDERING AROUND NEW YORK A FEW MONTHS AGO.
ANY IDEAS?
NO.
NOT A CLUE.

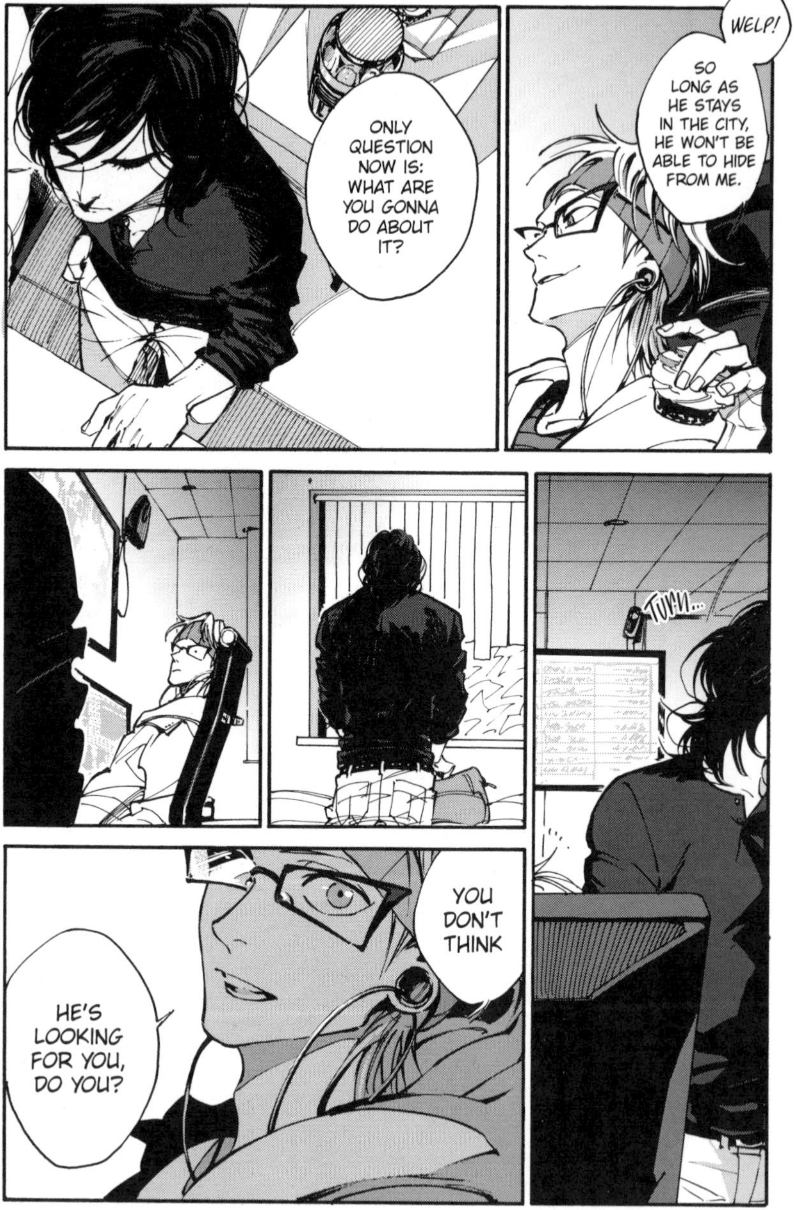
WELP!
SO LONG AS HE STAYS IN THE CITY, HE WON'T BE ABLE TO HIDE FROM ME.
ONLY QUESTION NOW IS: WHAT ARE YOU GONNA DO ABOUT IT?
TURN...
YOU DON'T THINK
HE'S LOOKING FOR YOU, DO YOU?

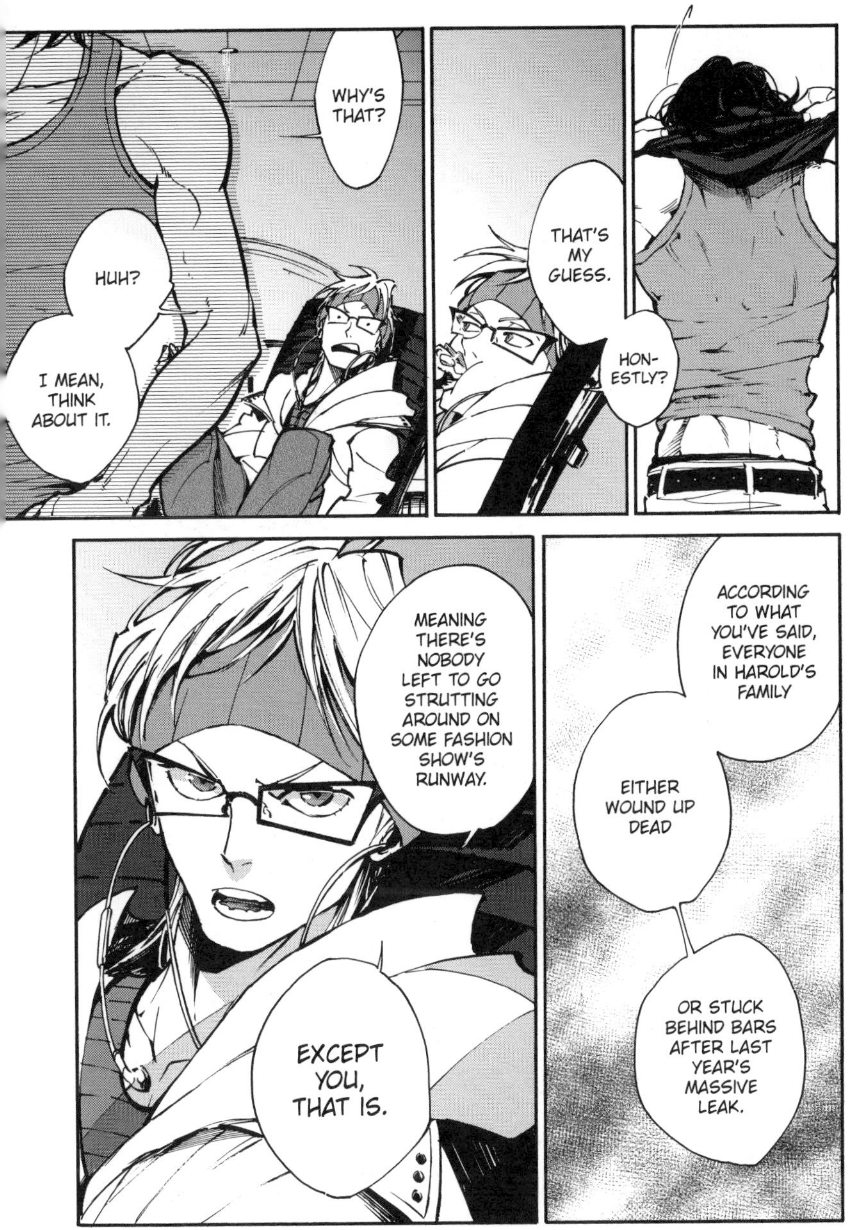
THAT'S MY GUESS.
HON-ESTLY?
WHY'S THAT?
HUH?
I MEAN, THINK ABOUT IT.
ACCORDING TO WHAT YOU'VE SAID, EVERYONE IN HAROLD'S FAMILY
EITHER WOUND UP DEAD
OR STUCK BEHIND BARS AFTER LAST YEAR'S MASSIVE LEAK.
MEANING THERE'S NOBODY LEFT TO GO STRUTTING AROUND ON SOME FASHION SHOW'S RUNWAY.
EXCEPT YOU, THAT IS.

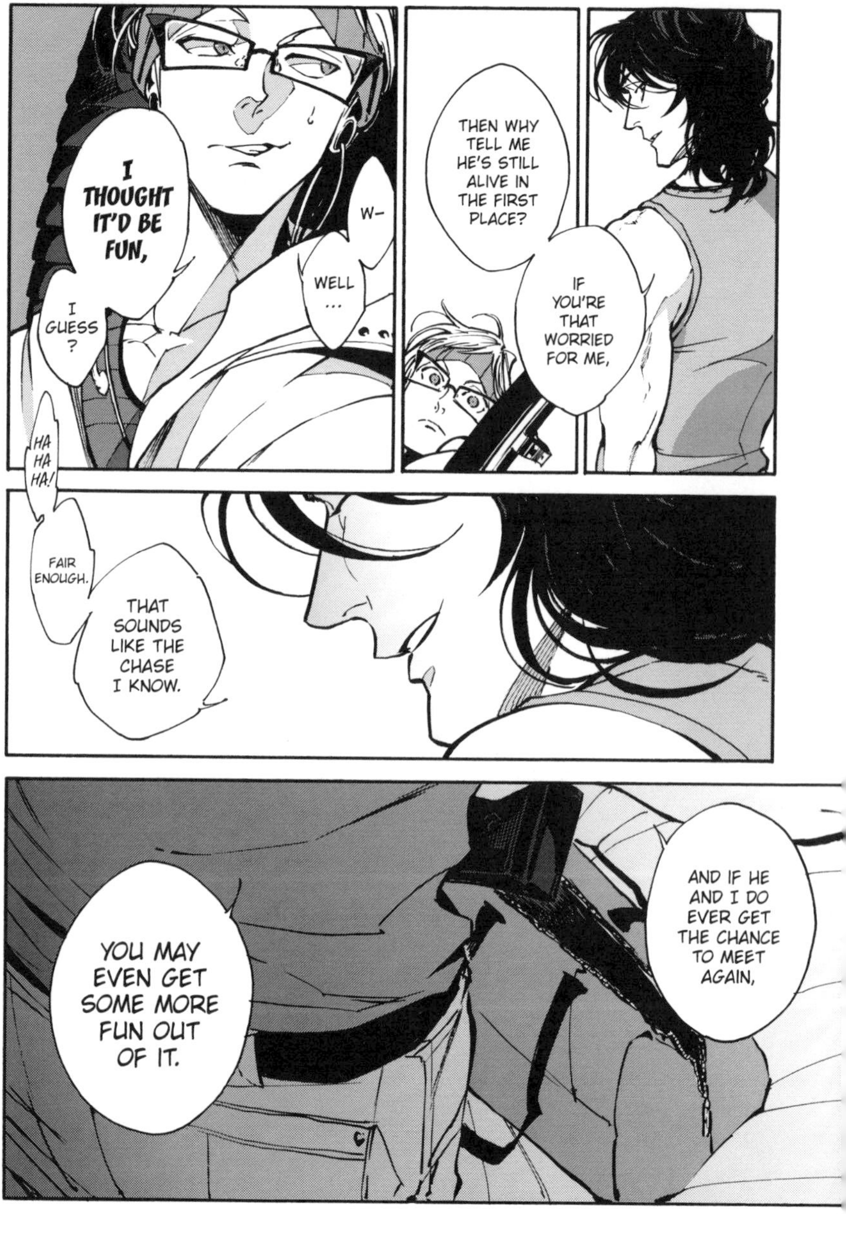
IF YOU'RE THAT WORRIED FOR ME,
THEN WHY TELL ME HE'S STILL ALIVE IN THE FIRST PLACE?
W-
WELL ...
I THOUGHT IT'D BE FUN,
I GUESS?
HA HA HA!
FAIR ENOUGH.
THAT SOUNDS LIKE THE CHASE I KNOW.
AND IF HE AND I DO EVER GET THE CHANCE TO MEET AGAIN,
YOU MAY EVEN GET SOME MORE FUN OUT OF IT.

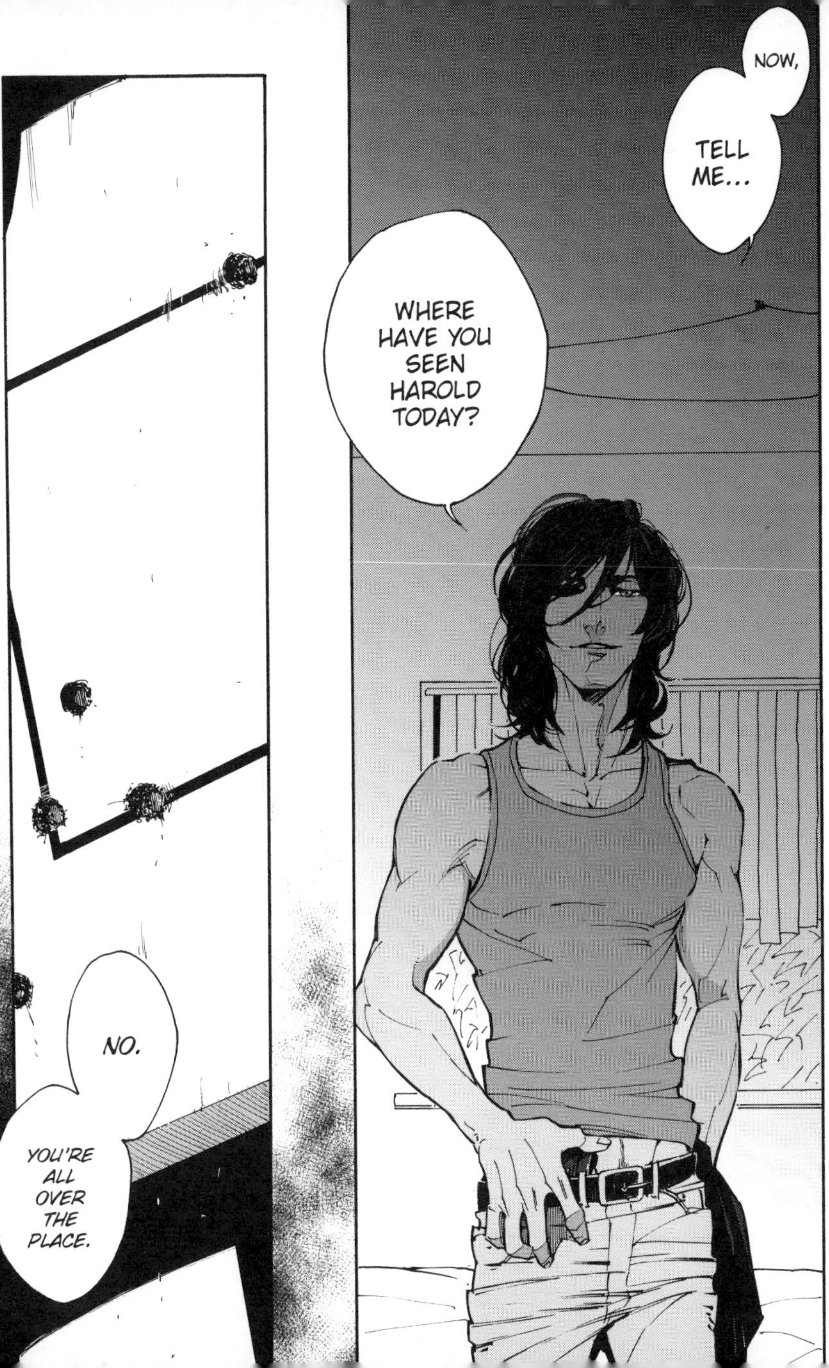
NOW,
TELL ME...
WHERE HAVE YOU SEEN HAROLD TODAY?
NO.
YOU'RE ALL OVER THE PLACE.

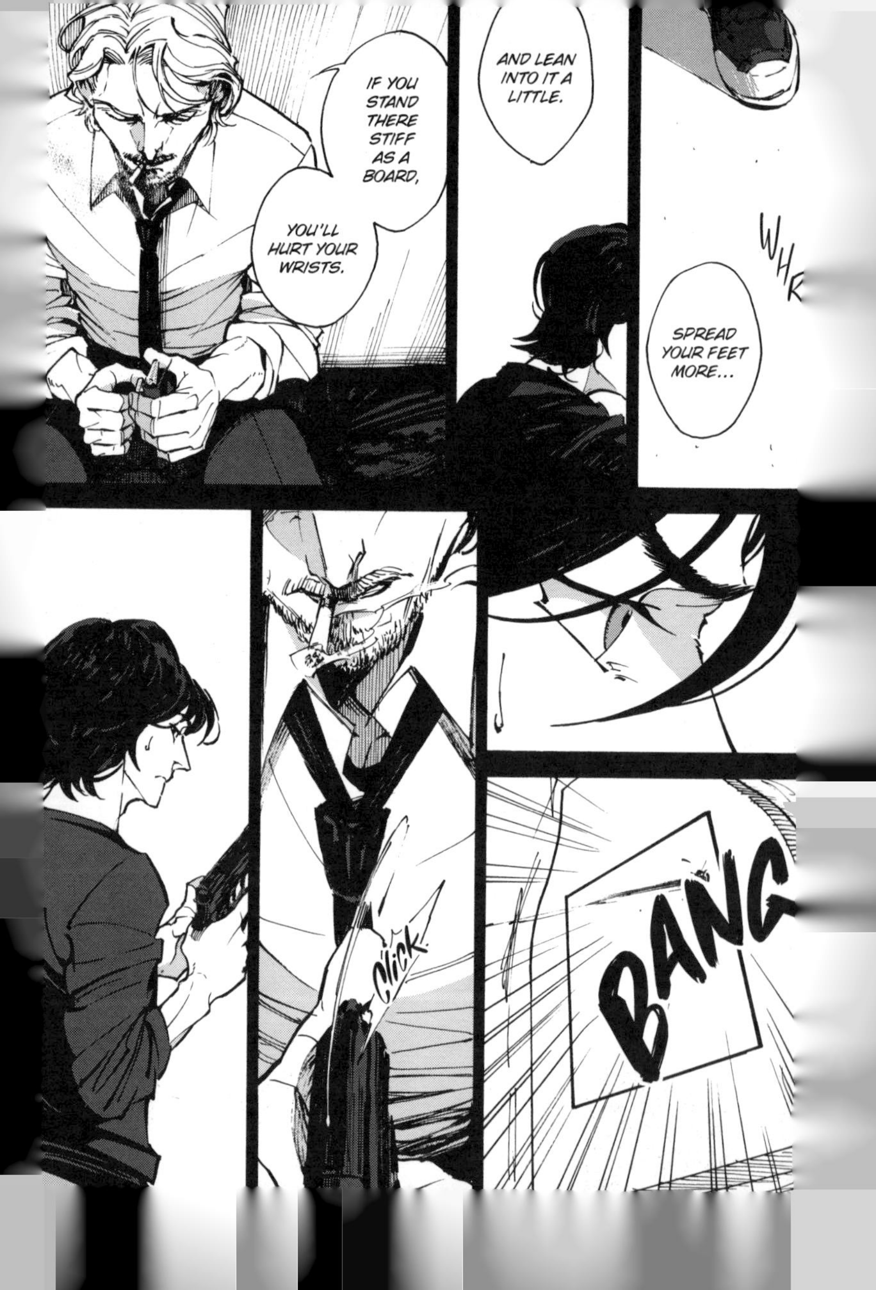
WHR
SPREAD YOUR FEET MORE...
AND LEAN INTO IT A LITTLE.
IF YOU STAND THERE STIFF AS A BOARD,
YOU'LL HURT YOUR WRISTS.
BANG
CLICK

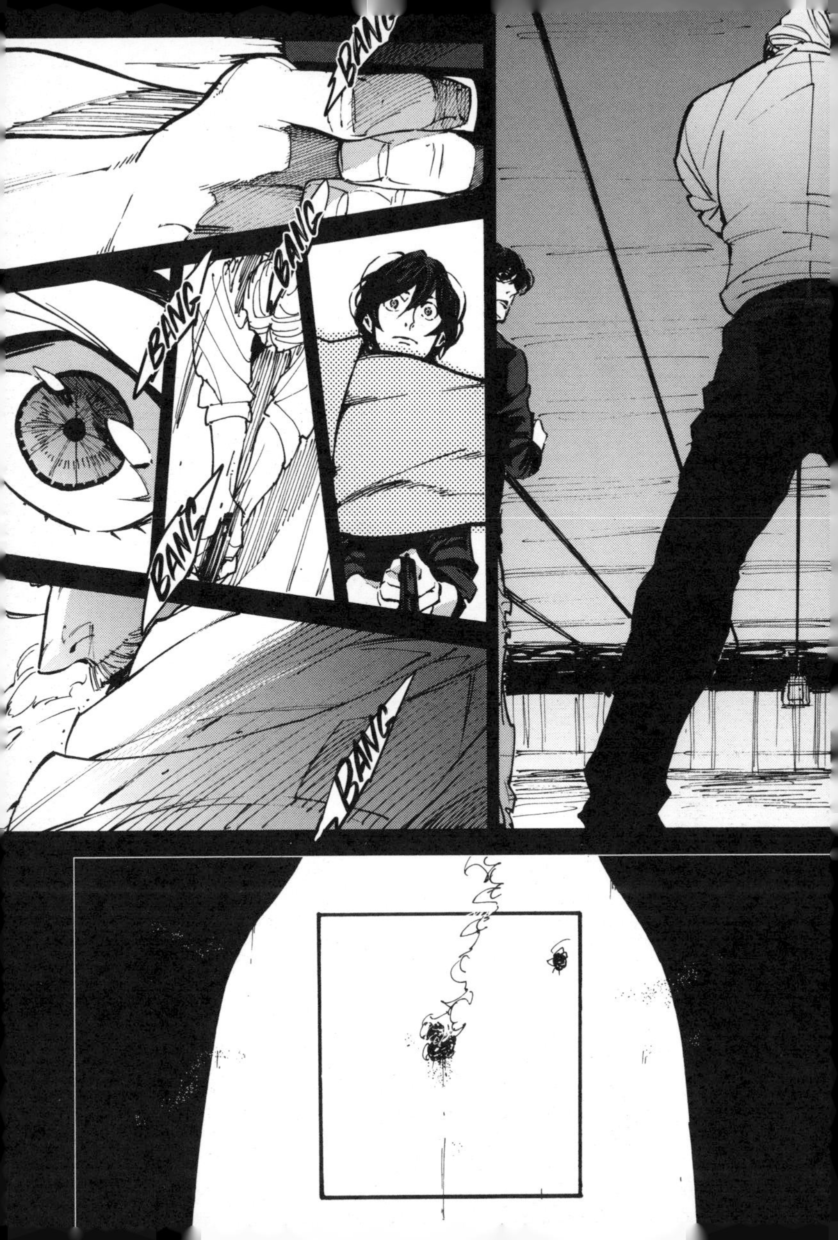
BANG
BANG
BANG
BANG
BANG
BANG

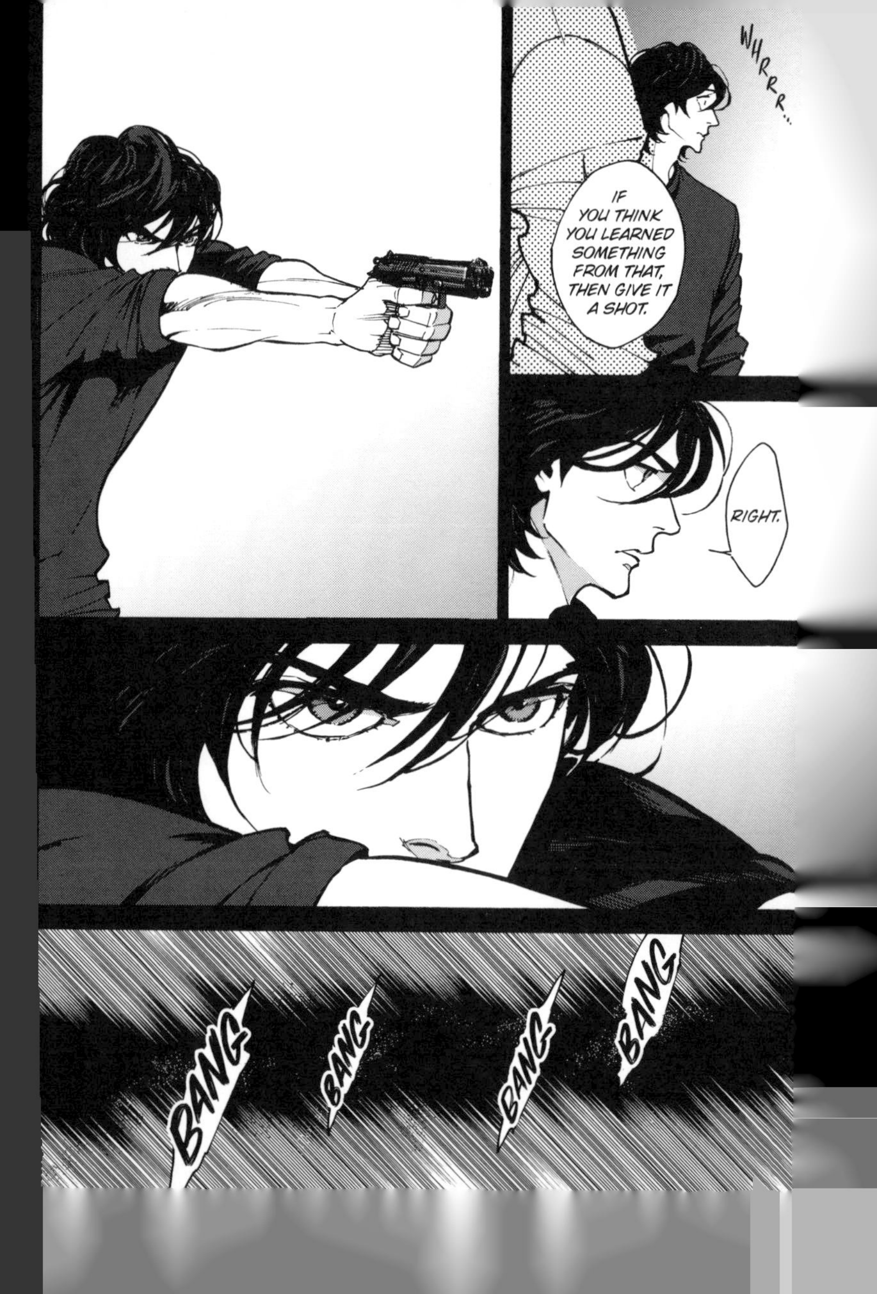
WHRRR...
IF YOU THINK YOU LEARNED SOMETHING FROM THAT, THEN GIVE IT A SHOT.
RIGHT.
BANG
BANG
BANG
BANG

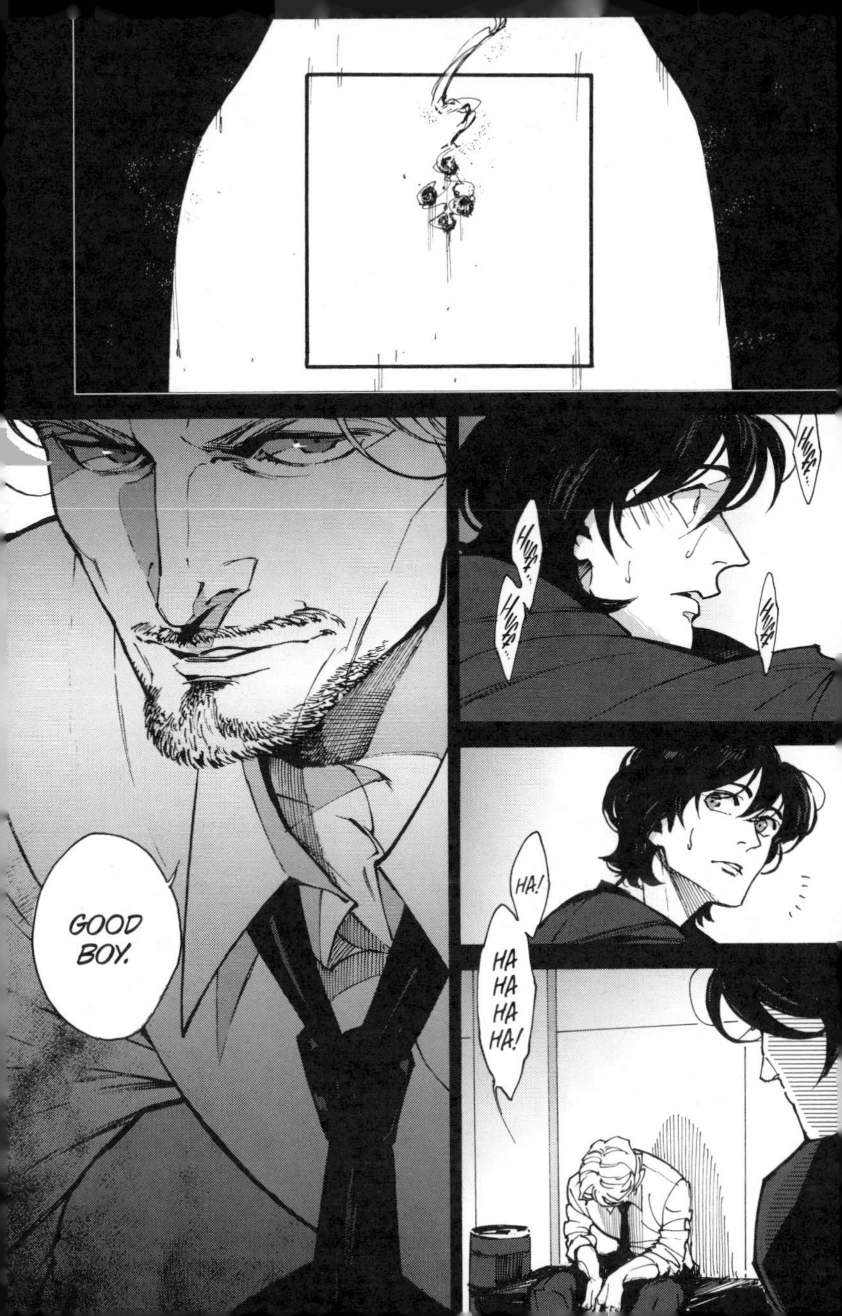
HUFF...
HUFF...
HUFF...
HUFF
HA!
HA HA HA HA!
GOOD BOY.

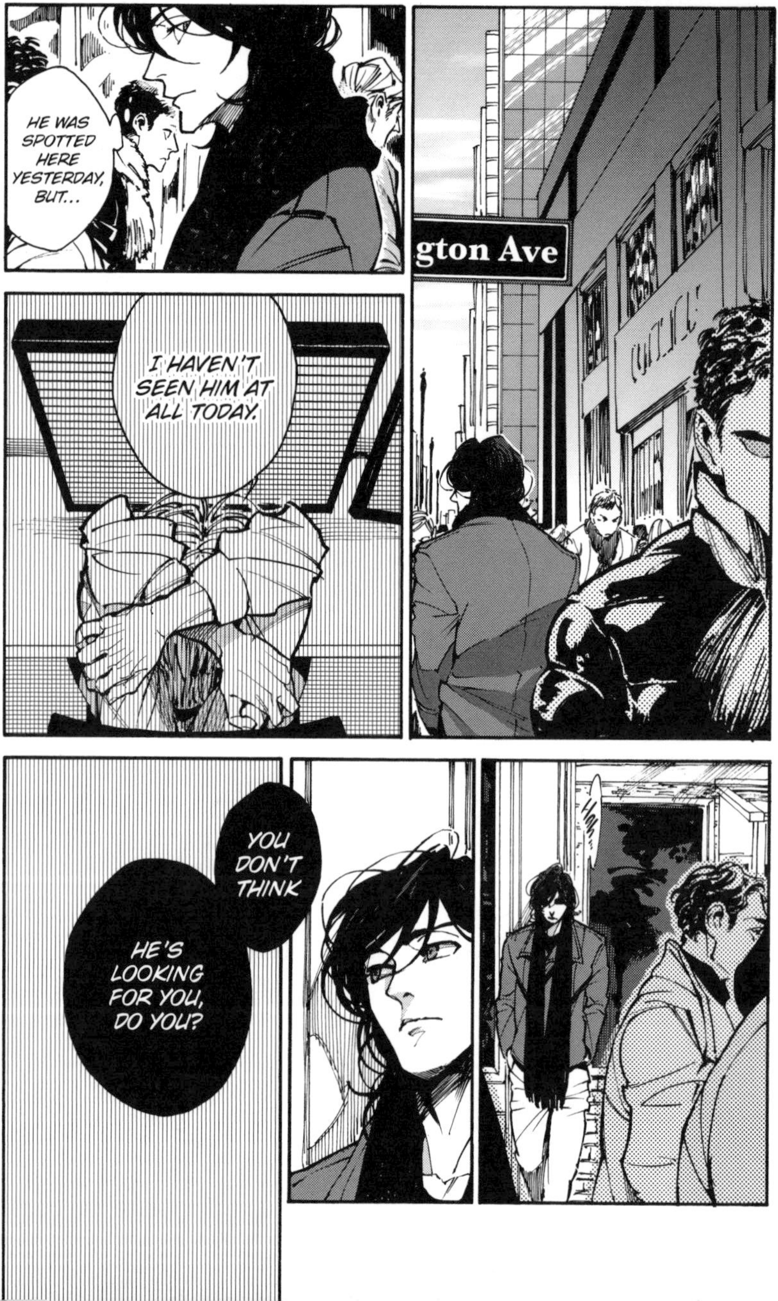
gton Ave
HE WAS SPOTTED HERE YESTERDAY, BUT...
I HAVEN'T SEEN HIM AT ALL TODAY.
YOU DON'T THINK
HE'S LOOKING FOR YOU, DO YOU?

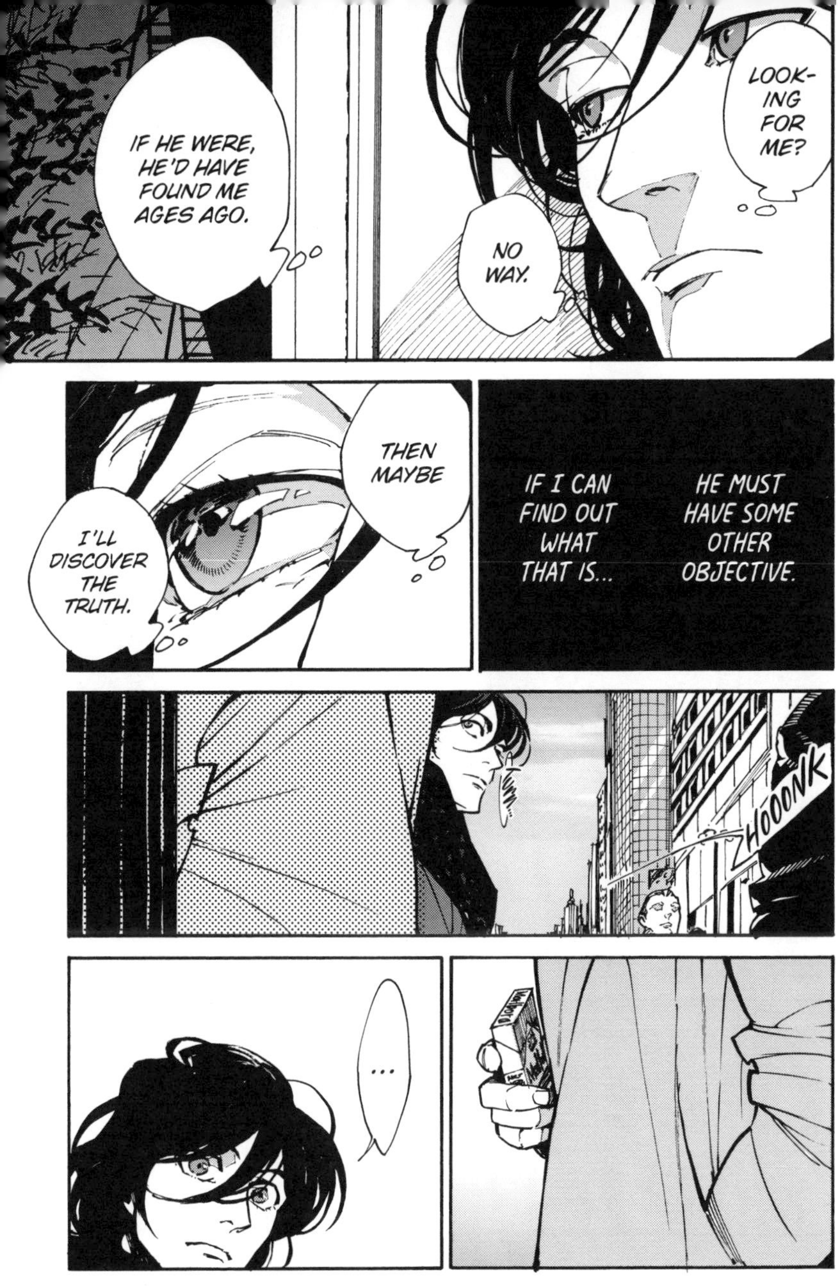
LOOKING FOR ME?
NO WAY.
IF HE WERE, HE'D HAVE FOUND ME AGES AGO.
HE MUST HAVE SOME OTHER OBJECTIVE.
IF I CAN FIND OUT WHAT THAT IS...
THEN MAYBE
I'LL DISCOVER THE TRUTH.
HOOONK
...

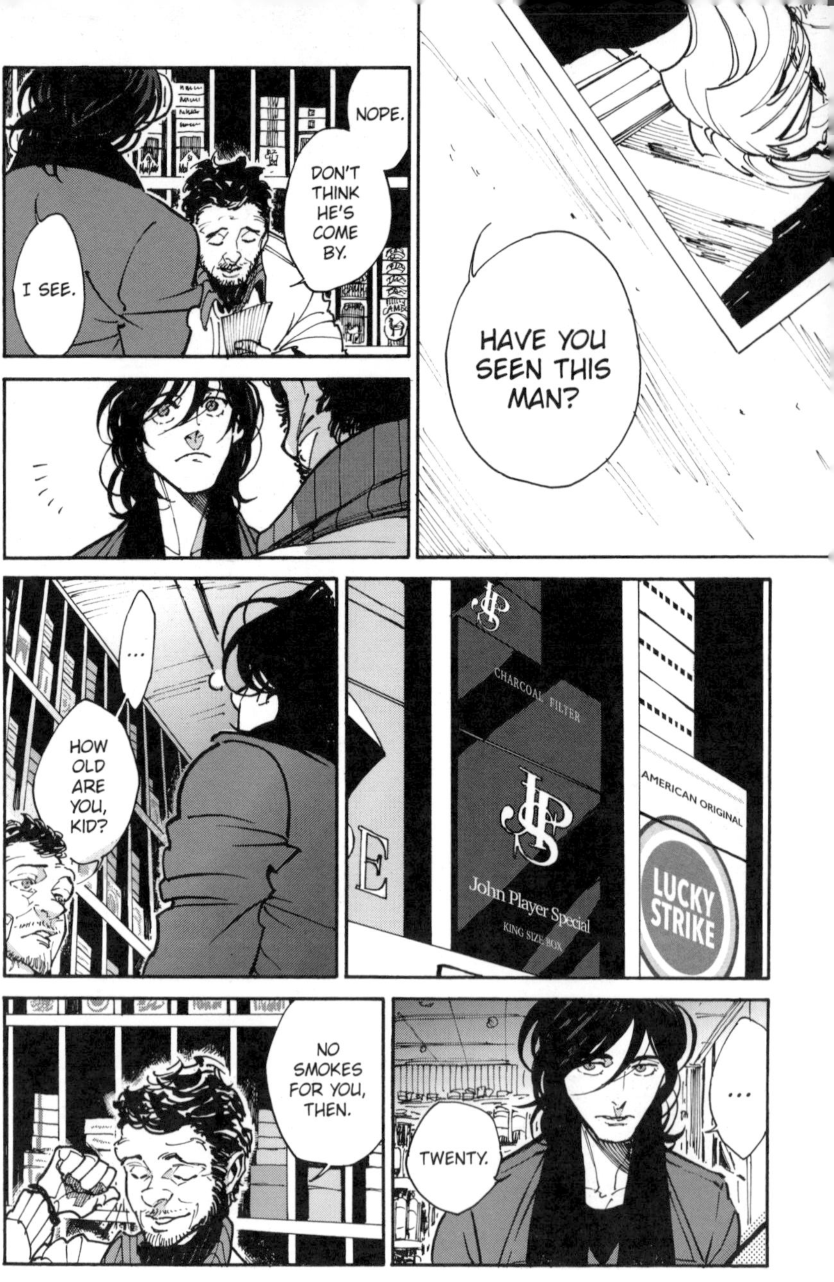
HAVE YOU SEEN THIS MAN?
NOPE.
DON'T THINK HE'S COME BY.
I SEE.
CHARCOAL FILTER
John Player Special
KING SIZE BOX
AMERICAN ORIGINAL
LUCKY STRIKE
...
HOW OLD ARE YOU, KID?
...
TWENTY.
NO SMOKES FOR YOU, THEN.

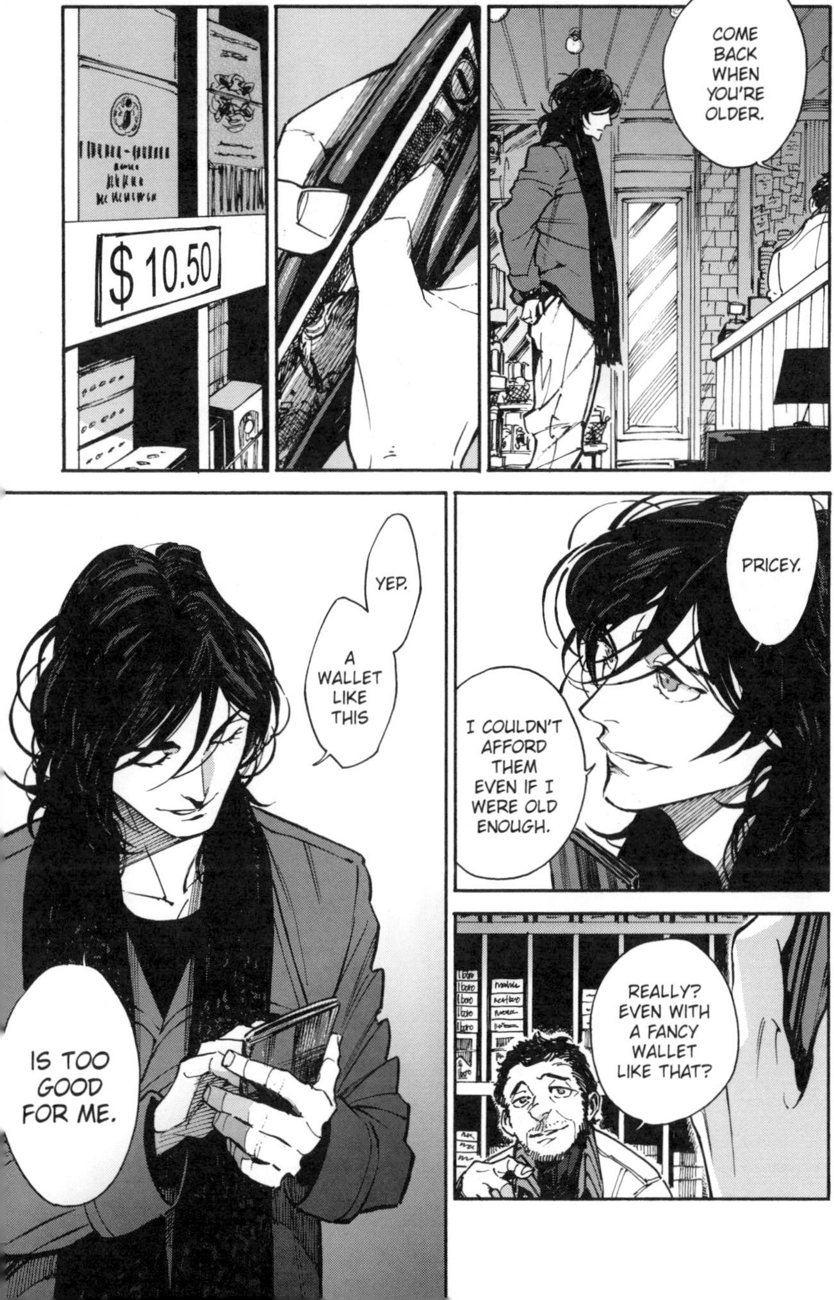
COME BACK WHEN YOU'RE OLDER.
$ 10.50
PRICEY.
I COULDN'T AFFORD THEM EVEN IF I WERE OLD ENOUGH.
REALLY? EVEN WITH A FANCY WALLET LIKE THAT?
YEP.
A WALLET LIKE THIS
IS TOO GOOD FOR ME.

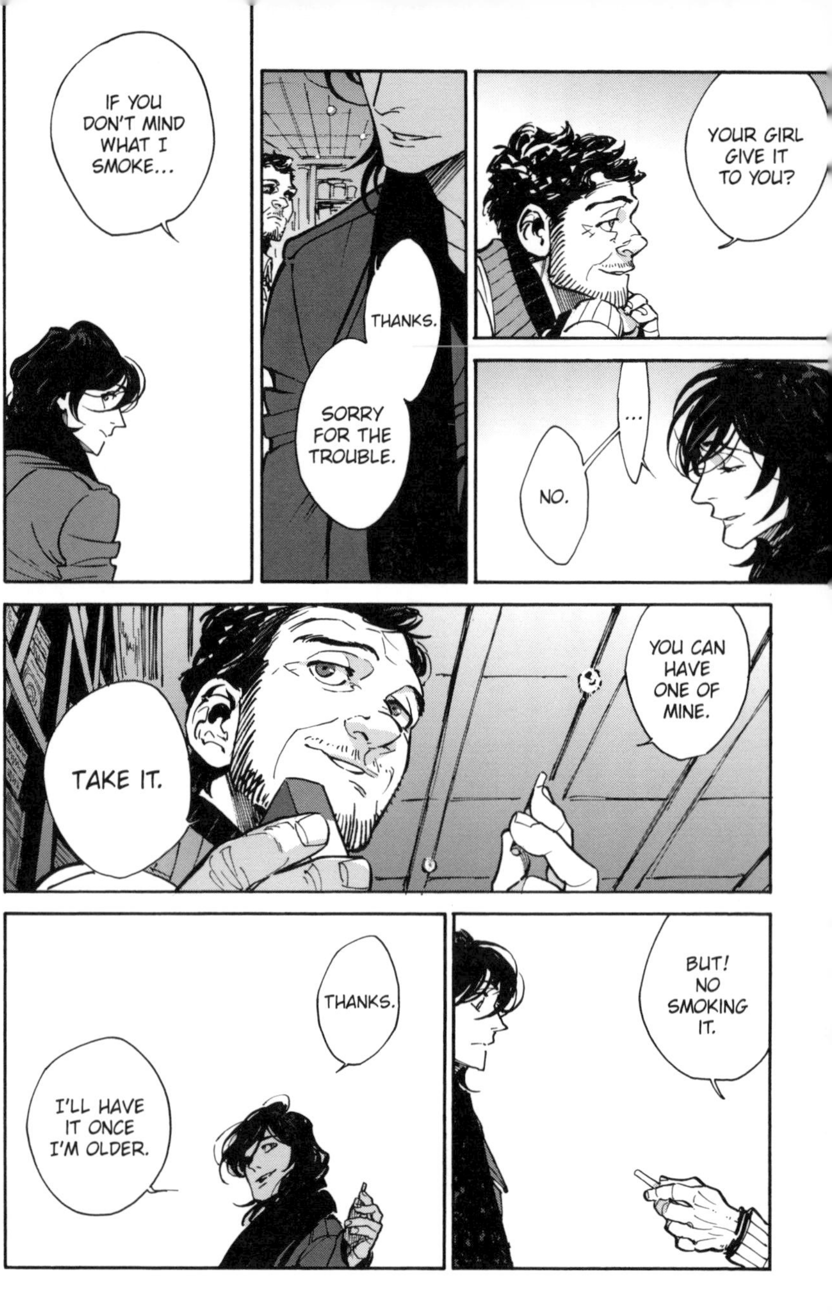
YOUR GIRL GIVE IT TO YOU?
...
NO.
THANKS.
SORRY FOR THE TROUBLE.
IF YOU DON'T MIND WHAT I SMOKE...
YOU CAN HAVE ONE OF MINE.
TAKE IT.
BUT! NO SMOKING IT.
THANKS.
I'LL HAVE IT ONCE I'M OLDER.

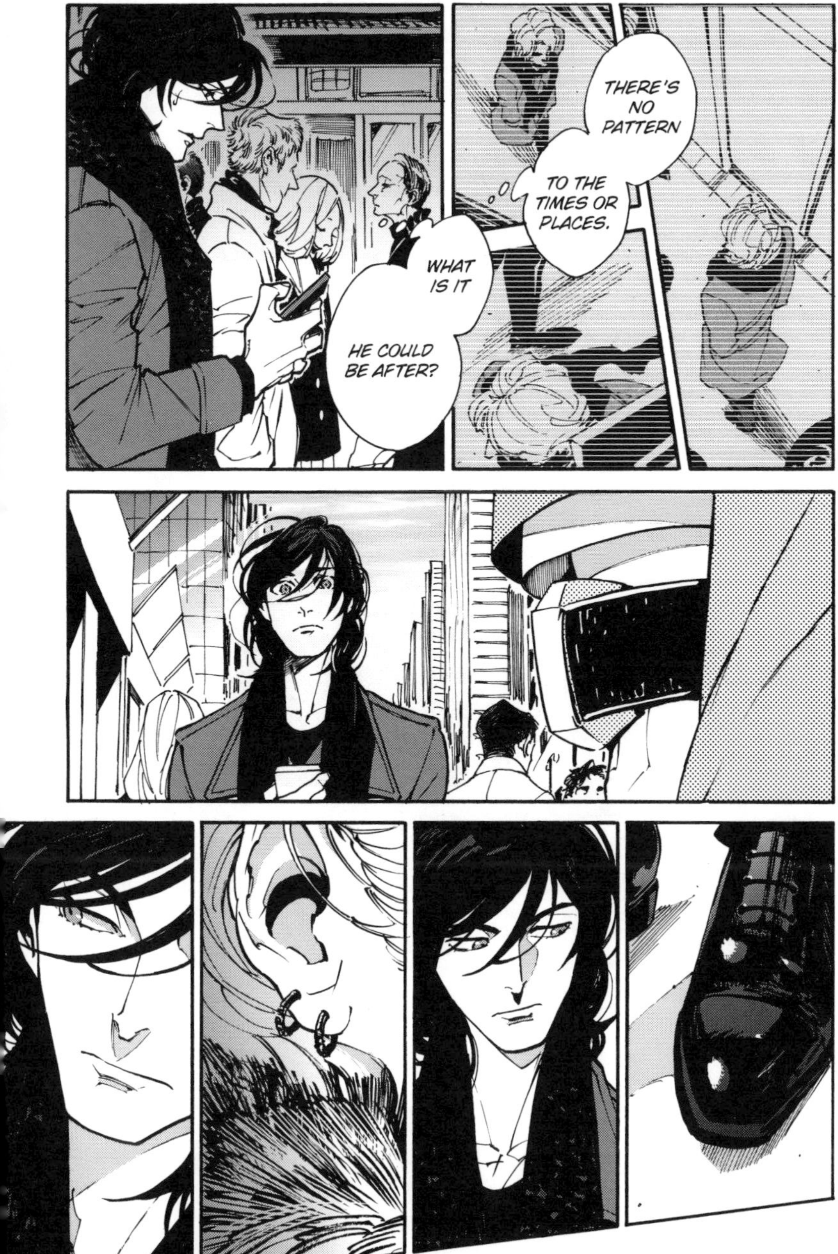
THERE'S NO PATTERN
TO THE TIMES OR PLACES.
WHAT IS IT
HE COULD BE AFTER?

I CAN'T HELP BUT GET LOST IN MY OWN THOUGHTS.

WHAT THE HELL AM I AFTER?

DAM-MIT.

ALL THE THINGS HE LIKED.

THINKING ABOUT WHAT HE WOULD WEAR.

ALL THE THINGS...

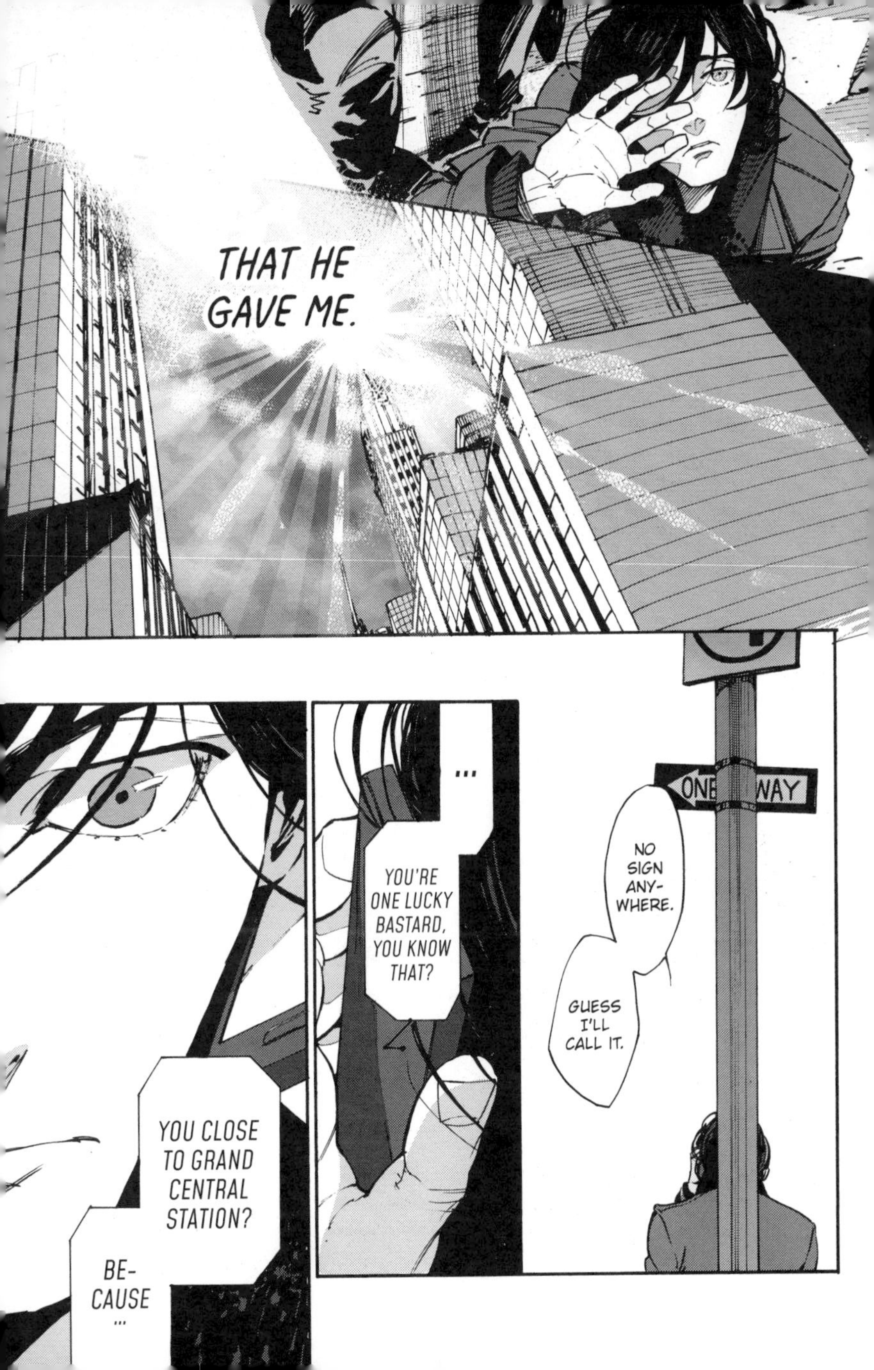
THAT HE GAVE ME.
ONE WAY
NO SIGN ANYWHERE.
GUESS I'LL CALL IT.
...
YOU'RE ONE LUCKY BASTARD, YOU KNOW THAT?
YOU CLOSE TO GRAND CENTRAL STATION?
BE-CAUSE ...

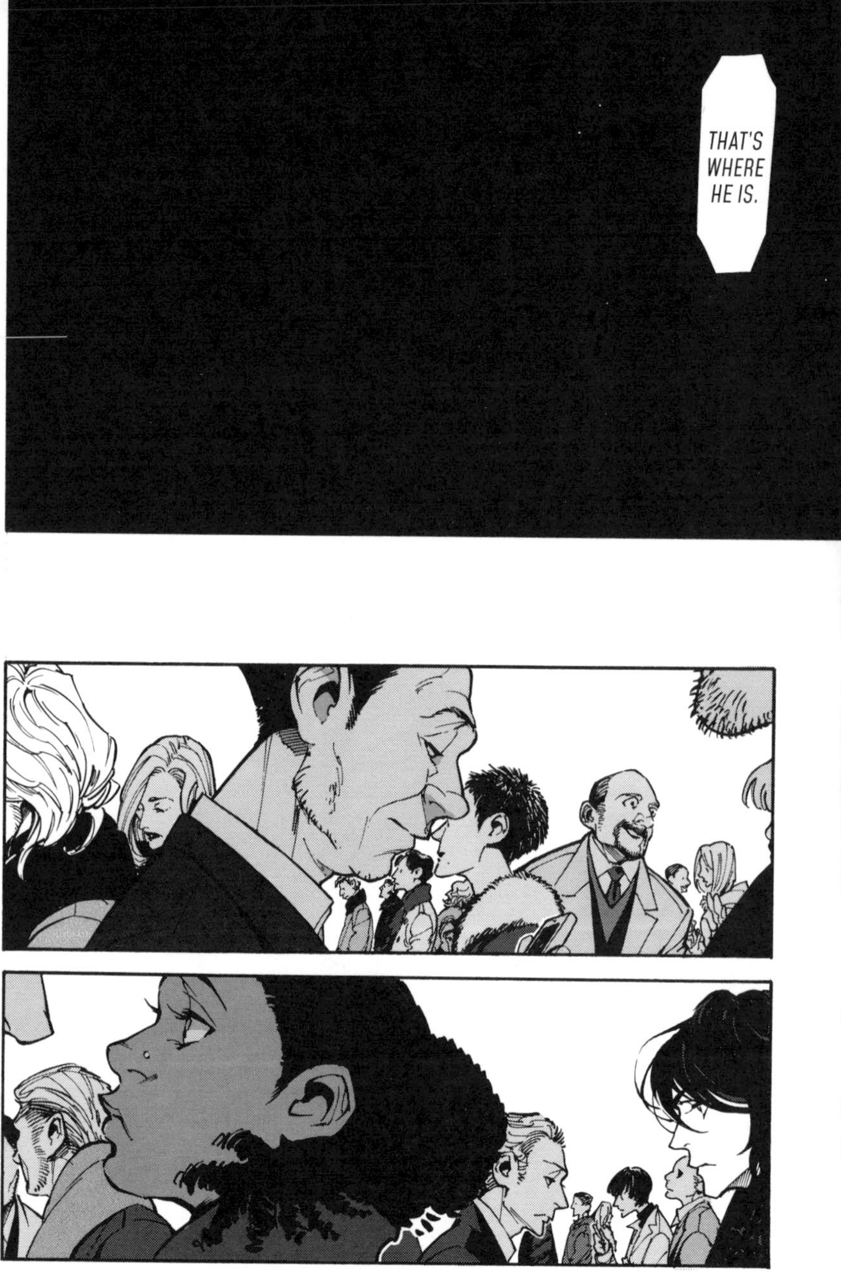
THAT'S WHERE HE IS.

I THINK

THAT'S HIM.

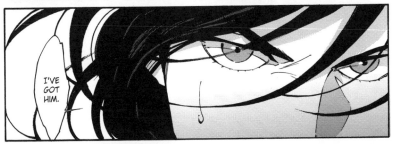

I'VE GOT HIM.

JUST A LITTLE MORE.

CLOS- ER.

CLOS- ER.

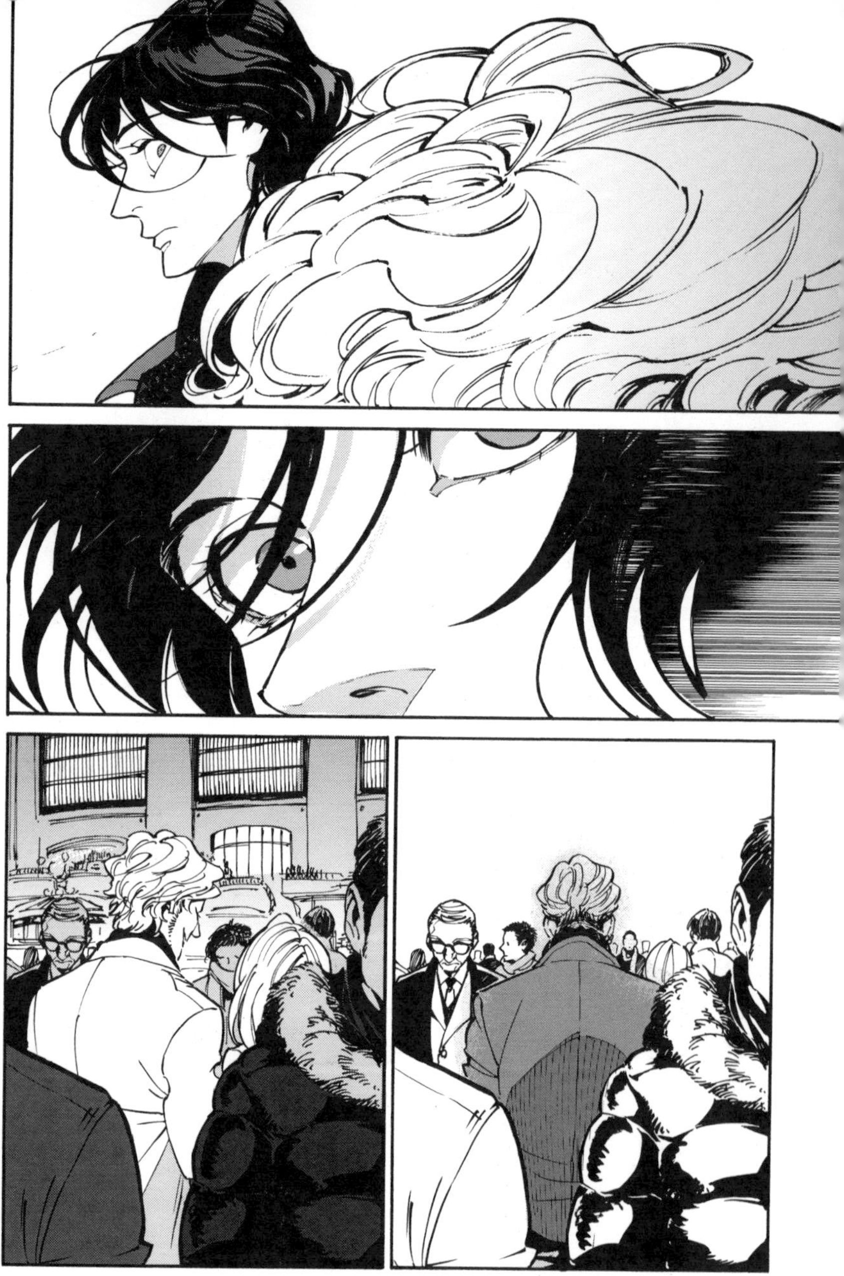

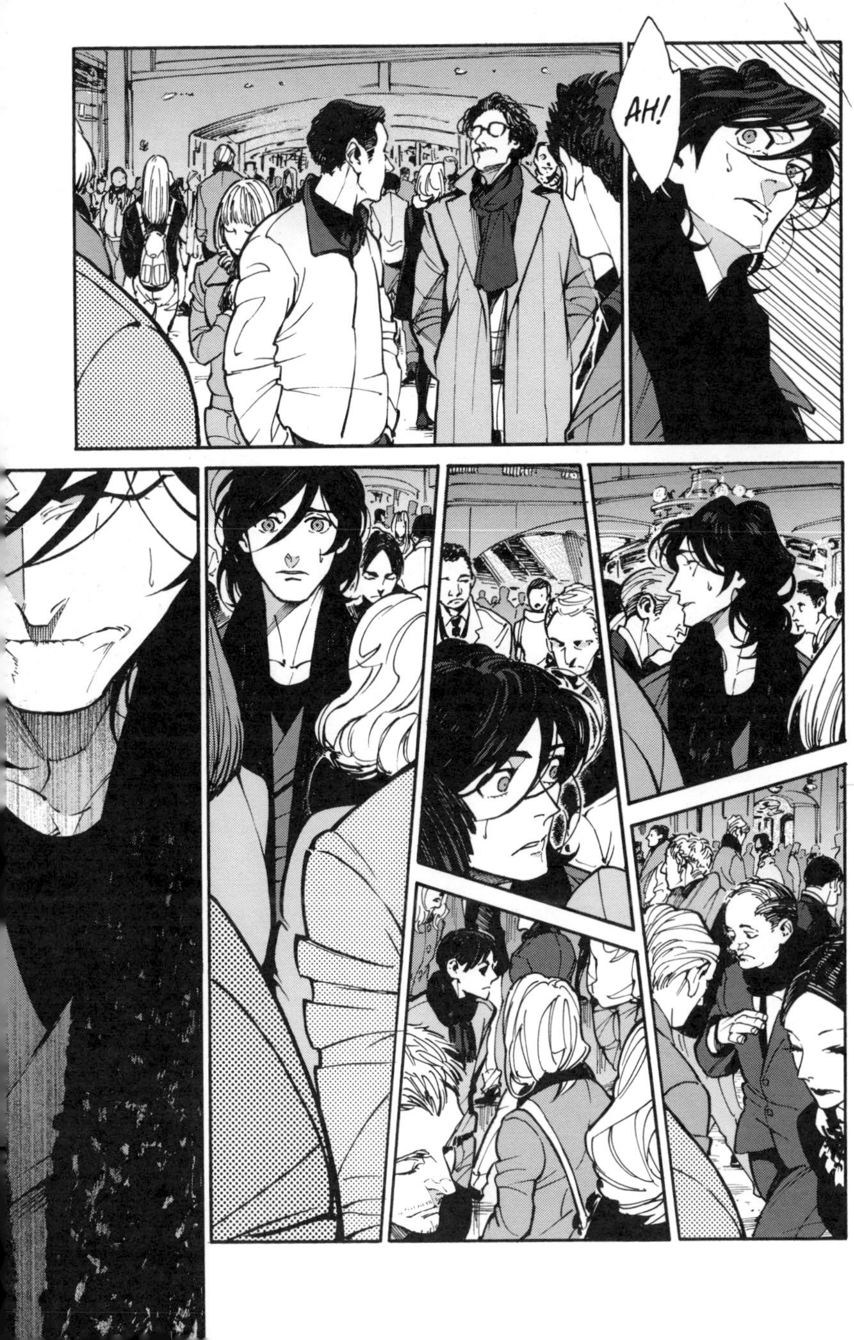
AH!

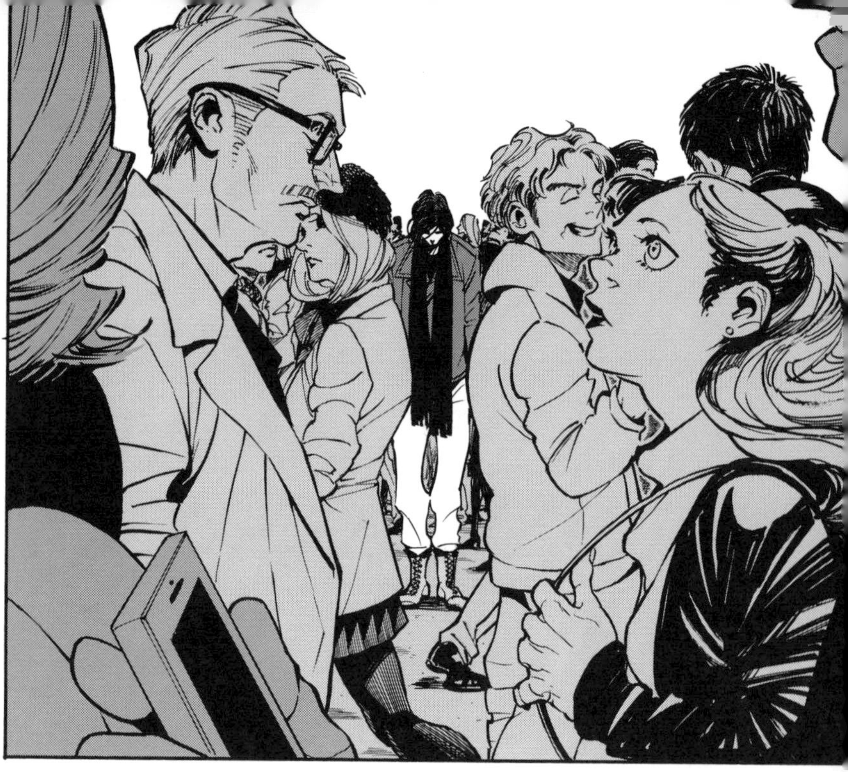
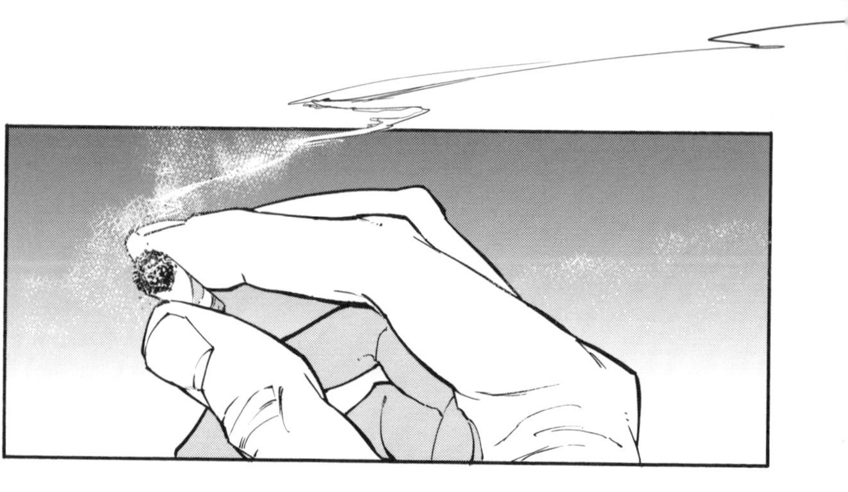

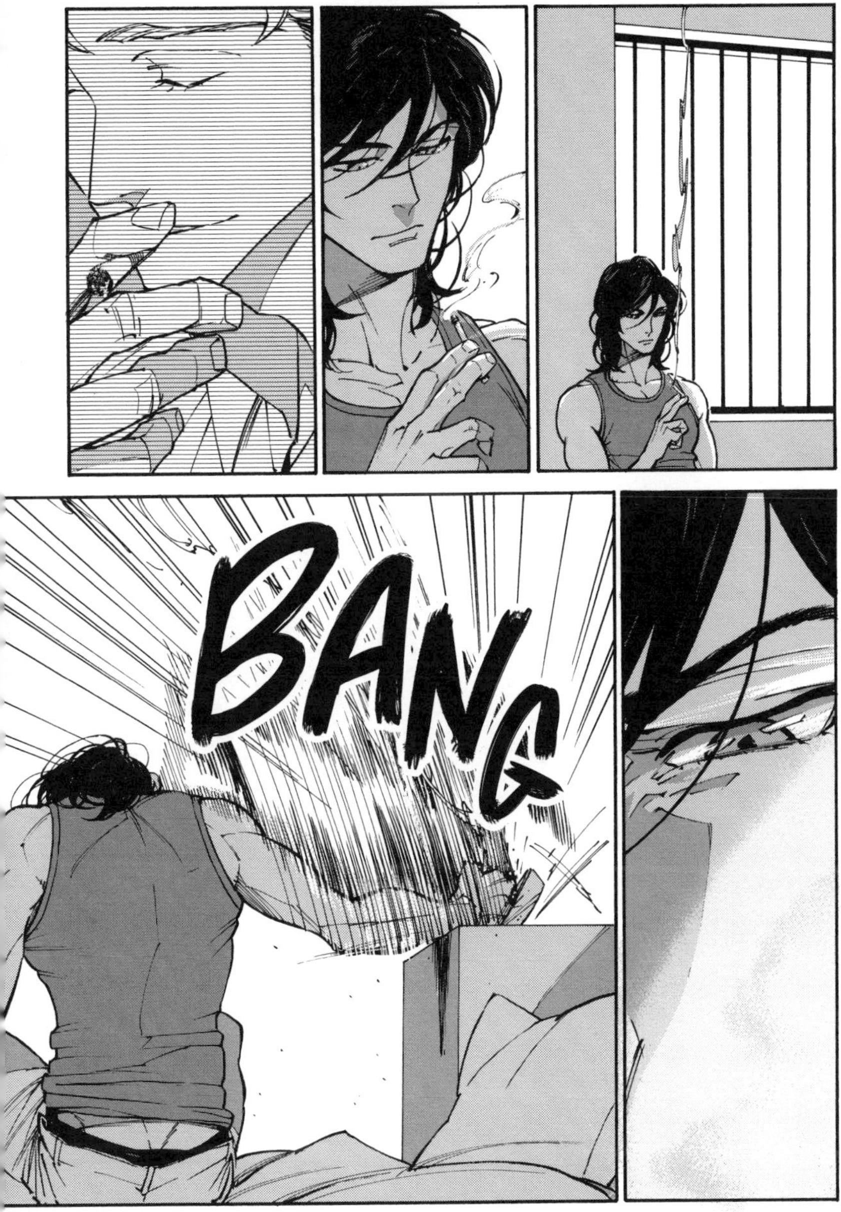
BANG

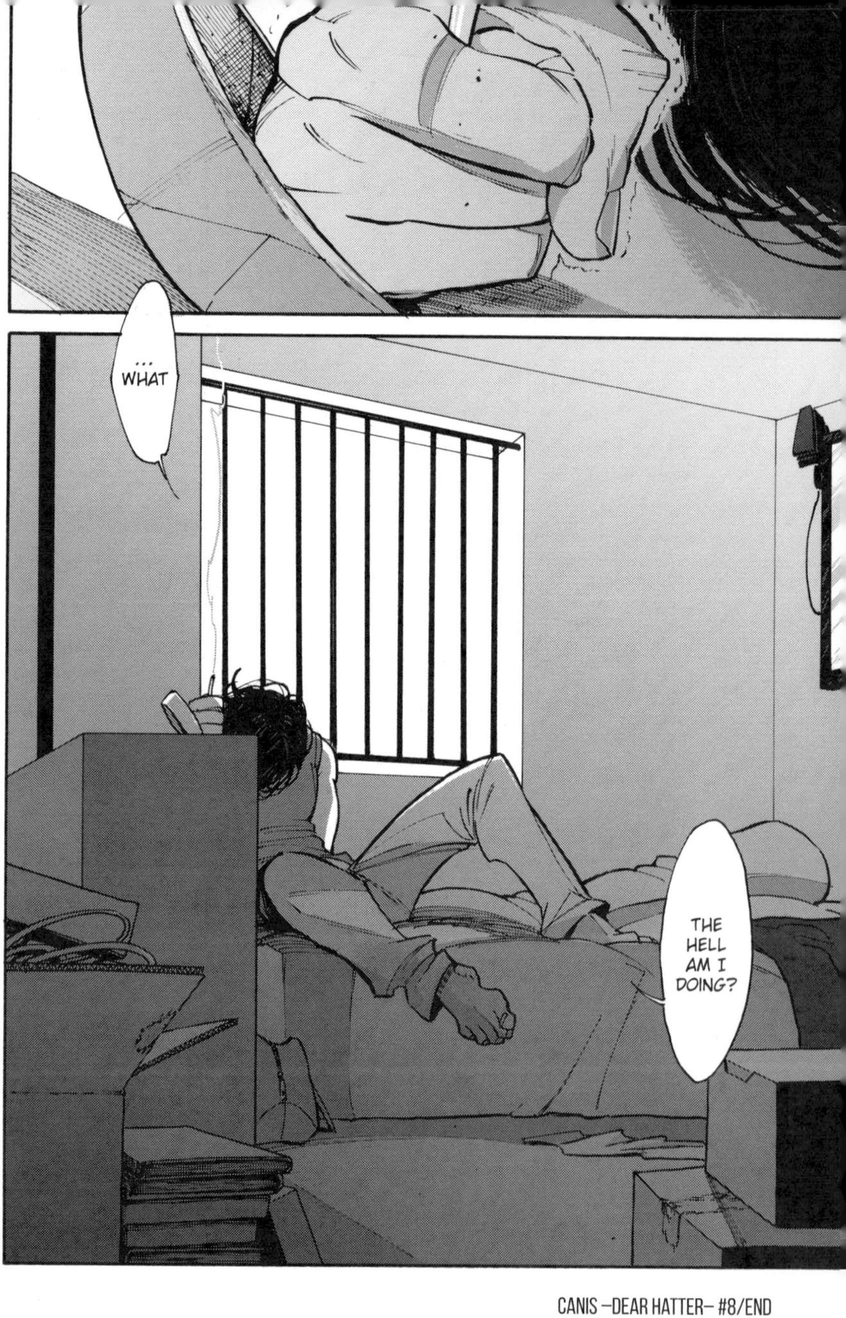
... WHAT
THE HELL AM I DOING?

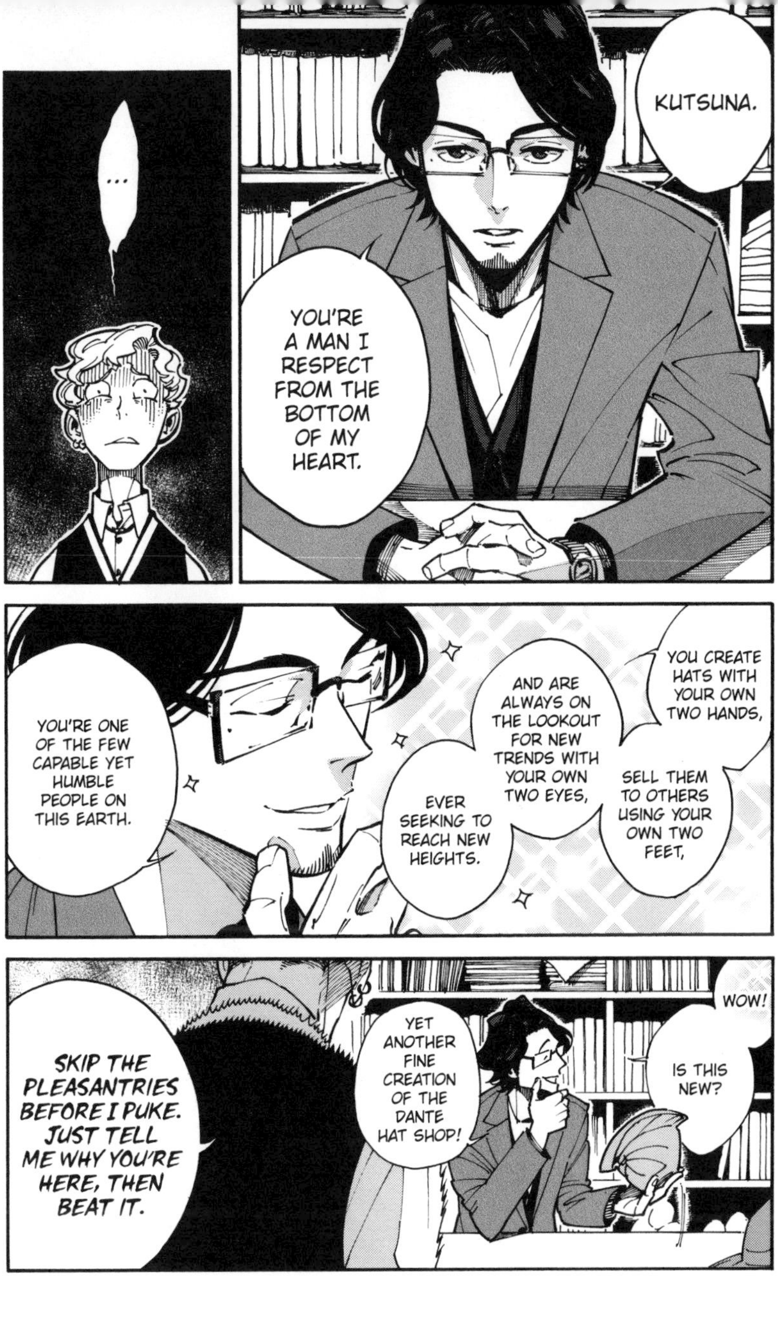
KUTSUNA.
YOU'RE A MAN I RESPECT FROM THE BOTTOM OF MY HEART.
...
YOU CREATE HATS WITH YOUR OWN TWO HANDS,
SELL THEM TO OTHERS USING YOUR OWN TWO FEET,
AND ARE ALWAYS ON THE LOOKOUT FOR NEW TRENDS WITH YOUR OWN TWO EYES,
EVER SEEKING TO REACH NEW HEIGHTS.
YOU'RE ONE OF THE FEW CAPABLE YET HUMBLE PEOPLE ON THIS EARTH.
WOW!
IS THIS NEW?
YET ANOTHER FINE CREATION OF THE DANTE HAT SHOP!
SKIP THE PLEASANTRIES BEFORE I PUKE. JUST TELL ME WHY YOU'RE HERE, THEN BEAT IT.

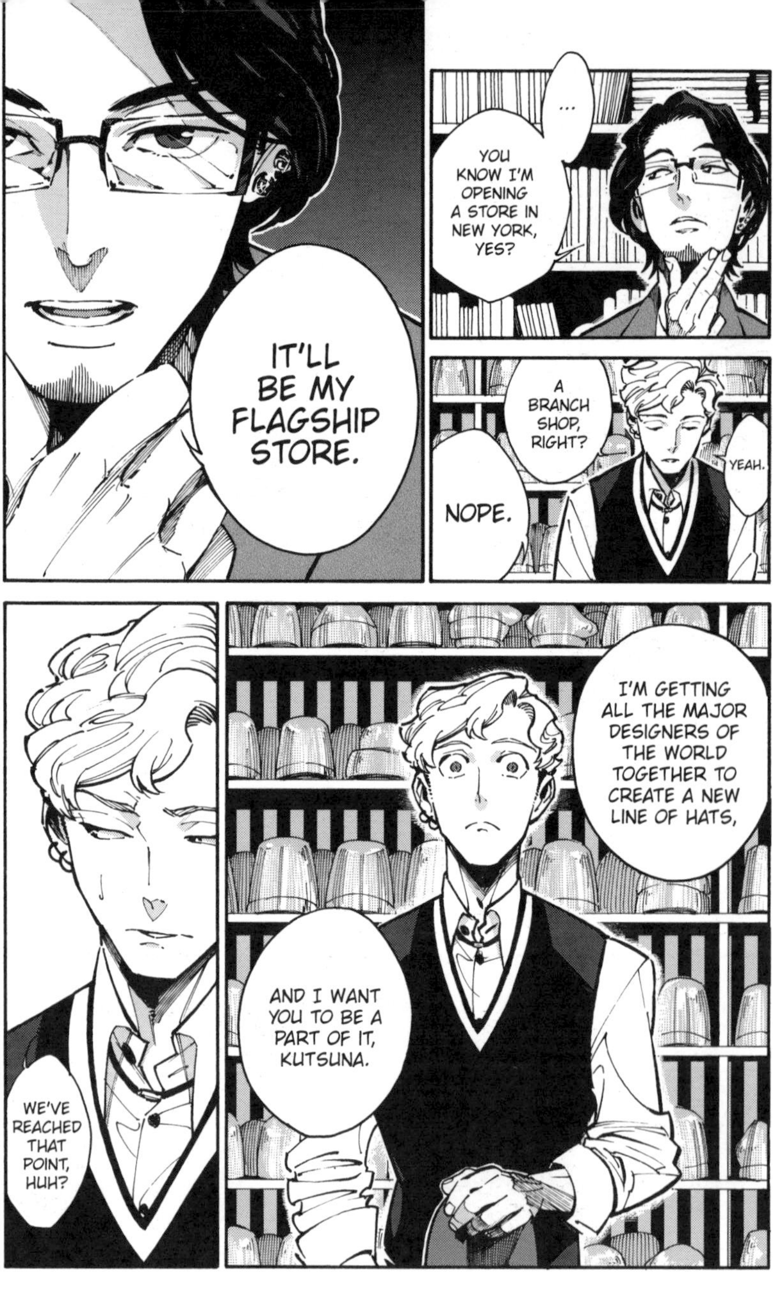
...
YOU KNOW I'M OPENING A STORE IN NEW YORK, YES?
YEAH.
A BRANCH SHOP, RIGHT?
NOPE.
IT'LL BE MY FLAGSHIP STORE.
I'M GETTING ALL THE MAJOR DESIGNERS OF THE WORLD TOGETHER TO CREATE A NEW LINE OF HATS,
AND I WANT YOU TO BE A PART OF IT, KUTSUNA.
WE'VE REACHED THAT POINT, HUH?

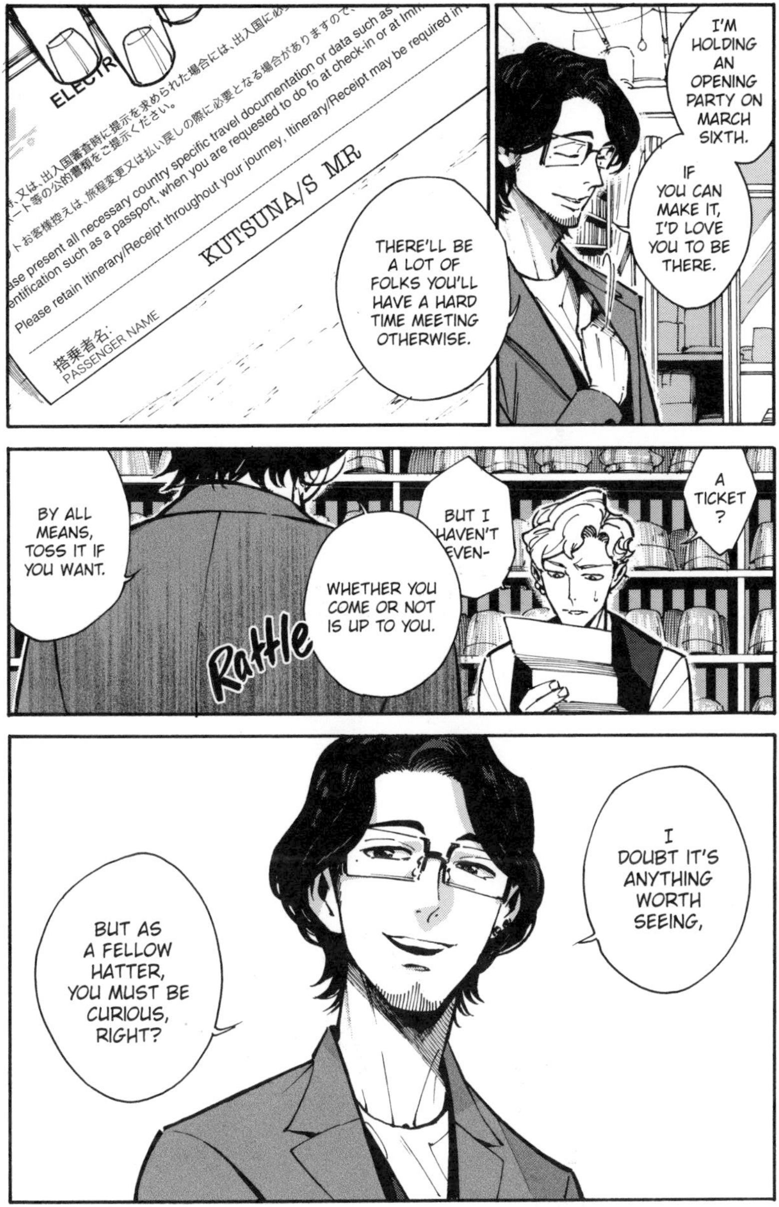
I'M HOLDING AN OPENING PARTY ON MARCH SIXTH.
IF YOU CAN MAKE IT, I'D LOVE YOU TO BE THERE.
THERE'LL BE A LOT OF FOLKS YOU'LL HAVE A HARD TIME MEETING OTHERWISE.
ELECTR
Please retain Itinerary/Receipt throughout your journey, Itinerary/Receipt may be required in
KUTSUNA/S MR
搭乗者名:
PASSENGER NAME
A TICKET?
BUT I HAVEN'T EVEN-
WHETHER YOU COME OR NOT IS UP TO YOU.
BY ALL MEANS, TOSS IT IF YOU WANT.
Rattle
I DOUBT IT'S ANYTHING WORTH SEEING,
BUT AS A FELLOW HATTER, YOU MUST BE CURIOUS, RIGHT?

I'LL THINK ABOUT IT.

...

Chapter.9

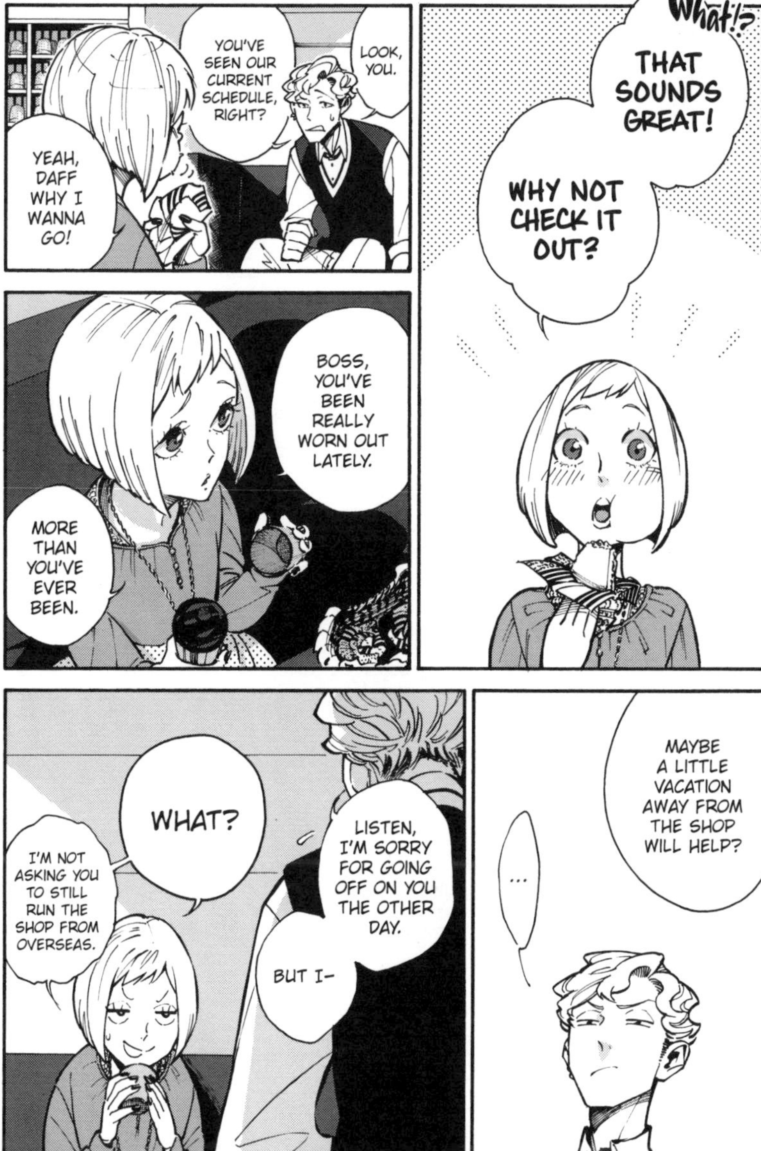
What!?
THAT SOUNDS GREAT!
WHY NOT CHECK IT OUT?
LOOK, YOU.
YOU'VE SEEN OUR CURRENT SCHEDULE, RIGHT?
YEAH, DAFF WHY I WANNA GO!
BOSS, YOU'VE BEEN REALLY WORN OUT LATELY.
MORE THAN YOU'VE EVER BEEN.
MAYBE A LITTLE VACATION AWAY FROM THE SHOP WILL HELP?
...
LISTEN, I'M SORRY FOR GOING OFF ON YOU THE OTHER DAY.
BUT I-
WHAT?
I'M NOT ASKING YOU TO STILL RUN THE SHOP FROM OVERSEAS.

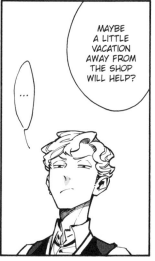

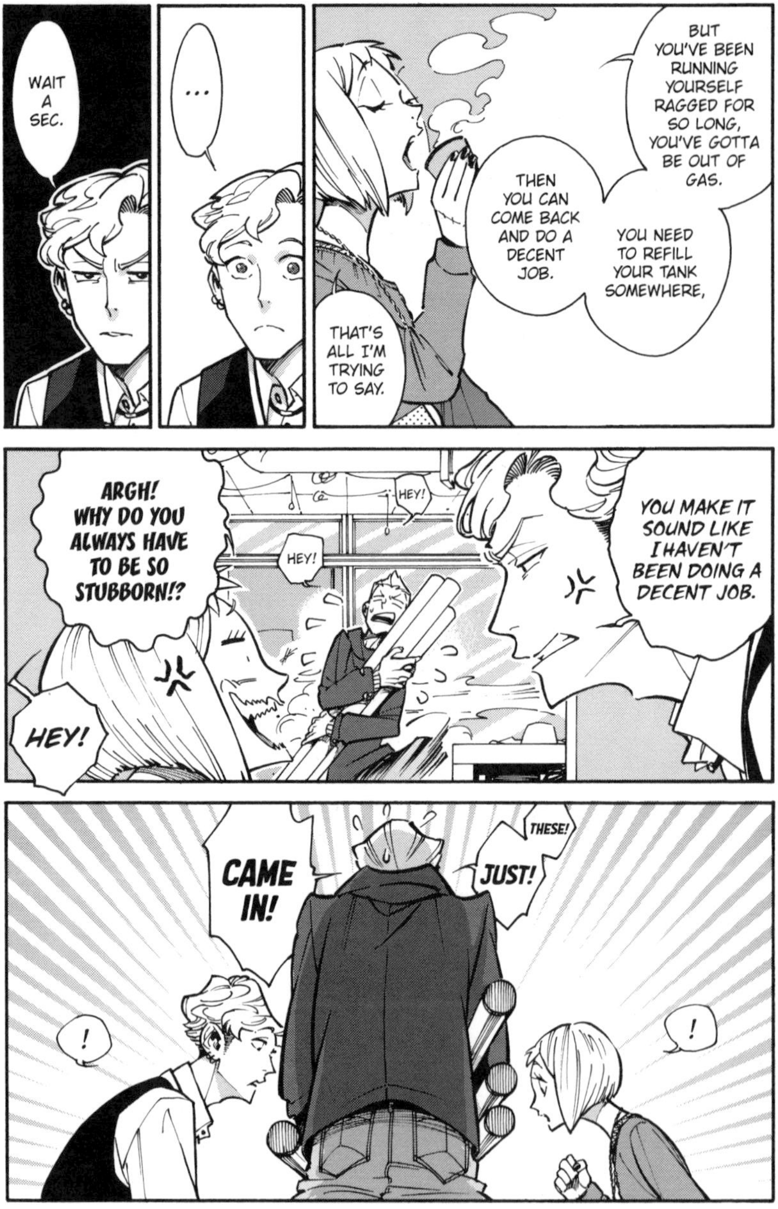
BUT YOU'VE BEEN RUNNING YOURSELF RAGGED FOR SO LONG, YOU'VE GOTTA BE OUT OF GAS.
YOU NEED TO REFILL YOUR TANK SOMEWHERE,
THEN YOU CAN COME BACK AND DO A DECENT JOB.
THAT'S ALL I'M TRYING TO SAY.
...
WAIT A SEC.
YOU MAKE IT SOUND LIKE I HAVEN'T BEEN DOING A DECENT JOB.
HEY!
HEY!
ARGH! WHY DO YOU ALWAYS HAVE TO BE SO STUBBORN!?
HEY!
THESE!
JUST!
CAME IN!
!
!

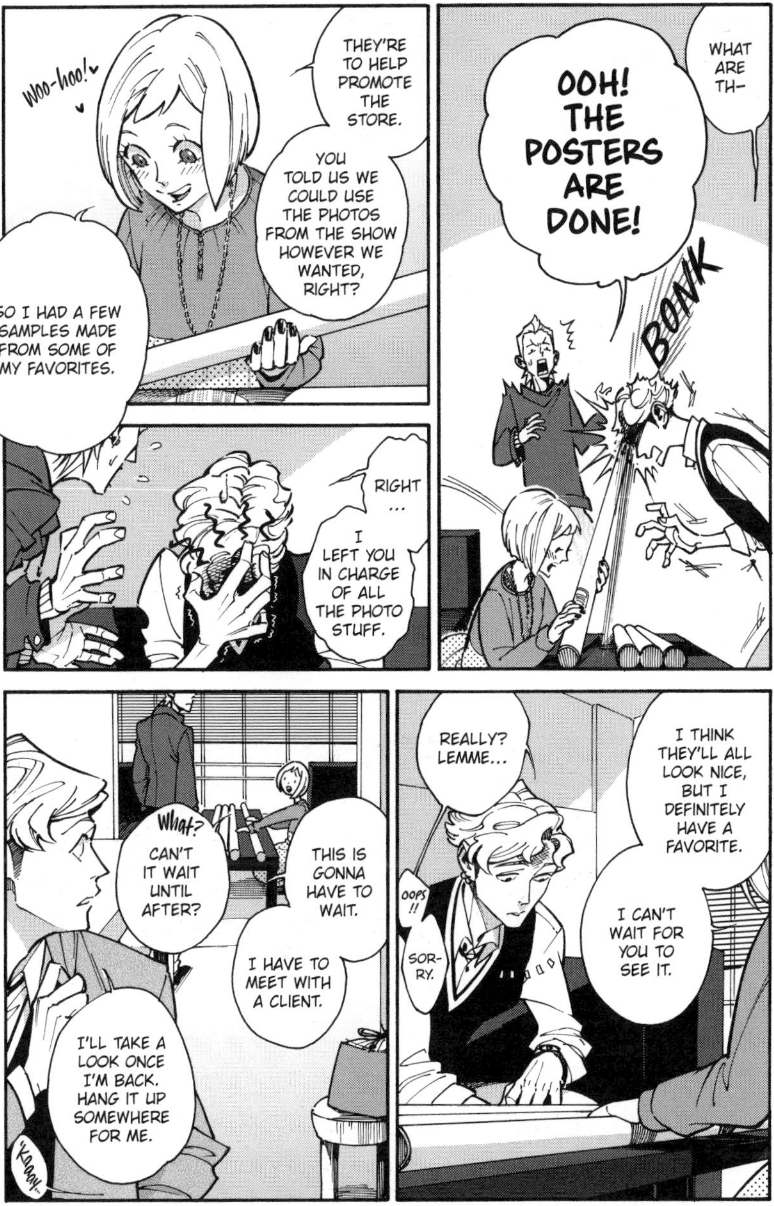
WHAT ARE TH-
OOH! THE POSTERS ARE DONE!
BONK
THEY'RE TO HELP PROMOTE THE STORE.
Woo-hoo!
YOU TOLD US WE COULD USE THE PHOTOS FROM THE SHOW HOWEVER WE WANTED, RIGHT?
SO I HAD A FEW SAMPLES MADE FROM SOME OF MY FAVORITES.
RIGHT...
I LEFT YOU IN CHARGE OF ALL THE PHOTO STUFF.
I THINK THEY'LL ALL LOOK NICE, BUT I DEFINITELY HAVE A FAVORITE.
REALLY? LEMME...
I CAN'T WAIT FOR YOU TO SEE IT.
OOPS!!
SOR-RY.
THIS IS GONNA HAVE TO WAIT.
What?
CAN'T IT WAIT UNTIL AFTER?
I HAVE TO MEET WITH A CLIENT.
I'LL TAKE A LOOK ONCE I'M BACK. HANG IT UP SOMEWHERE FOR ME.
Kaaay..

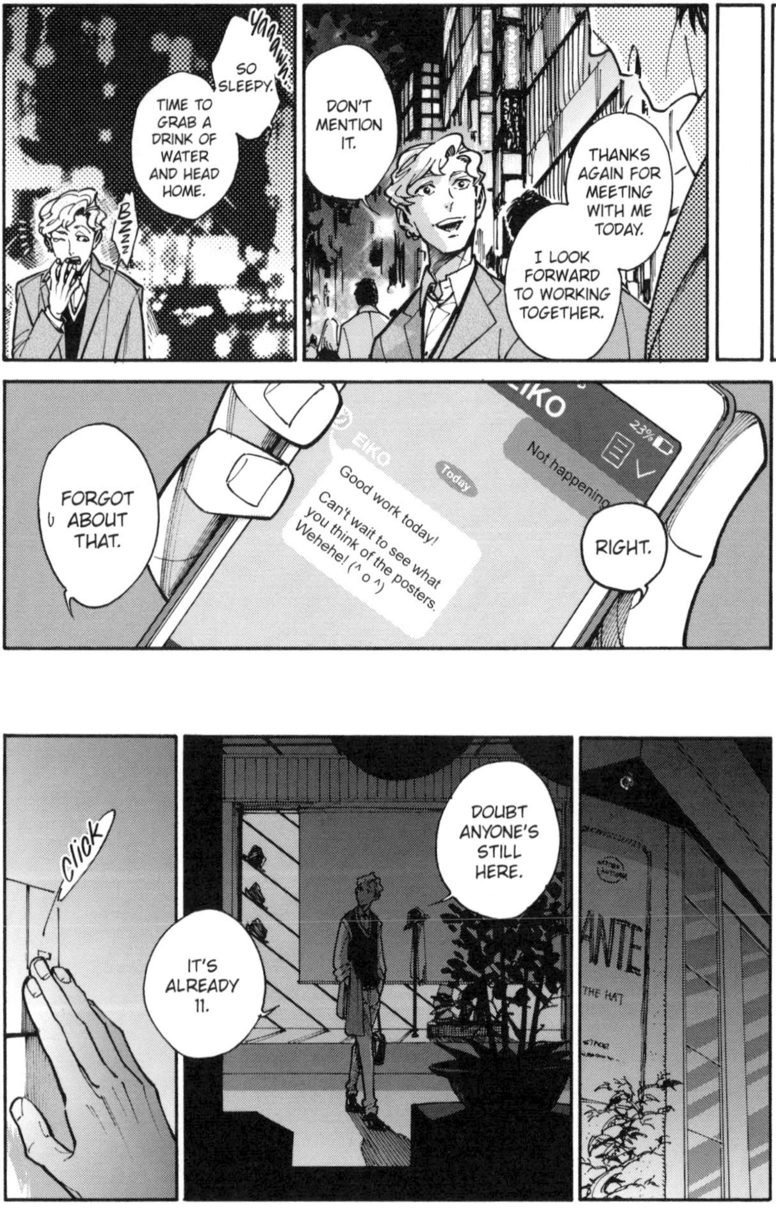
THANKS AGAIN FOR MEETING WITH ME TODAY.
I LOOK FORWARD TO WORKING TOGETHER.
DON'T MENTION IT.
yaaawn
SO SLEEPY.
TIME TO GRAB A DRINK OF WATER AND HEAD HOME.
BZzz
EIKO
23%
Not happening
RIGHT.
EIKO
Today
Good work today!
Can't wait to see what you think of the posters.
Wehehe! (^ o ^)
FORGOT ABOUT THAT.
THE HAT
DOUBT ANYONE'S STILL HERE.
IT'S ALREADY 11.
click

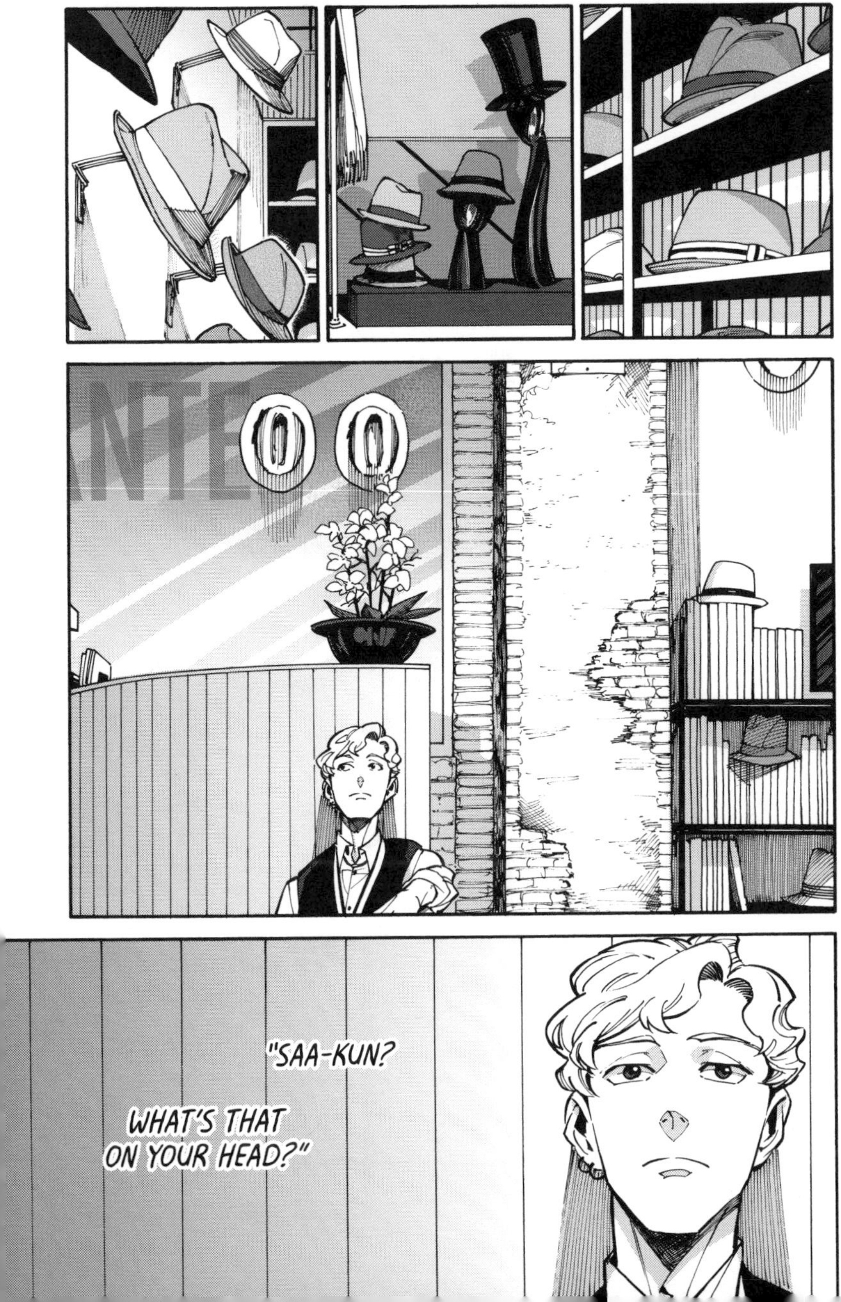
"SAA-KUN?
WHAT'S THAT ON YOUR HEAD?"

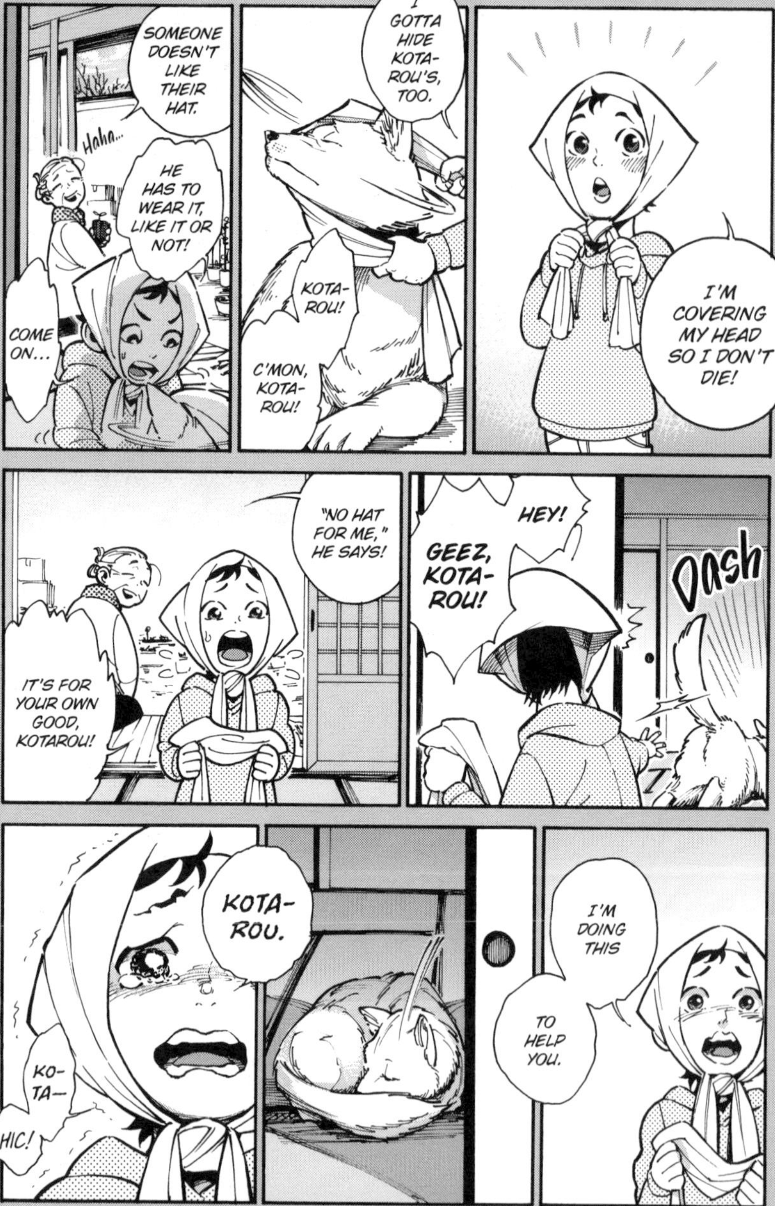
I'M COVERING MY HEAD SO I DON'T DIE!
I GOTTA HIDE KOTA-ROU'S, TOO.
KOTA-ROU!
C'MON, KOTA-ROU!
SOMEONE DOESN'T LIKE THEIR HAT.
Haha...
HE HAS TO WEAR IT, LIKE IT OR NOT!
COME ON...
HEY!
GEEZ, KOTA-ROU!
Dash
"NO HAT FOR ME," HE SAYS!
IT'S FOR YOUR OWN GOOD, KOTAROU!
I'M DOING THIS
TO HELP YOU.
KOTA-ROU.
KO-TA—
HIC!

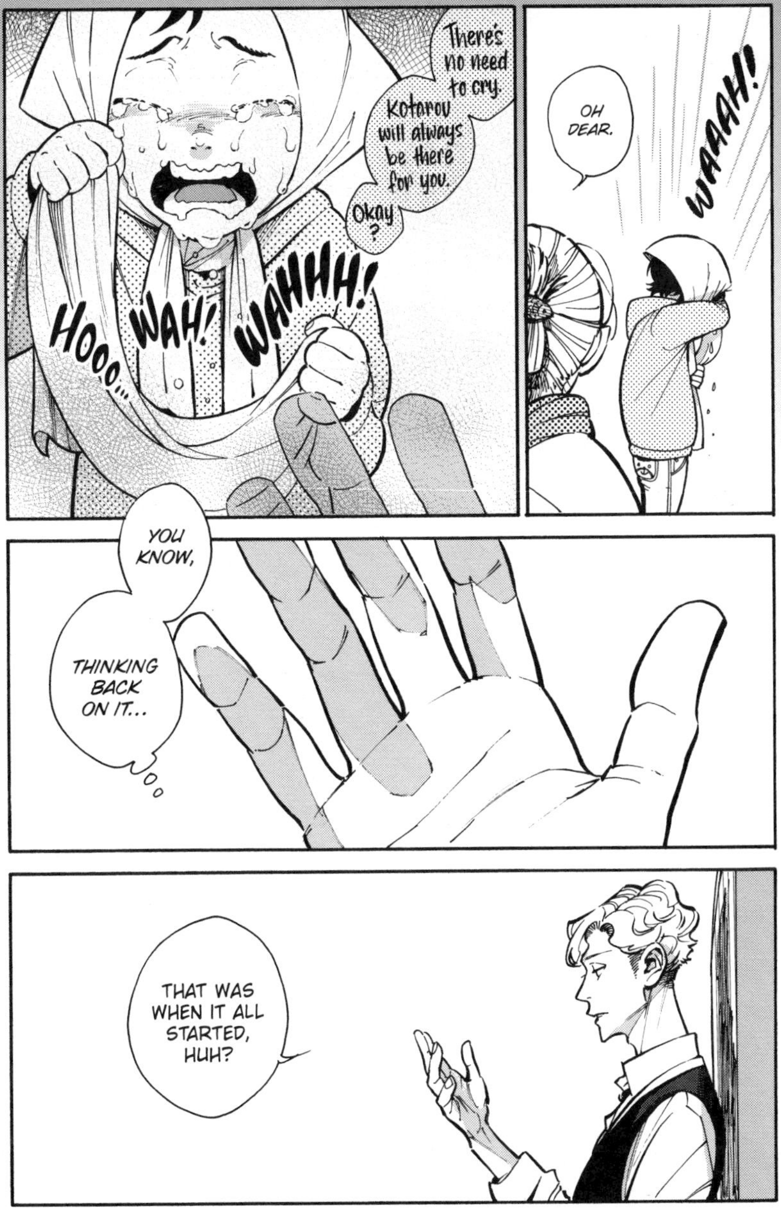
OH DEAR.
WAAAH!
There's no need to cry.
Kotarou will always be there for you.
Okay?
HOOO...
WAH!
WAHHH!
YOU KNOW,
THINKING BACK ON IT...
THAT WAS WHEN IT ALL STARTED, HUH?

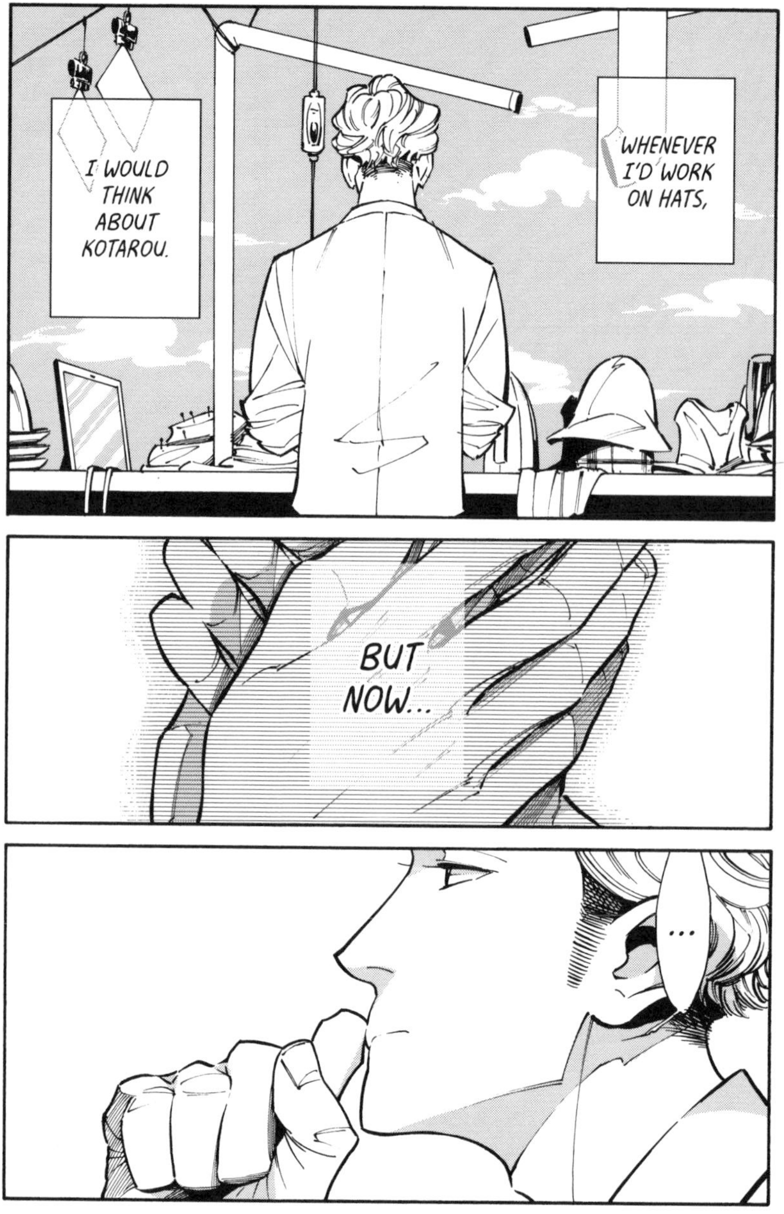
WHENEVER I'D WORK ON HATS,
I WOULD THINK ABOUT KOTAROU.
BUT NOW...
...

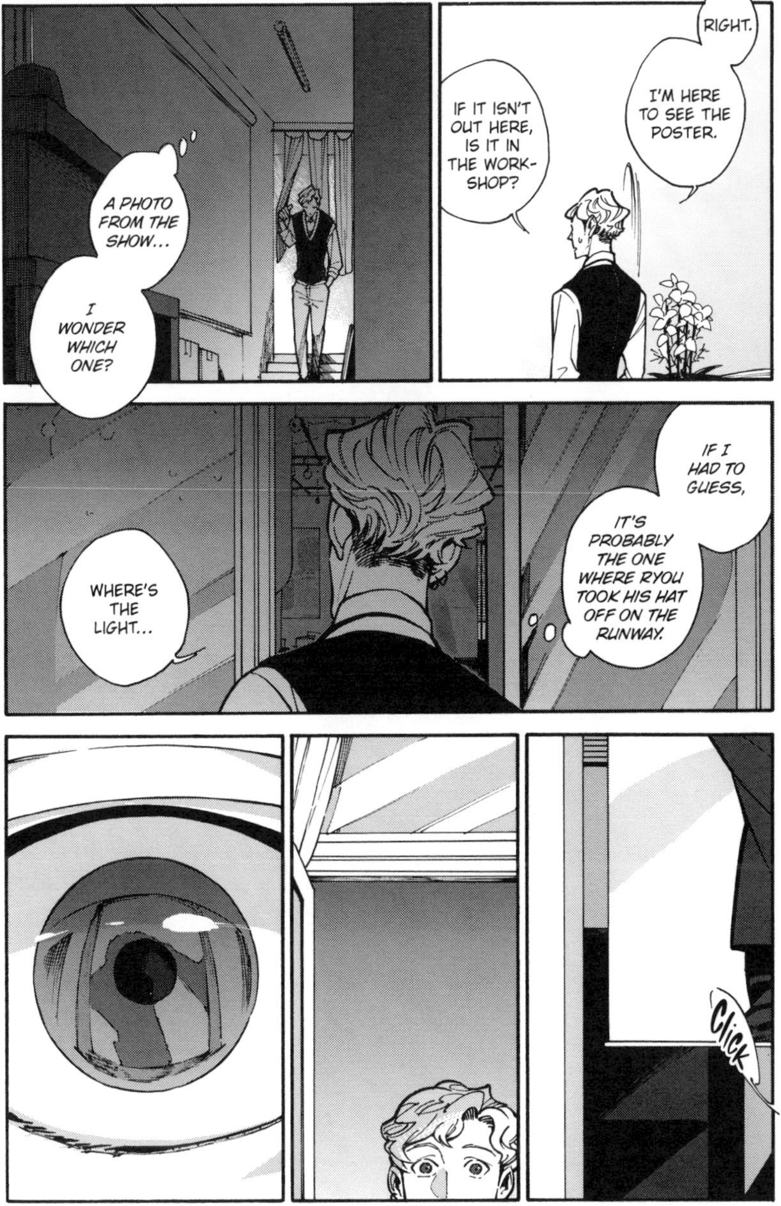
RIGHT.
I'M HERE TO SEE THE POSTER.
IF IT ISN'T OUT HERE, IS IT IN THE WORK-SHOP?
A PHOTO FROM THE SHOW...
I WONDER WHICH ONE?
IF I HAD TO GUESS,
IT'S PROBABLY THE ONE WHERE RYOU TOOK HIS HAT OFF ON THE RUNWAY.
WHERE'S THE LIGHT...
CLICK

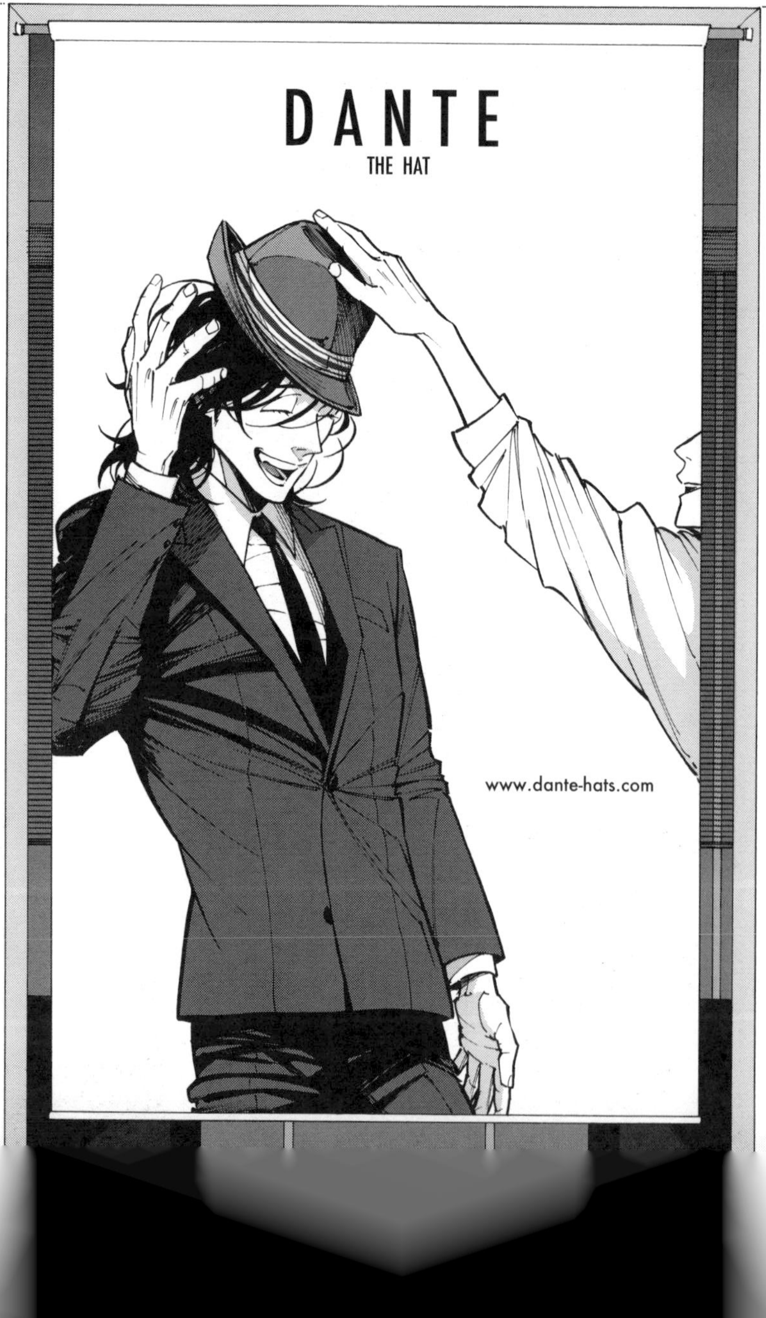
DANTE
THE HAT
www.dante-hats.com

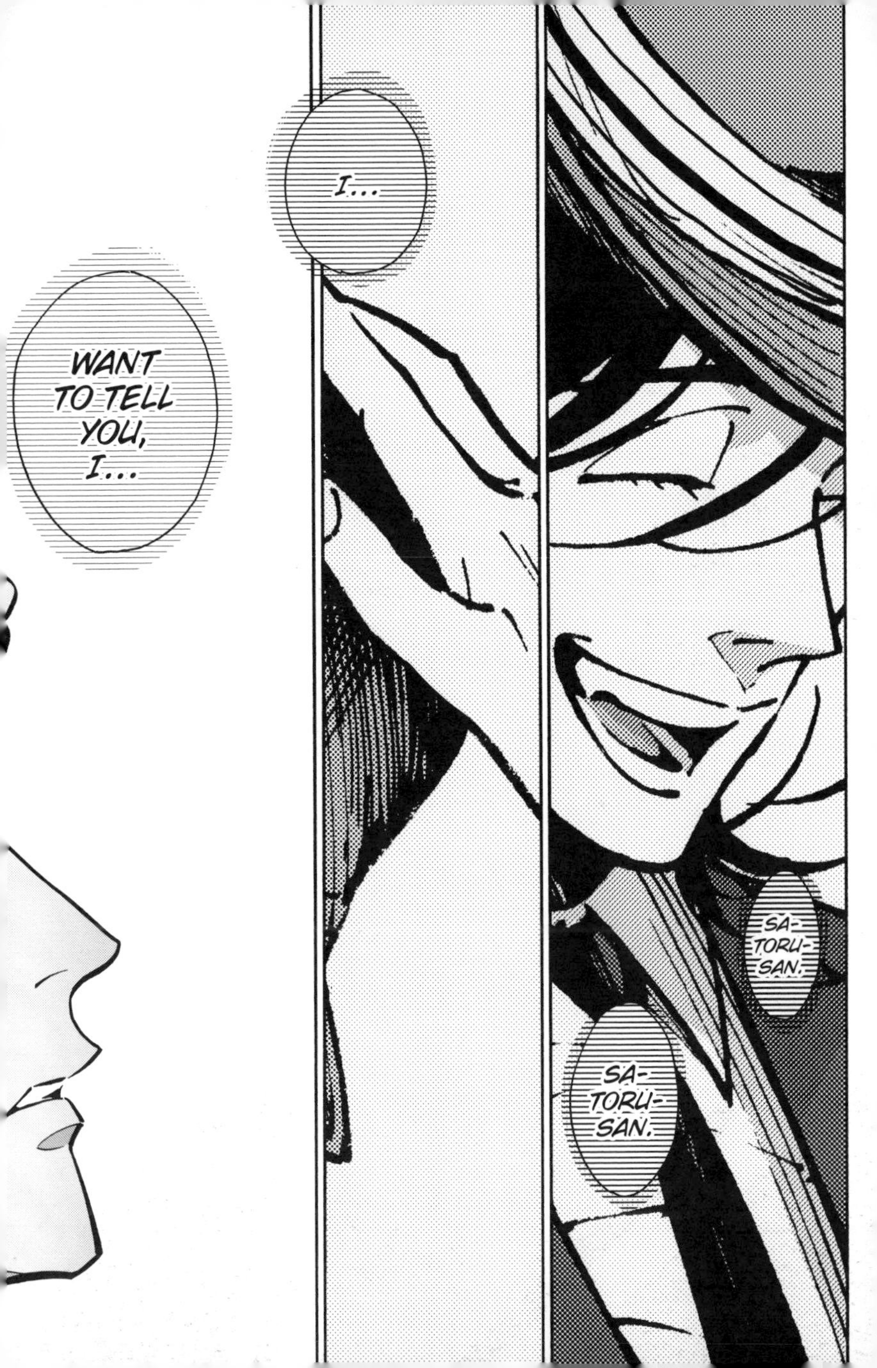
SA-TORU-SAN.
SA-TORU-SAN.
I...
WANT TO TELL YOU, I...

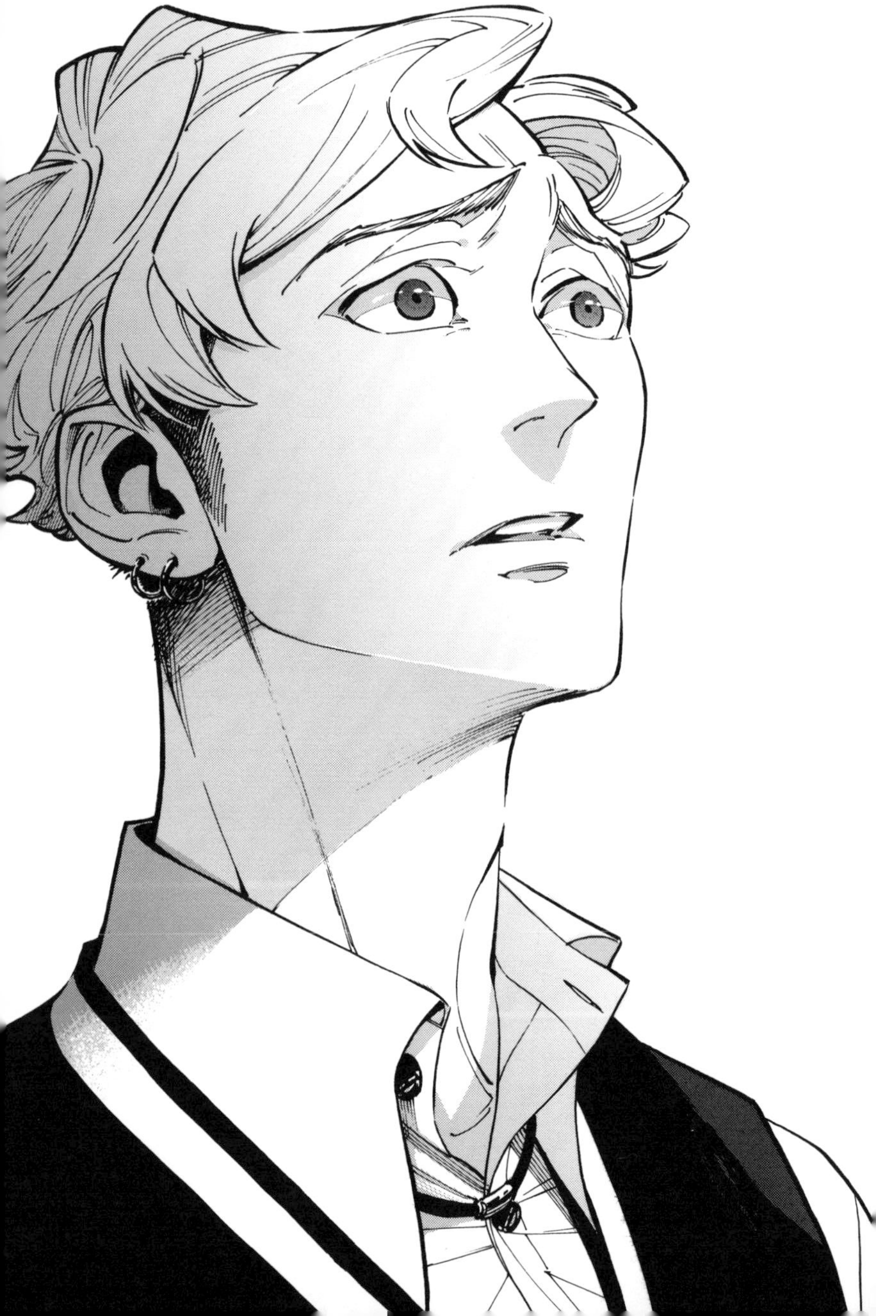

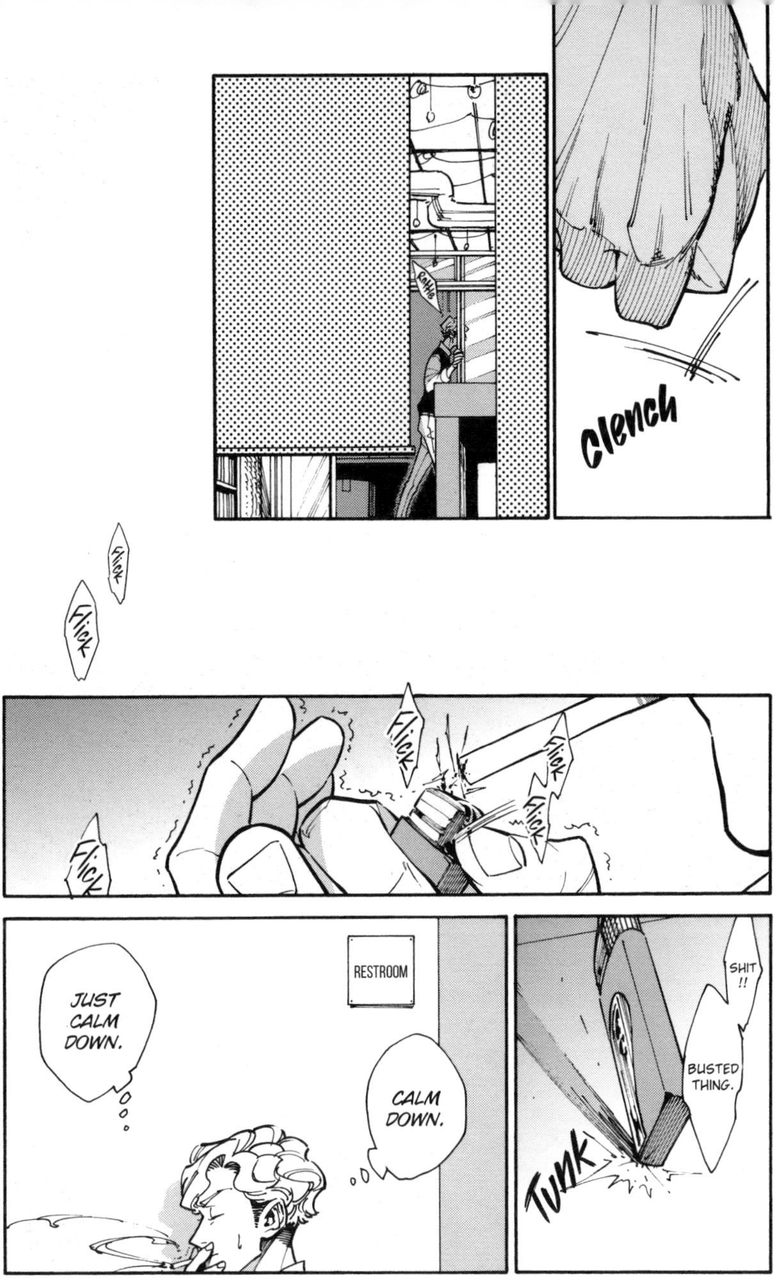
Clench
Rattle
Flick
Flick
Flick
Flick
Flick
Flick
SHIT !!
BUSTED THING.
TUNK
RESTROOM
CALM DOWN.
JUST CALM DOWN.

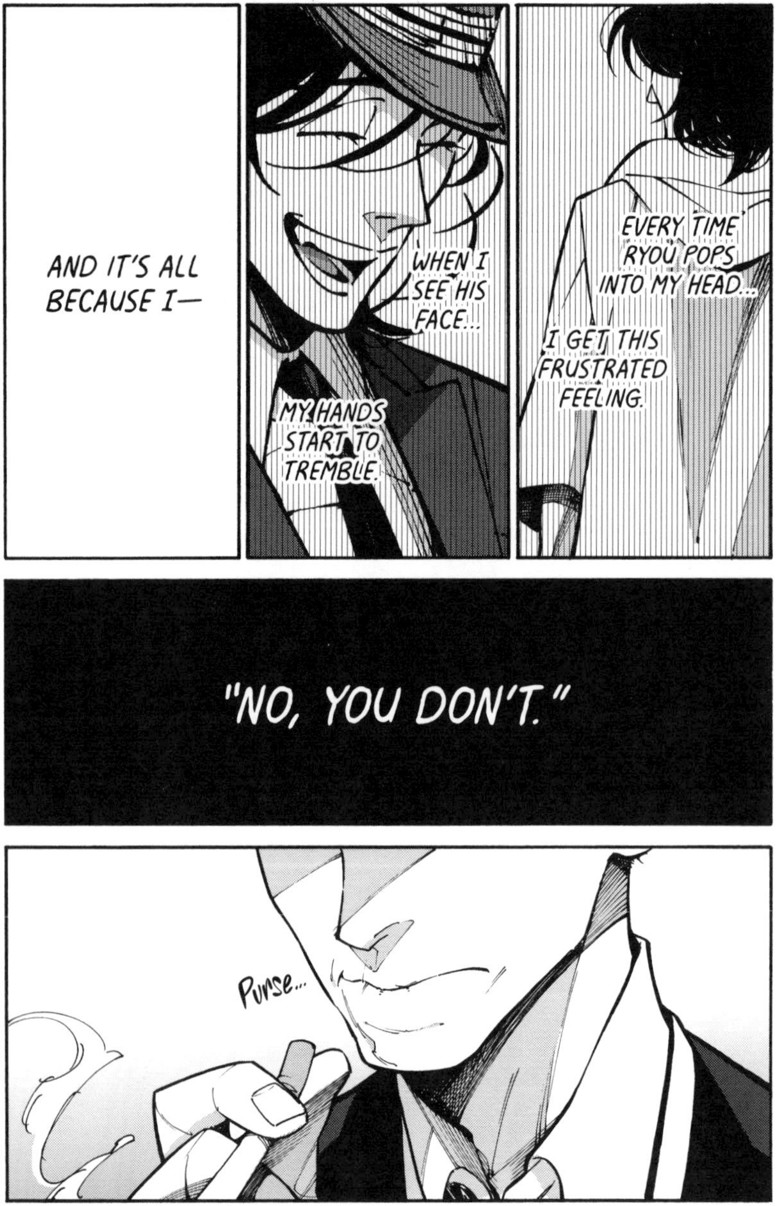
EVERY TIME RYOU POPS INTO MY HEAD...
I GET THIS FRUSTRATED FEELING.
WHEN I SEE HIS FACE...
MY HANDS START TO TREMBLE.
AND IT'S ALL BECAUSE I—
"NO, YOU DON'T."
Purse...

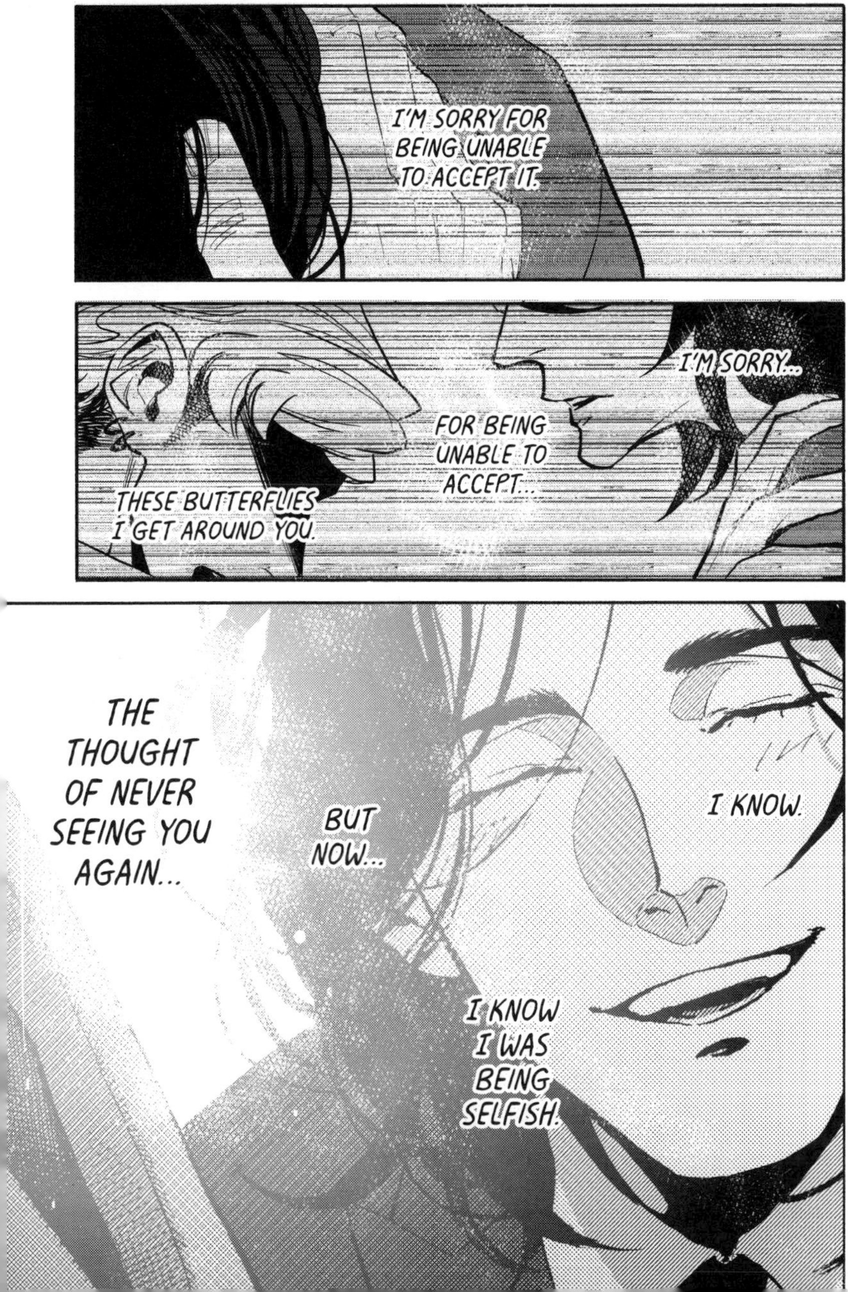
I'M SORRY FOR BEING UNABLE TO ACCEPT IT.
I'M SORRY...
FOR BEING UNABLE TO ACCEPT...
THESE BUTTERFLIES I GET AROUND YOU.
I KNOW.
I KNOW I WAS BEING SELFISH.
BUT NOW...
THE THOUGHT OF NEVER SEEING YOU AGAIN...

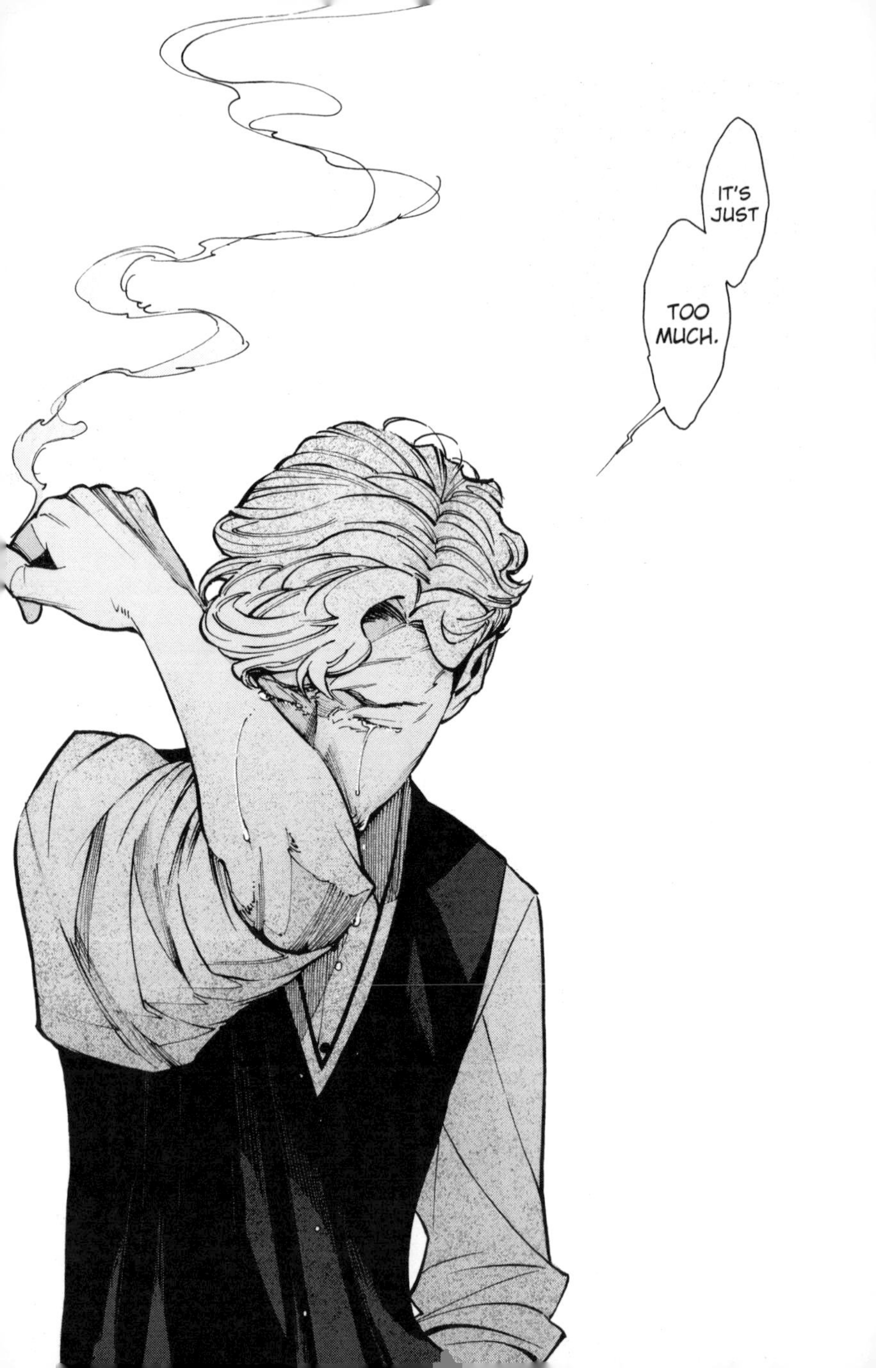
IT'S JUST TOO MUCH.

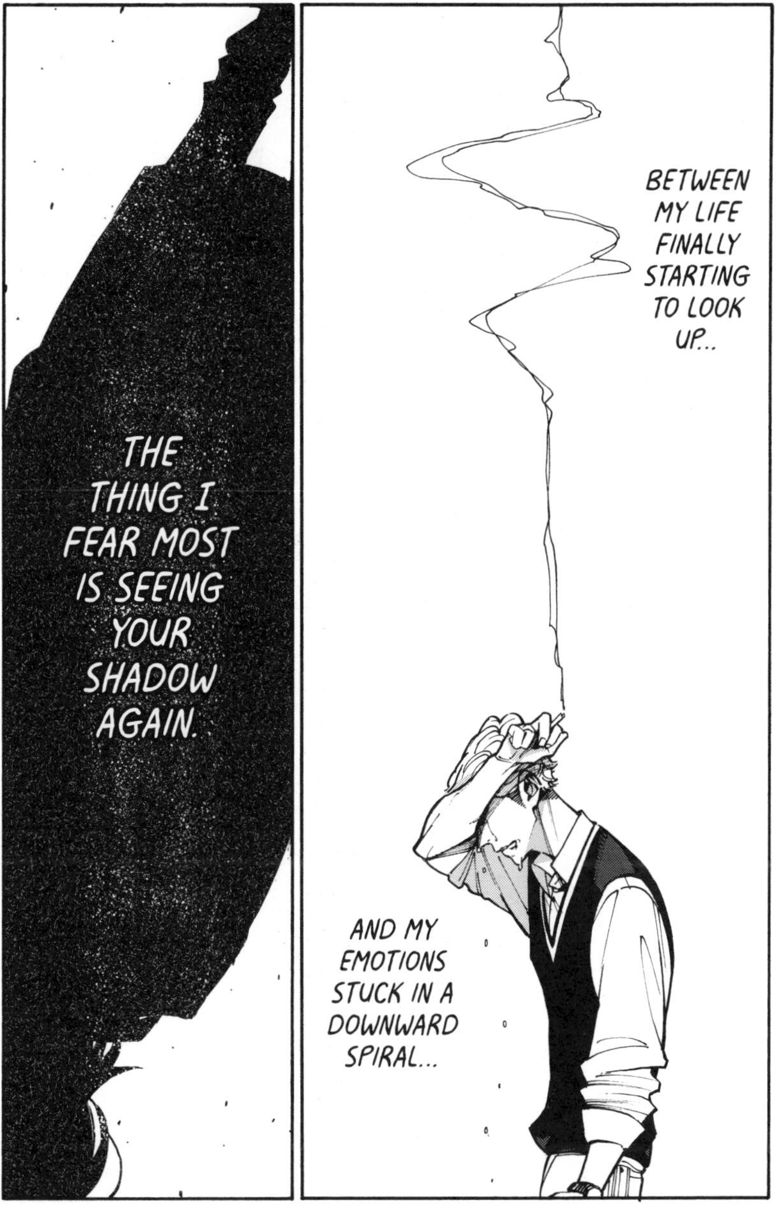
BETWEEN MY LIFE FINALLY STARTING TO LOOK UP...
AND MY EMOTIONS STUCK IN A DOWNWARD SPIRAL...
THE THING I FEAR MOST IS SEEING YOUR SHADOW AGAIN.

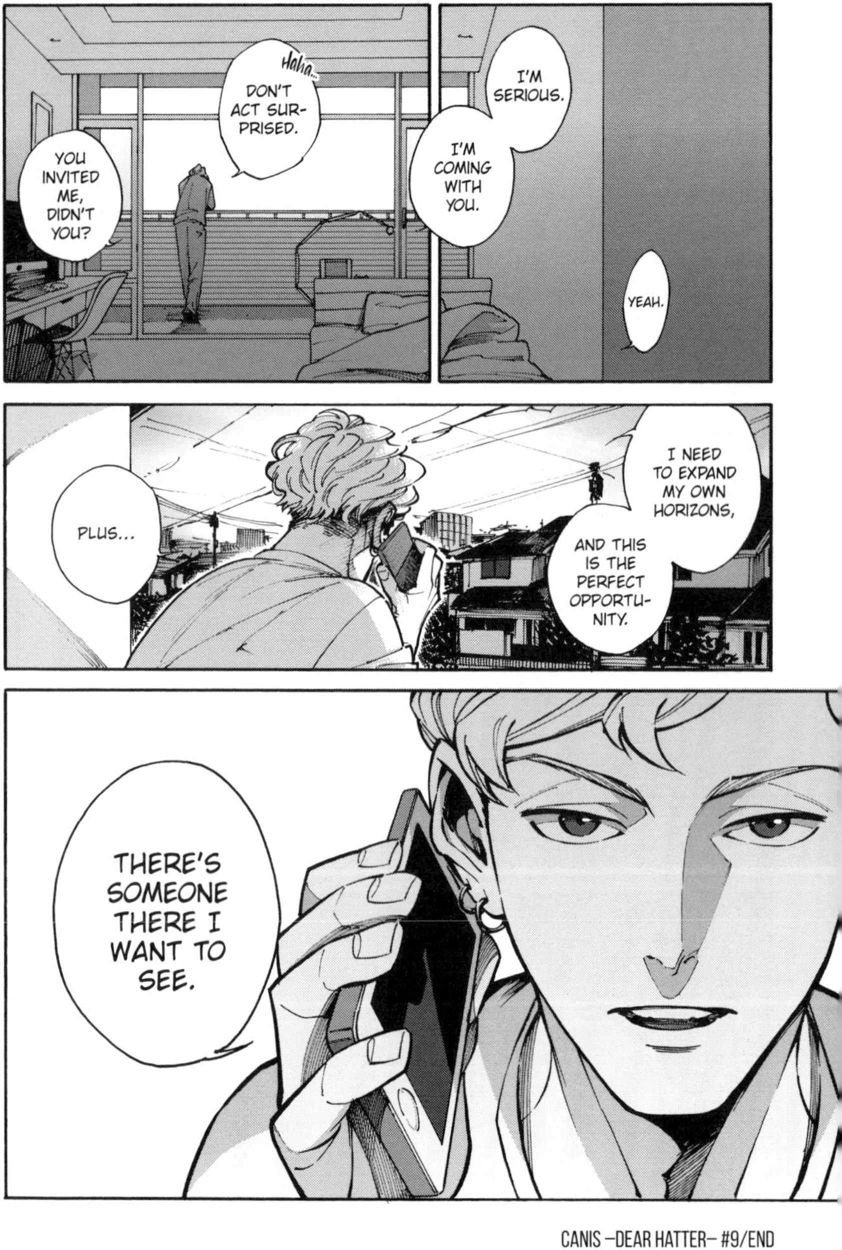
I'M SERIOUS.
I'M COMING WITH YOU.
YEAH.
Haha...
DON'T ACT SURPRISED.
YOU INVITED ME, DIDN'T YOU?
I NEED TO EXPAND MY OWN HORIZONS,
AND THIS IS THE PERFECT OPPORTUNITY.
PLUS...
THERE'S SOMEONE THERE I WANT TO SEE.

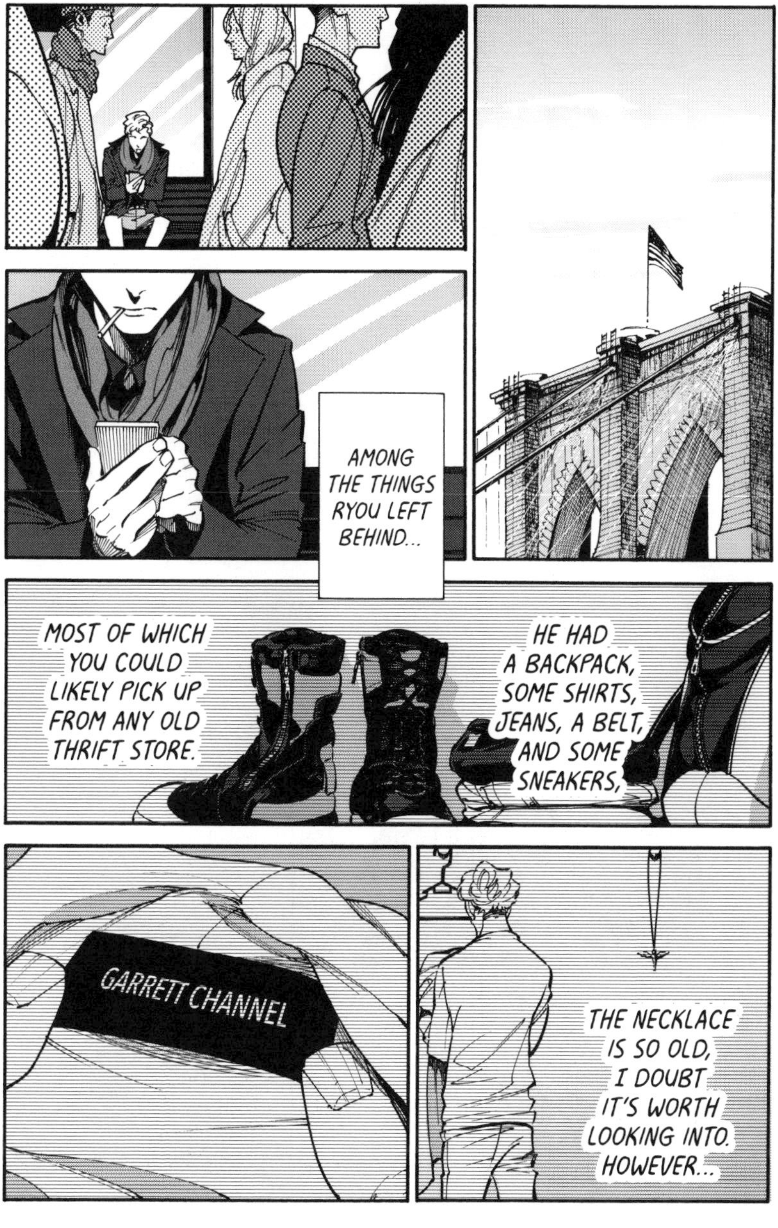
AMONG THE THINGS RYOU LEFT BEHIND...
HE HAD A BACKPACK, SOME SHIRTS, JEANS, A BELT, AND SOME SNEAKERS,
MOST OF WHICH YOU COULD LIKELY PICK UP FROM ANY OLD THRIFT STORE.
THE NECKLACE IS SO OLD, I DOUBT IT'S WORTH LOOKING INTO. HOWEVER...
GARRETT CHANNEL

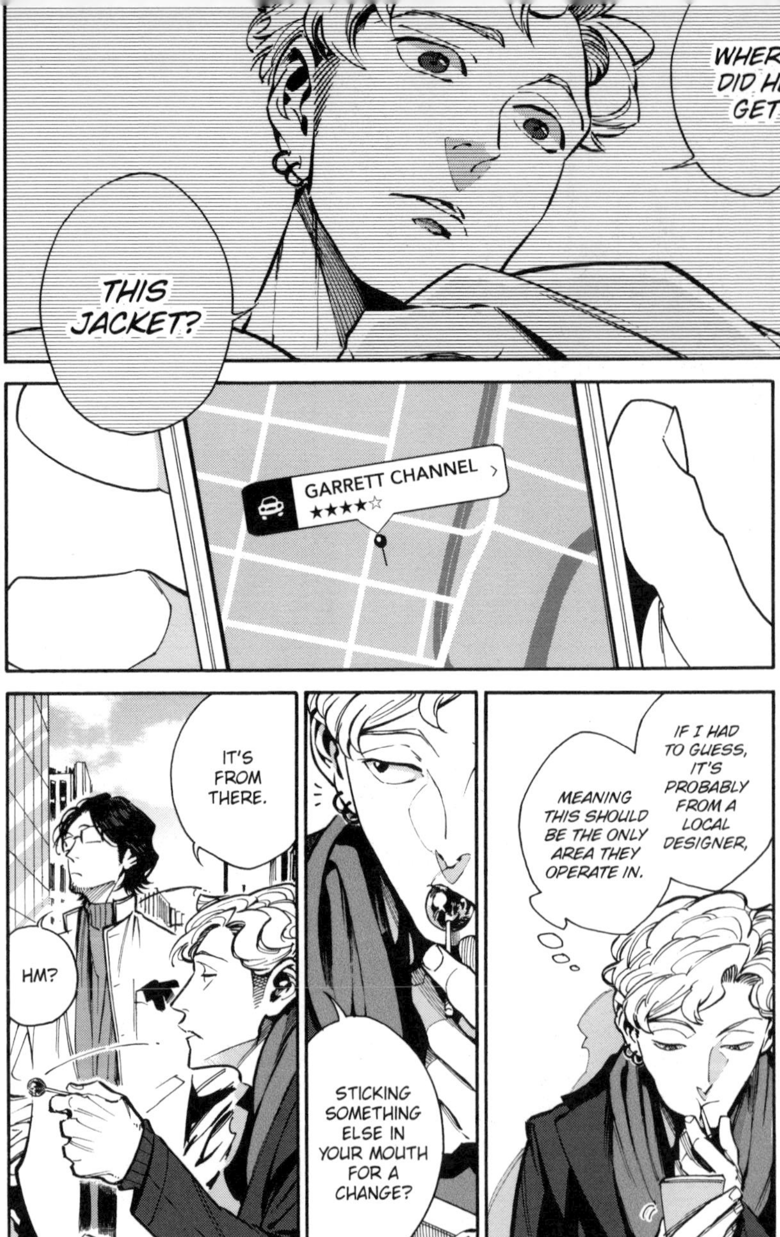
WHERE DID HE GET
THIS JACKET?
GARRETT CHANNEL
★★★★☆
IF I HAD TO GUESS, IT'S PROBABLY FROM A LOCAL DESIGNER,
MEANING THIS SHOULD BE THE ONLY AREA THEY OPERATE IN.
STICKING SOMETHING ELSE IN YOUR MOUTH FOR A CHANGE?
IT'S FROM THERE.
HM?

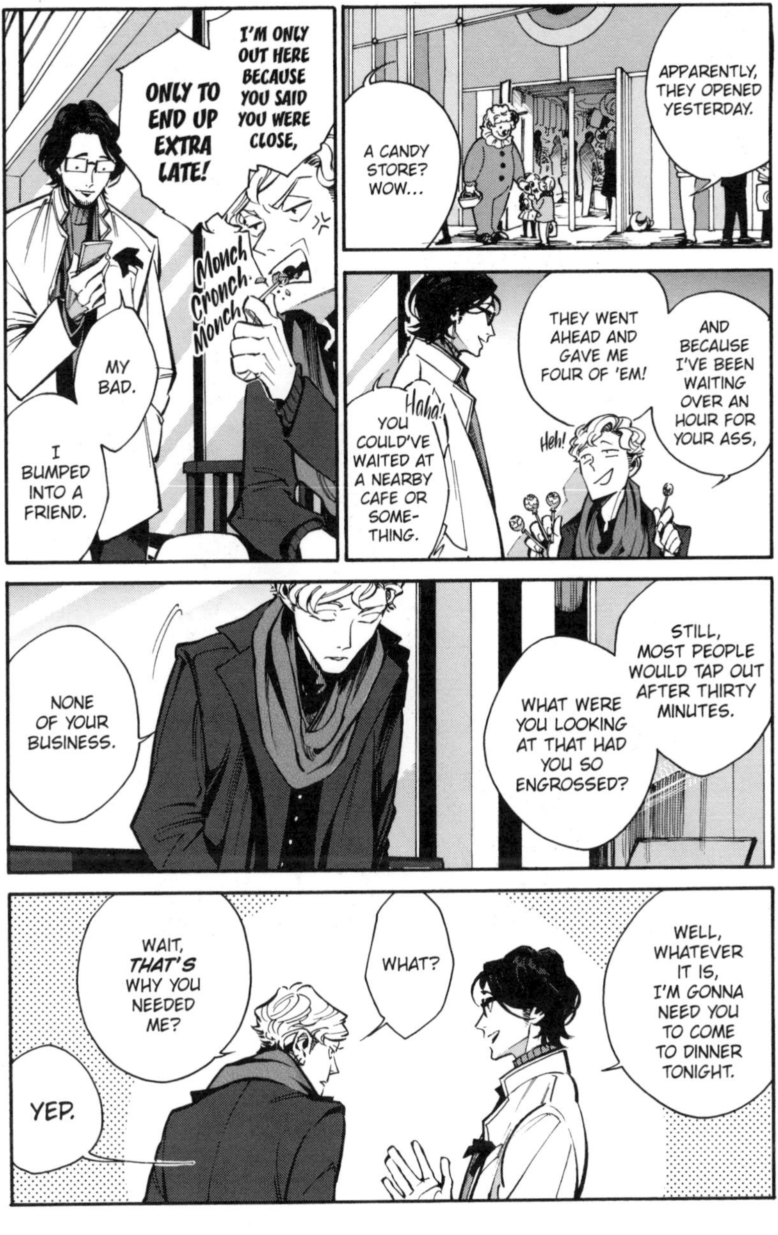
APPARENTLY, THEY OPENED YESTERDAY.
A CANDY STORE? WOW...
AND BECAUSE I'VE BEEN WAITING OVER AN HOUR FOR YOUR ASS,
THEY WENT AHEAD AND GAVE ME FOUR OF 'EM!
Heh!
Haha!
YOU COULD'VE WAITED AT A NEARBY CAFE OR SOME-THING.
I'M ONLY OUT HERE BECAUSE YOU SAID YOU WERE CLOSE,
ONLY TO END UP EXTRA LATE!
Monch Cronch Monch
MY BAD.
I BUMPED INTO A FRIEND.
STILL, MOST PEOPLE WOULD TAP OUT AFTER THIRTY MINUTES.
WHAT WERE YOU LOOKING AT THAT HAD YOU SO ENGROSSED?
NONE OF YOUR BUSINESS.
WELL, WHATEVER IT IS, I'M GONNA NEED YOU TO COME TO DINNER TONIGHT.
WHAT?
WAIT, *THAT'S* WHY YOU NEEDED ME?
YEP.

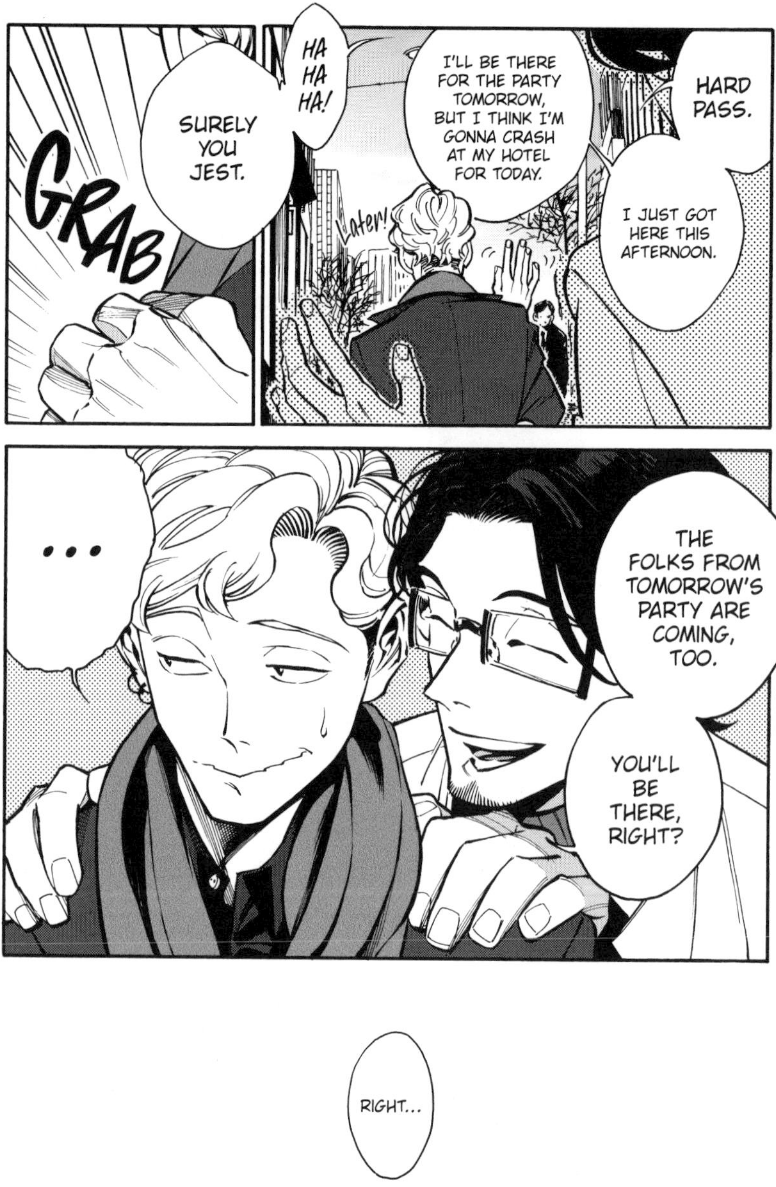
HARD PASS.
I JUST GOT HERE THIS AFTERNOON.
I'LL BE THERE FOR THE PARTY TOMORROW, BUT I THINK I'M GONNA CRASH AT MY HOTEL FOR TODAY.
Later!
HA HA HA!
SURELY YOU JEST.
GRAB
THE FOLKS FROM TOMORROW'S PARTY ARE COMING, TOO.
YOU'LL BE THERE, RIGHT?
...
RIGHT...

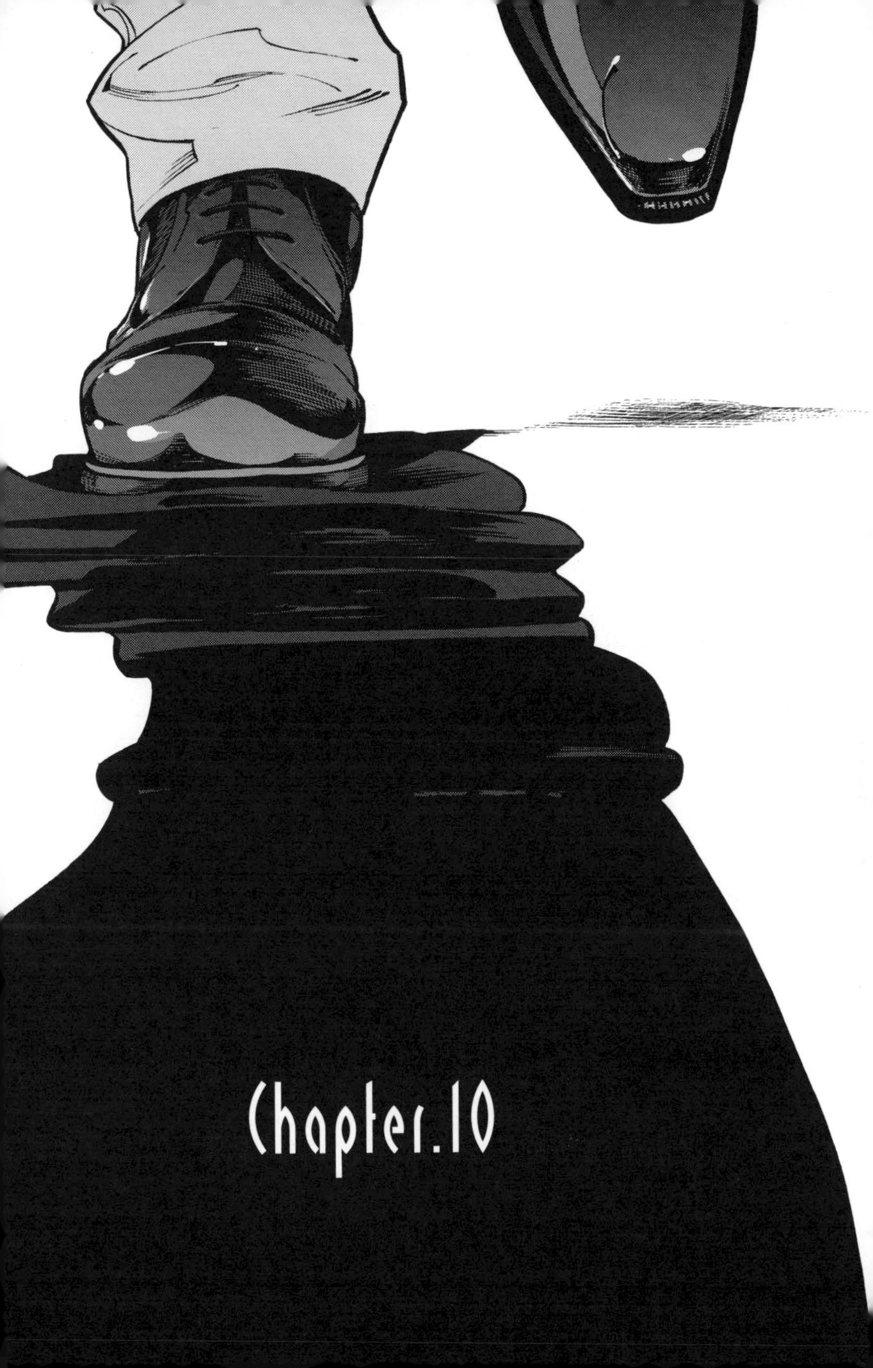
Chapter.10

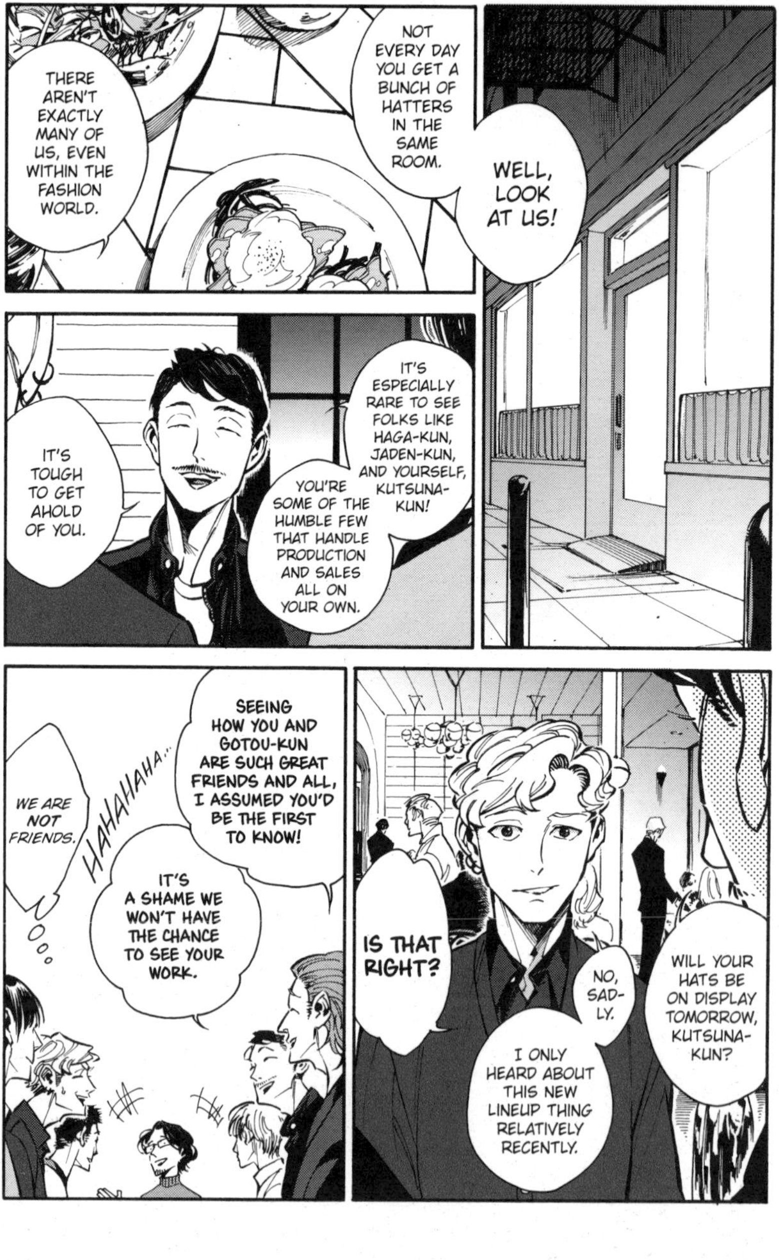
WELL, LOOK AT US!
NOT EVERY DAY YOU GET A BUNCH OF HATTERS IN THE SAME ROOM.
THERE AREN'T EXACTLY MANY OF US, EVEN WITHIN THE FASHION WORLD.
IT'S ESPECIALLY RARE TO SEE FOLKS LIKE HAGA-KUN, JADEN-KUN, AND YOURSELF, KUTSUNA-KUN!
YOU'RE SOME OF THE HUMBLE FEW THAT HANDLE PRODUCTION AND SALES ALL ON YOUR OWN.
IT'S TOUGH TO GET AHOLD OF YOU.
WILL YOUR HATS BE ON DISPLAY TOMORROW, KUTSUNA-KUN?
NO, SADLY.
I ONLY HEARD ABOUT THIS NEW LINEUP THING RELATIVELY RECENTLY.
IS THAT RIGHT?
SEEING HOW YOU AND GOTOU-KUN ARE SUCH GREAT FRIENDS AND ALL, I ASSUMED YOU'D BE THE FIRST TO KNOW!
IT'S A SHAME WE WON'T HAVE THE CHANCE TO SEE YOUR WORK.
HAHAHAHA...
WE ARE NOT FRIENDS.

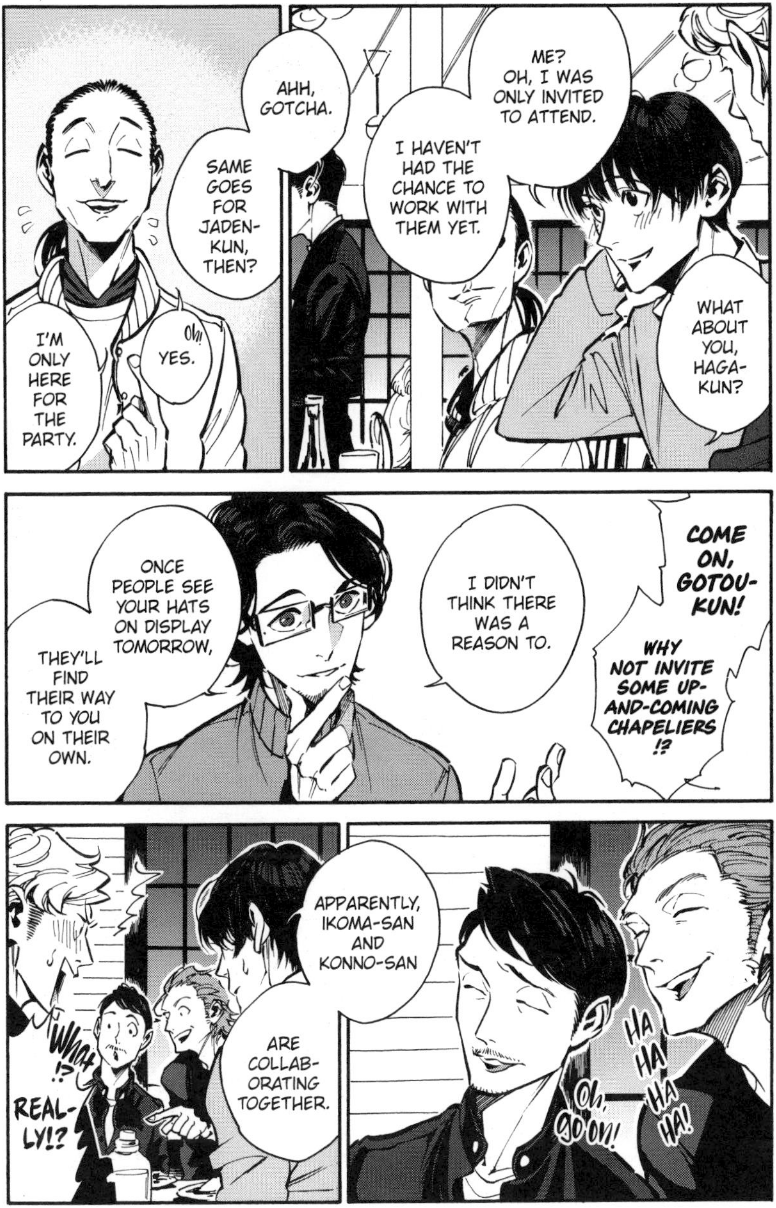
WHAT ABOUT YOU, HAGA-KUN?
ME? OH, I WAS ONLY INVITED TO ATTEND.
I HAVEN'T HAD THE CHANCE TO WORK WITH THEM YET.
AHH, GOTCHA.
SAME GOES FOR JADEN-KUN, THEN?
Oh! YES.
I'M ONLY HERE FOR THE PARTY.
COME ON, GOTOU-KUN!
WHY NOT INVITE SOME UP-AND-COMING CHAPELIERS!?
I DIDN'T THINK THERE WAS A REASON TO.
ONCE PEOPLE SEE YOUR HATS ON DISPLAY TOMORROW,
THEY'LL FIND THEIR WAY TO YOU ON THEIR OWN.
HA HA HA HA!
Oh, go on!
APPARENTLY, IKOMA-SAN AND KONNO-SAN
ARE COLLAB-ORATING TOGETHER.
What!?
REAL-LY!?

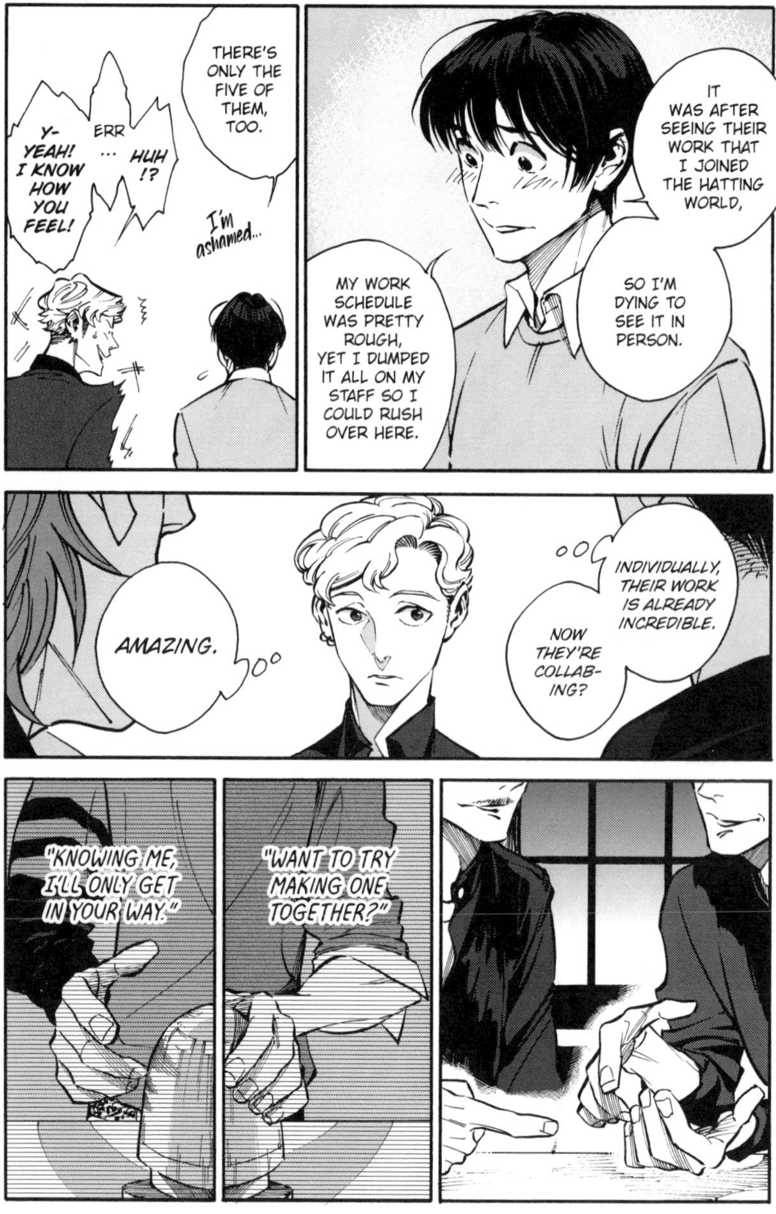
IT WAS AFTER SEEING THEIR WORK THAT I JOINED THE HATTING WORLD,
SO I'M DYING TO SEE IT IN PERSON.
MY WORK SCHEDULE WAS PRETTY ROUGH, YET I DUMPED IT ALL ON MY STAFF SO I COULD RUSH OVER HERE.
THERE'S ONLY THE FIVE OF THEM, TOO.
HUH !?
ERR ...
Y-YEAH! I KNOW HOW YOU FEEL!
I'm ashamed...
INDIVIDUALLY, THEIR WORK IS ALREADY INCREDIBLE.
NOW THEY'RE COLLAB-ING?
AMAZING.
"WANT TO TRY MAKING ONE TOGETHER?"
"KNOWING ME, I'LL ONLY GET IN YOUR WAY."

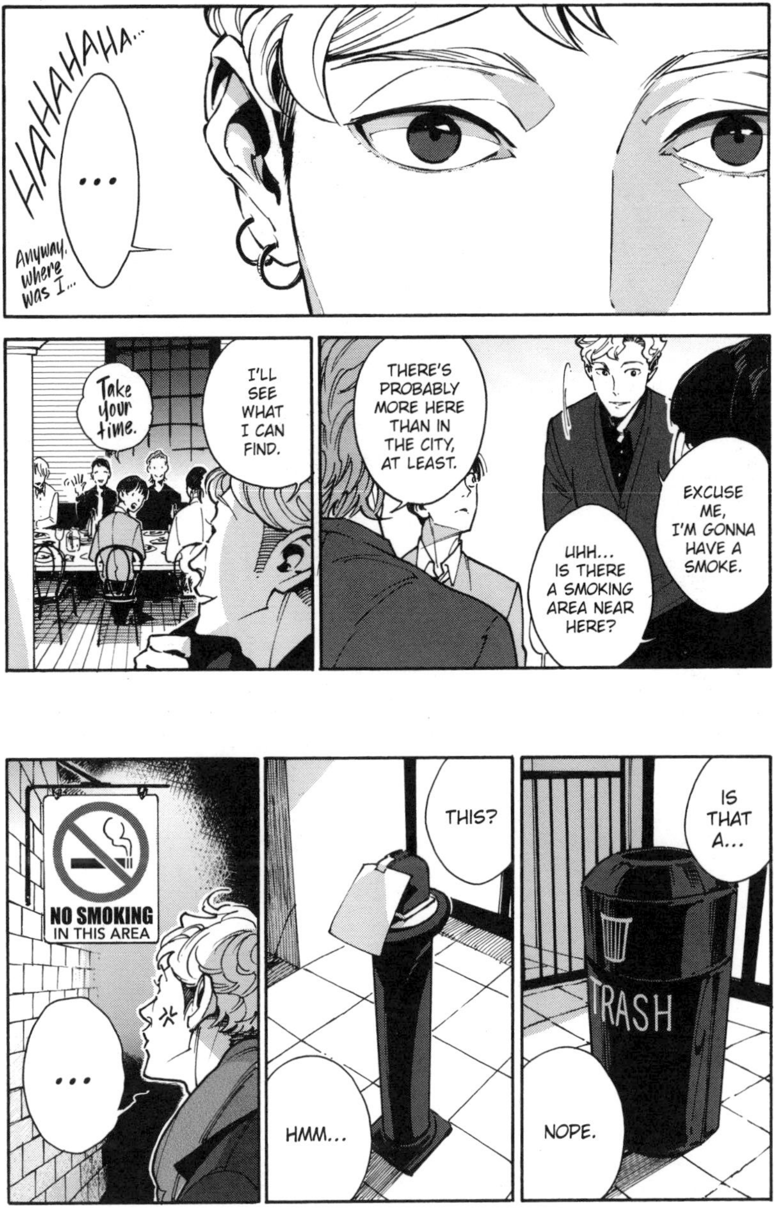
HAHAHAHA...
...
Anyway. where was I...
EXCUSE ME, I'M GONNA HAVE A SMOKE.
UHH... IS THERE A SMOKING AREA NEAR HERE?
THERE'S PROBABLY MORE HERE THAN IN THE CITY, AT LEAST.
I'LL SEE WHAT I CAN FIND.
Take your time.
IS THAT A...
TRASH
NOPE.
THIS?
HMM...
NO SMOKING IN THIS AREA
...

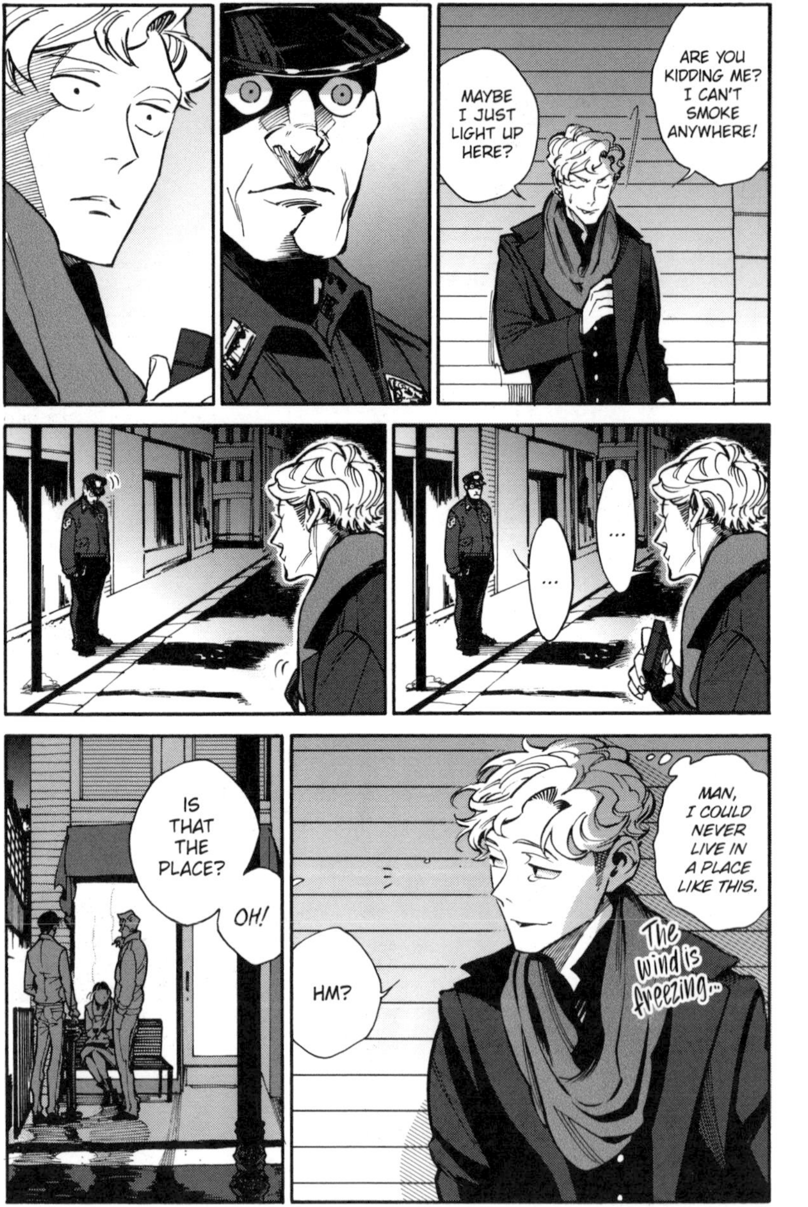
ARE YOU KIDDING ME? I CAN'T SMOKE ANYWHERE!
MAYBE I JUST LIGHT UP HERE?
...
...
MAN, I COULD NEVER LIVE IN A PLACE LIKE THIS.
The wind is freezing...
HM?
IS THAT THE PLACE?
OH!

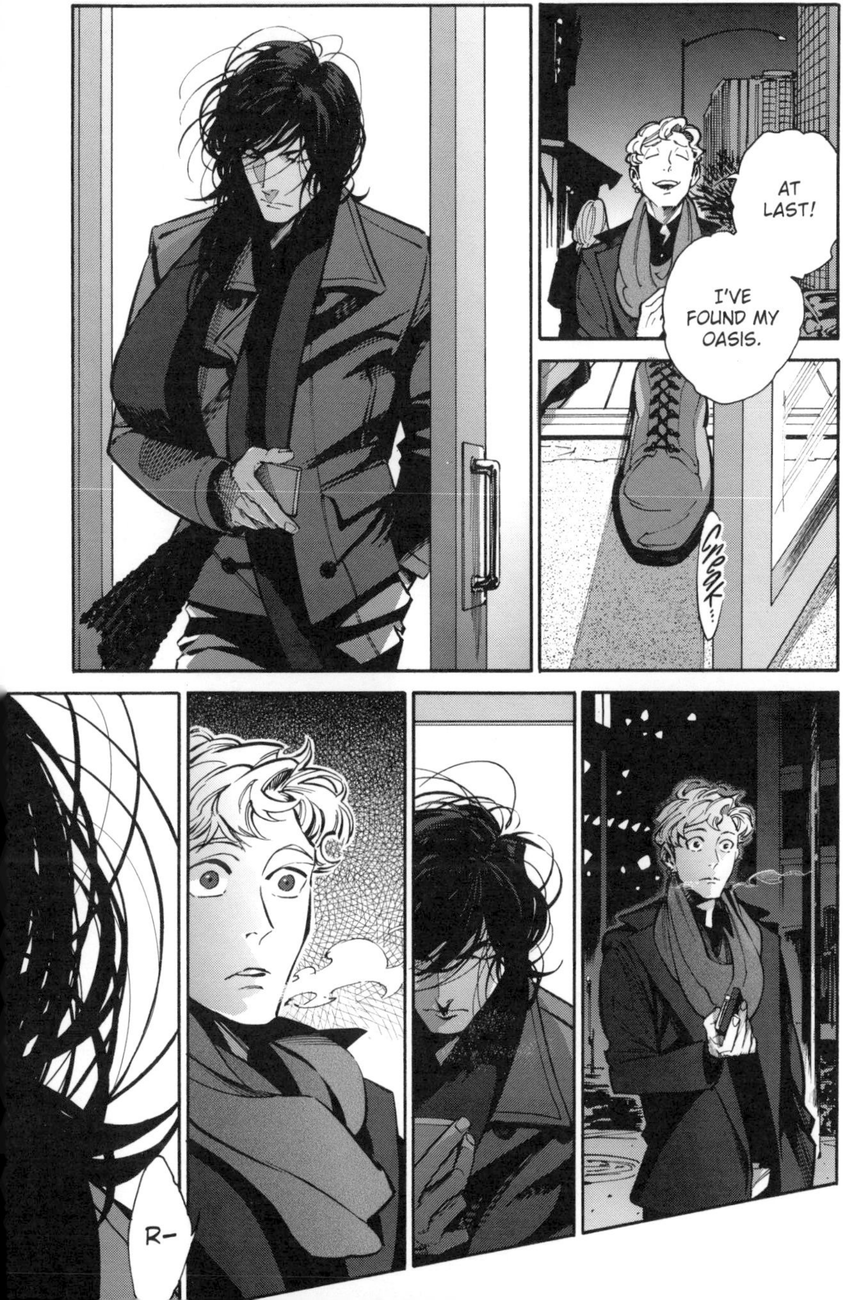
AT LAST!
I'VE FOUND MY OASIS.
Creak...
R–

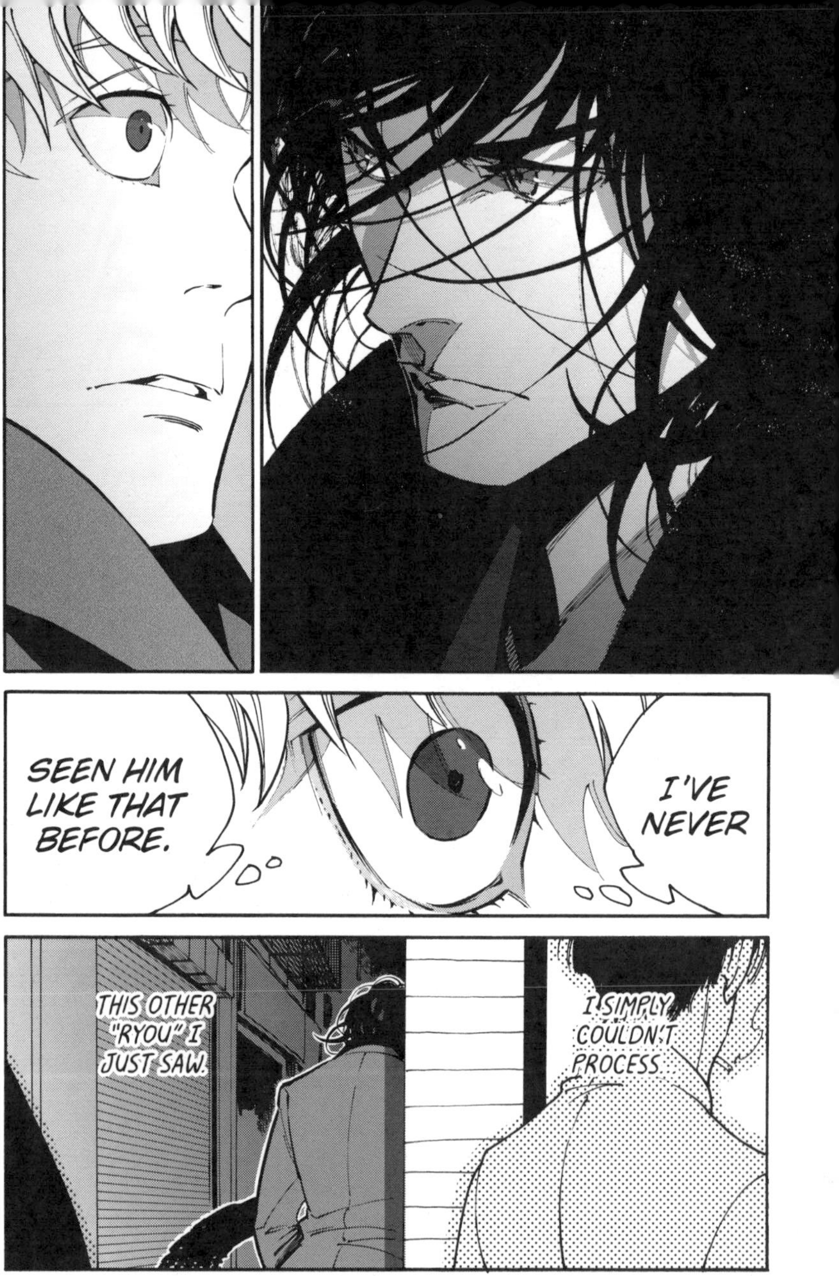
I'VE NEVER
SEEN HIM LIKE THAT BEFORE.
I SIMPLY COULDN'T PROCESS
THIS OTHER "RYOU" I JUST SAW.

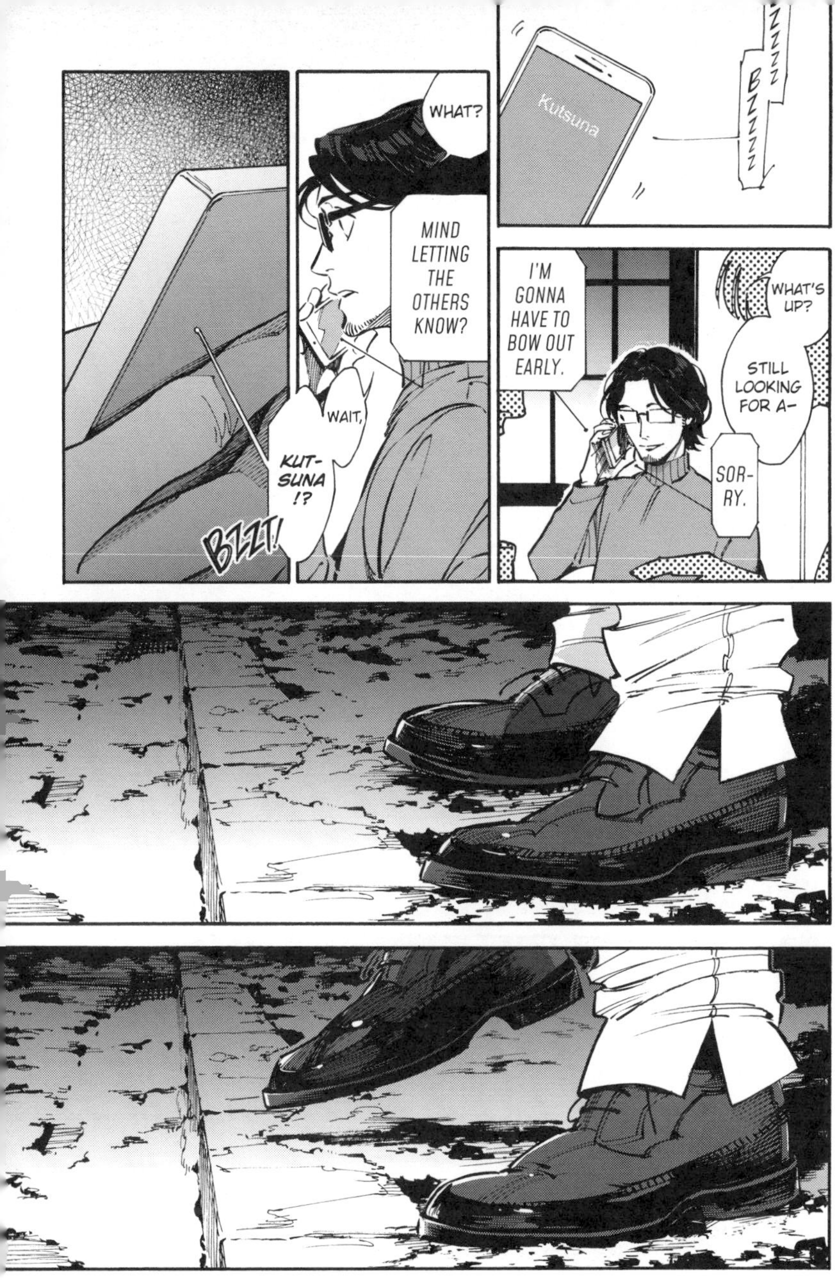
Kutsuna
ZZZZ
BZZZZ
WHAT'S UP?
STILL LOOKING FOR A-
SOR-RY.
I'M GONNA HAVE TO BOW OUT EARLY.
WHAT?
MIND LETTING THE OTHERS KNOW?
WAIT,
KUT-SUNA!?
BZZT!

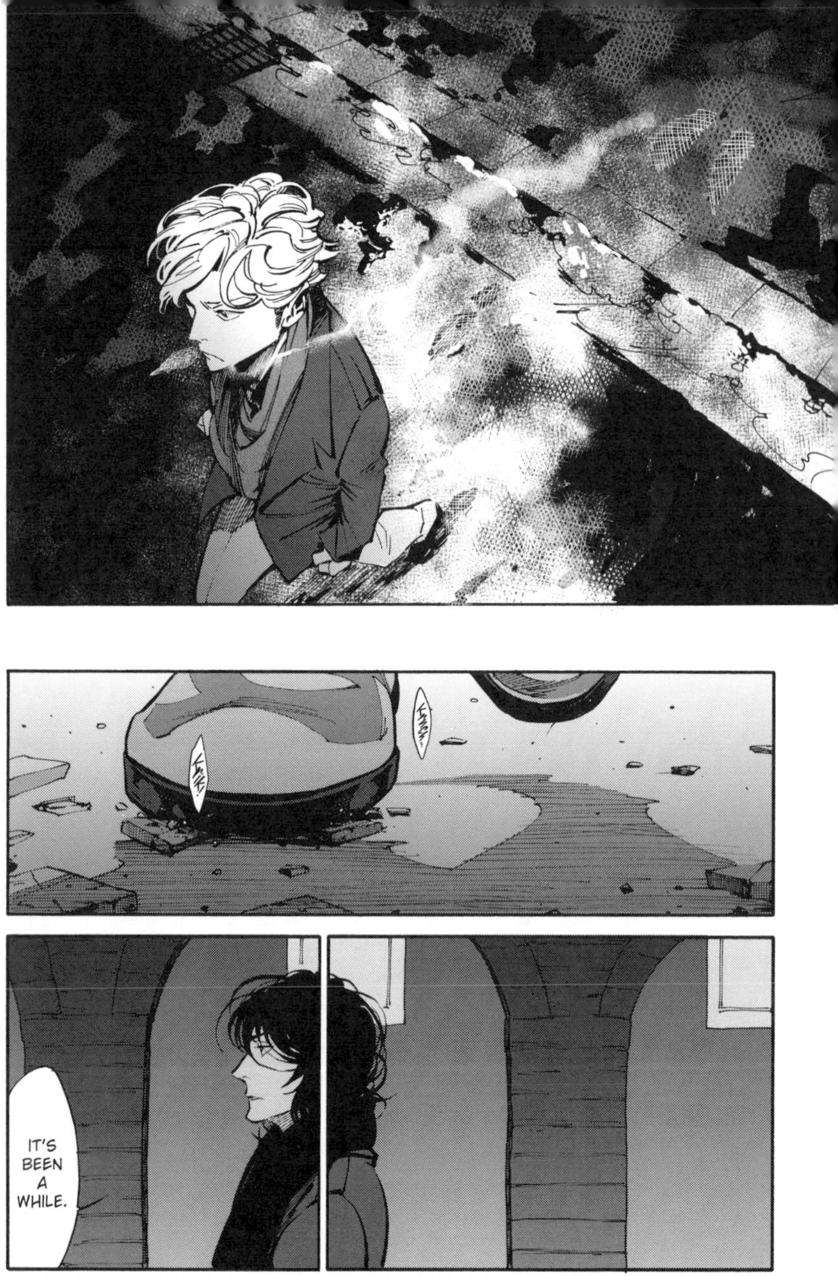
KRICK...
KRIK!
IT'S BEEN A WHILE.

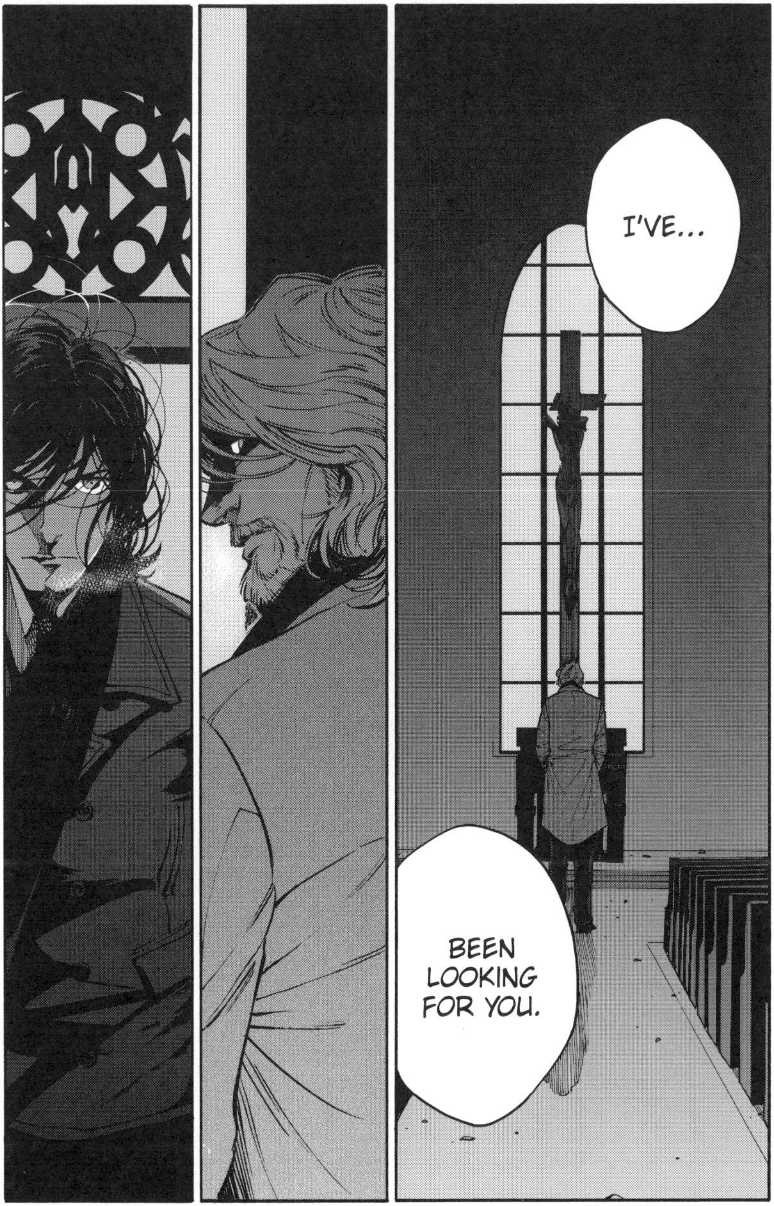
I'VE...
BEEN LOOKING FOR YOU.

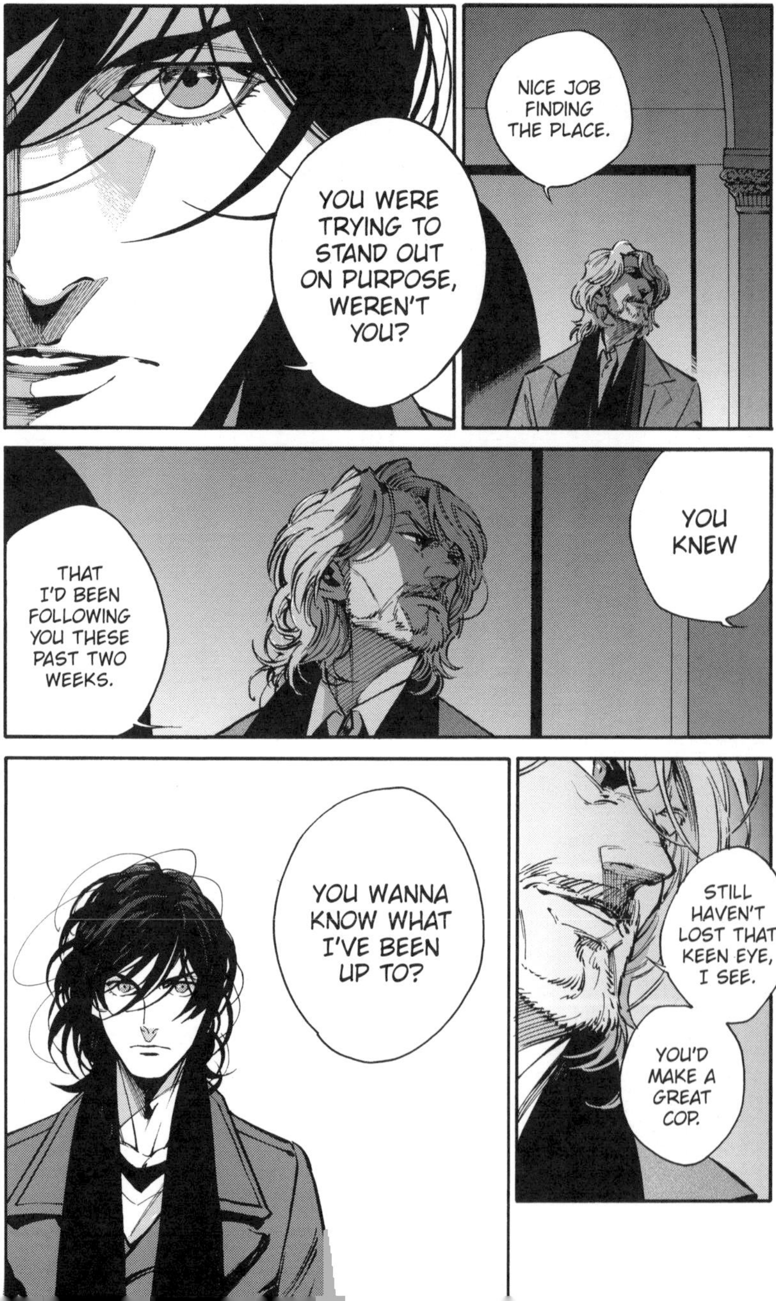
NICE JOB FINDING THE PLACE.
YOU WERE TRYING TO STAND OUT ON PURPOSE, WEREN'T YOU?
YOU KNEW
THAT I'D BEEN FOLLOWING YOU THESE PAST TWO WEEKS.
STILL HAVEN'T LOST THAT KEEN EYE, I SEE.
YOU'D MAKE A GREAT COP.
YOU WANNA KNOW WHAT I'VE BEEN UP TO?

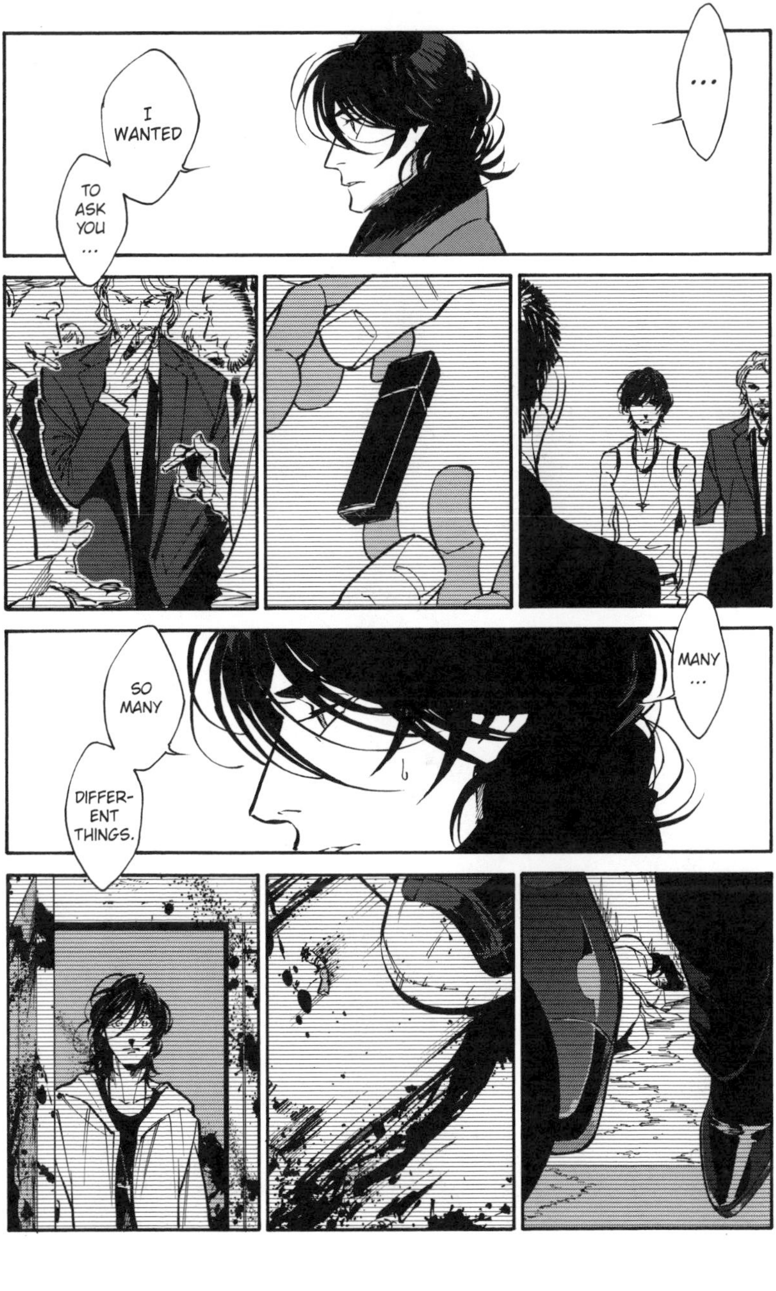
...
I WANTED
TO ASK YOU ...
MANY ...
SO MANY
DIFFERENT THINGS.

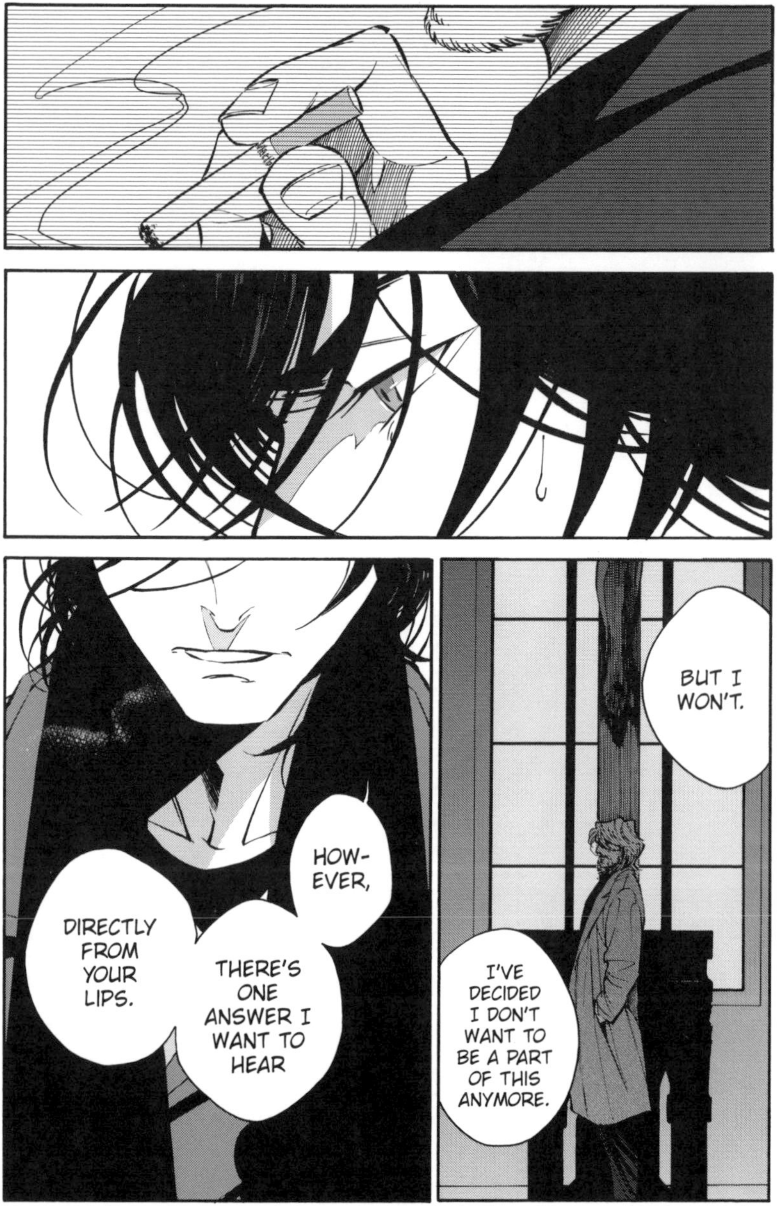
BUT I WON'T.
I'VE DECIDED I DON'T WANT TO BE A PART OF THIS ANYMORE.
HOW-EVER,
THERE'S ONE ANSWER I WANT TO HEAR
DIRECTLY FROM YOUR LIPS.

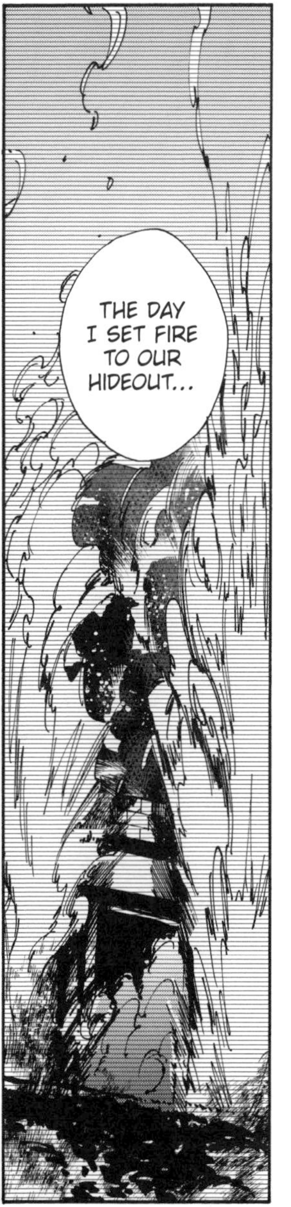
THE DAY I SET FIRE TO OUR HIDEOUT...
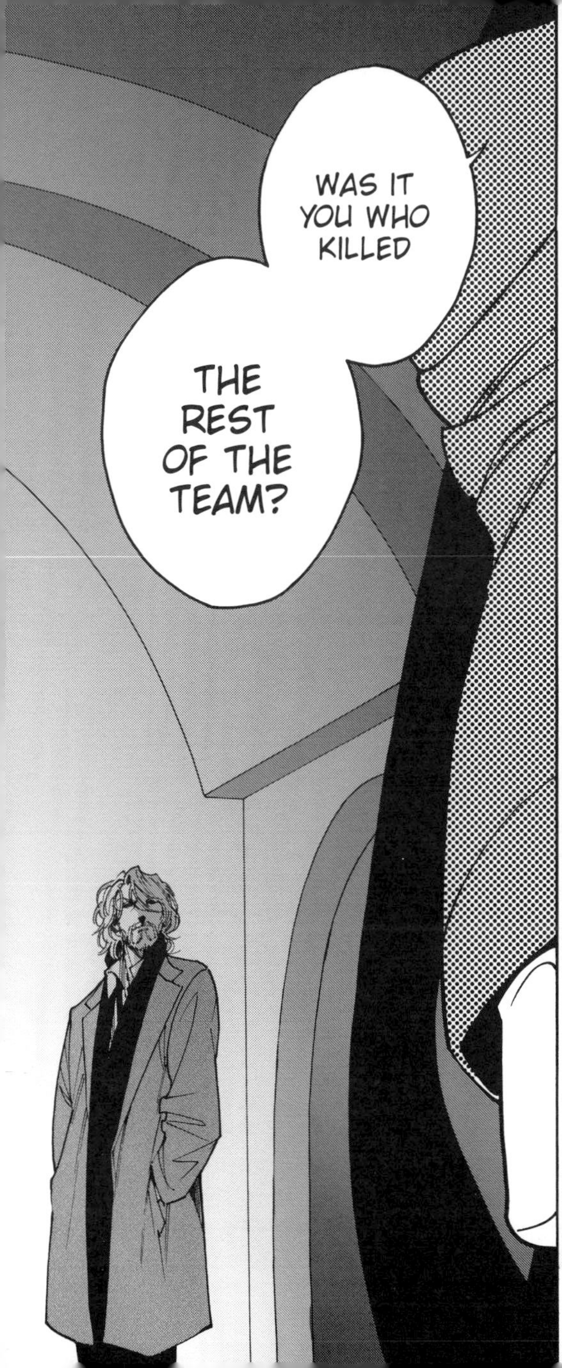
WAS IT YOU WHO KILLED
THE REST OF THE TEAM?

IT
WAS.

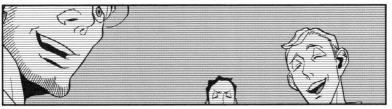

HA
HA!

HA
...

HA
HA
...

I
KNEW
IT.

I-
I
SEE.

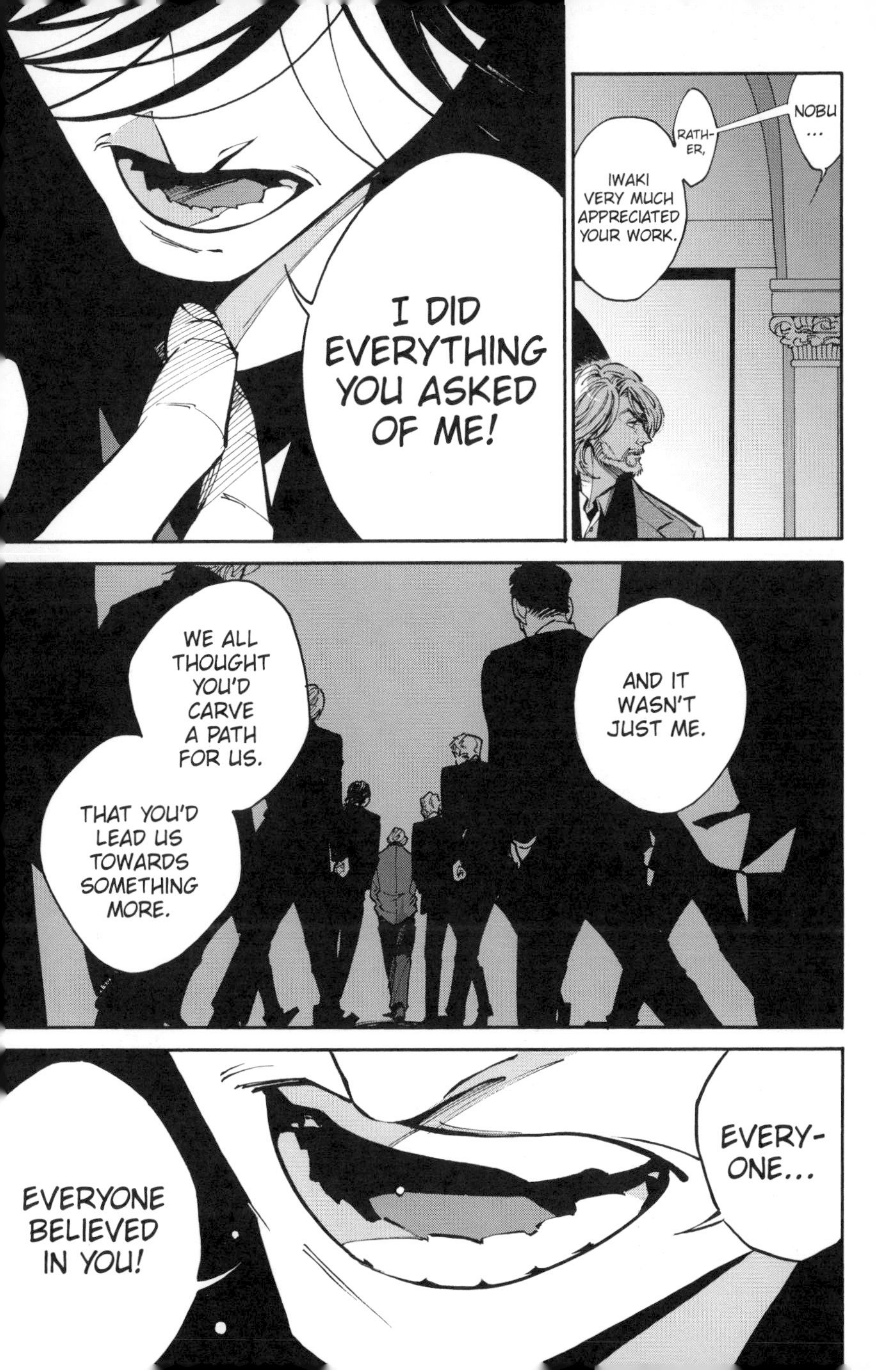
NOBU...
RATH-ER,
IWAKI VERY MUCH APPRECIATED YOUR WORK.
I DID EVERYTHING YOU ASKED OF ME!
AND IT WASN'T JUST ME.
WE ALL THOUGHT YOU'D CARVE A PATH FOR US.
THAT YOU'D LEAD US TOWARDS SOMETHING MORE.
EVERY-ONE...
EVERYONE BELIEVED IN YOU!

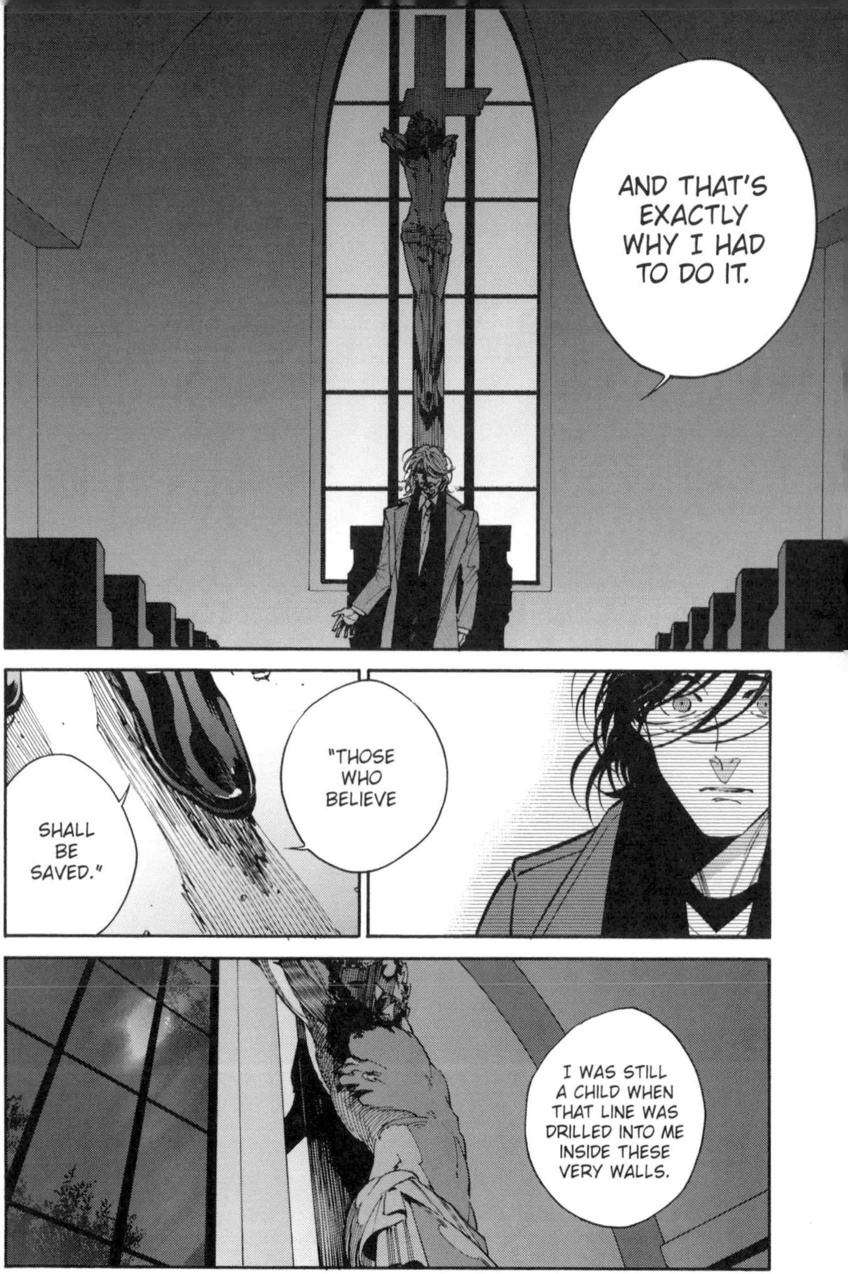
AND THAT'S EXACTLY WHY I HAD TO DO IT.
"THOSE WHO BELIEVE
SHALL BE SAVED."
I WAS STILL A CHILD WHEN THAT LINE WAS DRILLED INTO ME INSIDE THESE VERY WALLS.

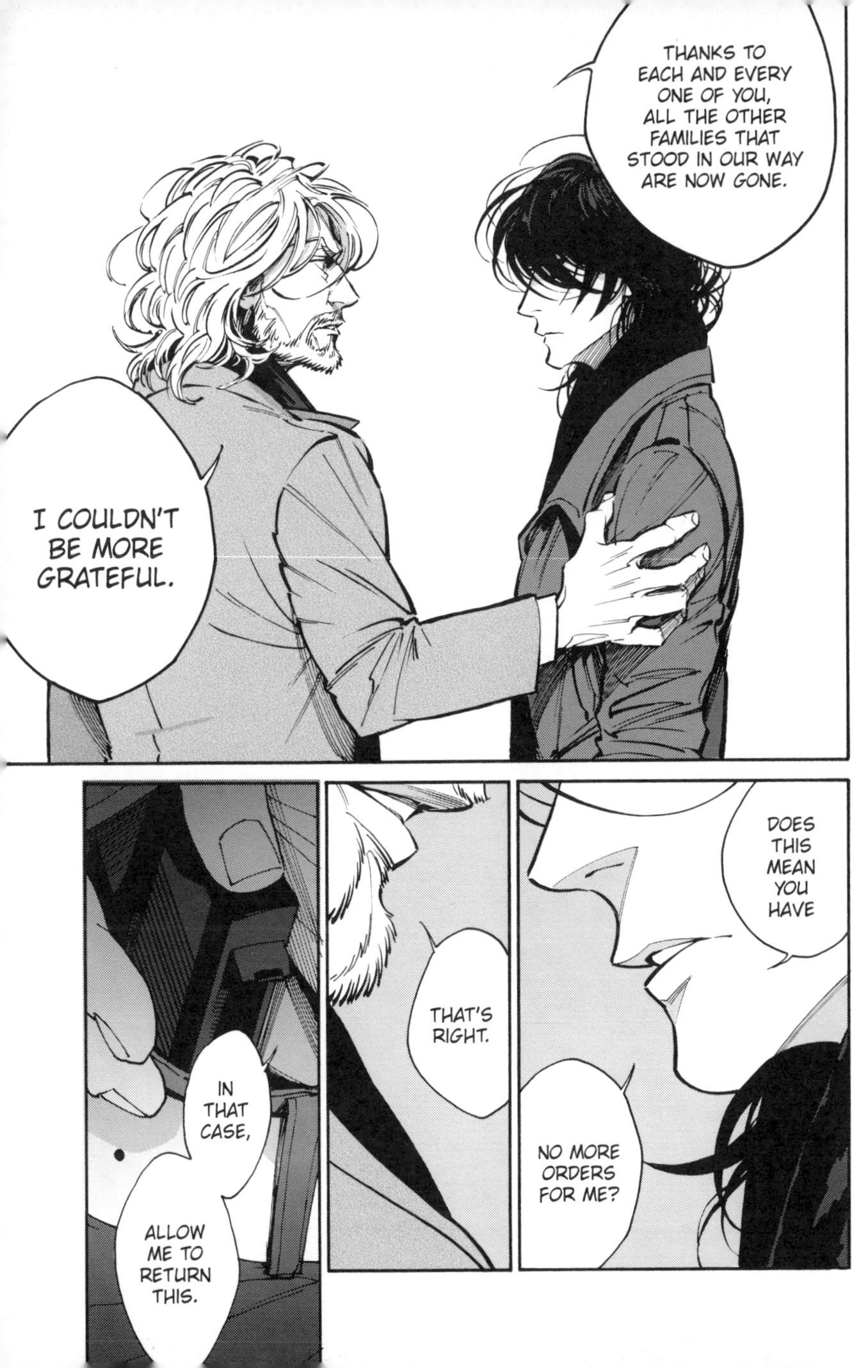
THANKS TO EACH AND EVERY ONE OF YOU, ALL THE OTHER FAMILIES THAT STOOD IN OUR WAY ARE NOW GONE.
I COULDN'T BE MORE GRATEFUL.
DOES THIS MEAN YOU HAVE
NO MORE ORDERS FOR ME?
THAT'S RIGHT.
IN THAT CASE,
ALLOW ME TO RETURN THIS.

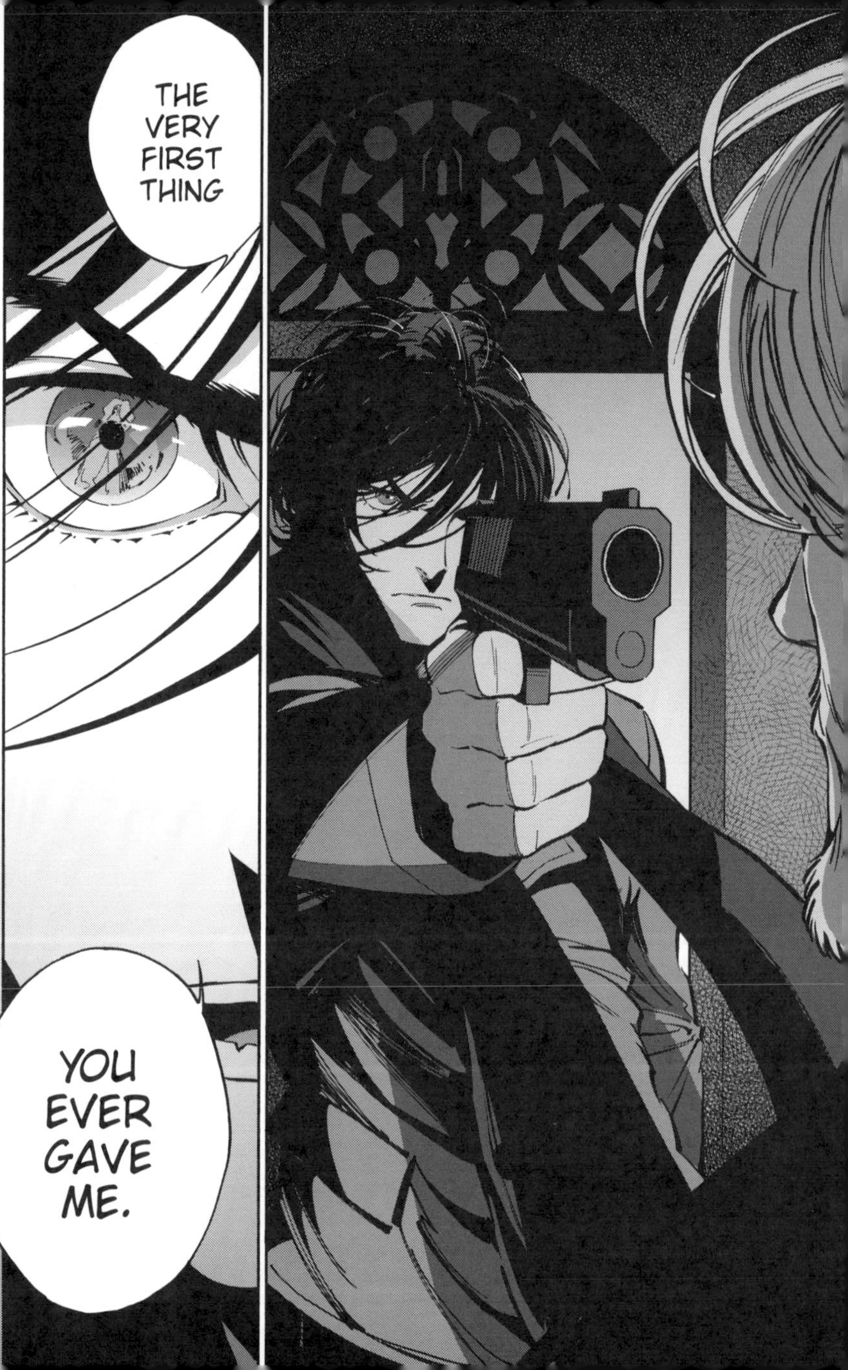
THE VERY FIRST THING
YOU EVER GAVE ME.

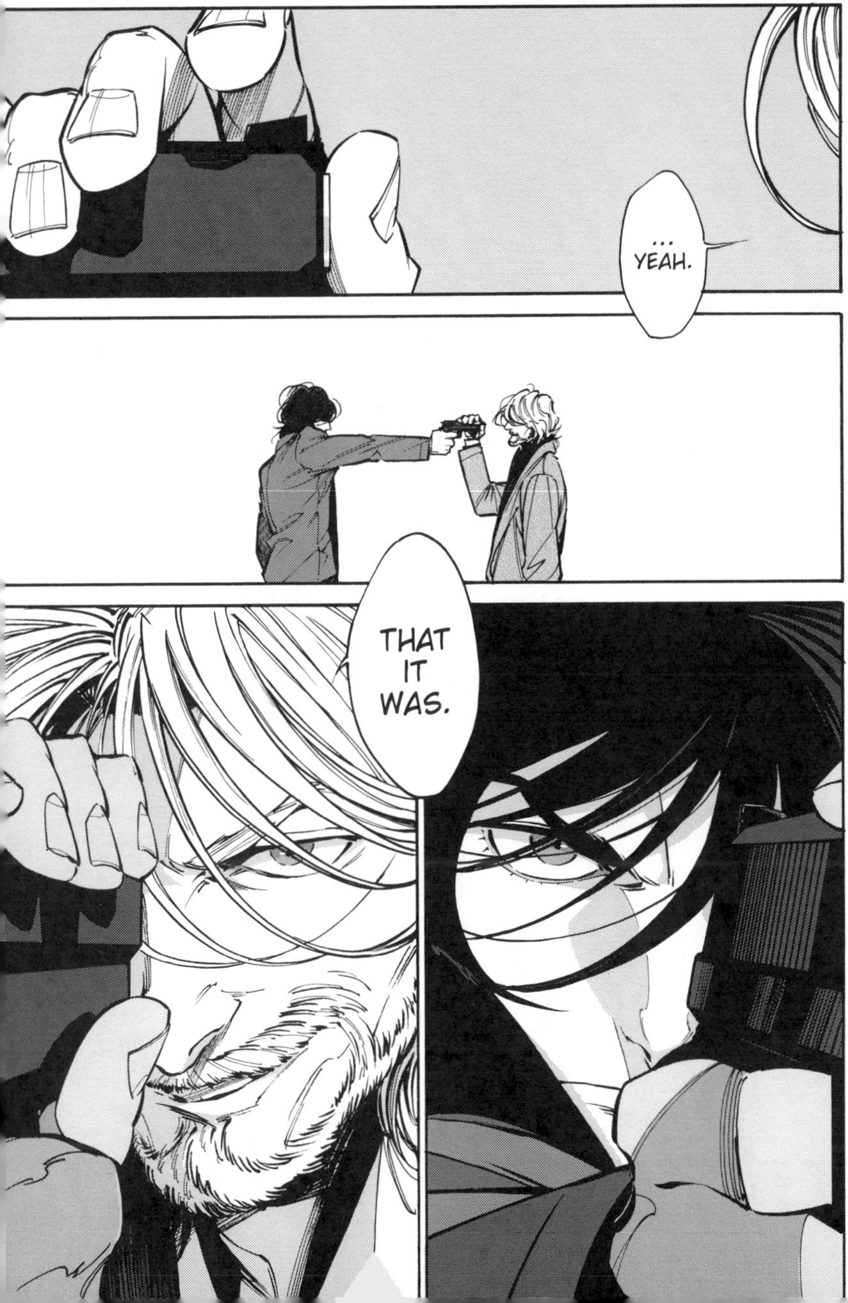
... YEAH.
THAT IT WAS.

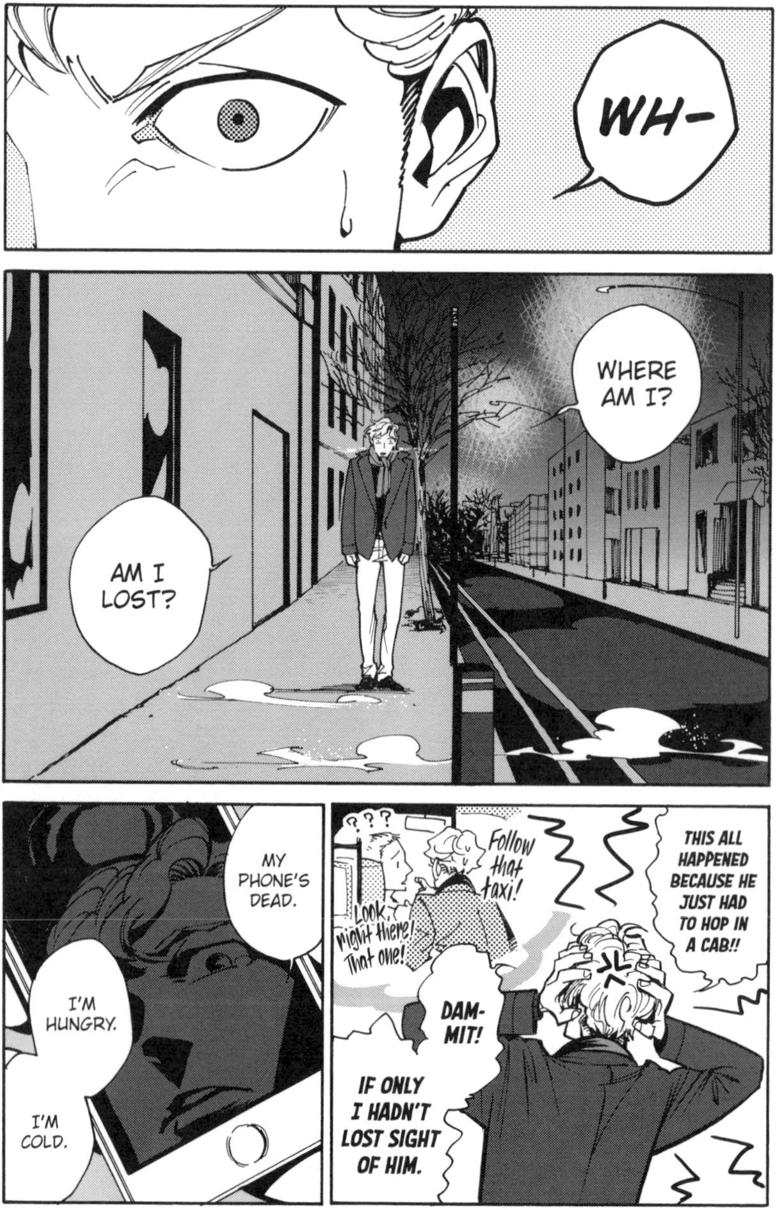
WH-
WHERE AM I?
AM I LOST?
THIS ALL HAPPENED BECAUSE HE JUST HAD TO HOP IN A CAB!!
Follow that taxi!
???
Look, right there! That one!
DAM-MIT!
IF ONLY I HADN'T LOST SIGHT OF HIM.
MY PHONE'S DEAD.
I'M HUNGRY.
I'M COLD.

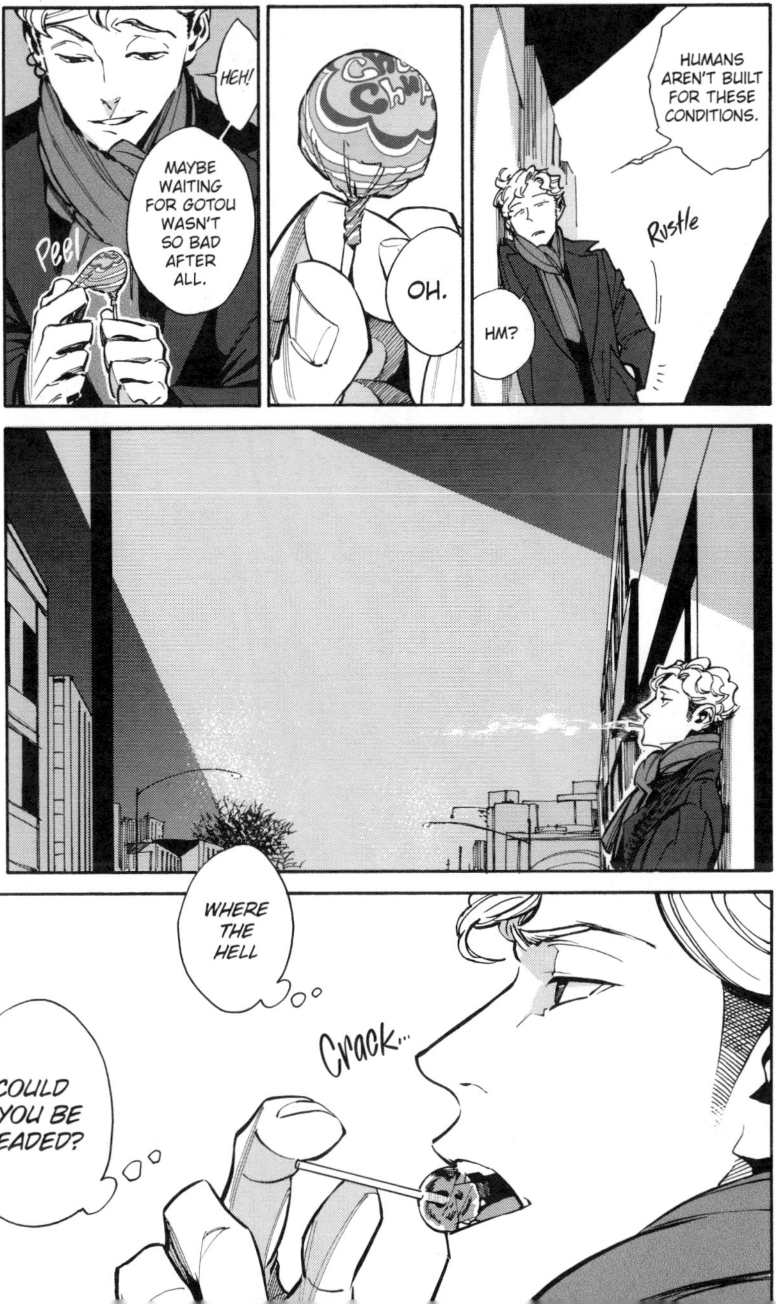
HUMANS AREN'T BUILT FOR THESE CONDITIONS.
Rustle
HM?
OH.
HEH!
MAYBE WAITING FOR GOTOU WASN'T SO BAD AFTER ALL.
Peel
WHERE THE HELL
Crack...
COULD RYOU BE HEADED?

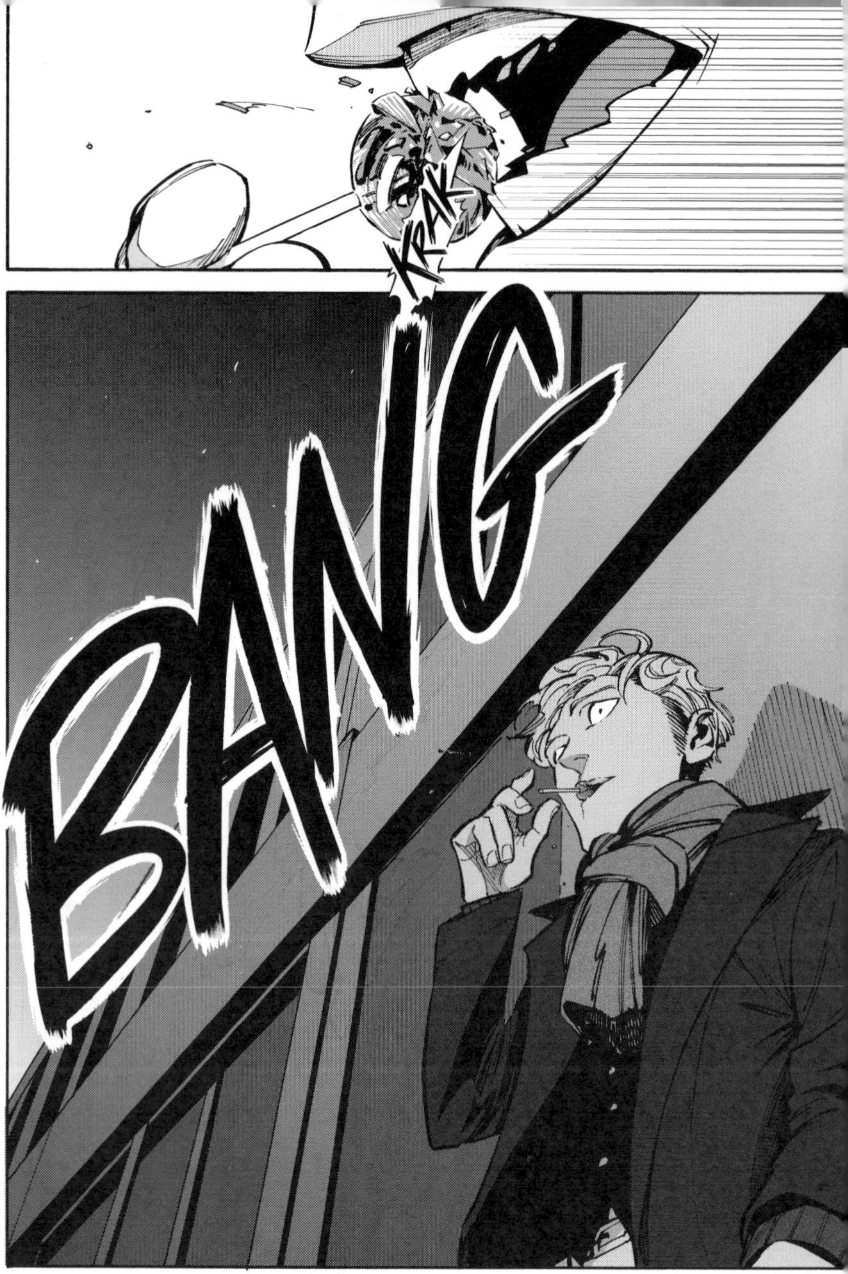
KRAK
BANG

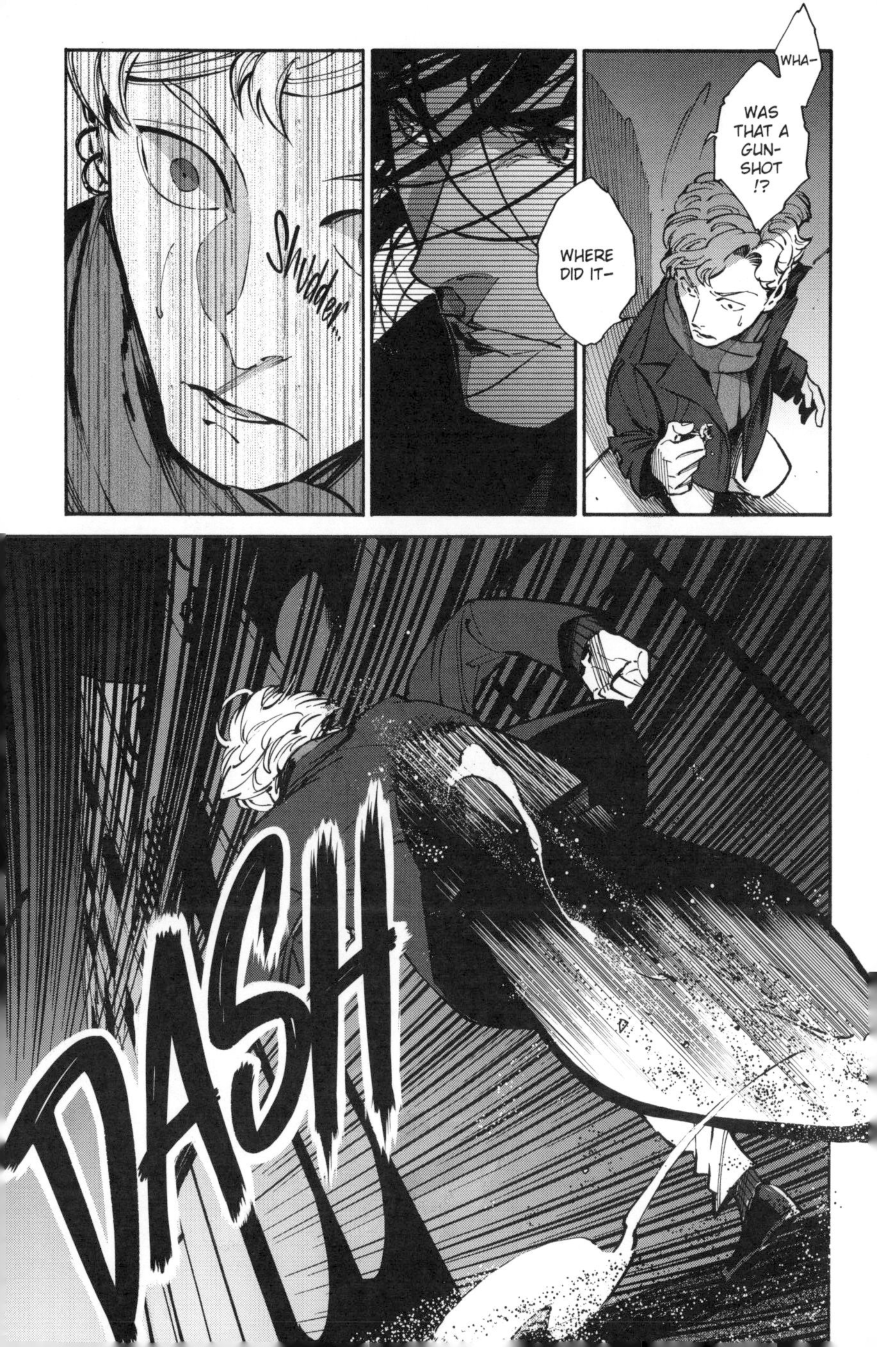
WHA-
WAS THAT A GUN-SHOT !?
WHERE DID IT-
Shudder...
DASH

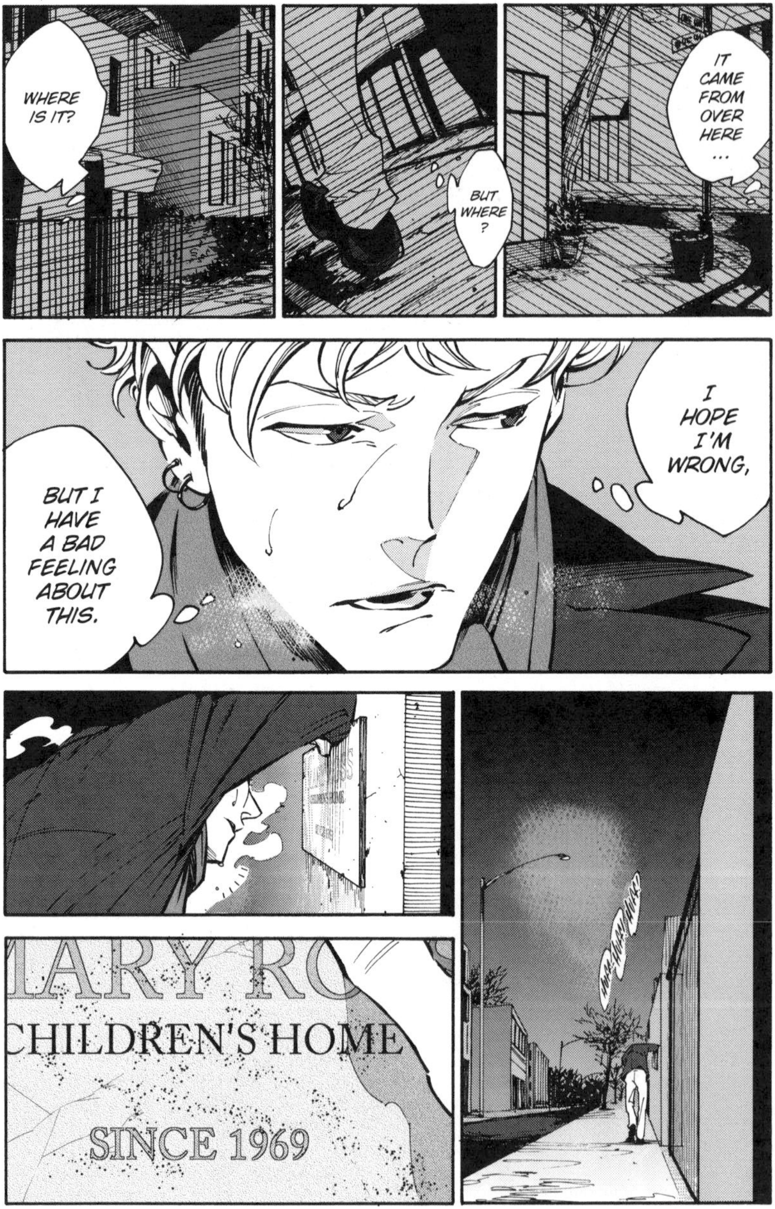
IT CAME FROM OVER HERE...
BUT WHERE?
WHERE IS IT?
I HOPE I'M WRONG,
BUT I HAVE A BAD FEELING ABOUT THIS.
HUFF! HUFF! HUFF!
MARY RO
CHILDREN'S HOME
SINCE 1969

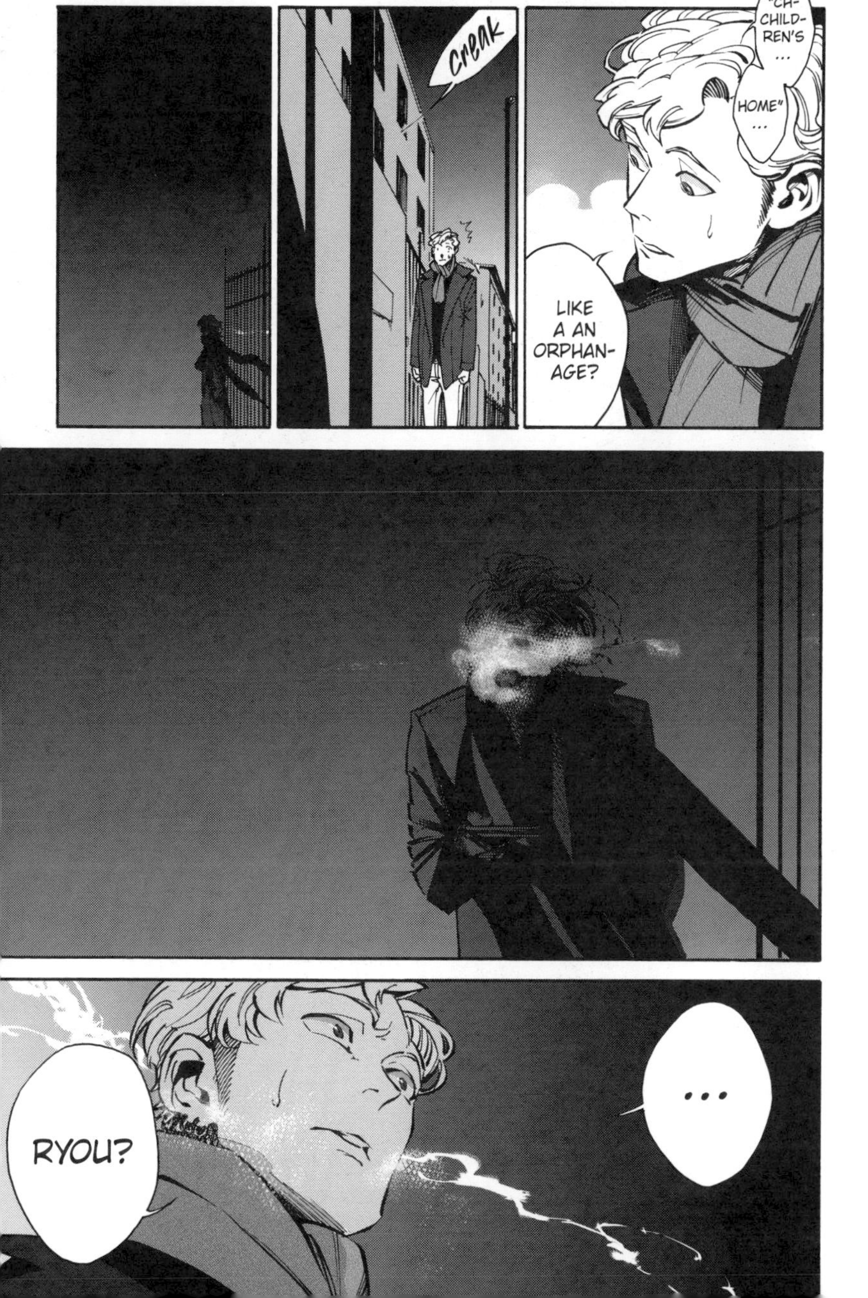
"CH-CHILDREN'S ...
HOME" ...
LIKE A AN ORPHANAGE?
Creak
...
RYOU?

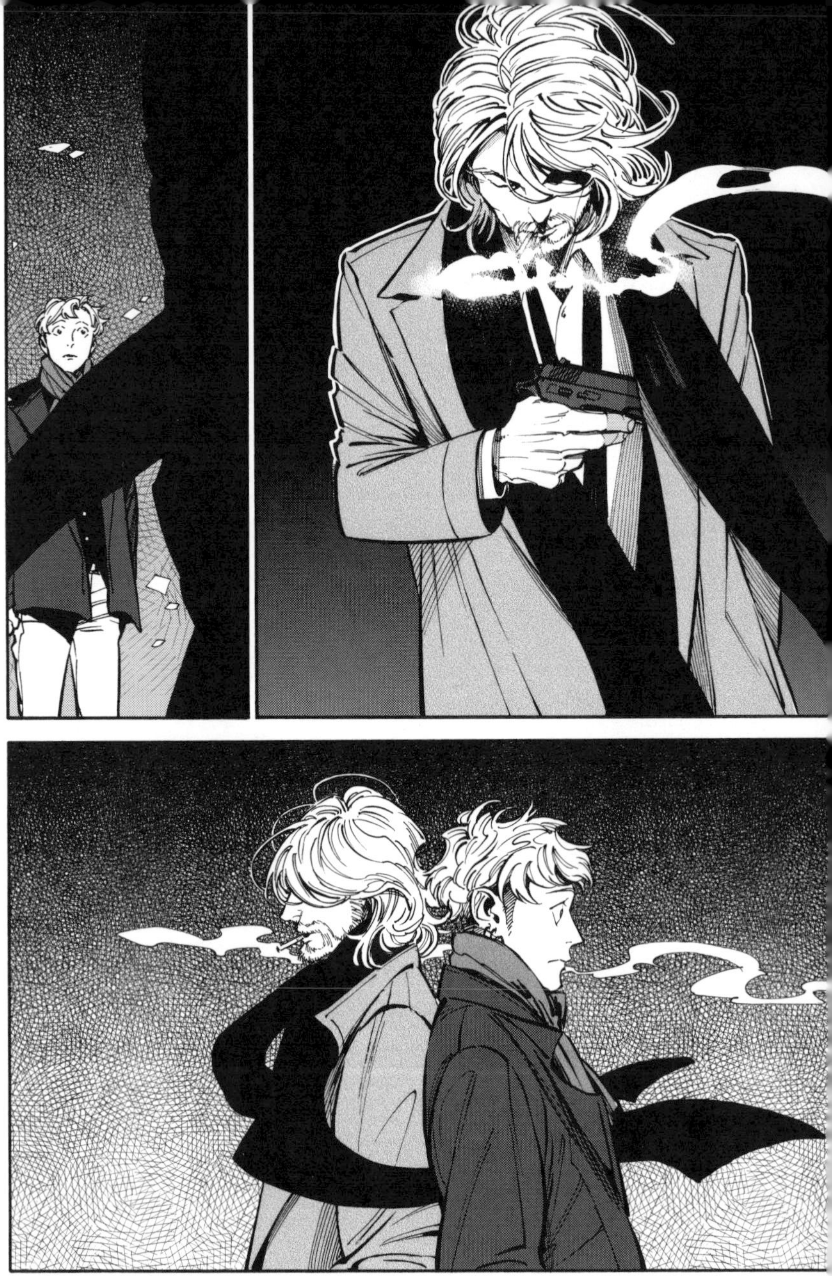

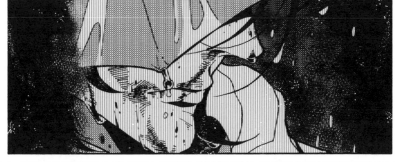

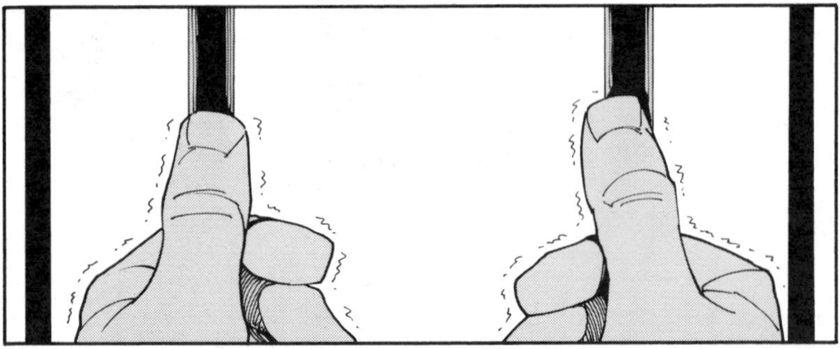

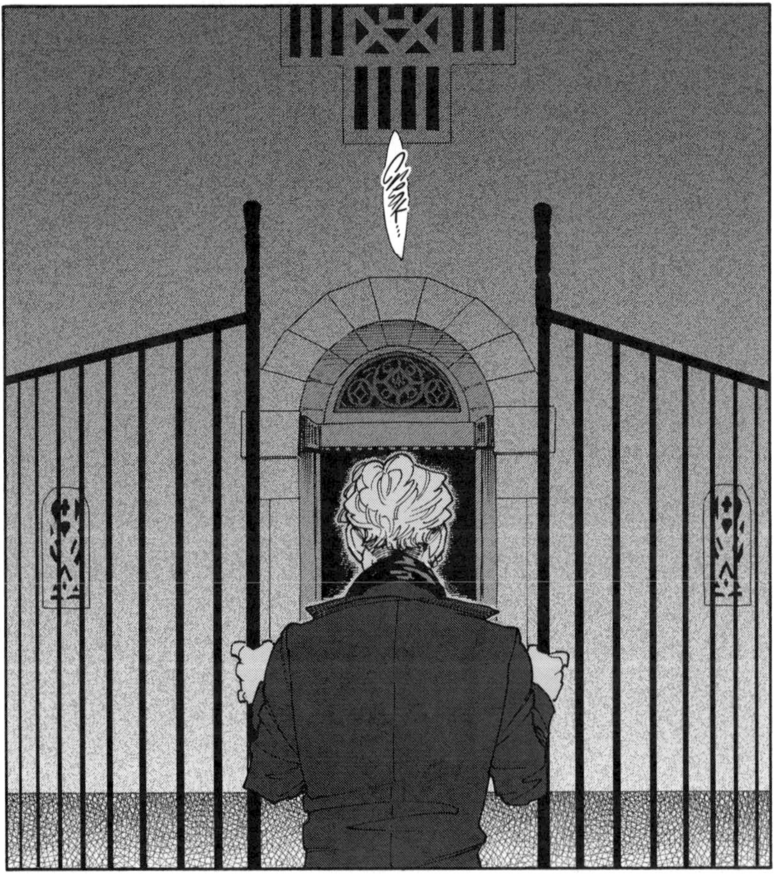
CREAK...

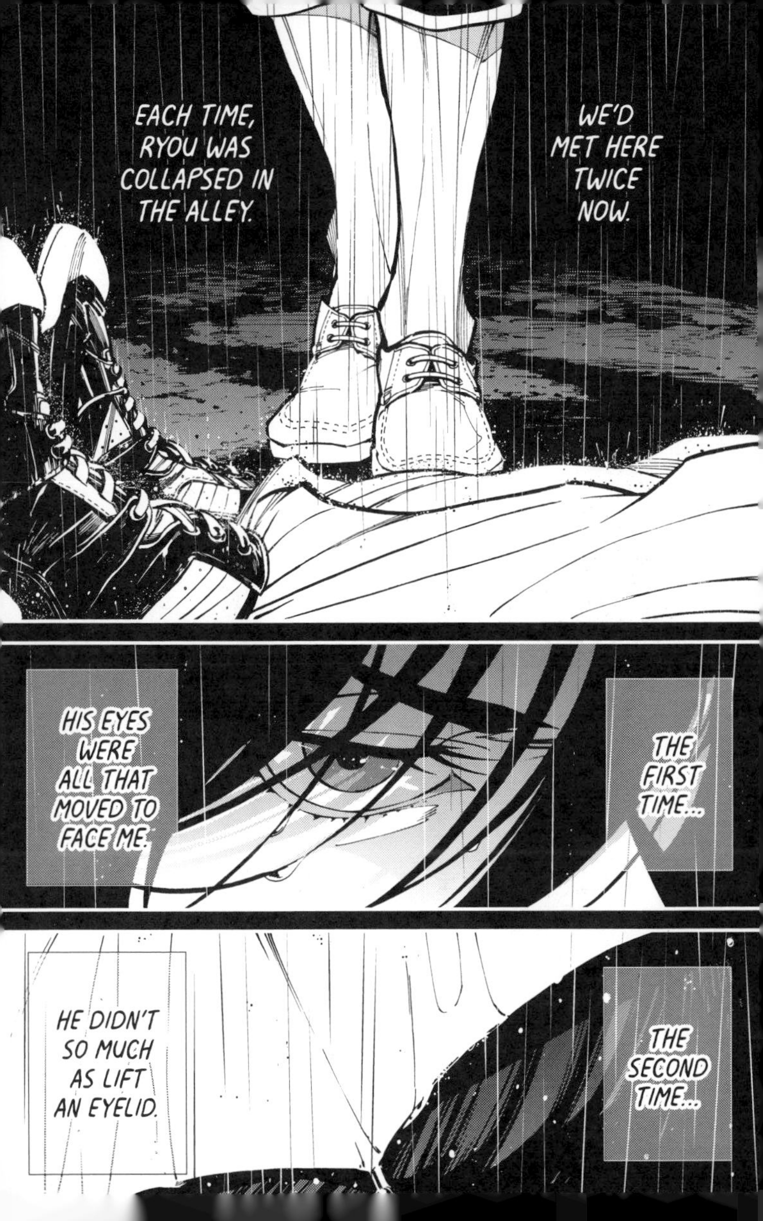
WE'D MET HERE TWICE NOW.
EACH TIME, RYOU WAS COLLAPSED IN THE ALLEY.
THE FIRST TIME...
HIS EYES WERE ALL THAT MOVED TO FACE ME.
THE SECOND TIME...
HE DIDN'T SO MUCH AS LIFT AN EYELID.

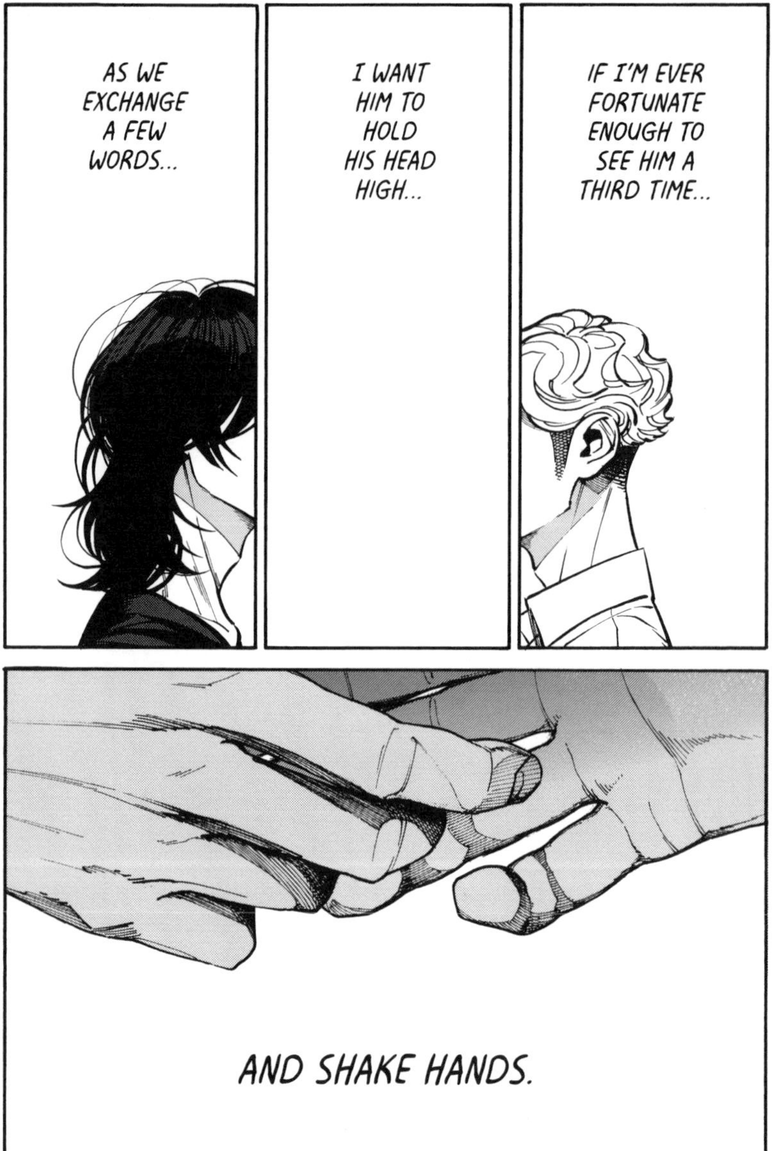
IF I'M EVER FORTUNATE ENOUGH TO SEE HIM A THIRD TIME...
I WANT HIM TO HOLD HIS HEAD HIGH...
AS WE EXCHANGE A FEW WORDS...
AND SHAKE HANDS.

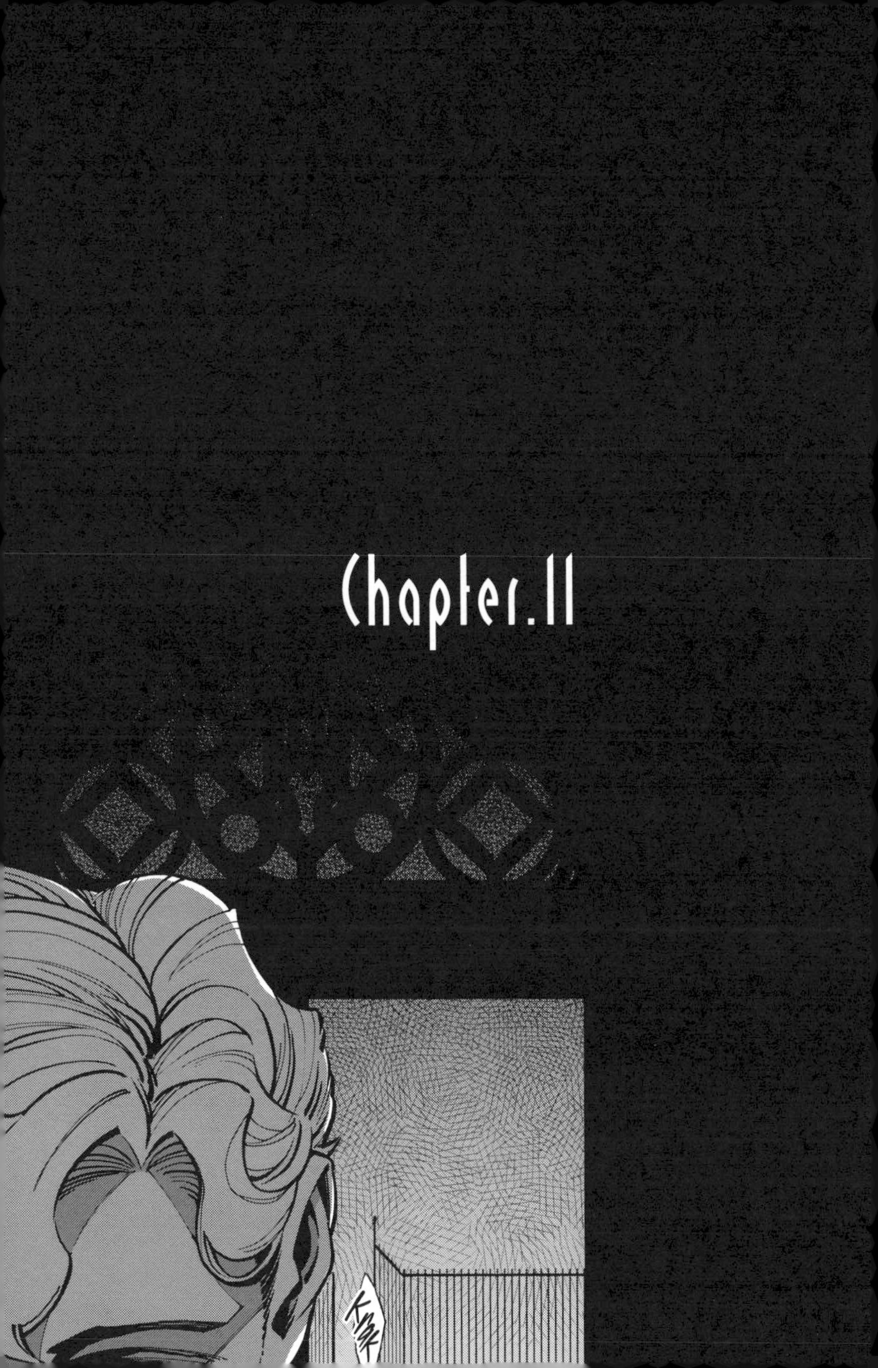
Chapter.11

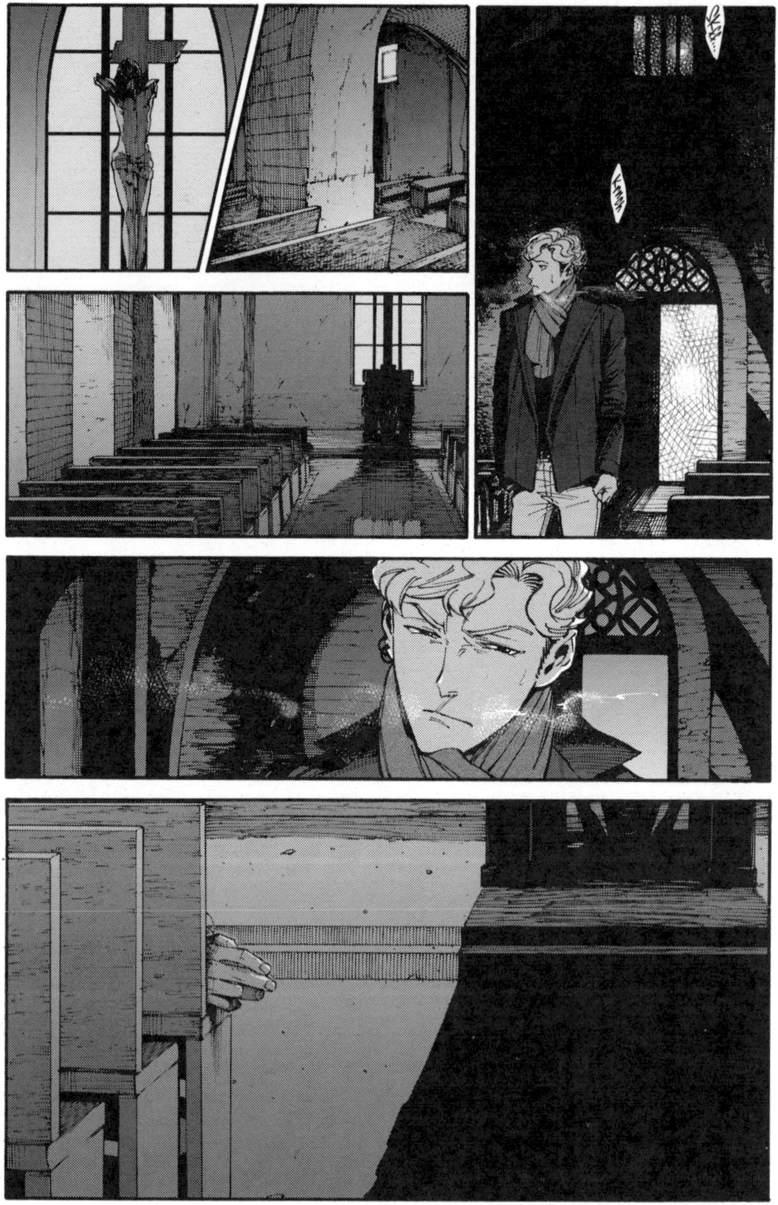
SKSH...

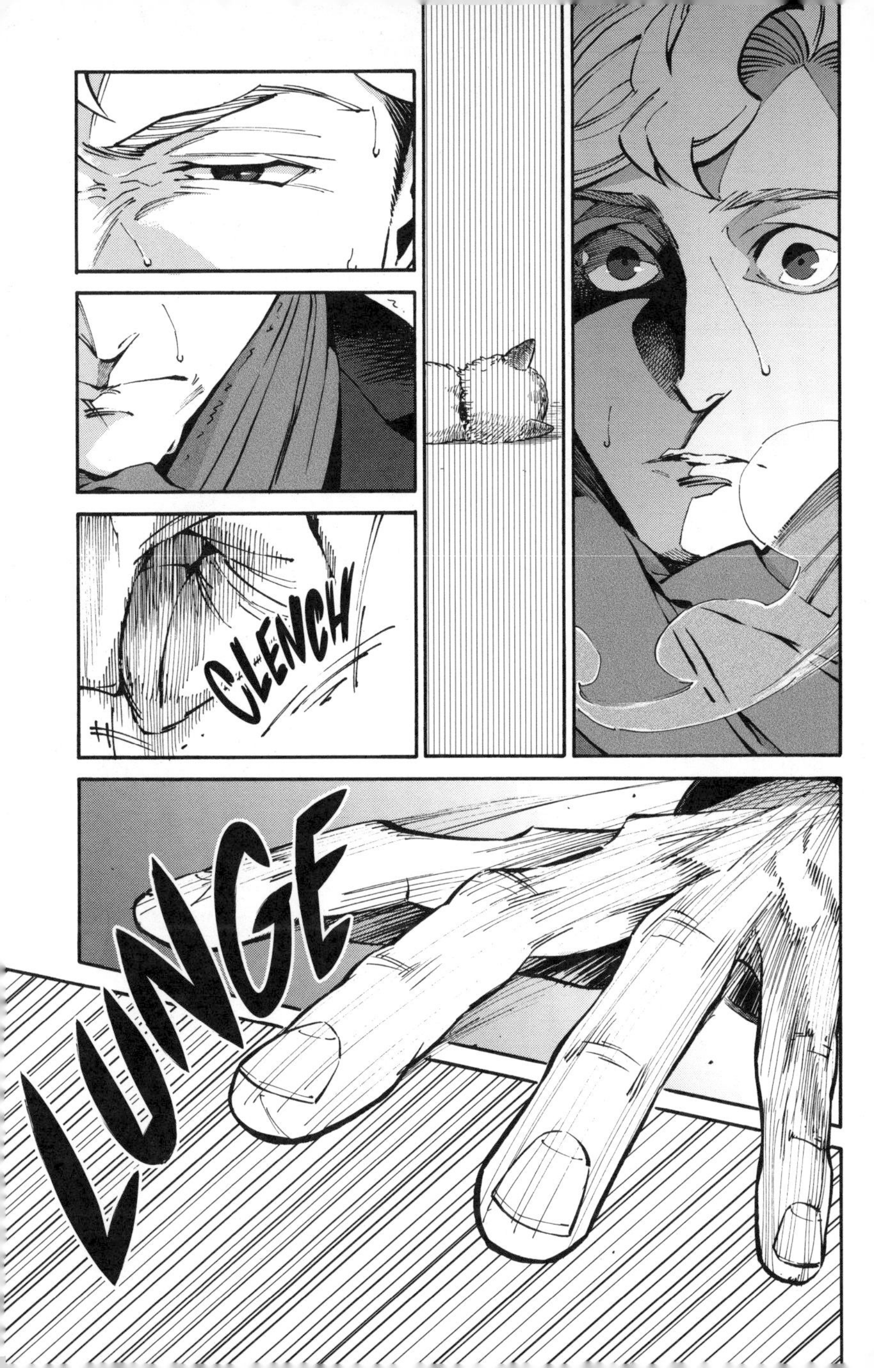
CLENCH
LUNGE

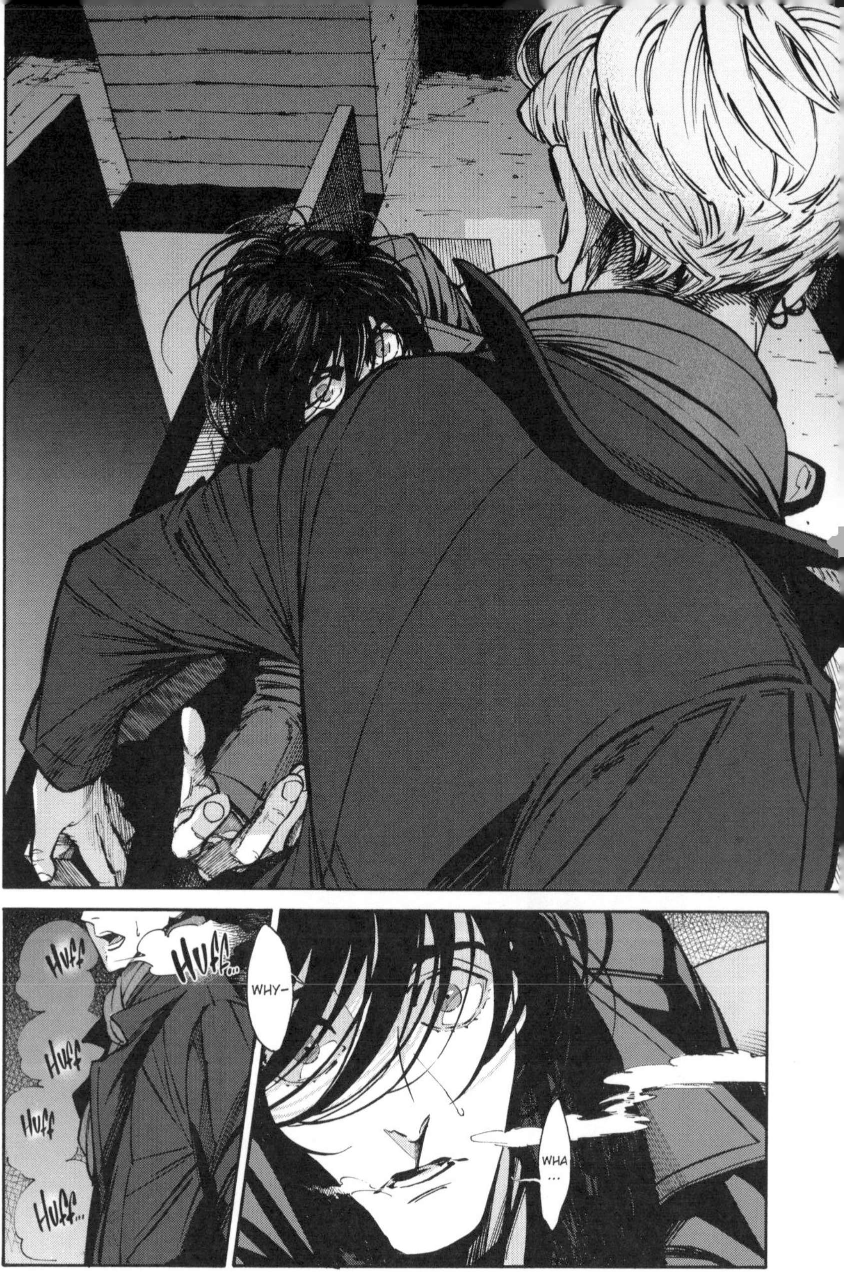
WHY-
WHA...
HUFF...
HUFF
HUFF
HUFF
HUFF...

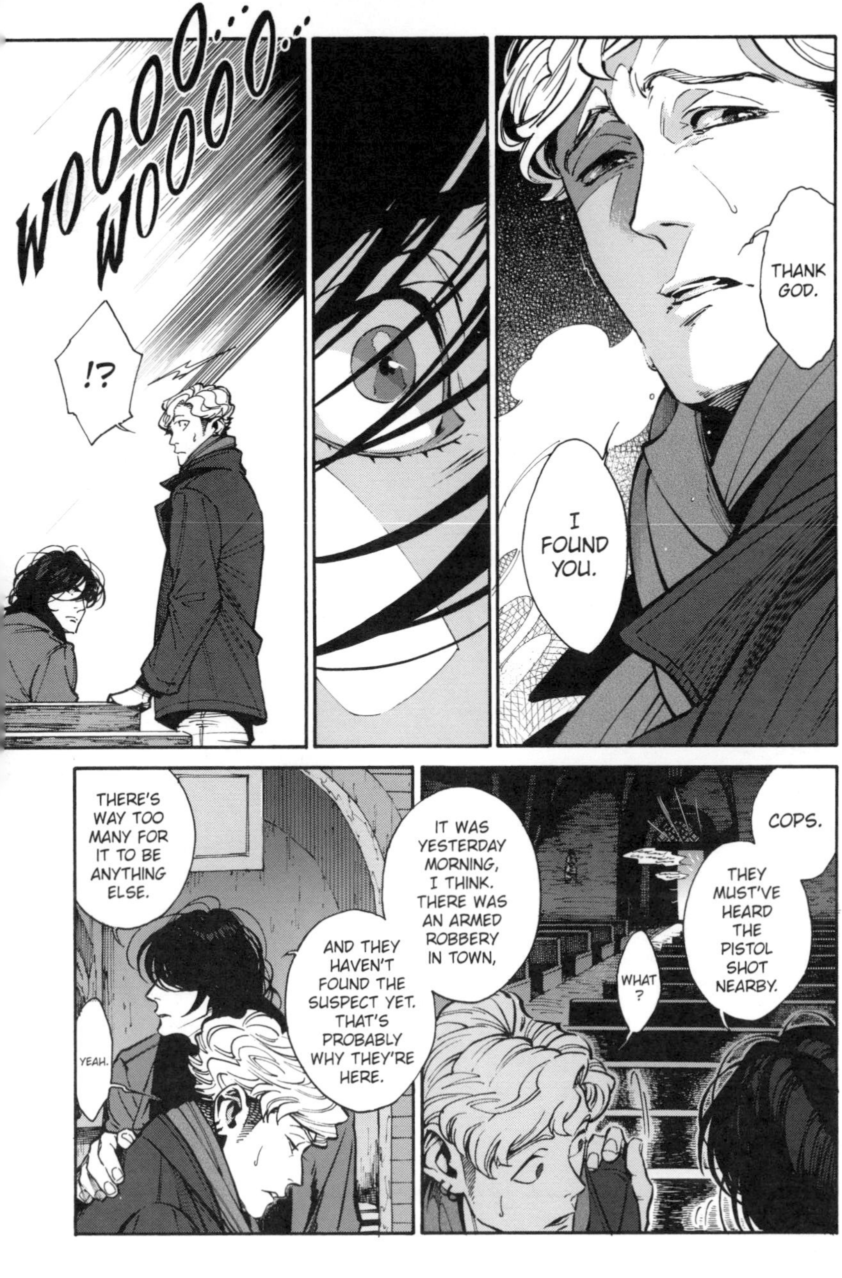
THANK GOD.
I FOUND YOU.
WOOOOO...
WOOOOO...
!?
COPS.
THEY MUST'VE HEARD THE PISTOL SHOT NEARBY.
WHAT?
IT WAS YESTERDAY MORNING, I THINK. THERE WAS AN ARMED ROBBERY IN TOWN,
AND THEY HAVEN'T FOUND THE SUSPECT YET. THAT'S PROBABLY WHY THEY'RE HERE.
THERE'S WAY TOO MANY FOR IT TO BE ANYTHING ELSE.
YEAH.

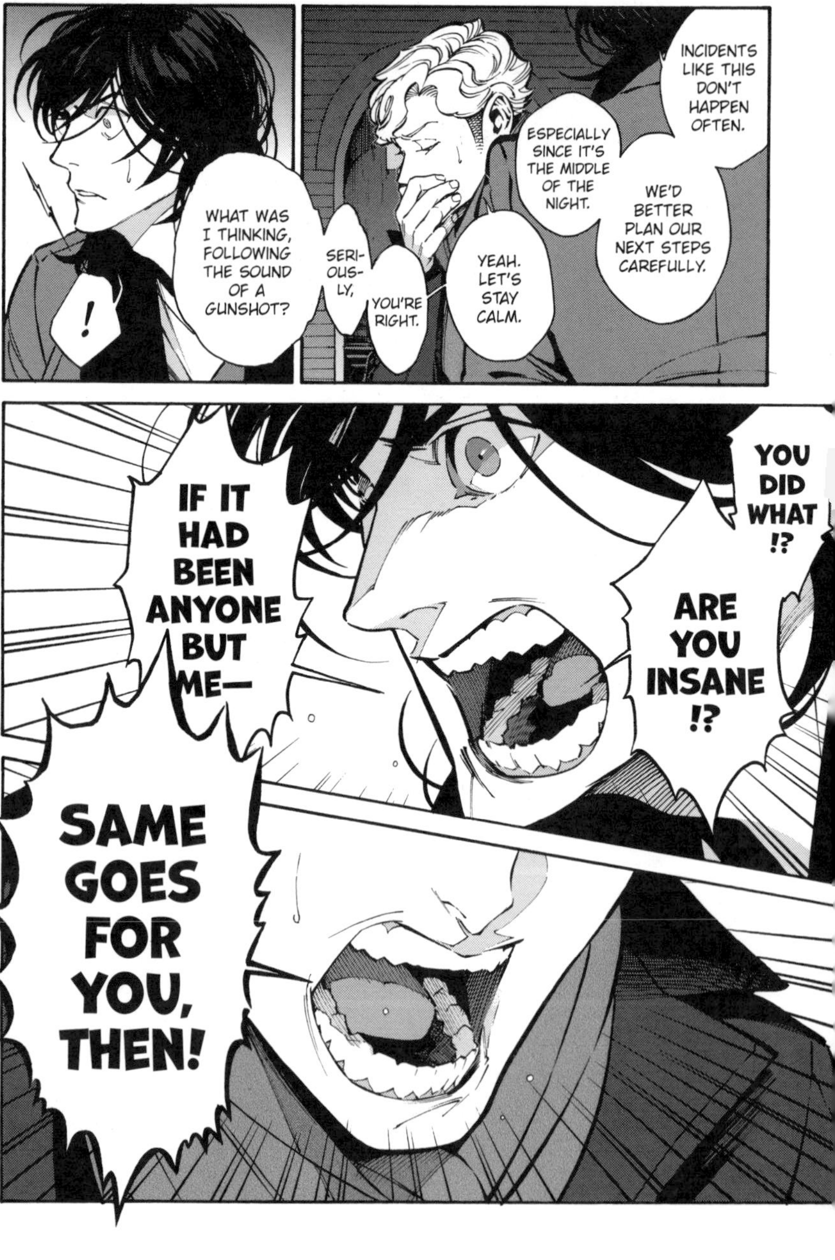
INCIDENTS LIKE THIS DON'T HAPPEN OFTEN.
ESPECIALLY SINCE IT'S THE MIDDLE OF THE NIGHT.
WE'D BETTER PLAN OUR NEXT STEPS CAREFULLY.
YEAH. LET'S STAY CALM.
YOU'RE RIGHT.
SERI-OUS-LY,
WHAT WAS I THINKING, FOLLOWING THE SOUND OF A GUNSHOT?
!
YOU DID WHAT!?
ARE YOU INSANE!?
IF IT HAD BEEN ANYONE BUT ME—
SAME GOES FOR YOU, THEN!

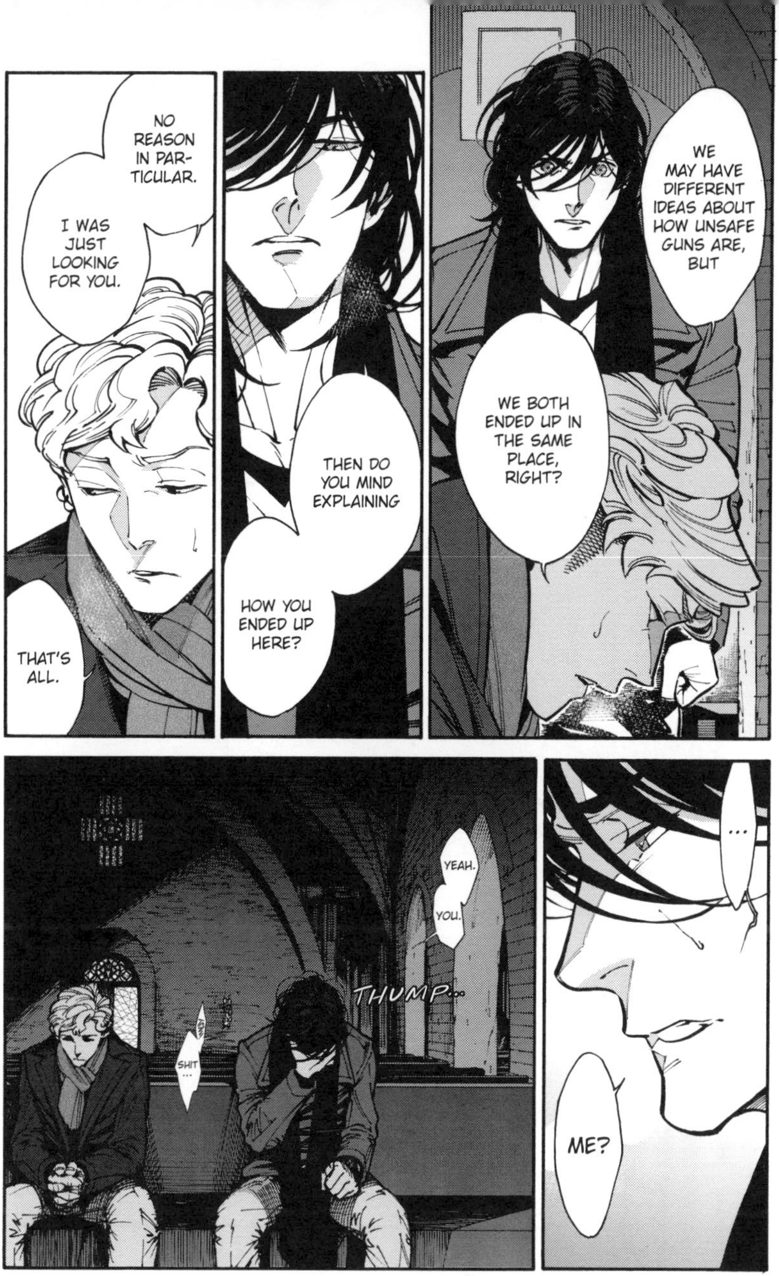
WE MAY HAVE DIFFERENT IDEAS ABOUT HOW UNSAFE GUNS ARE, BUT
WE BOTH ENDED UP IN THE SAME PLACE, RIGHT?
THEN DO YOU MIND EXPLAINING
HOW YOU ENDED UP HERE?
NO REASON IN PAR-TICULAR.
I WAS JUST LOOKING FOR YOU.
THAT'S ALL.
...
ME?
YEAH.
YOU.
THUMP...
SHIT...

SORRY FOR WHAT?

IT WAS MY OWN CHOICE TO COME HERE.

...I'M SORRY.

HE HAD A...

THAT I SAW LEAVE THE BUILDING EARLIER.

THERE WAS A MAN

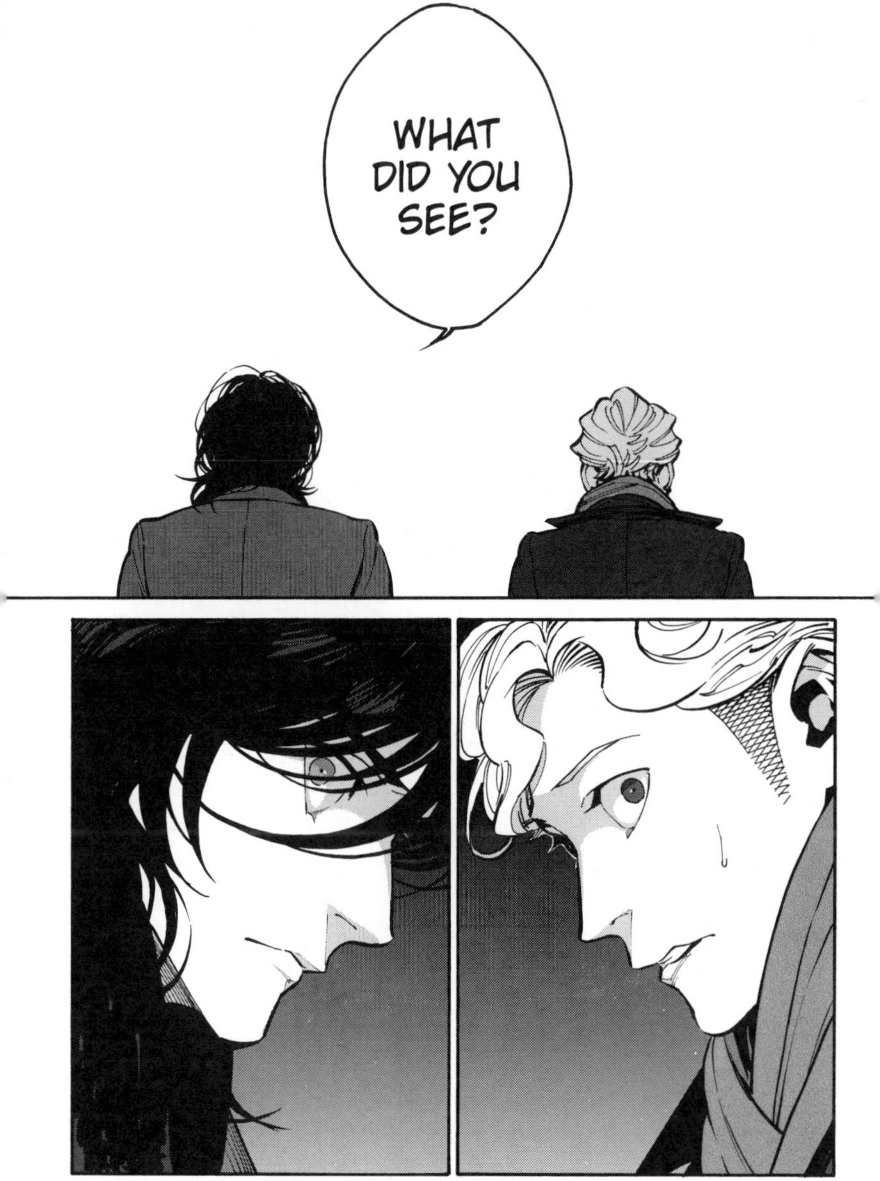
WHAT DID YOU SEE?

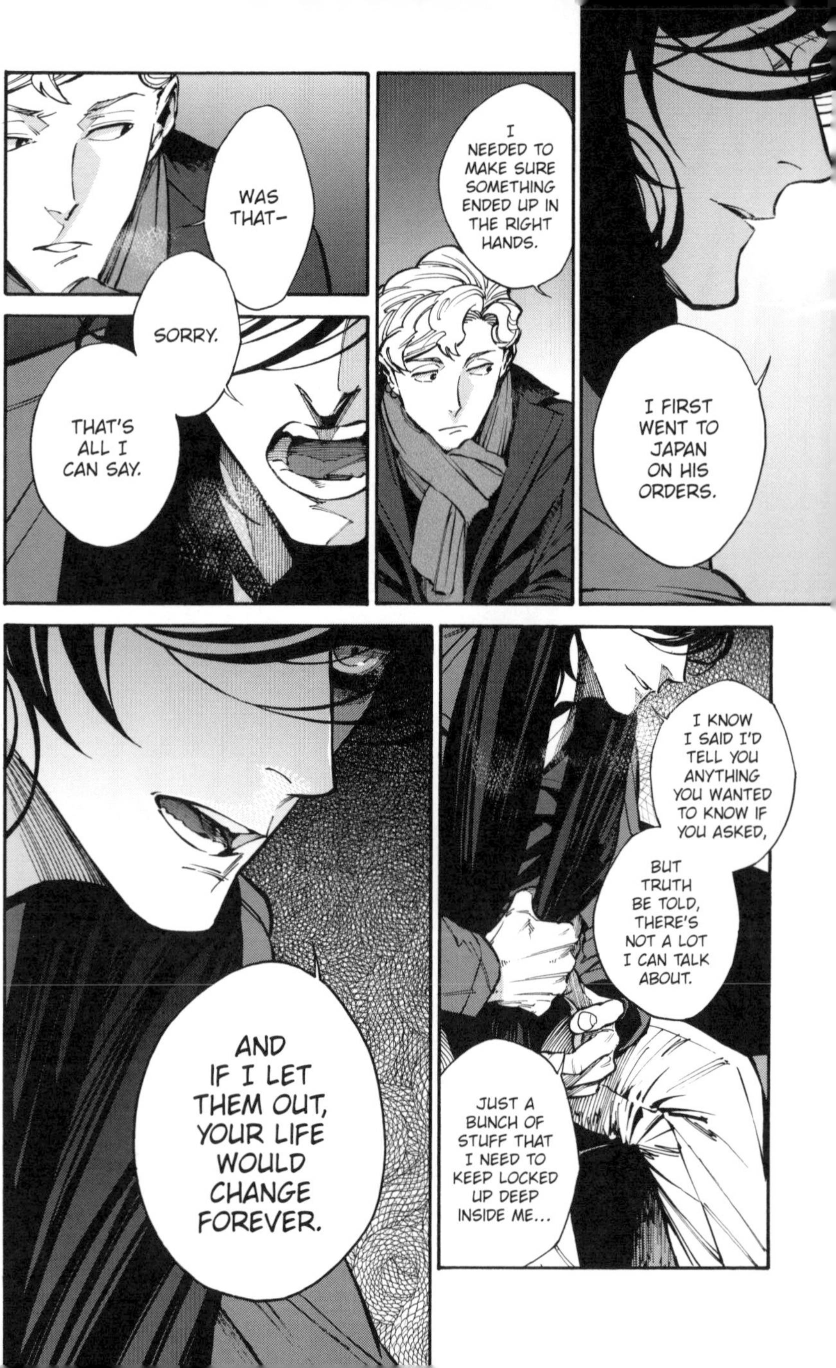
I FIRST WENT TO JAPAN ON HIS ORDERS.
I NEEDED TO MAKE SURE SOMETHING ENDED UP IN THE RIGHT HANDS.
WAS THAT–
SORRY.
THAT'S ALL I CAN SAY.
I KNOW I SAID I'D TELL YOU ANYTHING YOU WANTED TO KNOW IF YOU ASKED,
BUT TRUTH BE TOLD, THERE'S NOT A LOT I CAN TALK ABOUT.
JUST A BUNCH OF STUFF THAT I NEED TO KEEP LOCKED UP DEEP INSIDE ME...
AND IF I LET THEM OUT, YOUR LIFE WOULD CHANGE FOREVER.

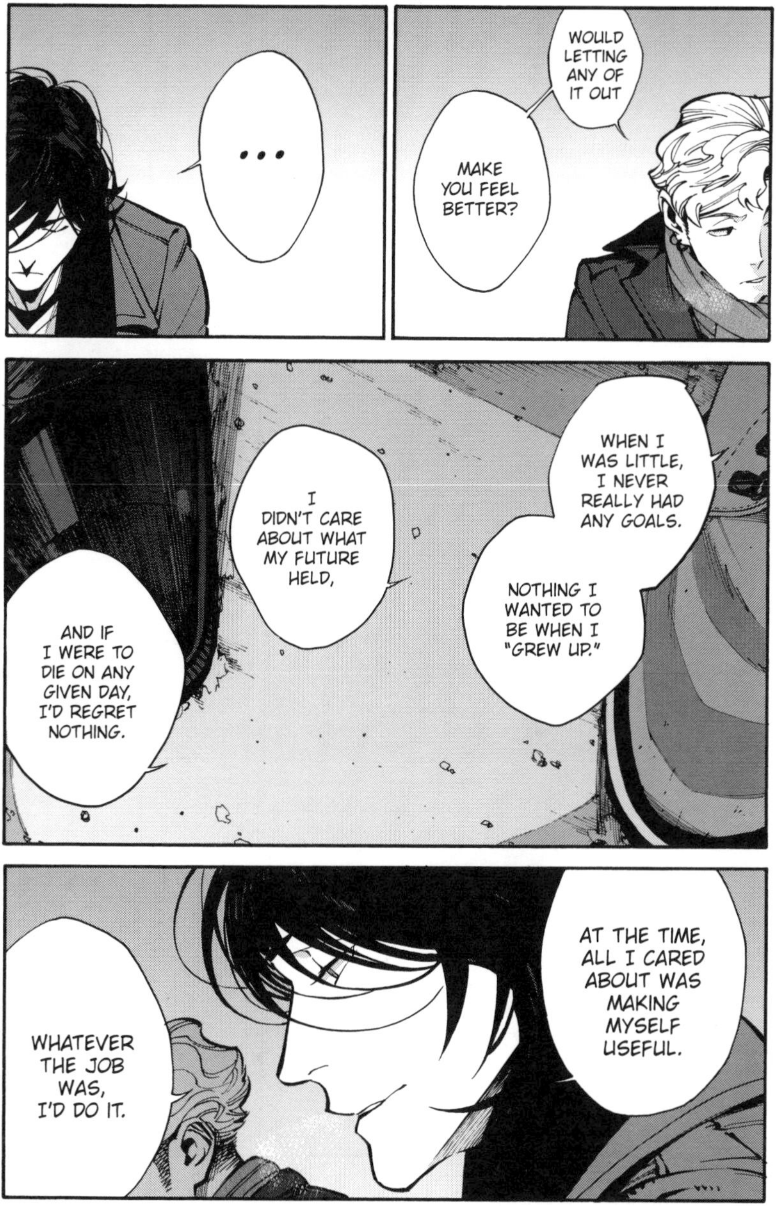
WOULD LETTING ANY OF IT OUT
MAKE YOU FEEL BETTER?
...
WHEN I WAS LITTLE, I NEVER REALLY HAD ANY GOALS.
NOTHING I WANTED TO BE WHEN I "GREW UP."
I DIDN'T CARE ABOUT WHAT MY FUTURE HELD,
AND IF I WERE TO DIE ON ANY GIVEN DAY, I'D REGRET NOTHING.
AT THE TIME, ALL I CARED ABOUT WAS MAKING MYSELF USEFUL.
WHATEVER THE JOB WAS, I'D DO IT.

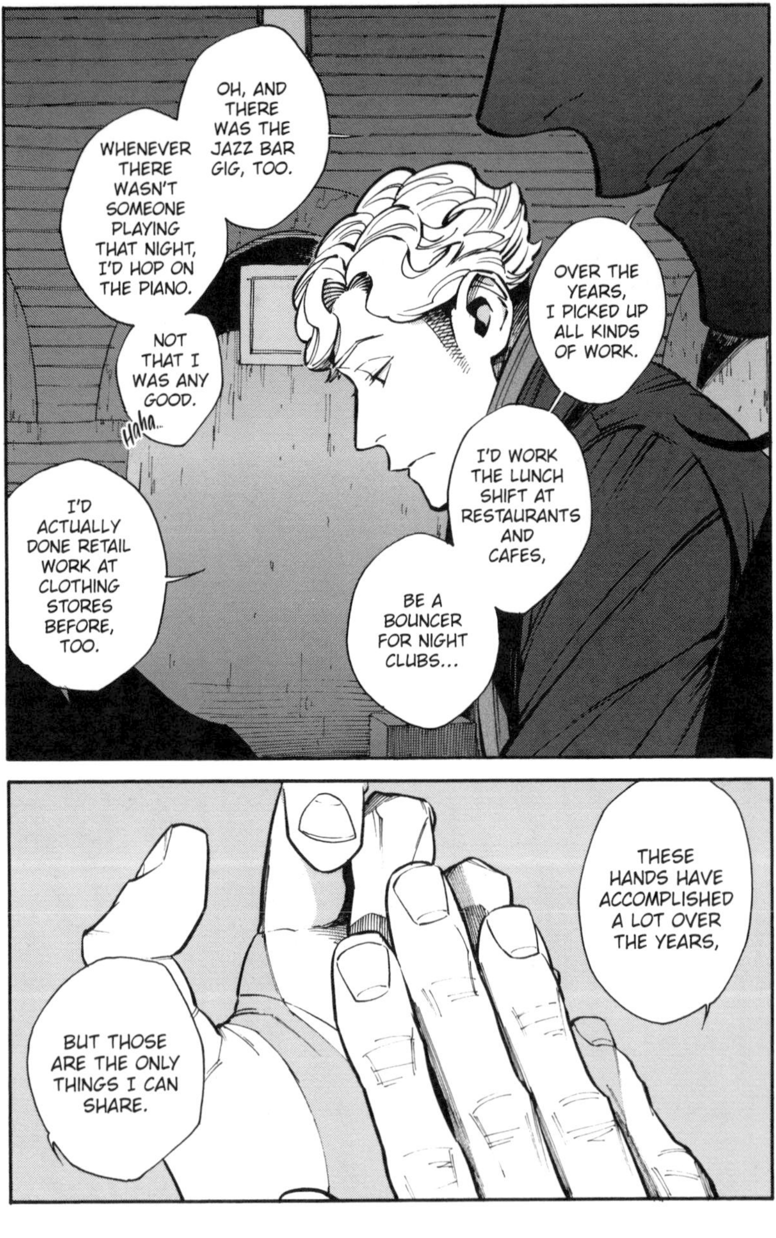
OVER THE YEARS, I PICKED UP ALL KINDS OF WORK.
I'D WORK THE LUNCH SHIFT AT RESTAURANTS AND CAFES,
BE A BOUNCER FOR NIGHT CLUBS...
I'D ACTUALLY DONE RETAIL WORK AT CLOTHING STORES BEFORE, TOO.
OH, AND THERE WAS THE JAZZ BAR GIG, TOO.
WHENEVER THERE WASN'T SOMEONE PLAYING THAT NIGHT, I'D HOP ON THE PIANO.
NOT THAT I WAS ANY GOOD.
Haha...
THESE HANDS HAVE ACCOMPLISHED A LOT OVER THE YEARS,
BUT THOSE ARE THE ONLY THINGS I CAN SHARE.

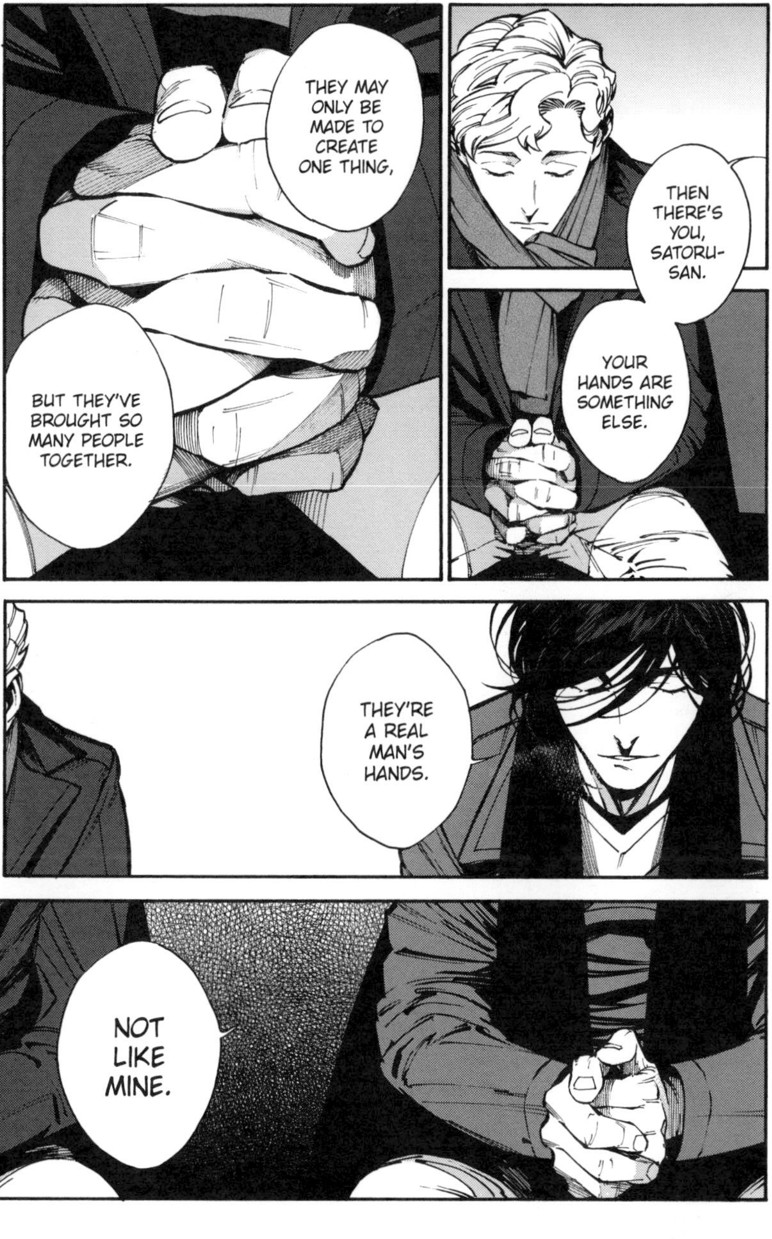
THEN THERE'S YOU, SATORU-SAN.
YOUR HANDS ARE SOMETHING ELSE.
THEY MAY ONLY BE MADE TO CREATE ONE THING,
BUT THEY'VE BROUGHT SO MANY PEOPLE TOGETHER.
THEY'RE A REAL MAN'S HANDS.
NOT LIKE MINE.

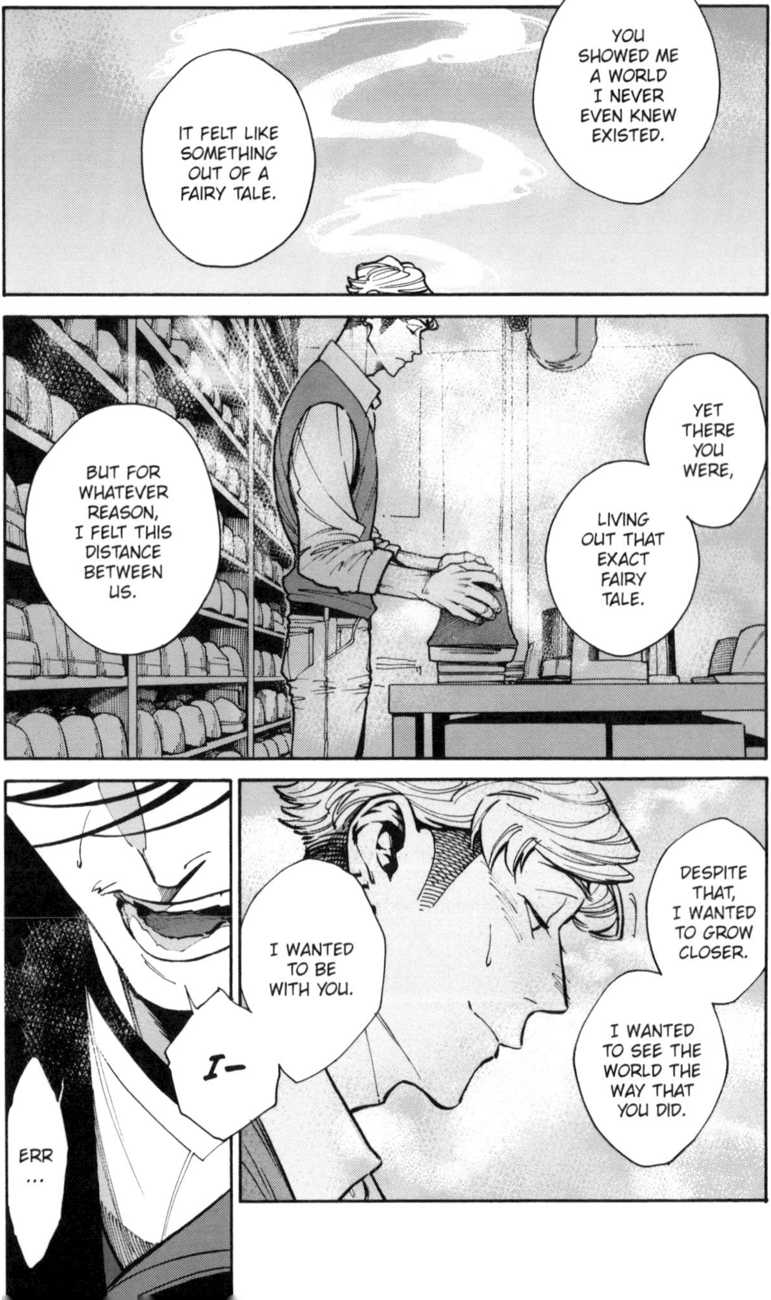
YOU SHOWED ME A WORLD I NEVER EVEN KNEW EXISTED.
IT FELT LIKE SOMETHING OUT OF A FAIRY TALE.
YET THERE YOU WERE,
LIVING OUT THAT EXACT FAIRY TALE.
BUT FOR WHATEVER REASON, I FELT THIS DISTANCE BETWEEN US.
DESPITE THAT, I WANTED TO GROW CLOSER.
I WANTED TO SEE THE WORLD THE WAY THAT YOU DID.
I WANTED TO BE WITH YOU.
I—
ERR ...

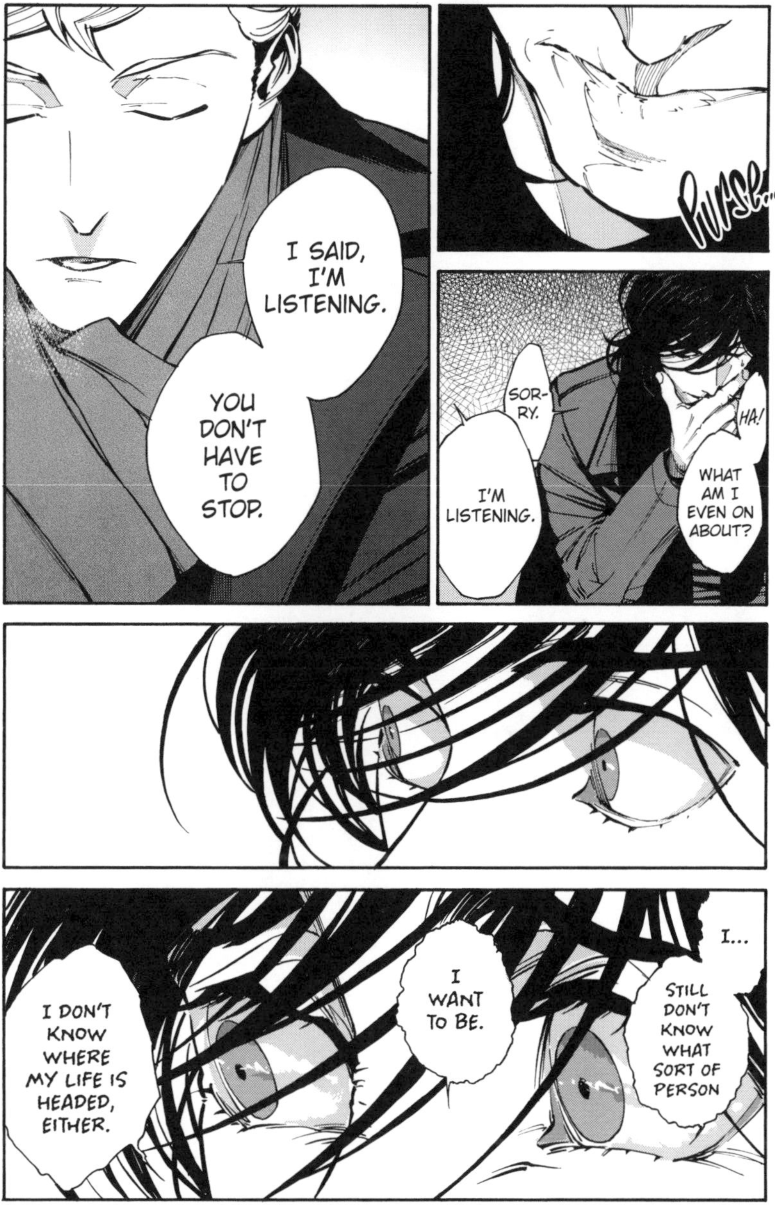
Purse...
HA!
WHAT AM I EVEN ON ABOUT?
SORRY.
I'M LISTENING.
I SAID, I'M LISTENING.
YOU DON'T HAVE TO STOP.
I...
STILL DON'T KNOW WHAT SORT OF PERSON
I WANT TO BE.
I DON'T KNOW WHERE MY LIFE IS HEADED, EITHER.

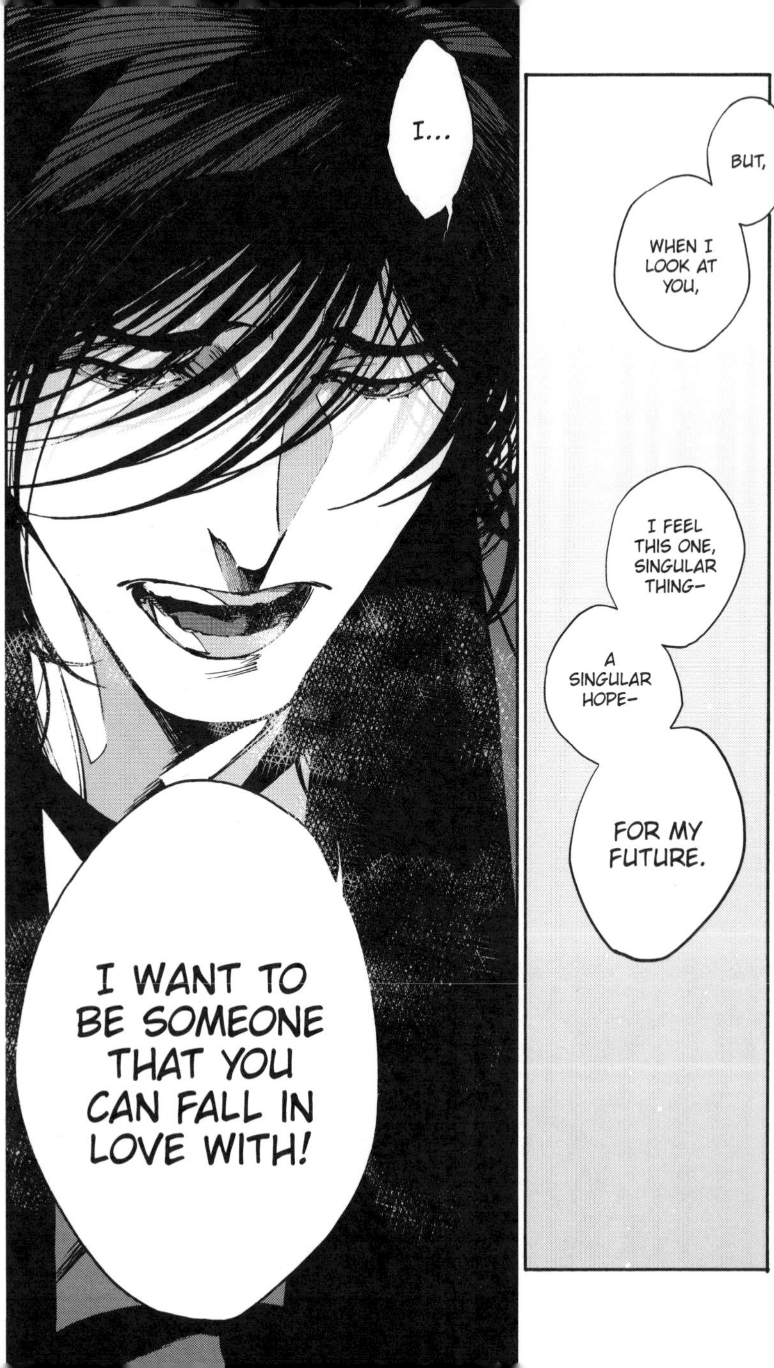
BUT,
WHEN I LOOK AT YOU,
I FEEL THIS ONE, SINGULAR THING-
A SINGULAR HOPE-
FOR MY FUTURE.
I...
I WANT TO BE SOMEONE THAT YOU CAN FALL IN LOVE WITH!

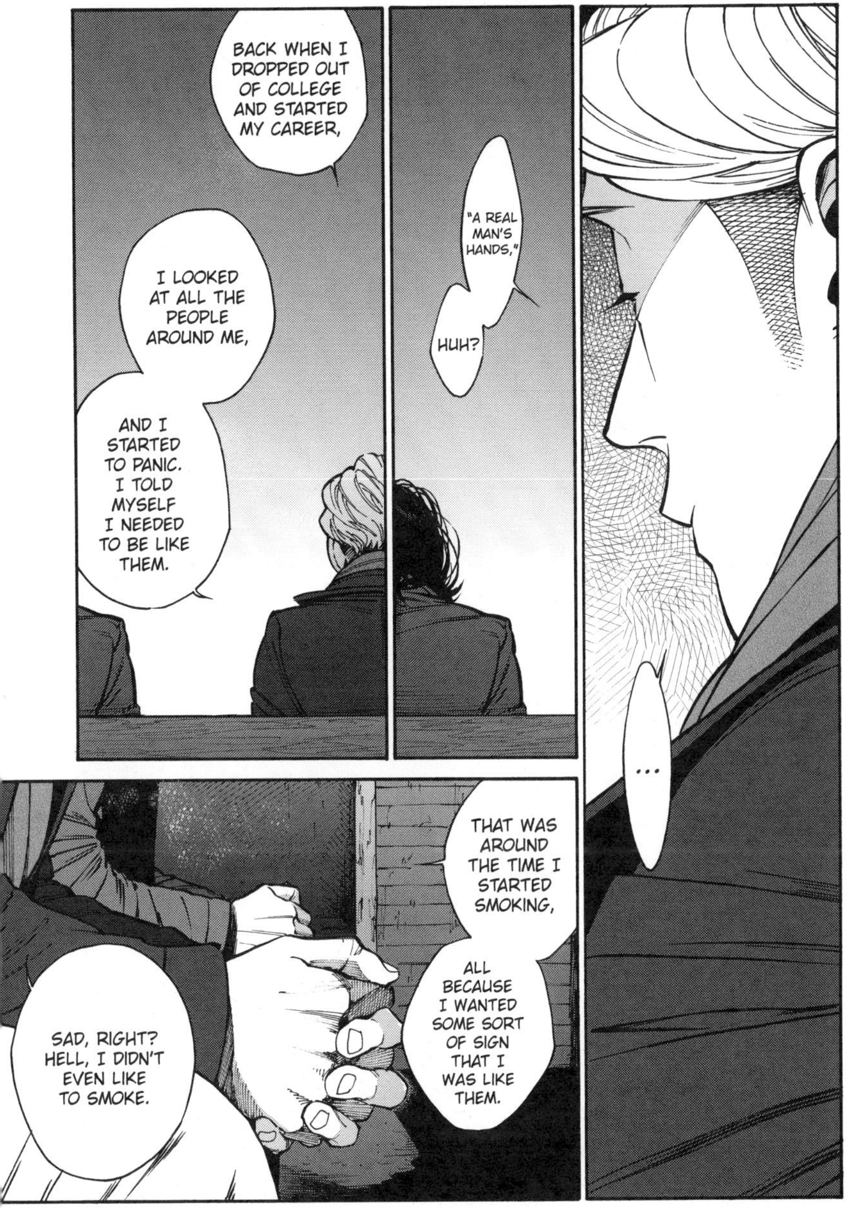
...
"A REAL MAN'S HANDS,"
HUH?
BACK WHEN I DROPPED OUT OF COLLEGE AND STARTED MY CAREER,
I LOOKED AT ALL THE PEOPLE AROUND ME,
AND I STARTED TO PANIC. I TOLD MYSELF I NEEDED TO BE LIKE THEM.
THAT WAS AROUND THE TIME I STARTED SMOKING,
ALL BECAUSE I WANTED SOME SORT OF SIGN THAT I WAS LIKE THEM.
SAD, RIGHT? HELL, I DIDN'T EVEN LIKE TO SMOKE.

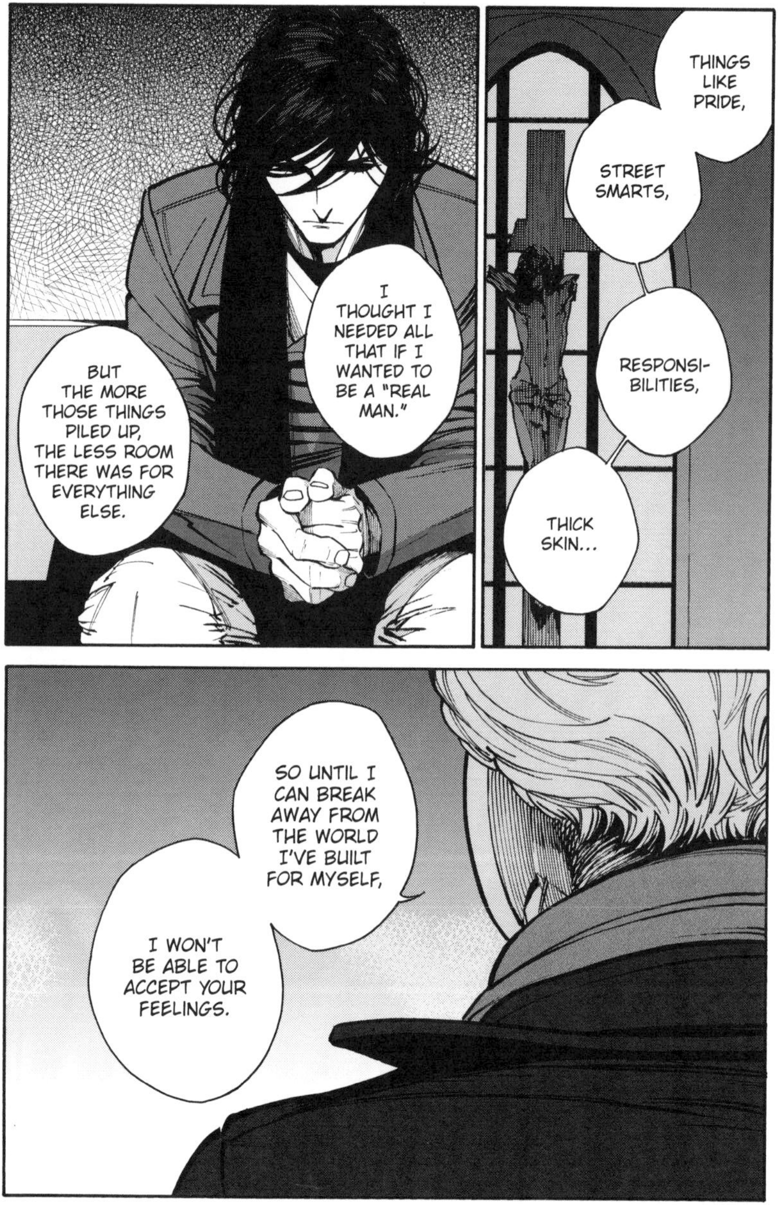
THINGS LIKE PRIDE,
STREET SMARTS,
RESPONSIBILITIES,
THICK SKIN...
I THOUGHT I NEEDED ALL THAT IF I WANTED TO BE A "REAL MAN."
BUT THE MORE THOSE THINGS PILED UP, THE LESS ROOM THERE WAS FOR EVERYTHING ELSE.
SO UNTIL I CAN BREAK AWAY FROM THE WORLD I'VE BUILT FOR MYSELF,
I WON'T BE ABLE TO ACCEPT YOUR FEELINGS.

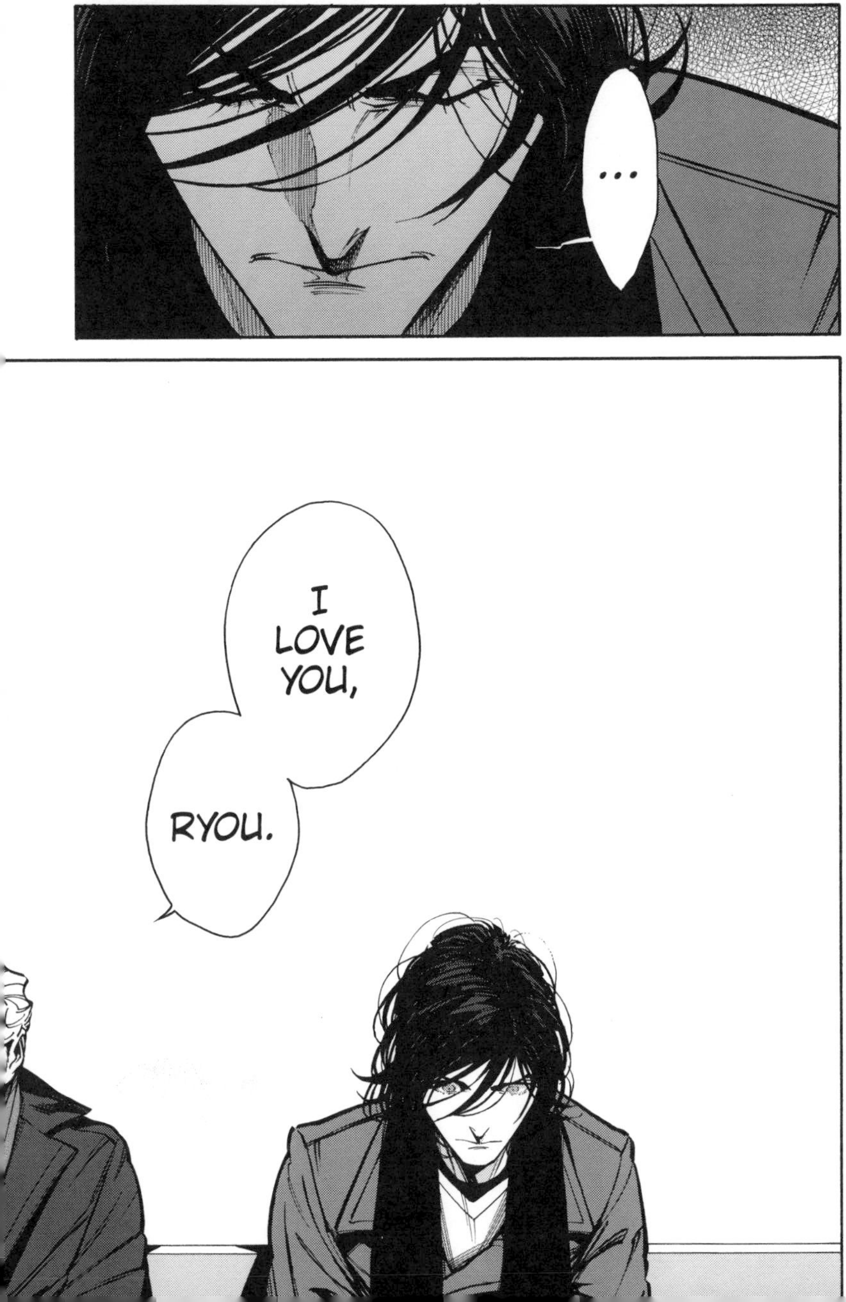
...
I LOVE YOU,
RYOU.

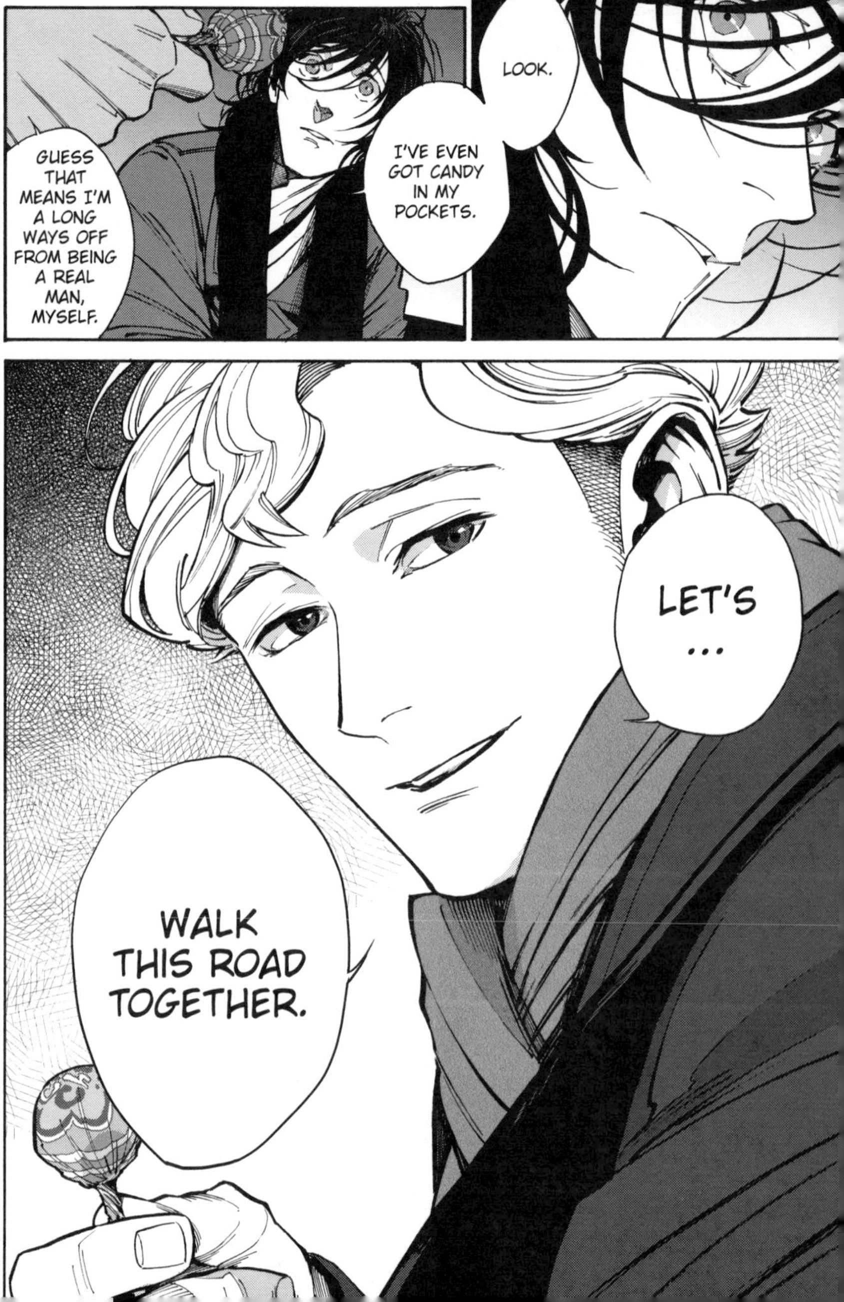
LOOK.
I'VE EVEN GOT CANDY IN MY POCKETS.
GUESS THAT MEANS I'M A LONG WAYS OFF FROM BEING A REAL MAN, MYSELF.
LET'S ...
WALK THIS ROAD TOGETHER.

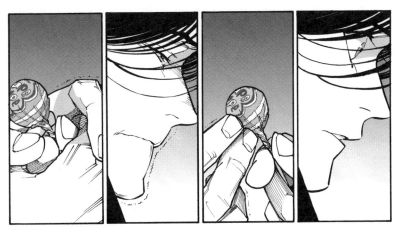

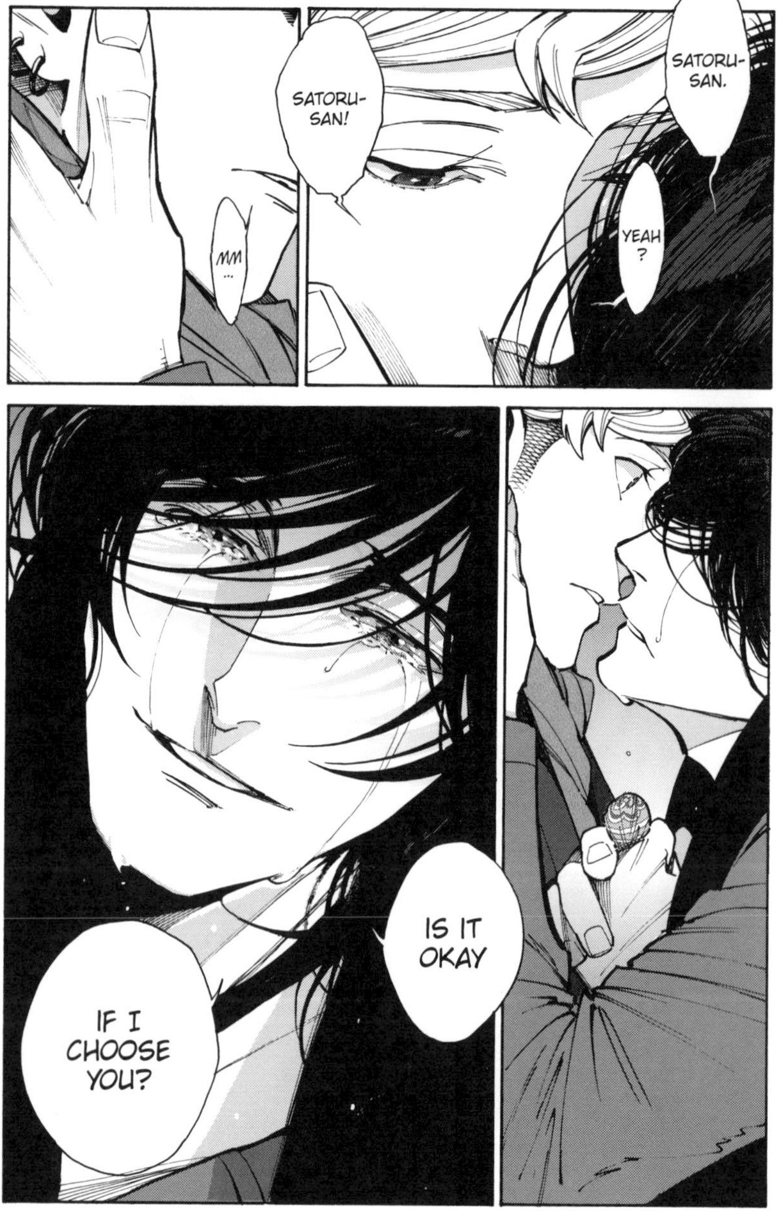
SATORU-SAN.
SATORU-SAN!
YEAH?
MM...
IS IT OKAY
IF I CHOOSE YOU?

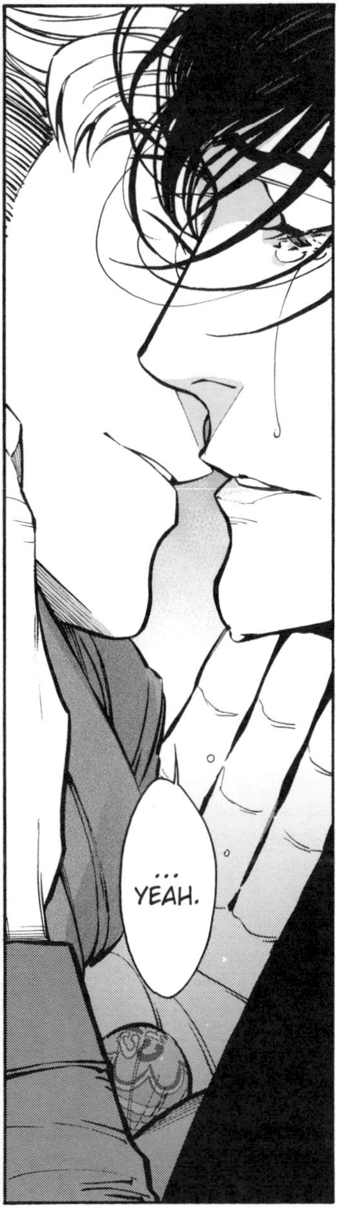
...
YEAH.
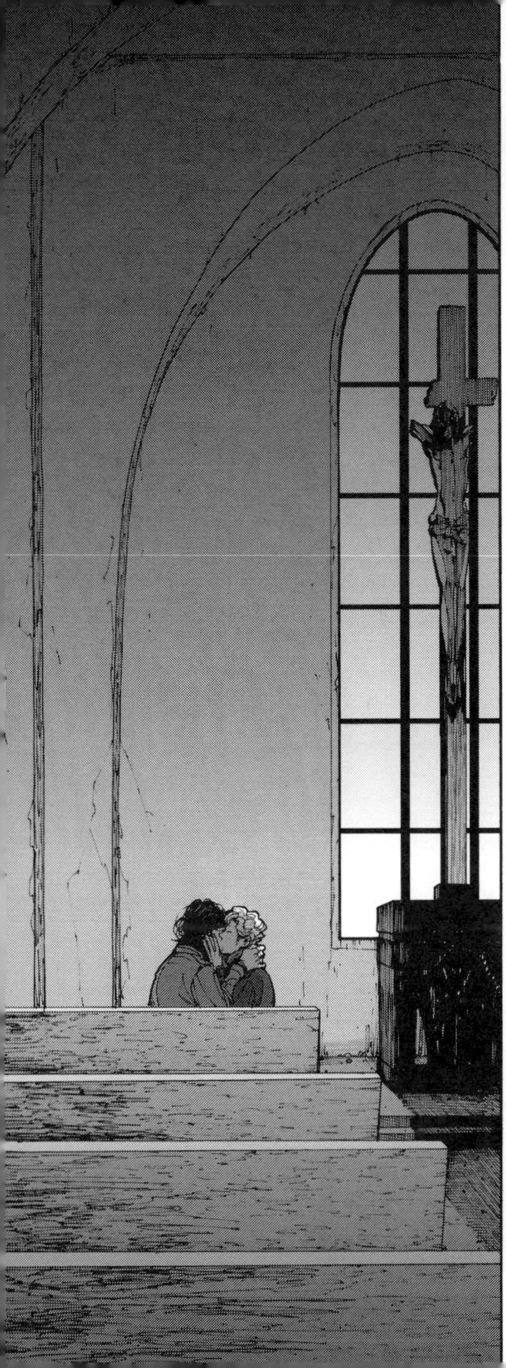

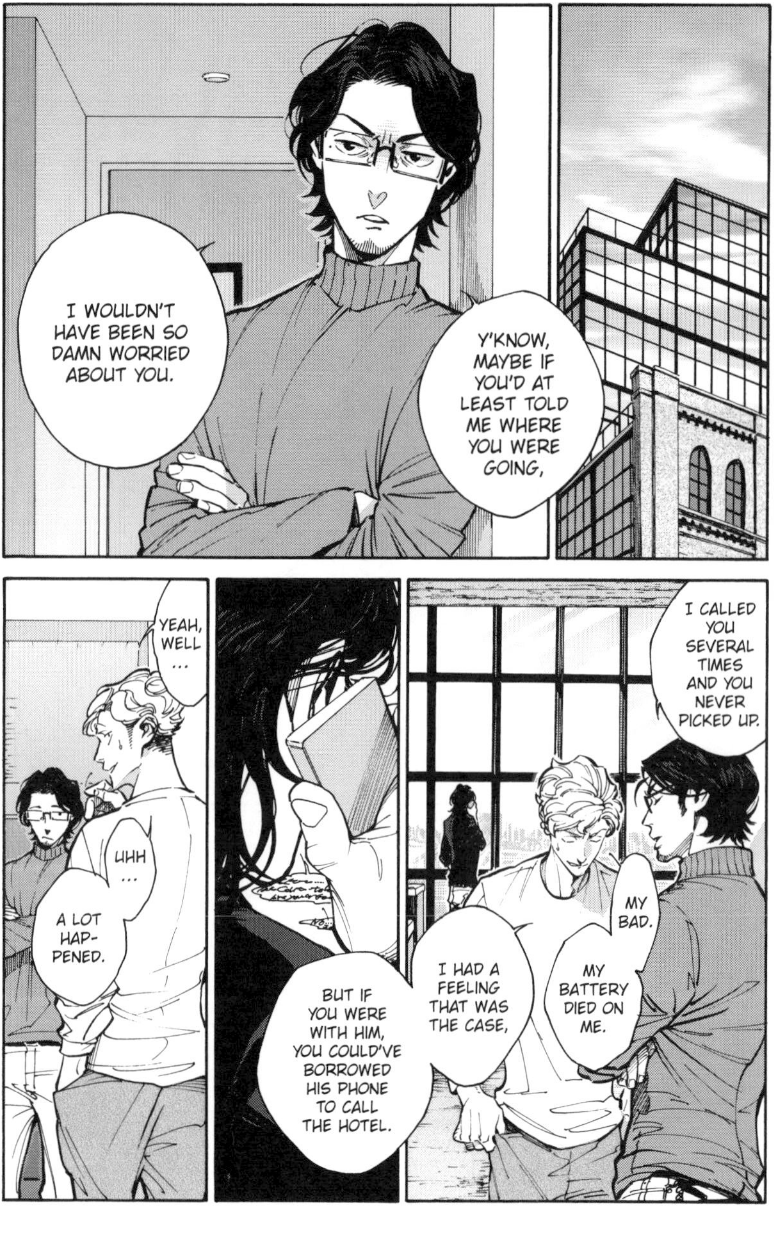
Y'KNOW, MAYBE IF YOU'D AT LEAST TOLD ME WHERE YOU WERE GOING,
I WOULDN'T HAVE BEEN SO DAMN WORRIED ABOUT YOU.
I CALLED YOU SEVERAL TIMES AND YOU NEVER PICKED UP.
MY BAD.
MY BATTERY DIED ON ME.
I HAD A FEELING THAT WAS THE CASE,
BUT IF YOU WERE WITH HIM, YOU COULD'VE BORROWED HIS PHONE TO CALL THE HOTEL.
YEAH, WELL ...
UHH ...
A LOT HAP-PENED.

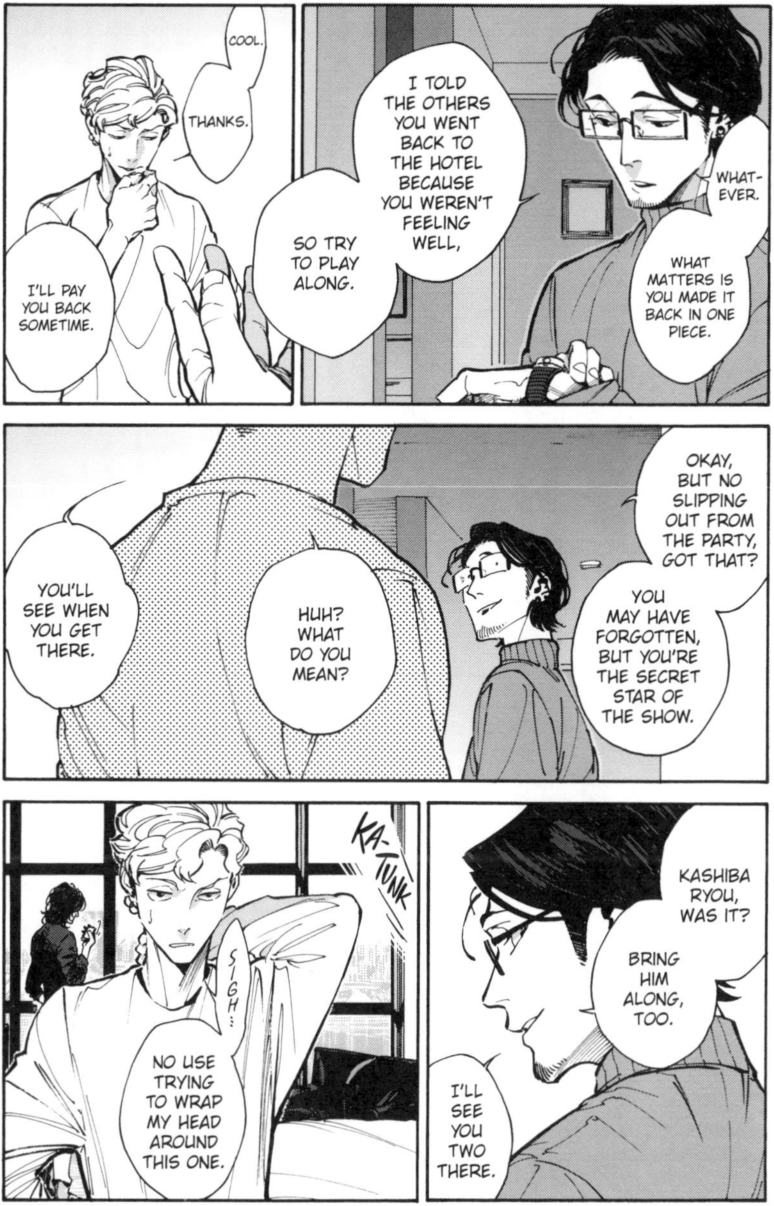
WHAT-EVER.
WHAT MATTERS IS YOU MADE IT BACK IN ONE PIECE.
I TOLD THE OTHERS YOU WENT BACK TO THE HOTEL BECAUSE YOU WEREN'T FEELING WELL,
SO TRY TO PLAY ALONG.
COOL.
THANKS.
I'LL PAY YOU BACK SOMETIME.
OKAY, BUT NO SLIPPING OUT FROM THE PARTY, GOT THAT?
YOU MAY HAVE FORGOTTEN, BUT YOU'RE THE SECRET STAR OF THE SHOW.
HUH? WHAT DO YOU MEAN?
YOU'LL SEE WHEN YOU GET THERE.
KASHIBA RYOU, WAS IT?
BRING HIM ALONG, TOO.
I'LL SEE YOU TWO THERE.
KA-TUNK
SIGH...
NO USE TRYING TO WRAP MY HEAD AROUND THIS ONE.

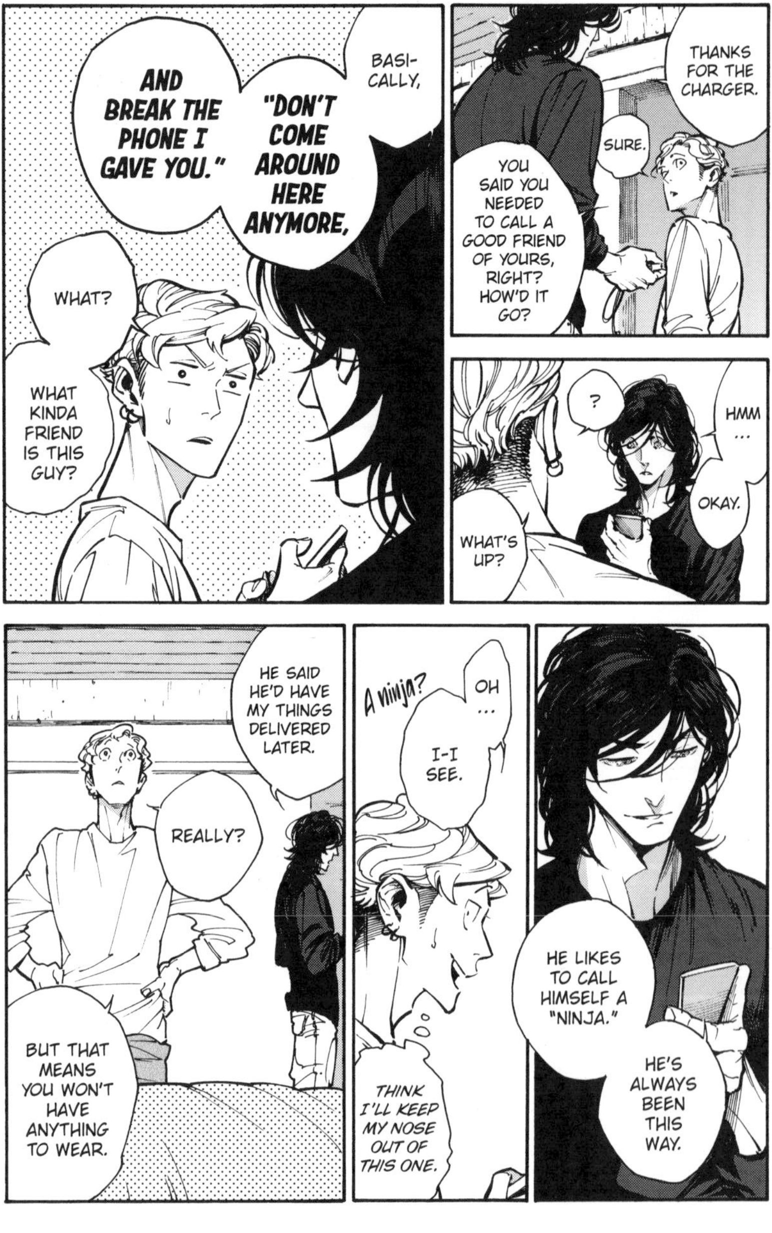
THANKS FOR THE CHARGER.
SURE.
YOU SAID YOU NEEDED TO CALL A GOOD FRIEND OF YOURS, RIGHT? HOW'D IT GO?
HMM ...
?
OKAY.
WHAT'S UP?
BASI-CALLY,
"DON'T COME AROUND HERE ANYMORE,
AND BREAK THE PHONE I GAVE YOU."
WHAT?
WHAT KINDA FRIEND IS THIS GUY?
HE LIKES TO CALL HIMSELF A "NINJA."
HE'S ALWAYS BEEN THIS WAY.
OH ...
A ninja?
I-I SEE.
THINK I'LL KEEP MY NOSE OUT OF THIS ONE.
HE SAID HE'D HAVE MY THINGS DELIVERED LATER.
REALLY?
BUT THAT MEANS YOU WON'T HAVE ANYTHING TO WEAR.

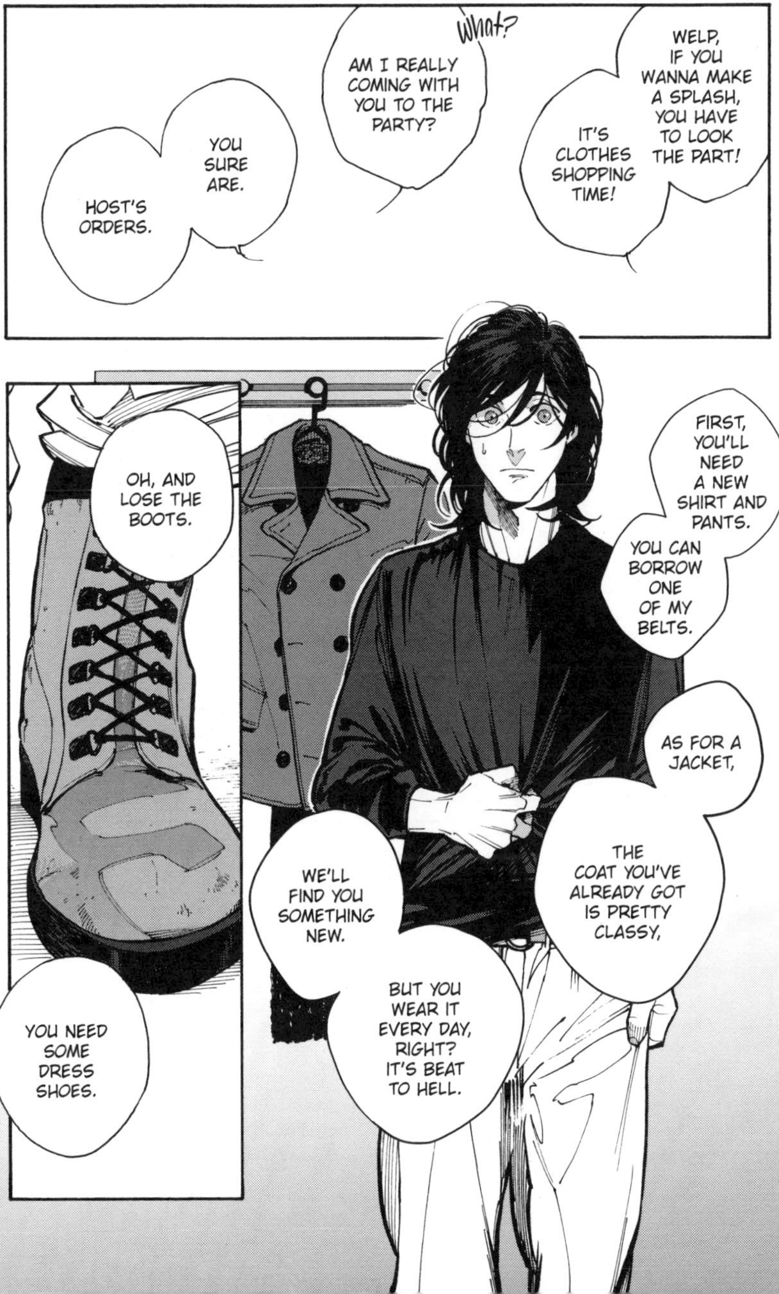
WELP, IF YOU WANNA MAKE A SPLASH, YOU HAVE TO LOOK THE PART!
IT'S CLOTHES SHOPPING TIME!
What?
AM I REALLY COMING WITH YOU TO THE PARTY?
YOU SURE ARE.
HOST'S ORDERS.
FIRST, YOU'LL NEED A NEW SHIRT AND PANTS.
YOU CAN BORROW ONE OF MY BELTS.
AS FOR A JACKET,
THE COAT YOU'VE ALREADY GOT IS PRETTY CLASSY,
BUT YOU WEAR IT EVERY DAY, RIGHT? IT'S BEAT TO HELL.
WE'LL FIND YOU SOMETHING NEW.
OH, AND LOSE THE BOOTS.
YOU NEED SOME DRESS SHOES.

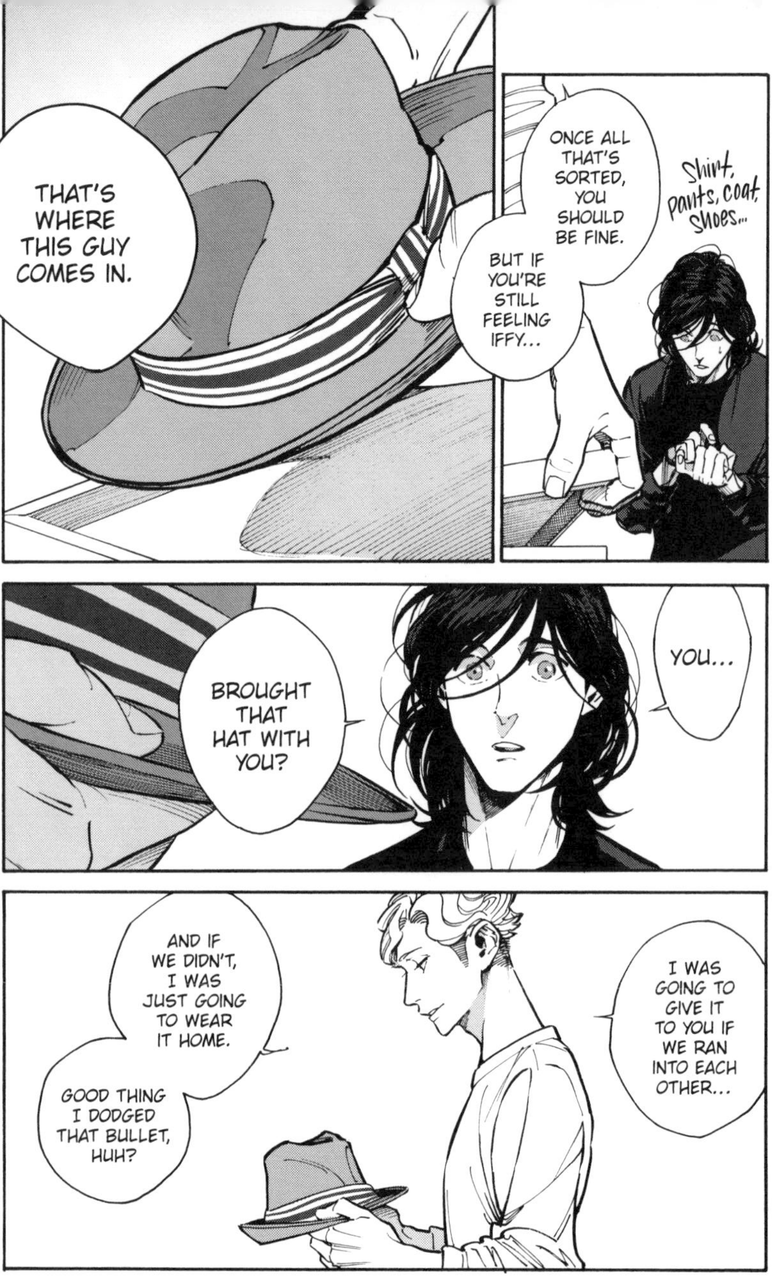
Shirt, pants, coat, shoes...
ONCE ALL THAT'S SORTED, YOU SHOULD BE FINE.
BUT IF YOU'RE STILL FEELING IFFY...
THAT'S WHERE THIS GUY COMES IN.
YOU...
BROUGHT THAT HAT WITH YOU?
I WAS GOING TO GIVE IT TO YOU IF WE RAN INTO EACH OTHER...
AND IF WE DIDN'T, I WAS JUST GOING TO WEAR IT HOME.
GOOD THING I DODGED THAT BULLET, HUH?

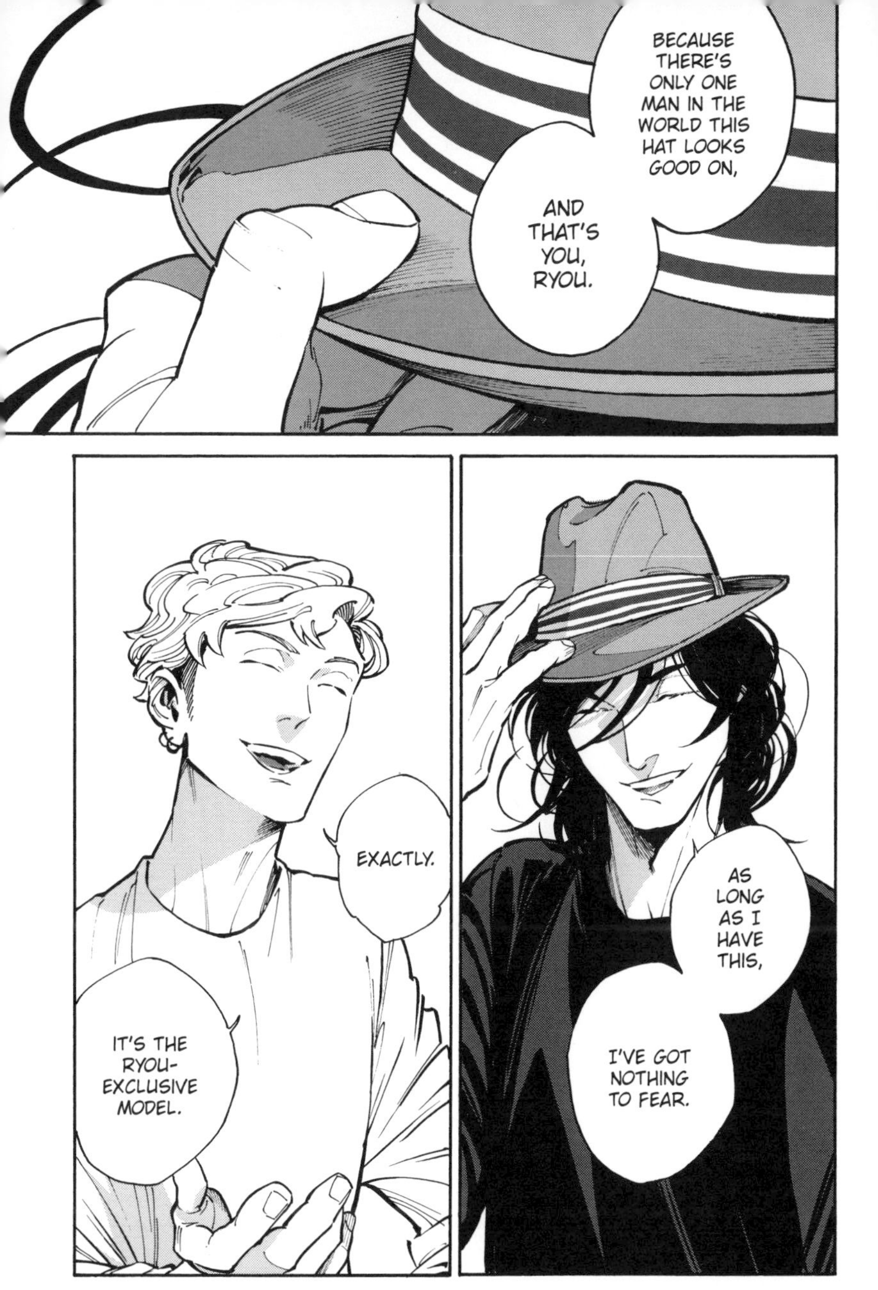
BECAUSE THERE'S ONLY ONE MAN IN THE WORLD THIS HAT LOOKS GOOD ON,
AND THAT'S YOU, RYOU.
AS LONG AS I HAVE THIS,
I'VE GOT NOTHING TO FEAR.
EXACTLY.
IT'S THE RYOU-EXCLUSIVE MODEL.

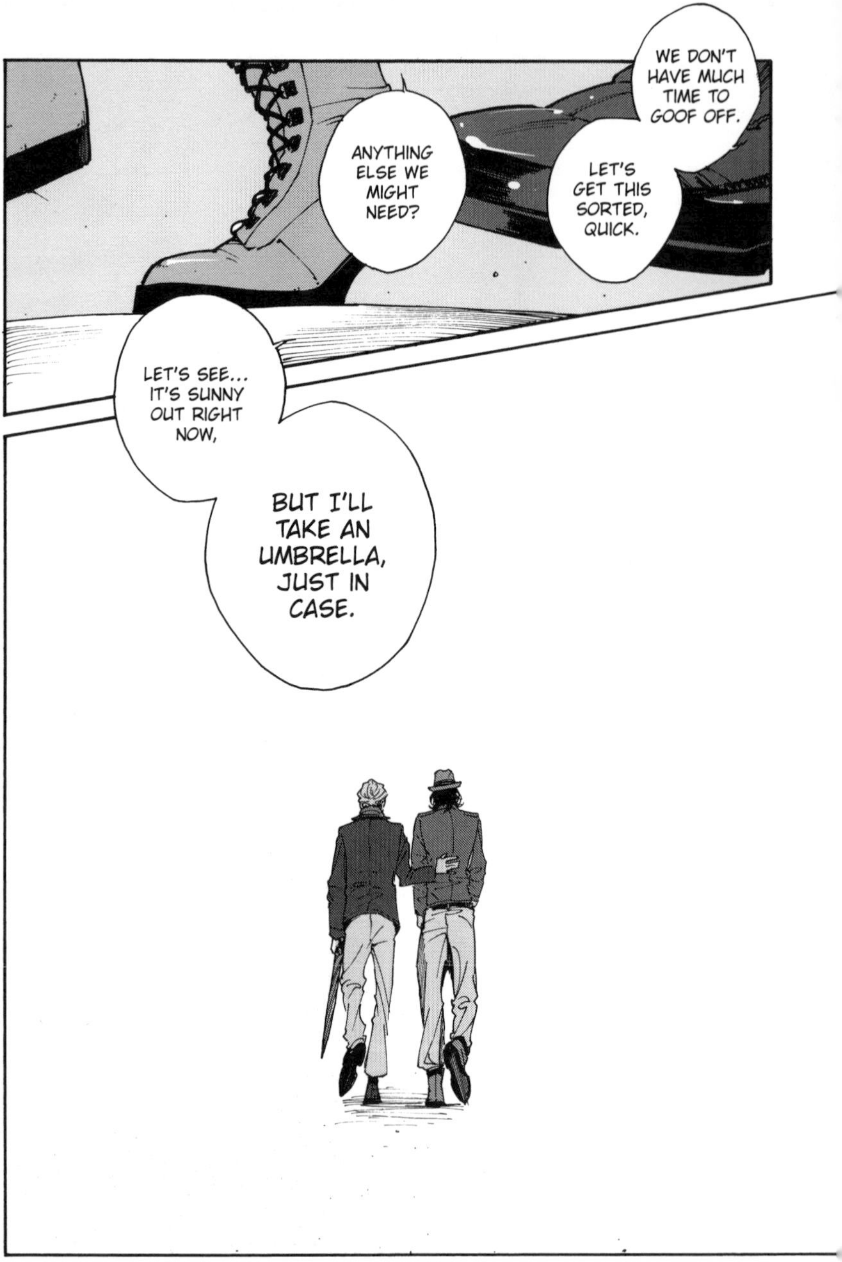
WE DON'T HAVE MUCH TIME TO GOOF OFF.
LET'S GET THIS SORTED, QUICK.
ANYTHING ELSE WE MIGHT NEED?
LET'S SEE... IT'S SUNNY OUT RIGHT NOW,
BUT I'LL TAKE AN UMBRELLA, JUST IN CASE.

CANIS —DEAR HATTER— 11/END

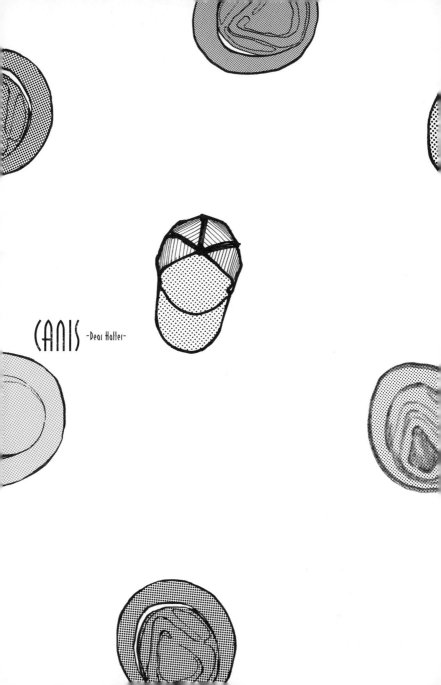

CANIS -Dear Hatter-

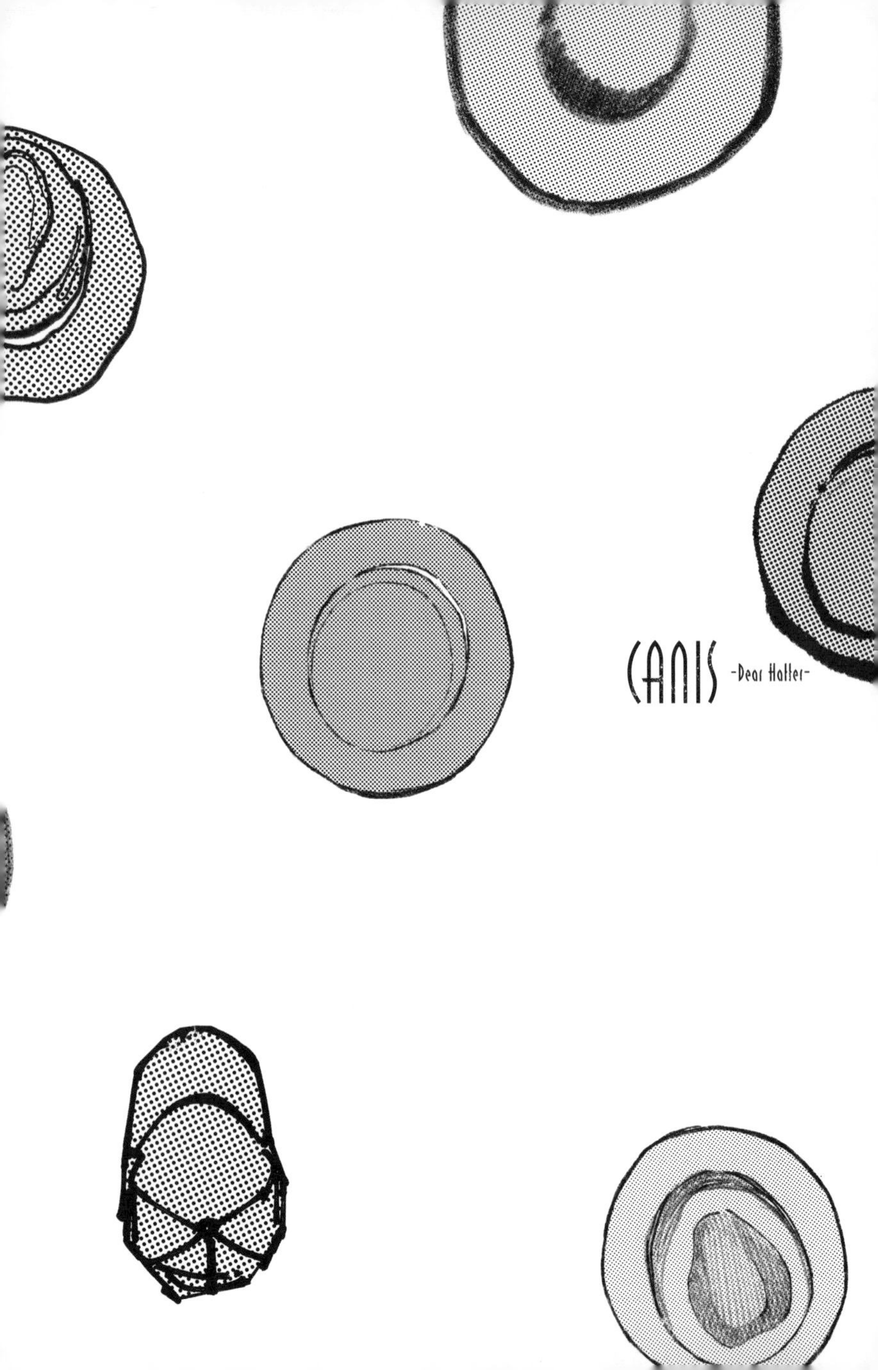
CANIS
-Dear Hatter-

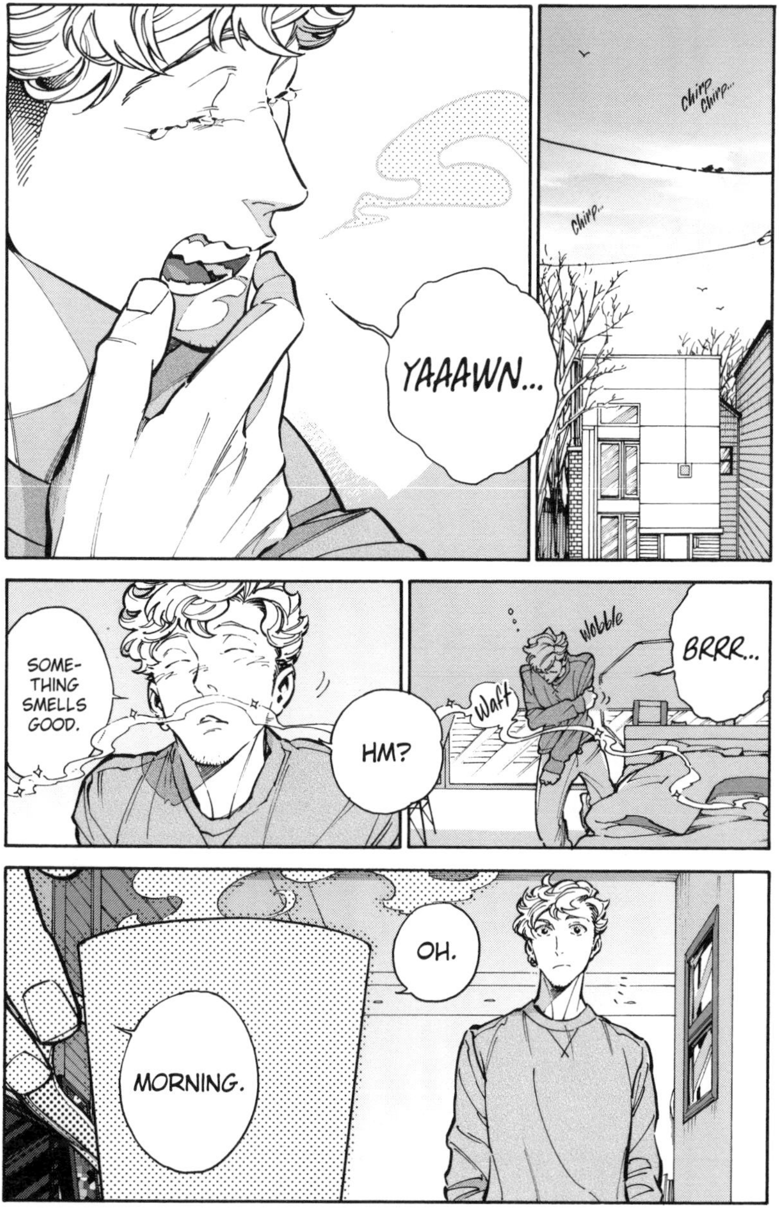
Chirp Chirp...
Chirp...
YAAAWN...
BRRR...
Wobble
Waft
HM?
SOME-THING SMELLS GOOD.
OH.
MORNING.

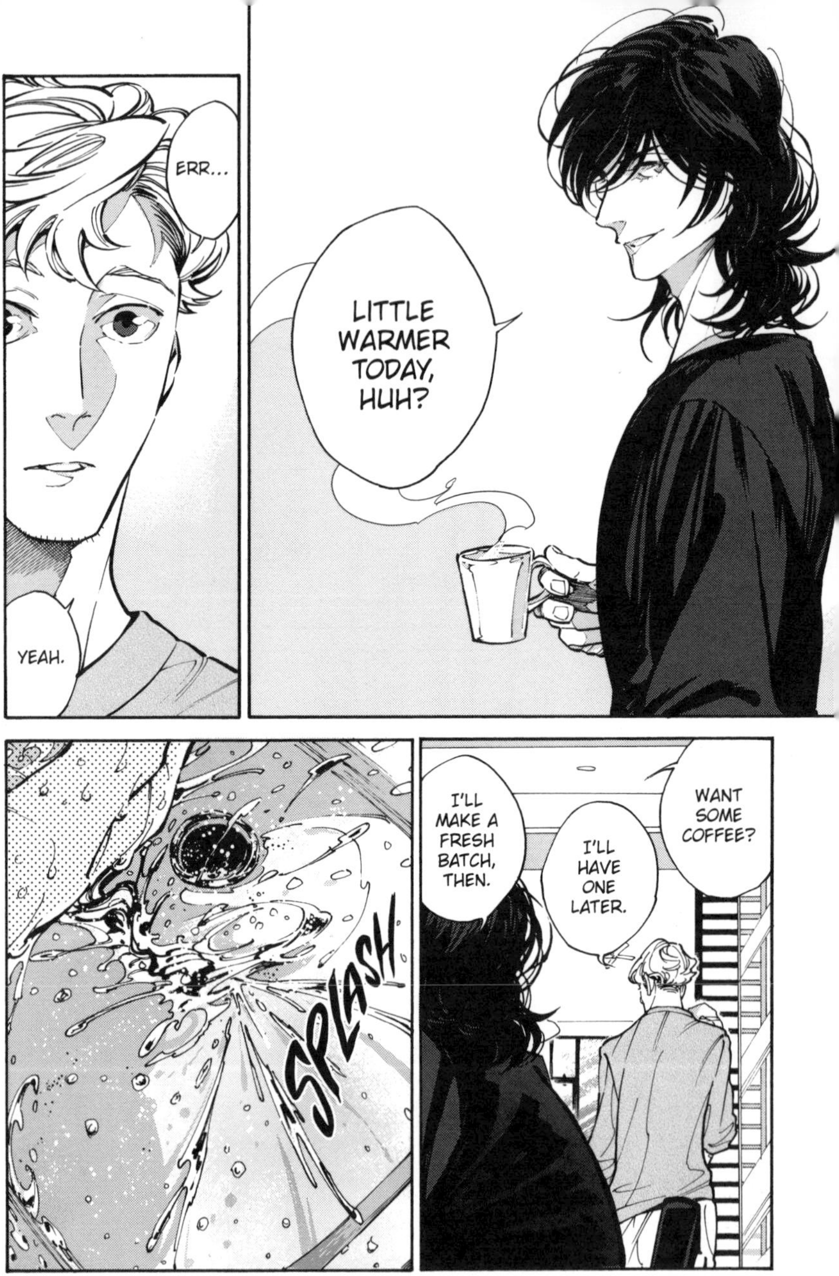
LITTLE WARMER TODAY, HUH?
ERR...
YEAH.
WANT SOME COFFEE?
I'LL HAVE ONE LATER.
I'LL MAKE A FRESH BATCH, THEN.
SPLASH

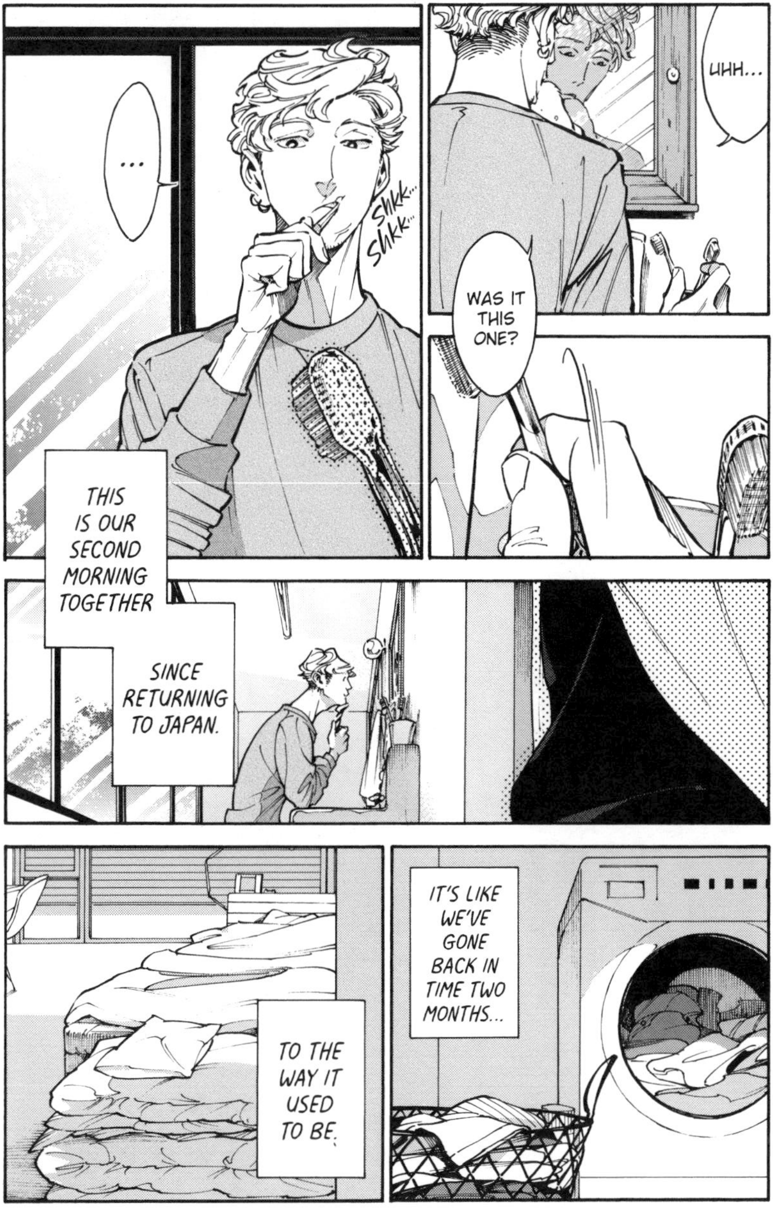
UHH...
WAS IT THIS ONE?
...
SHKK... SHKK...
THIS IS OUR SECOND MORNING TOGETHER
SINCE RETURNING TO JAPAN.
IT'S LIKE WE'VE GONE BACK IN TIME TWO MONTHS...
TO THE WAY IT USED TO BE.

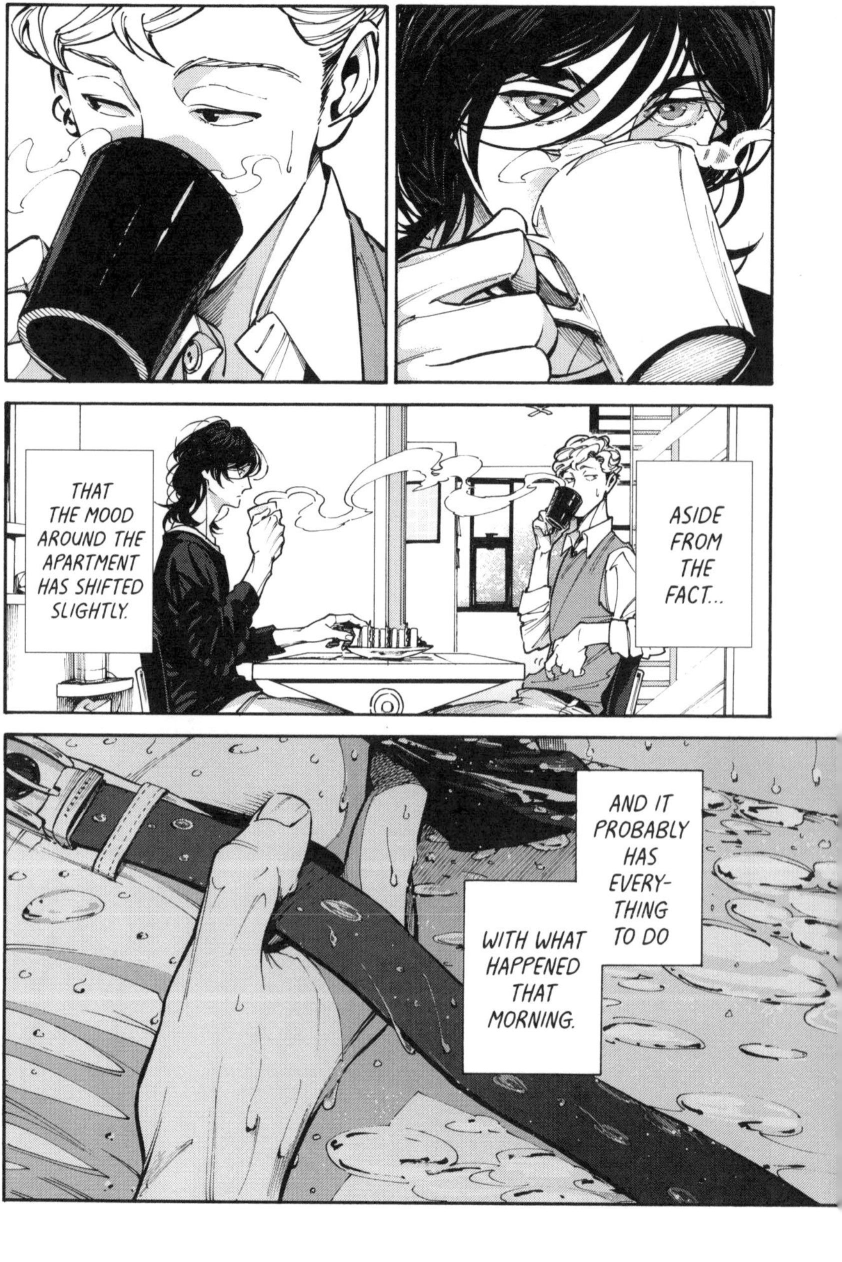
ASIDE FROM THE FACT...
THAT THE MOOD AROUND THE APARTMENT HAS SHIFTED SLIGHTLY.
AND IT PROBABLY HAS EVERY-THING TO DO
WITH WHAT HAPPENED THAT MORNING.

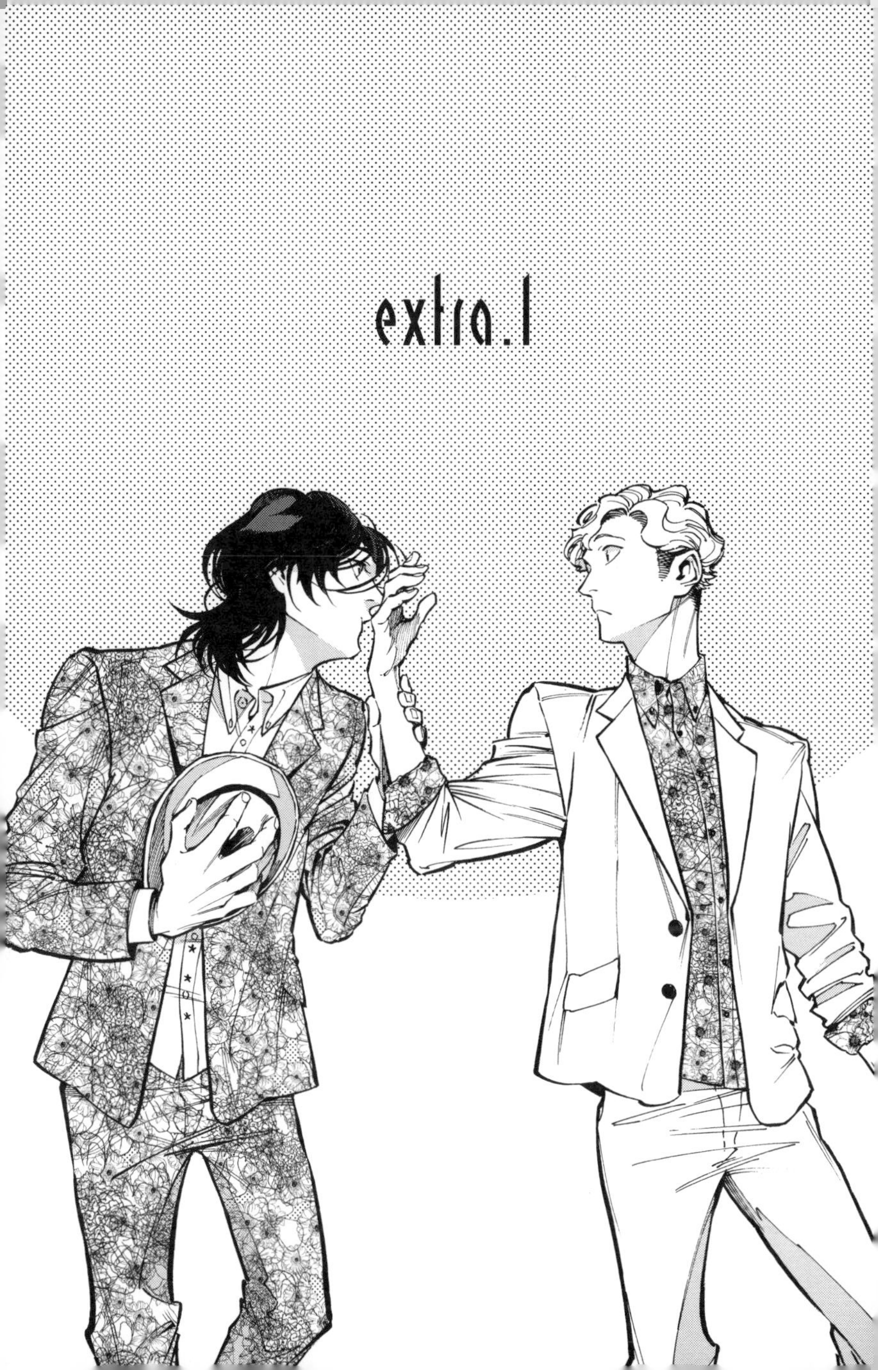
extra.1

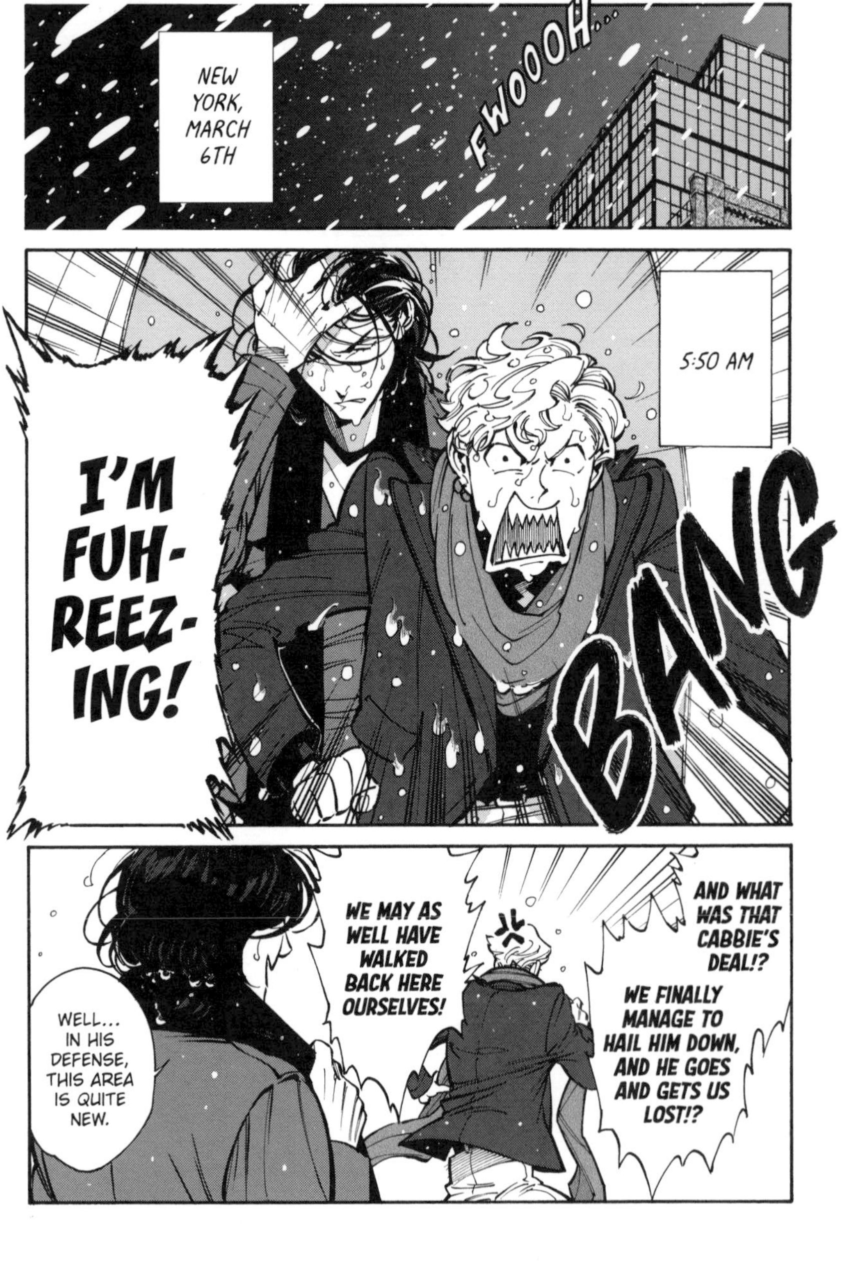

NEW YORK, MARCH 6TH
FWOOOH...
5:50 AM
BANG
I'M FUH-REEZ-ING!
AND WHAT WAS THAT CABBIE'S DEAL!?
WE FINALLY MANAGE TO HAIL HIM DOWN, AND HE GOES AND GETS US LOST!?
WE MAY AS WELL HAVE WALKED BACK HERE OURSELVES!
WELL... IN HIS DEFENSE, THIS AREA IS QUITE NEW.

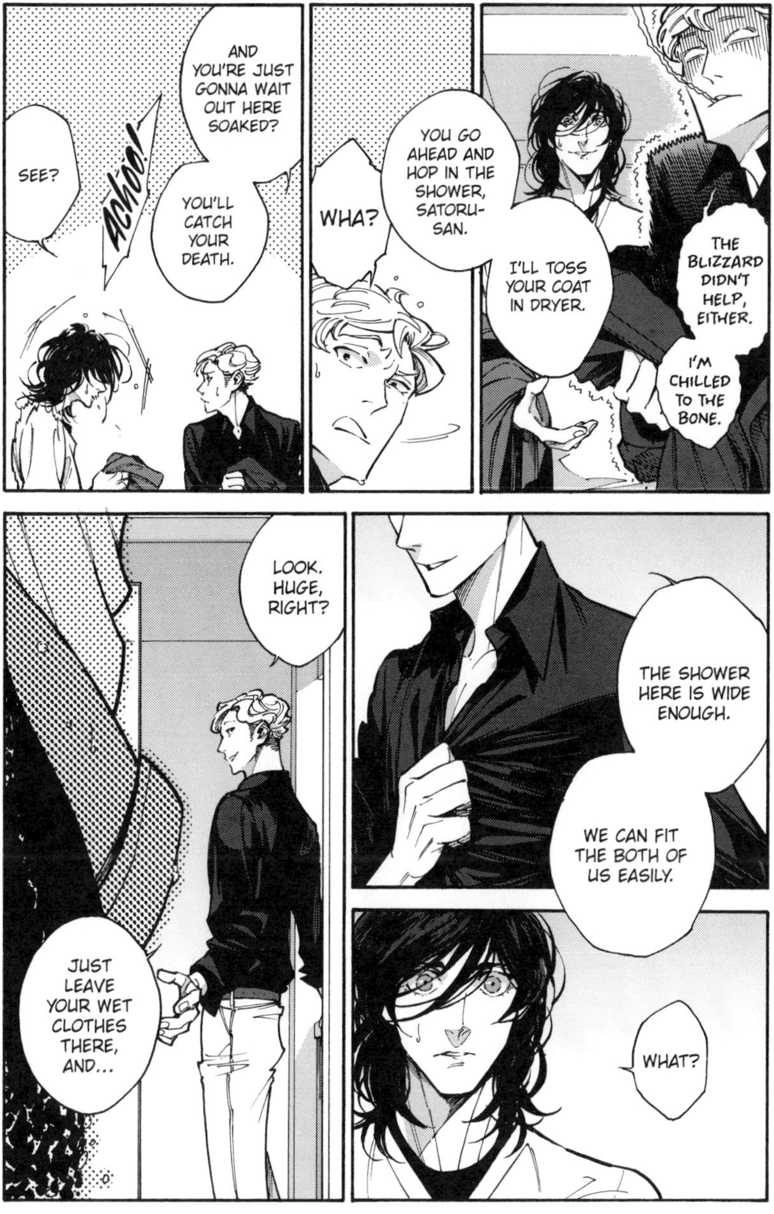
THE BLIZZARD DIDN'T HELP, EITHER.
I'M CHILLED TO THE BONE.
I'LL TOSS YOUR COAT IN DRYER.
YOU GO AHEAD AND HOP IN THE SHOWER, SATORU-SAN.
WHA?
AND YOU'RE JUST GONNA WAIT OUT HERE SOAKED?
YOU'LL CATCH YOUR DEATH.
Achoo!
SEE?
THE SHOWER HERE IS WIDE ENOUGH.
WE CAN FIT THE BOTH OF US EASILY.
WHAT?
LOOK. HUGE, RIGHT?
JUST LEAVE YOUR WET CLOTHES THERE, AND...

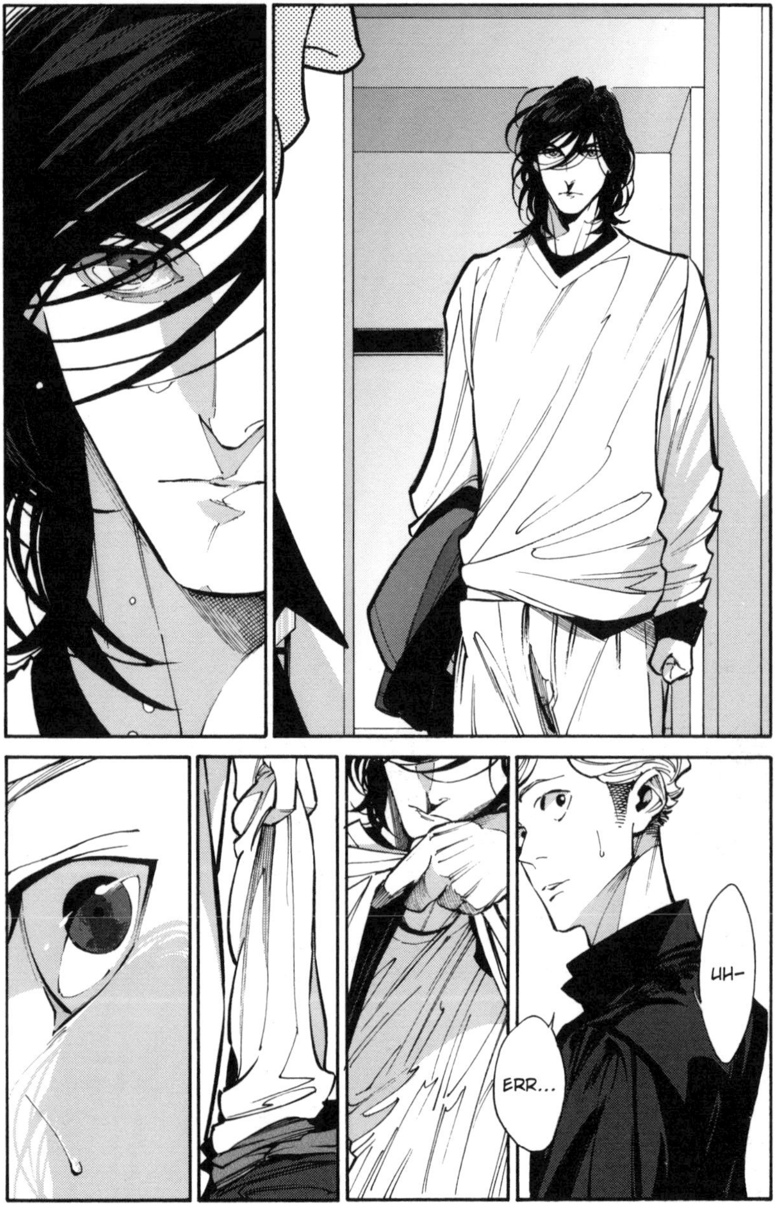
UH-
ERR...

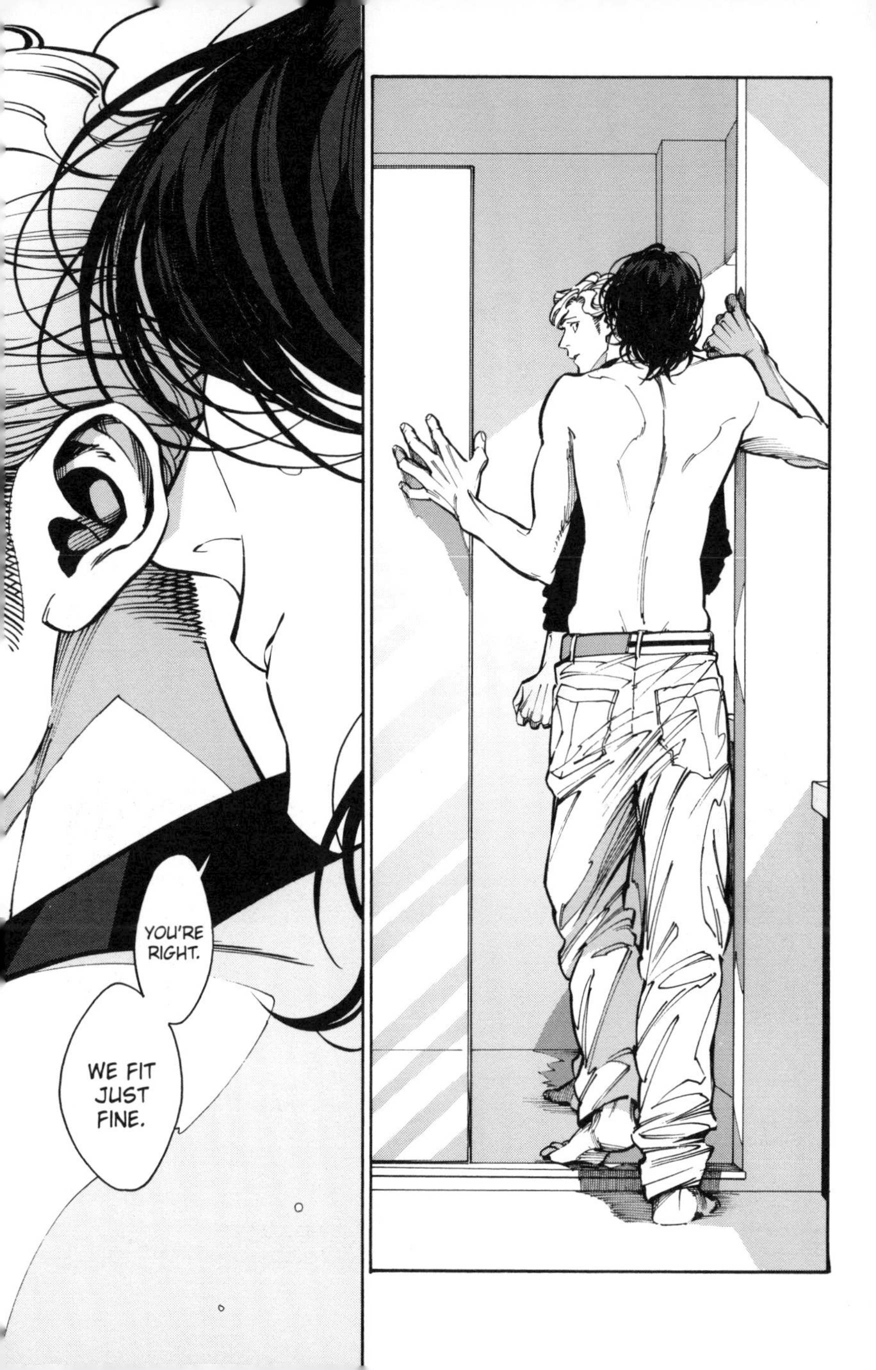
YOU'RE RIGHT.
WE FIT JUST FINE.

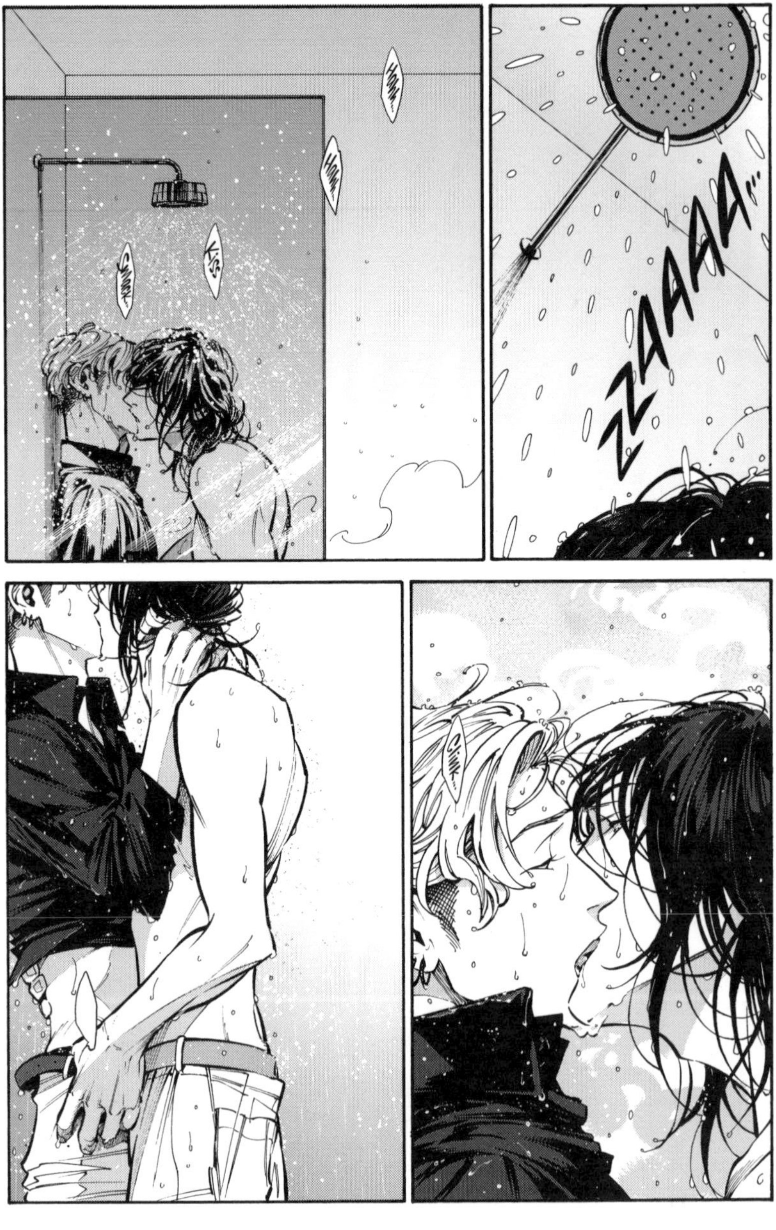
ZZAAAAA...
Hmm...
Hmm...
Kiss
Smack...
Clink...

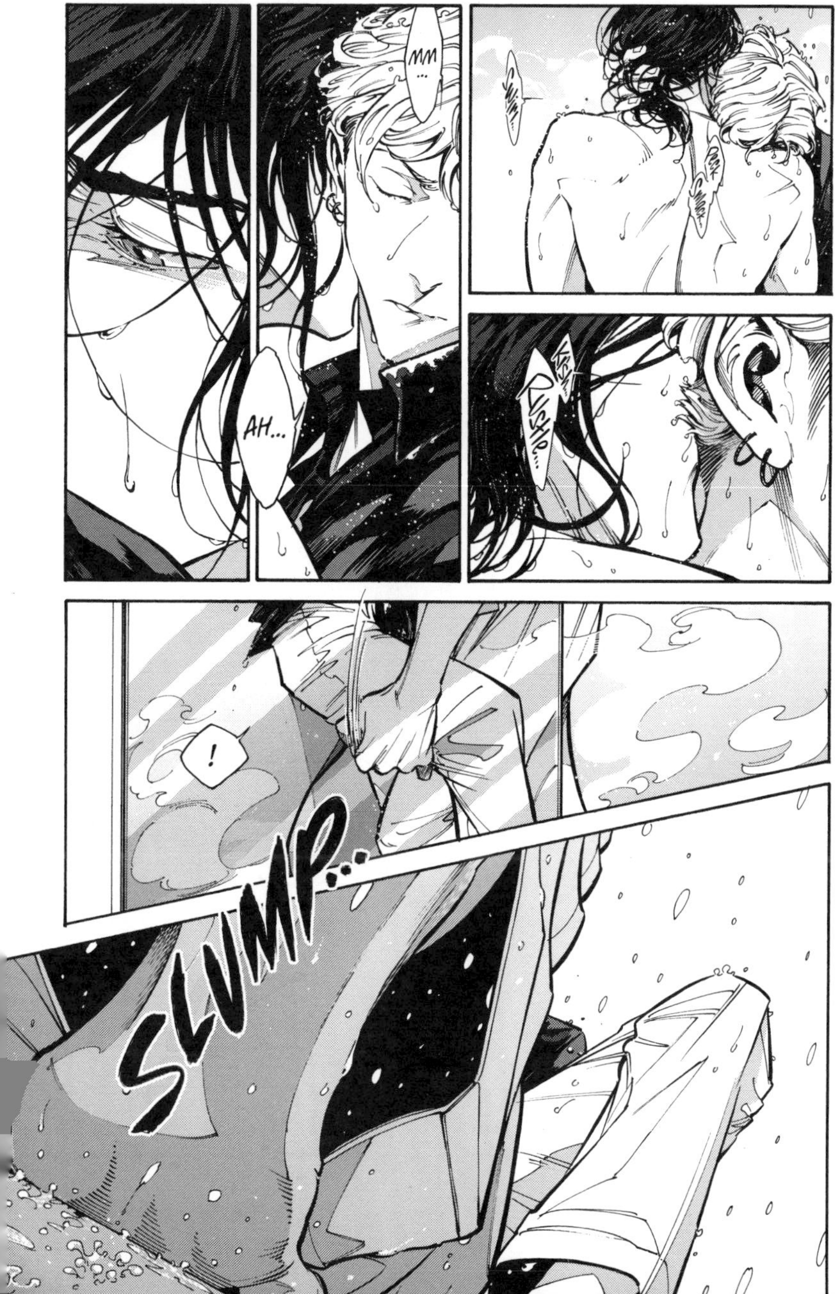
SWIM...
PECK
SMOOCH...
KISH...
RUSTLE...
MM...
AH...
!
SLUMP..

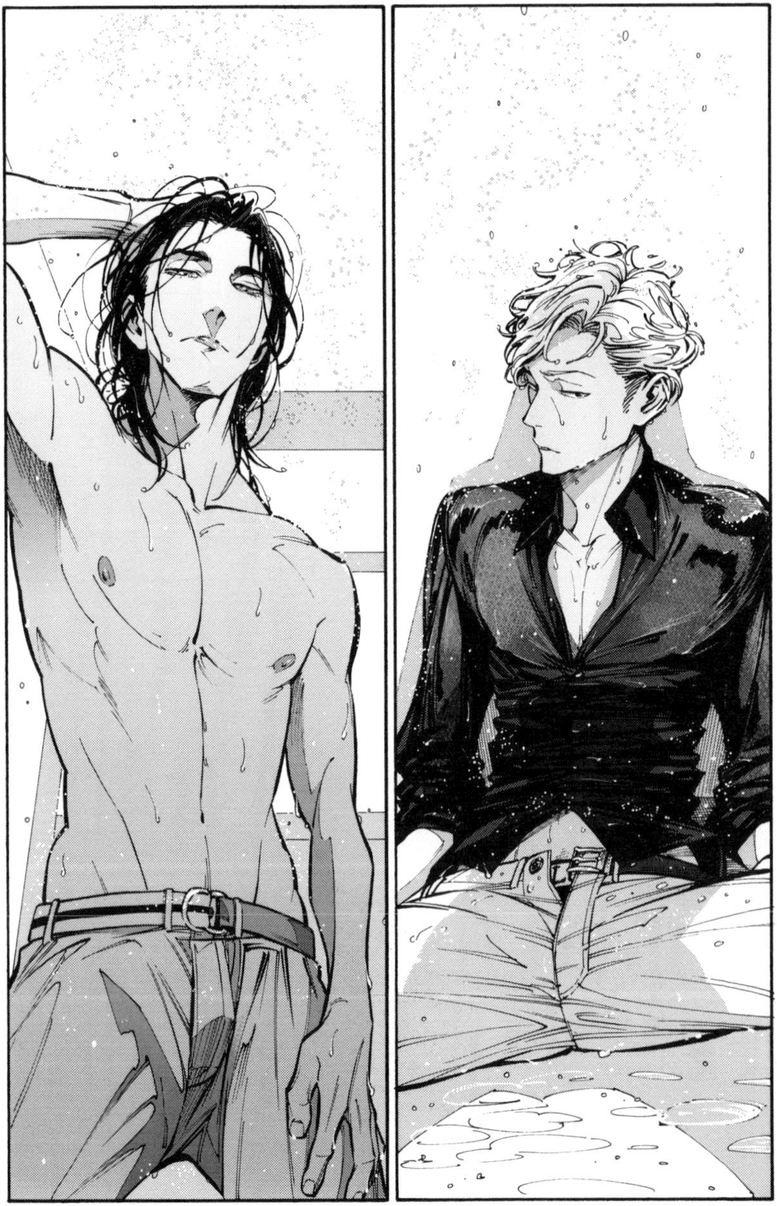

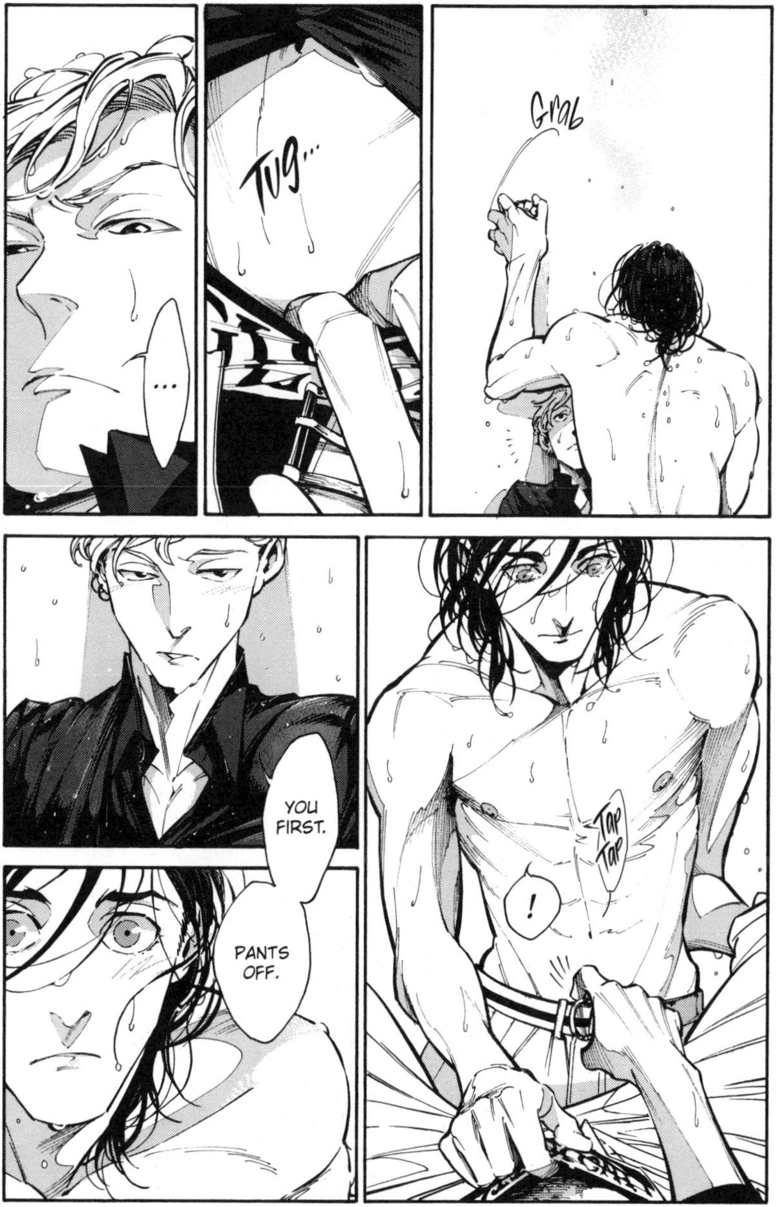
Grab
Tug...
...
Tap Tap
!
YOU FIRST.
PANTS OFF.

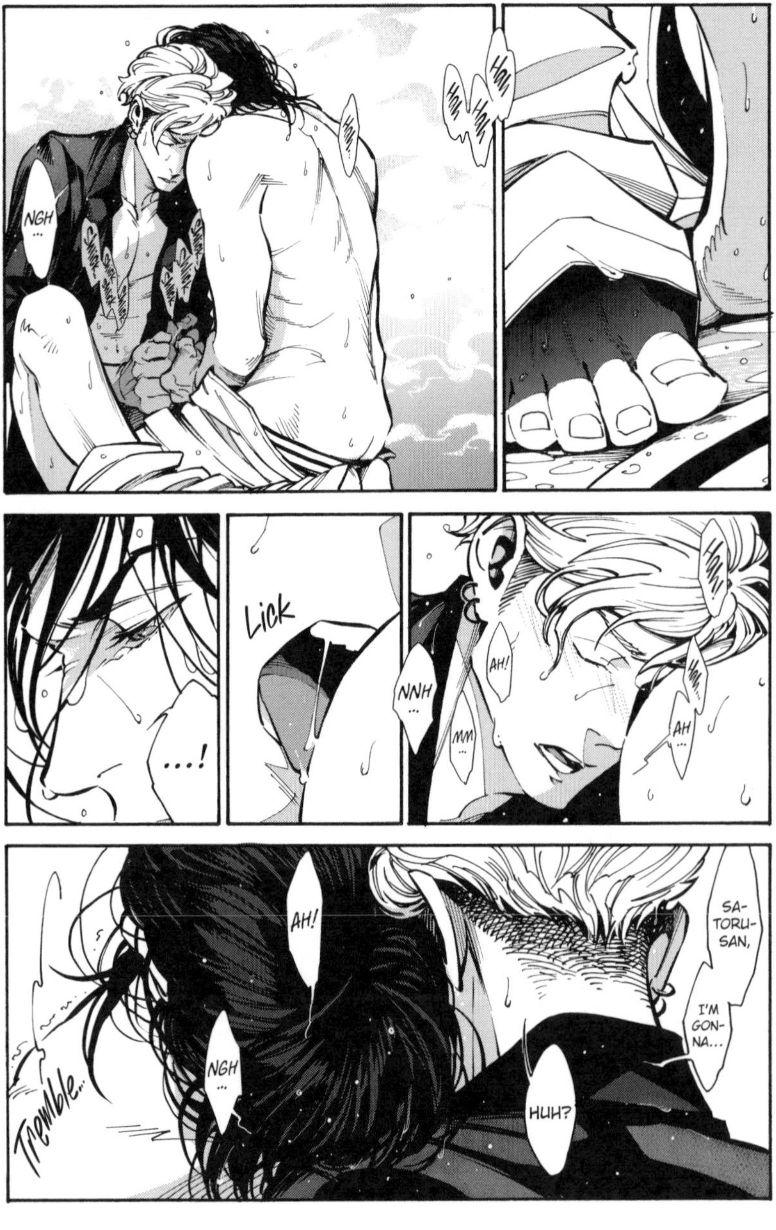
Hah
Hah
Hah
Hah...
NGH...
Shlick
Shlick
Shlick
Shlick
Shlick
Shlick
Hah
Hah
AH!
AH...
NNH...
MM...
Lick
...!
SA-TORU-SAN,
I'M GON-NA...
AH!
HUH?
NGH...
Tremble...

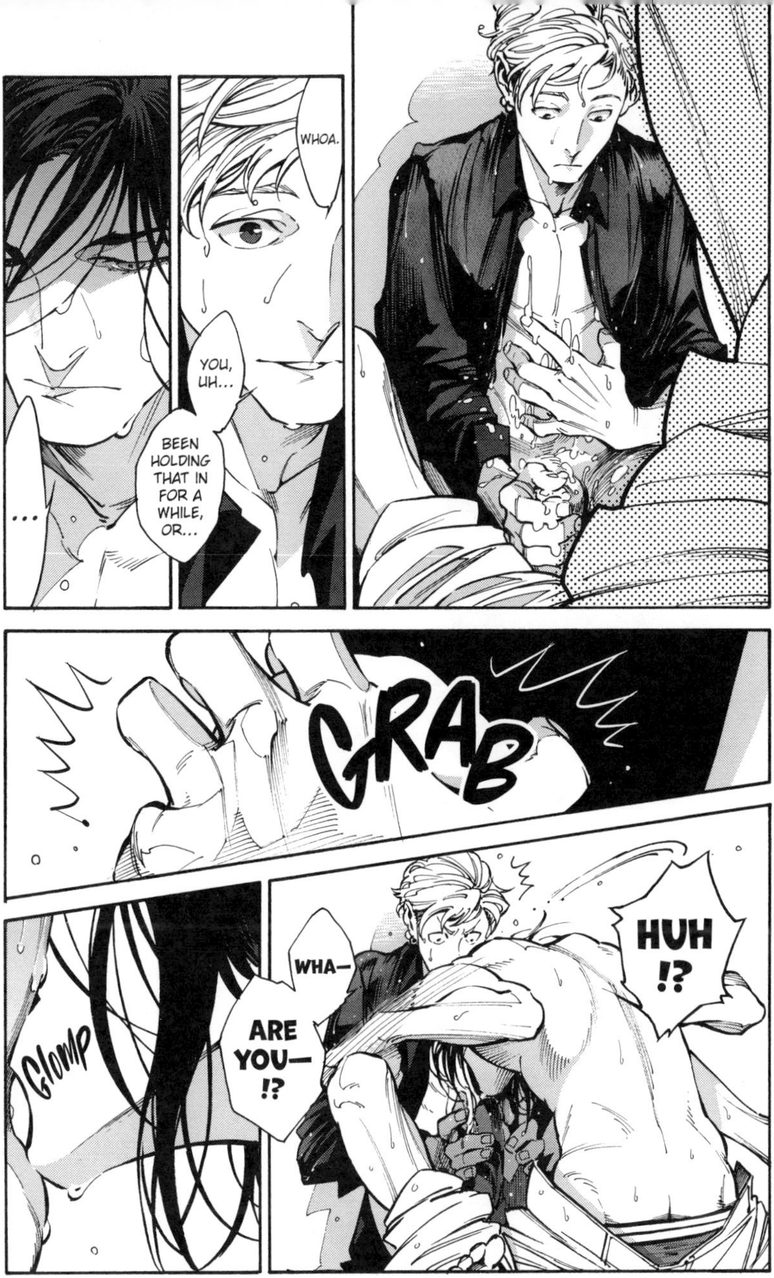
WHOA.
YOU, UH...
BEEN HOLDING THAT IN FOR A WHILE, OR...
...
GRAB
HUH!?
WHA—
ARE YOU—!?
Glomp

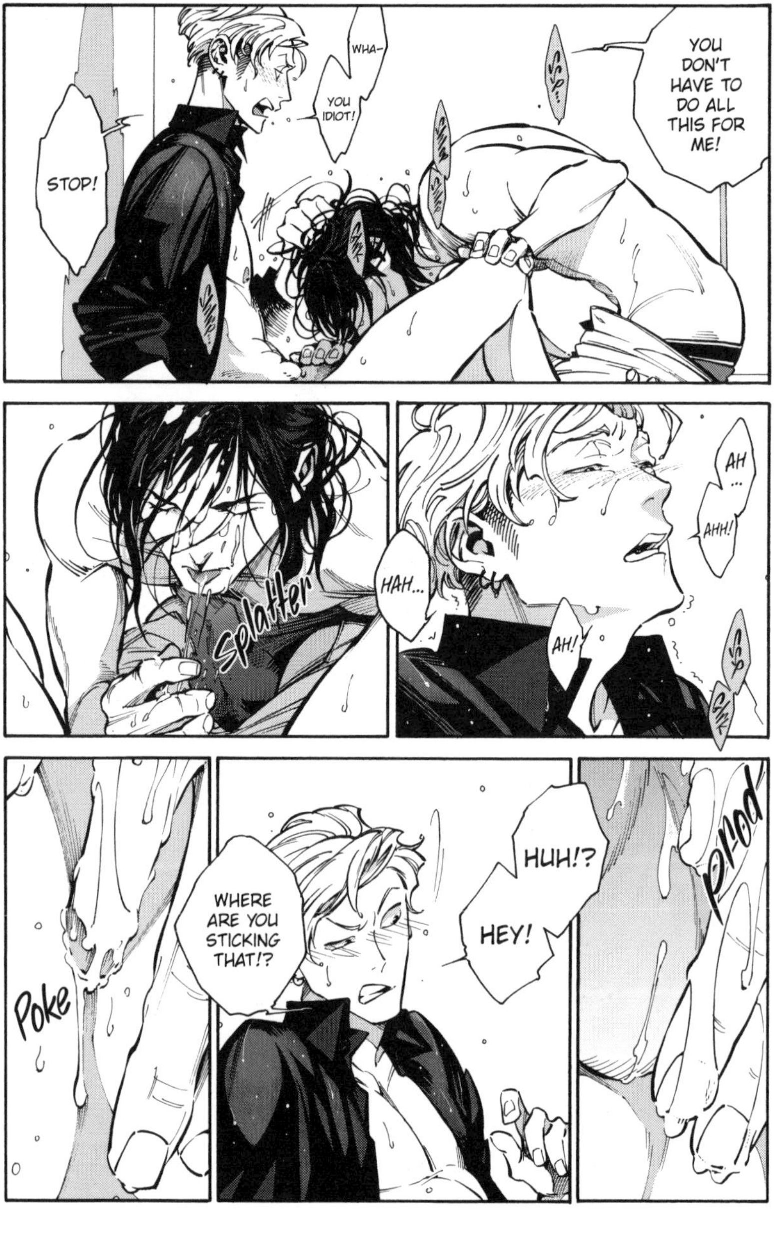
YOU DON'T HAVE TO DO ALL THIS FOR ME!
WHA-
YOU IDIOT!
STOP!
AH ... AHH!
HAH...
AH!
Splatter
prod
HUH!?
HEY!
WHERE ARE YOU STICKING THAT!?
Poke

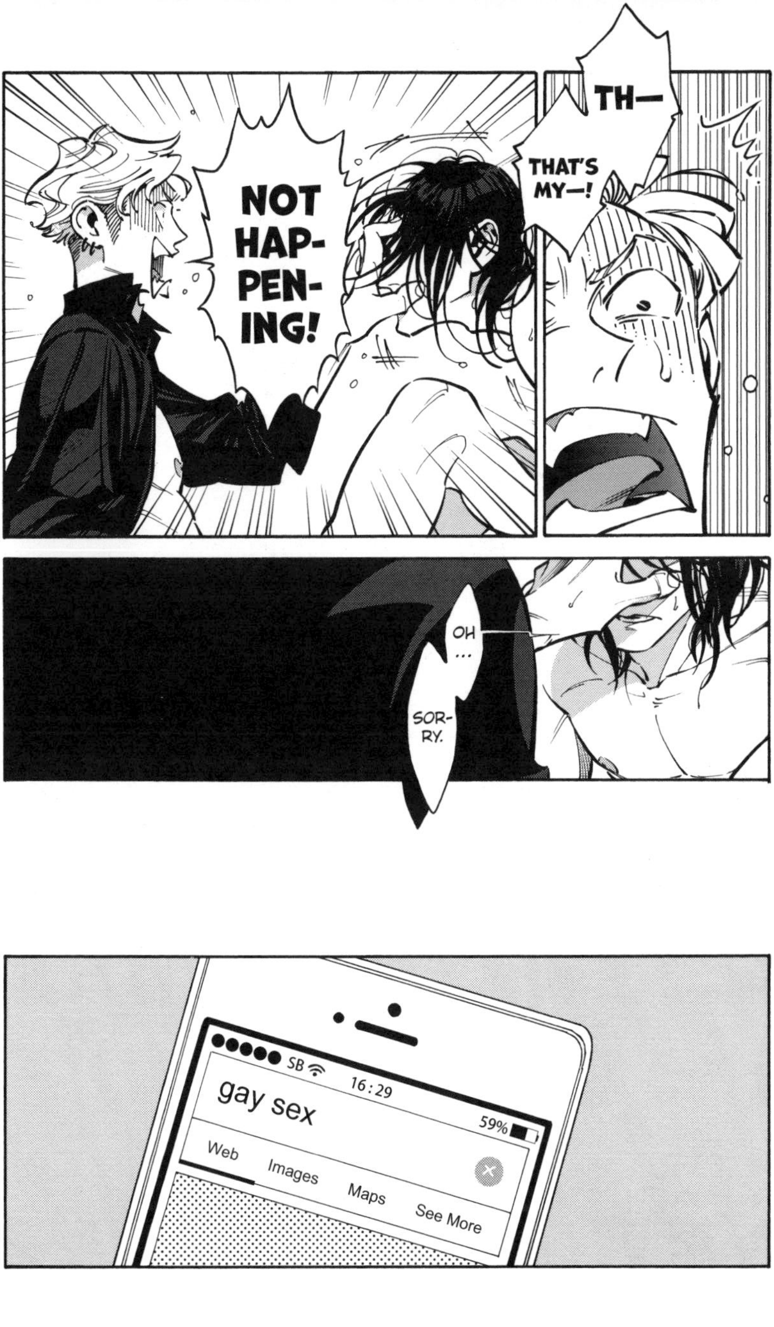
TH—
THAT'S MY—!
NOT HAP-PEN-ING!
OH ...
SOR-RY.
SB
16:29
gay sex
59%
Web
Images
Maps
See More

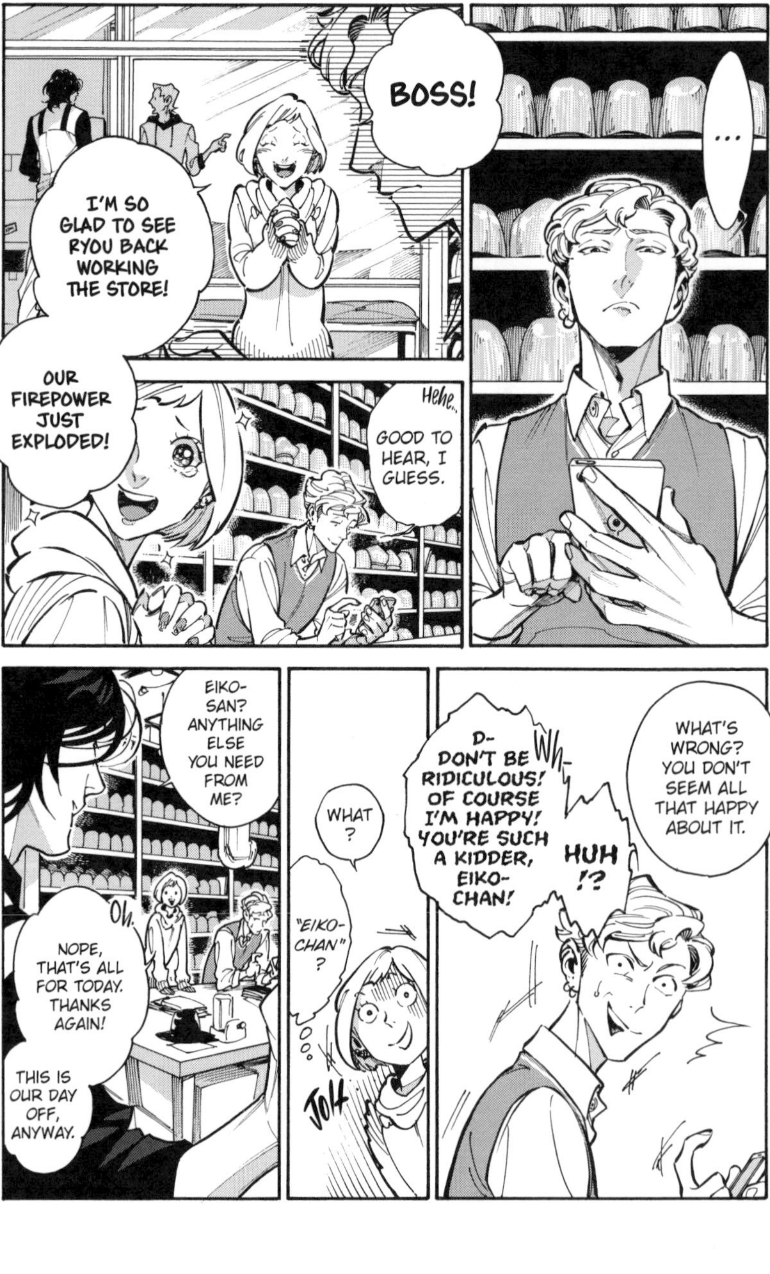
...
BOSS!
I'M SO GLAD TO SEE RYOU BACK WORKING THE STORE!
OUR FIREPOWER JUST EXPLODED!
Hehe..
GOOD TO HEAR, I GUESS.
WHAT'S WRONG? YOU DON'T SEEM ALL THAT HAPPY ABOUT IT.
HUH !?
Wh-
D- DON'T BE RIDICULOUS! OF COURSE I'M HAPPY! YOU'RE SUCH A KIDDER, EIKO-CHAN!
WHAT ?
"EIKO-CHAN" ?
JOLT
EIKO-SAN? ANYTHING ELSE YOU NEED FROM ME?
Oh.
NOPE, THAT'S ALL FOR TODAY. THANKS AGAIN!
THIS IS OUR DAY OFF, ANYWAY.

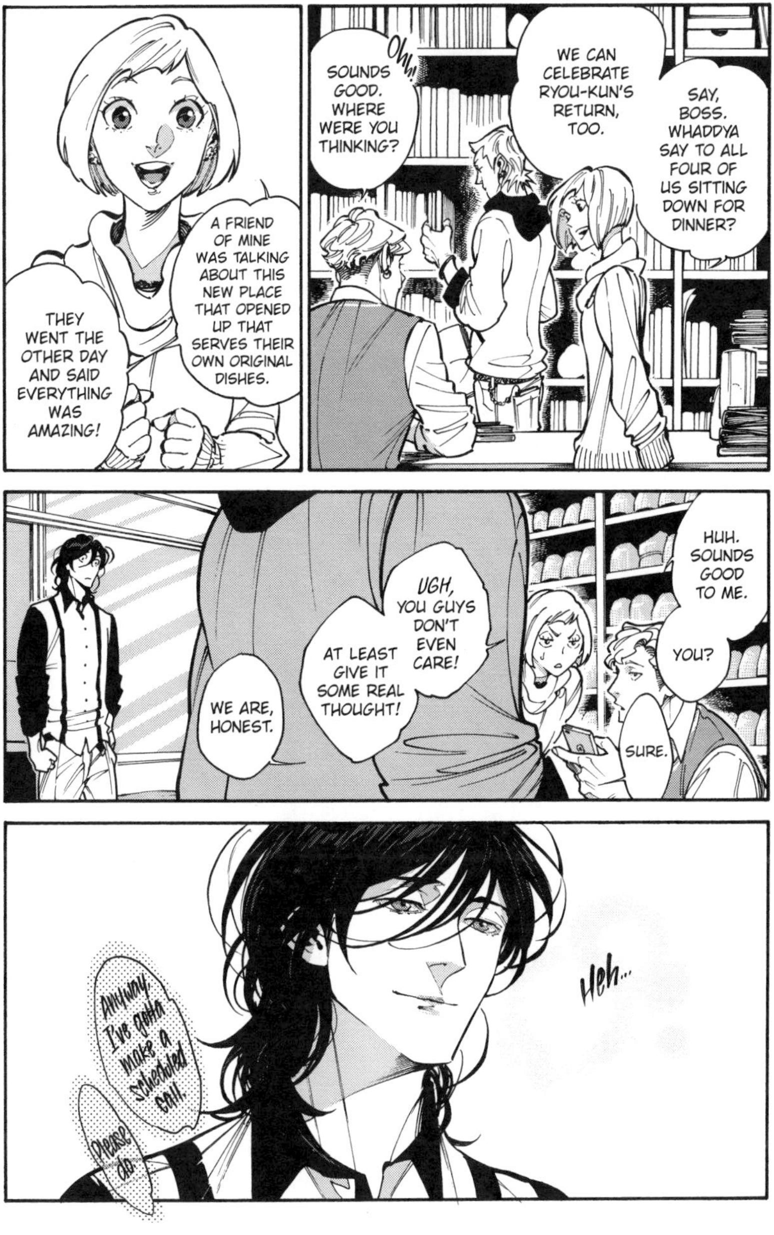
SAY, BOSS. WHADDYA SAY TO ALL FOUR OF US SITTING DOWN FOR DINNER?
WE CAN CELEBRATE RYOU-KUN'S RETURN, TOO.
Ohh!
SOUNDS GOOD. WHERE WERE YOU THINKING?
A FRIEND OF MINE WAS TALKING ABOUT THIS NEW PLACE THAT OPENED UP THAT SERVES THEIR OWN ORIGINAL DISHES.
THEY WENT THE OTHER DAY AND SAID EVERYTHING WAS AMAZING!
HUH. SOUNDS GOOD TO ME.
YOU?
SURE.
UGH, YOU GUYS DON'T EVEN CARE!
AT LEAST GIVE IT SOME REAL THOUGHT!
WE ARE, HONEST.
Heh...
Anyway, I've gotta make a scheduled call.
Please do.

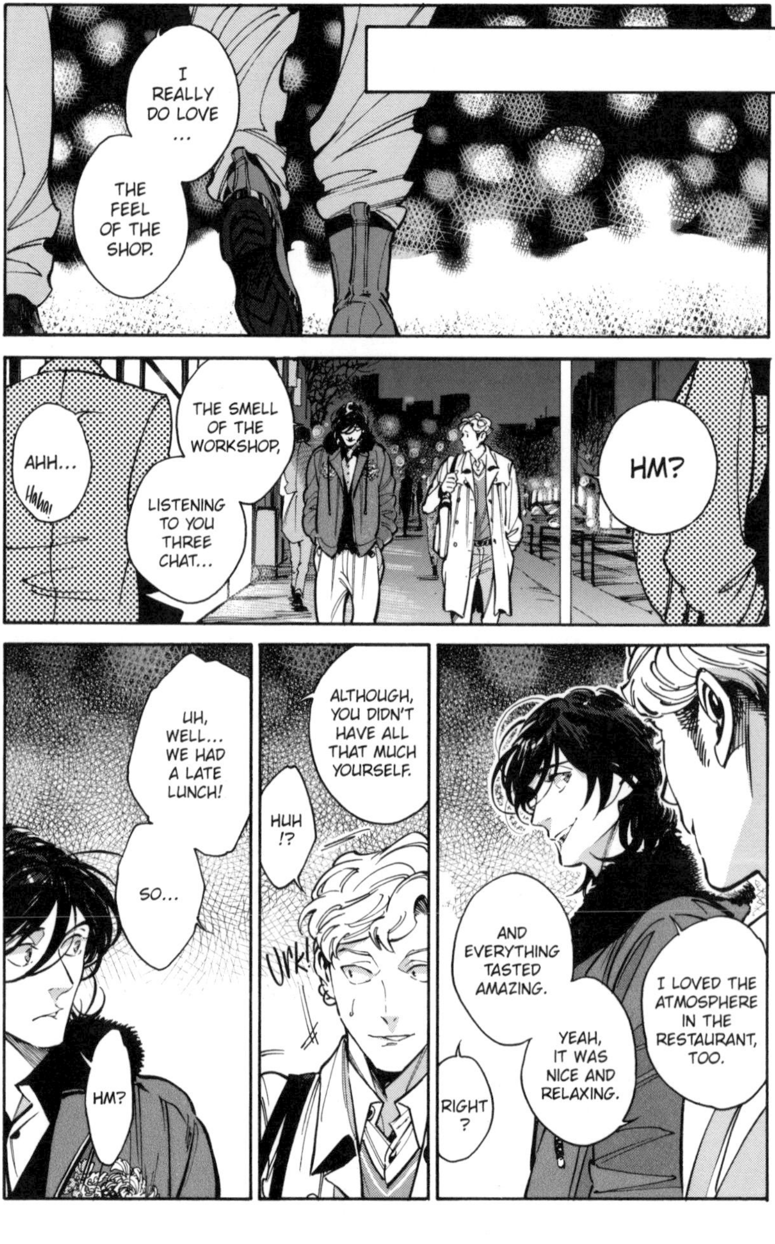
I REALLY DO LOVE ...
THE FEEL OF THE SHOP.
HM?
THE SMELL OF THE WORKSHOP,
LISTENING TO YOU THREE CHAT...
AHH...
Haha!
I LOVED THE ATMOSPHERE IN THE RESTAURANT, TOO.
AND EVERYTHING TASTED AMAZING.
YEAH, IT WAS NICE AND RELAXING.
RIGHT?
ALTHOUGH, YOU DIDN'T HAVE ALL THAT MUCH YOURSELF.
HUH!?
Urk!
UH, WELL... WE HAD A LATE LUNCH!
SO...
HM?

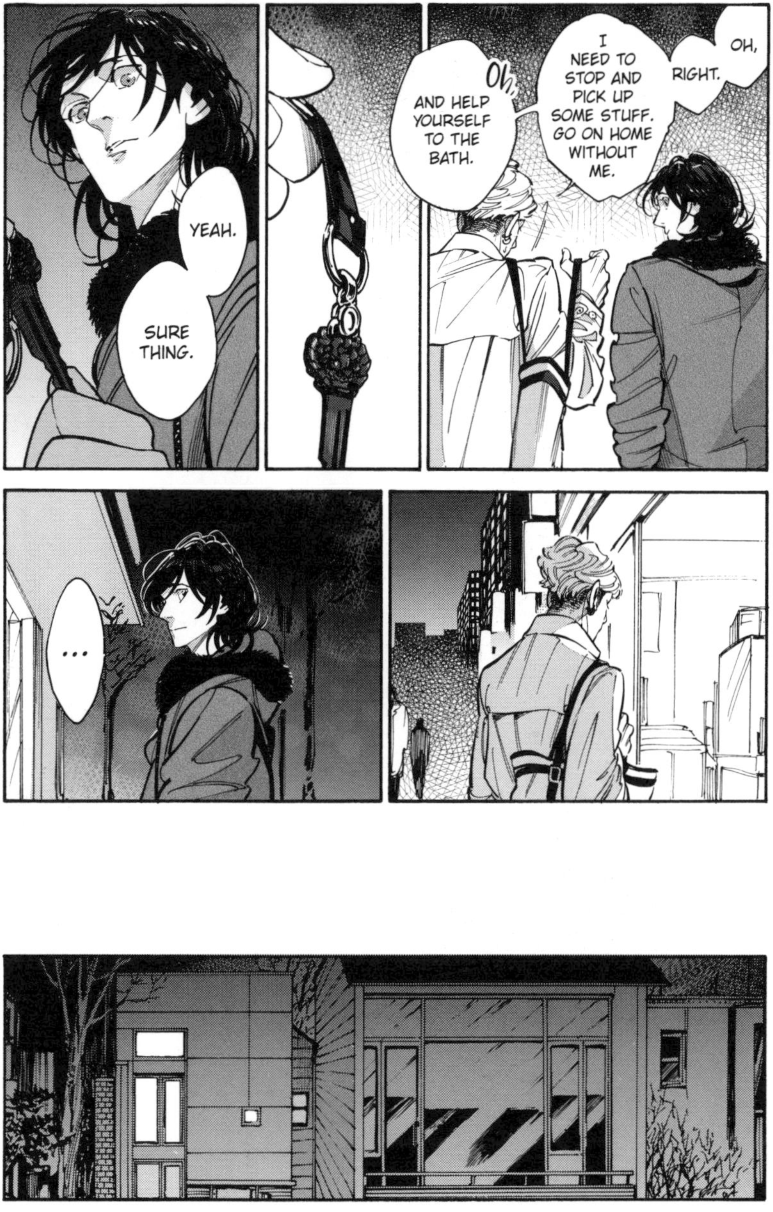
OH, RIGHT.
I NEED TO STOP AND PICK UP SOME STUFF. GO ON HOME WITHOUT ME.
Oh
AND HELP YOURSELF TO THE BATH.
YEAH.
SURE THING.
...

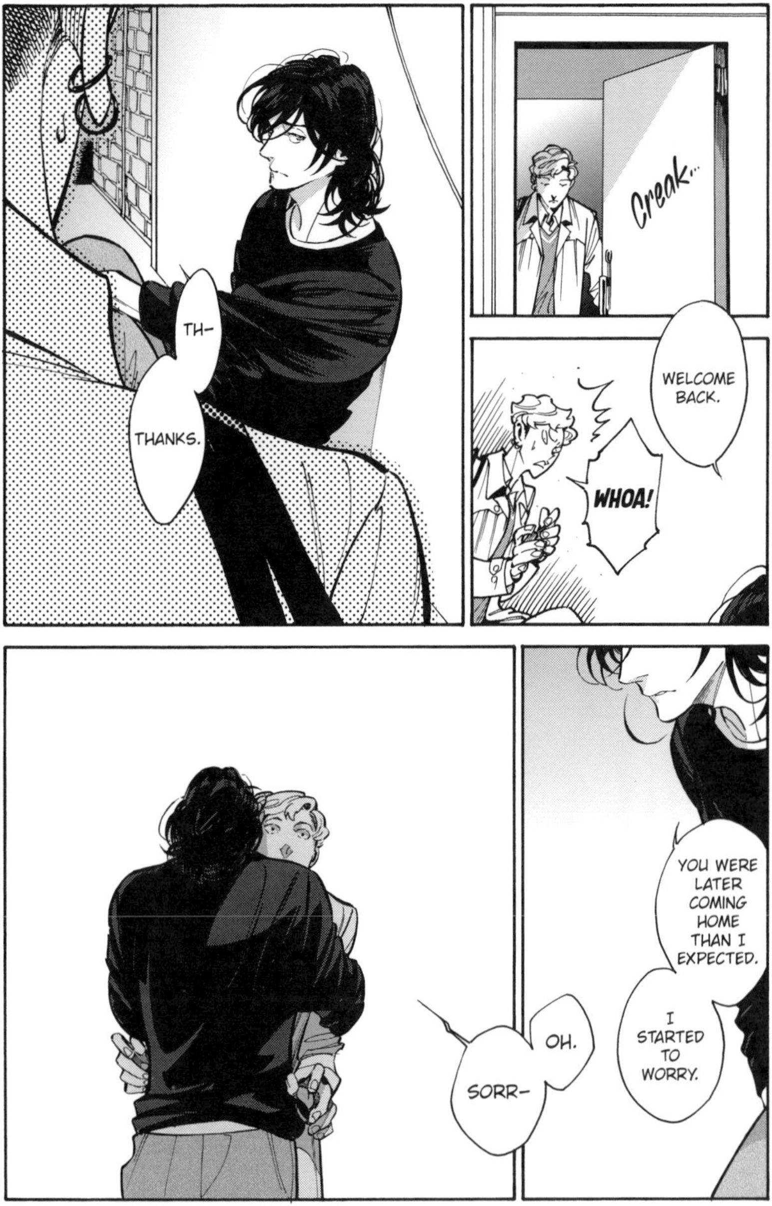
Creak...
WELCOME BACK.
WHOA!
TH-
THANKS.
YOU WERE LATER COMING HOME THAN I EXPECTED.
I STARTED TO WORRY.
OH.
SORR-

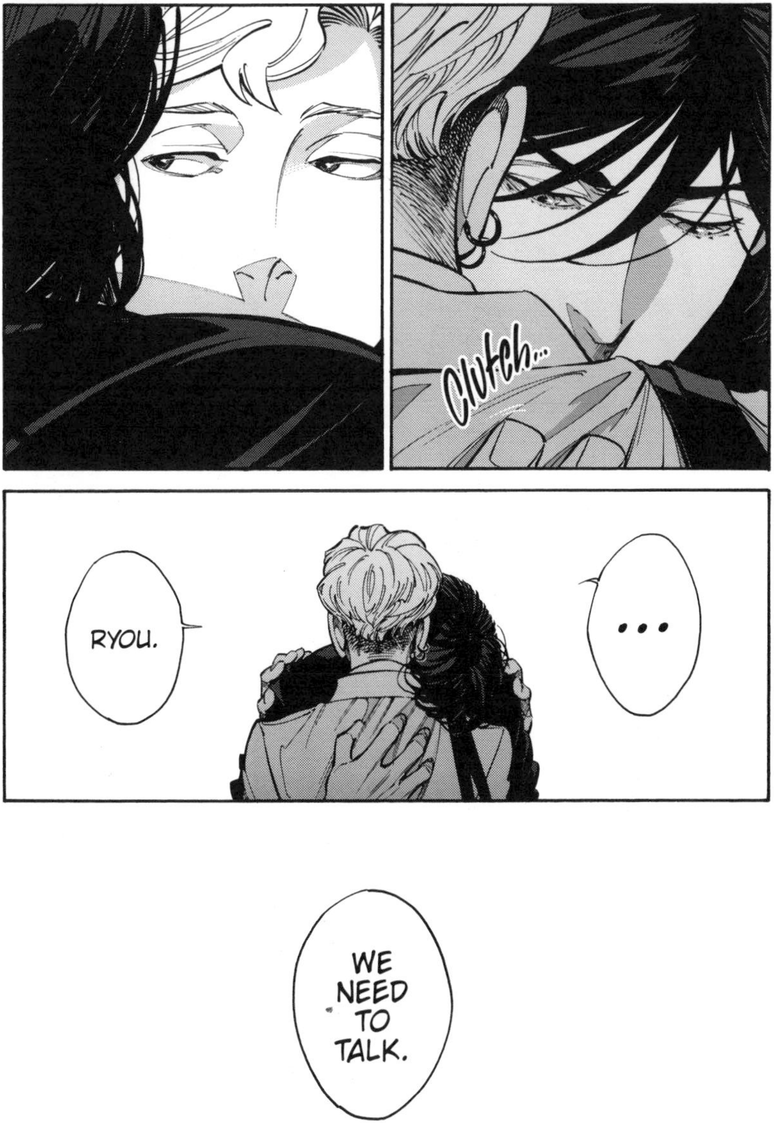
Clutch...
...
RYOU.
WE NEED TO TALK.

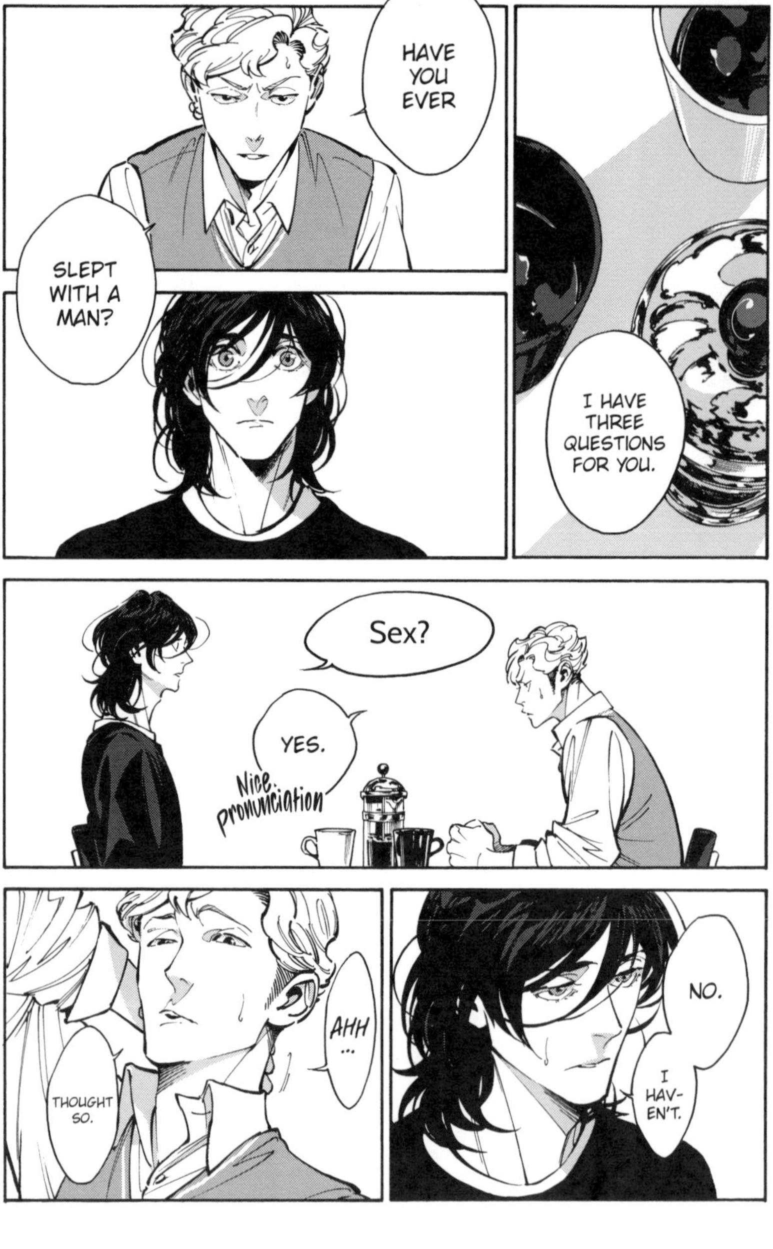
I HAVE THREE QUESTIONS FOR YOU.
HAVE YOU EVER
SLEPT WITH A MAN?
Sex?
YES.
Nice pronunciation
NO.
I HAV-EN'T.
AHH ...
THOUGHT SO.

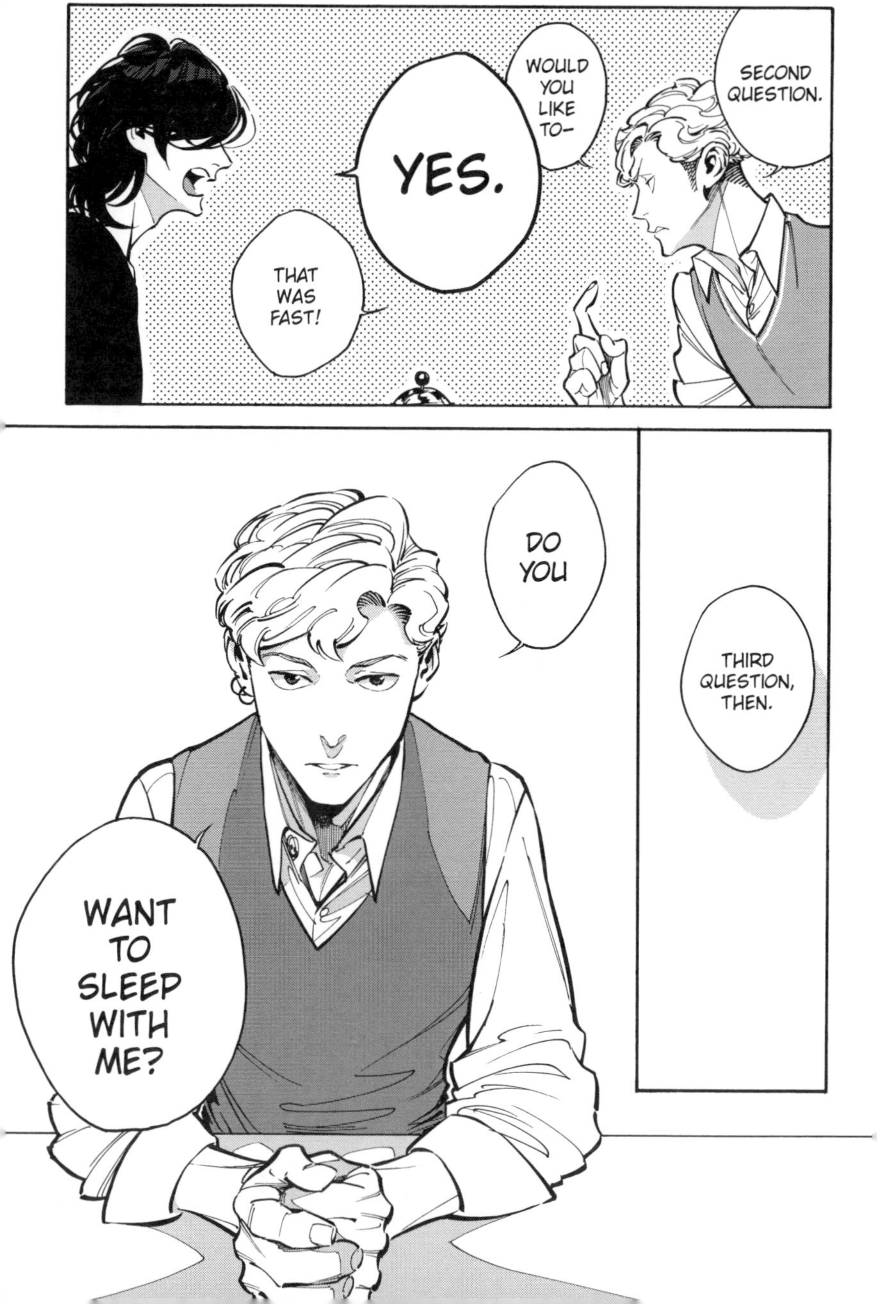
SECOND QUESTION.
WOULD YOU LIKE TO—
YES.
THAT WAS FAST!
THIRD QUESTION, THEN.
DO YOU
WANT TO SLEEP WITH ME?

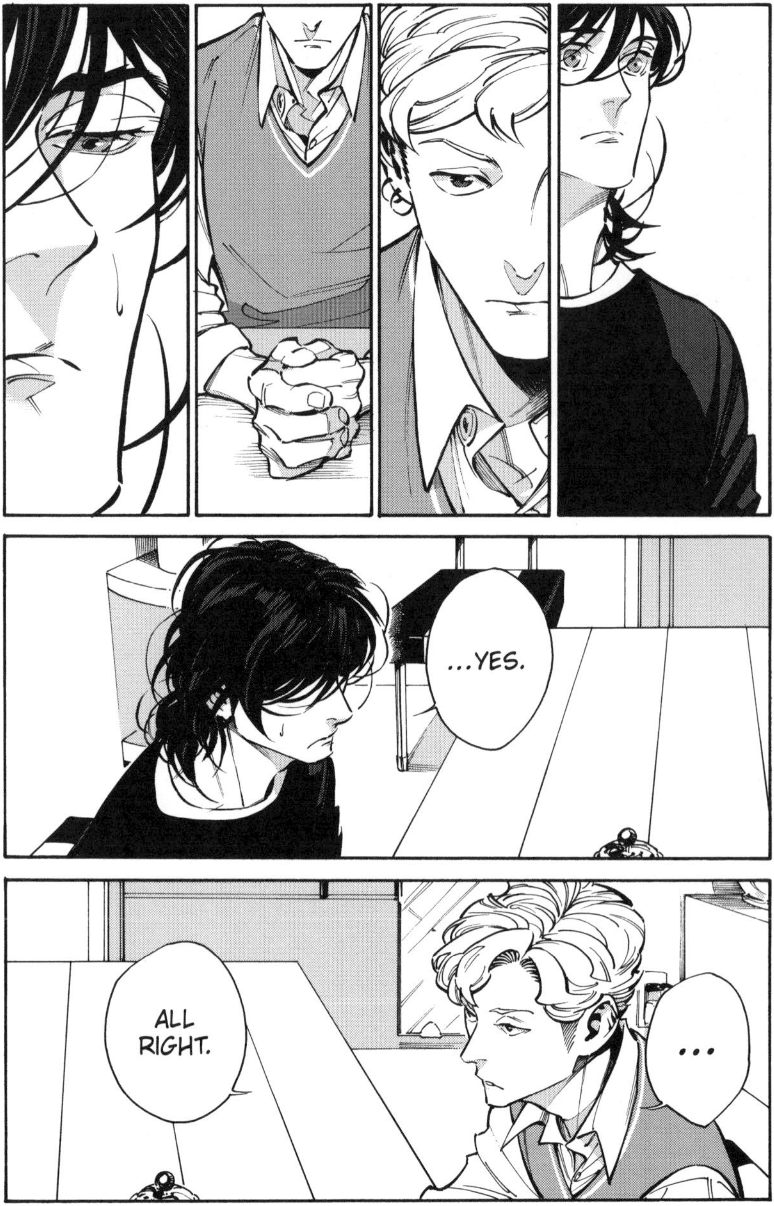
...YES.
...
ALL RIGHT.

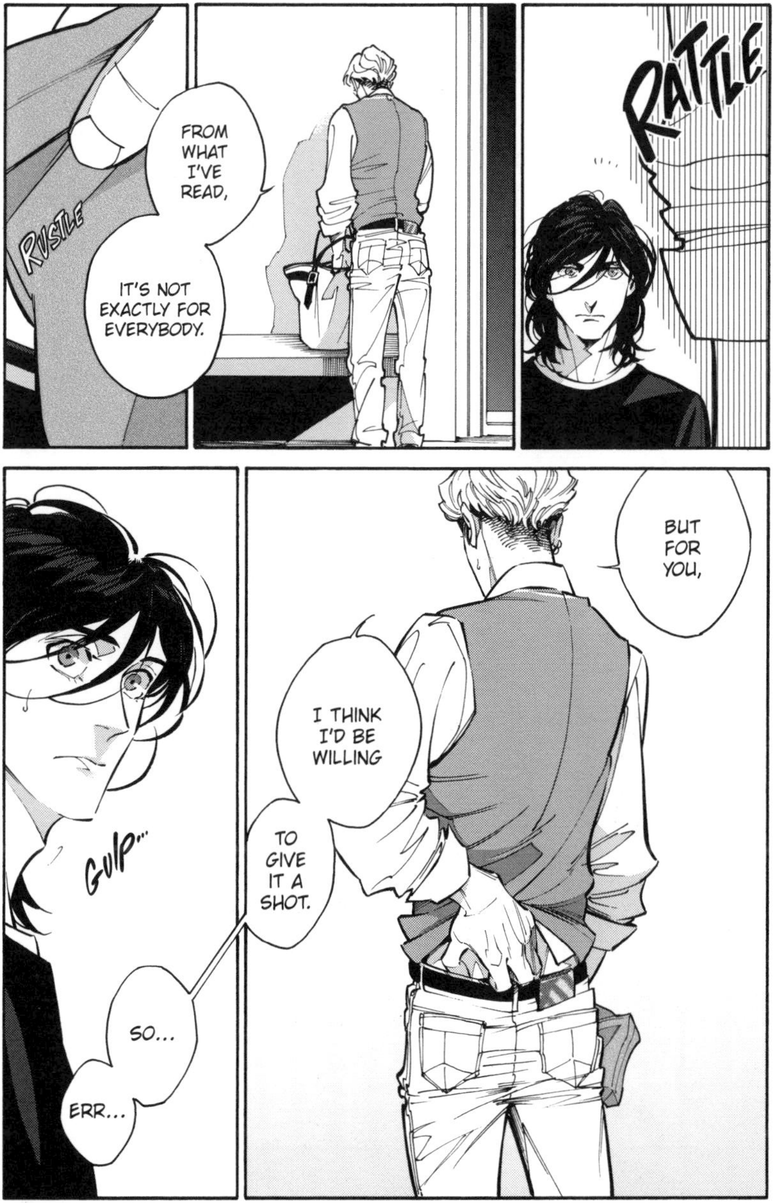
RATTLE
FROM WHAT I'VE READ,
IT'S NOT EXACTLY FOR EVERYBODY.
RUSTLE
BUT FOR YOU,
I THINK I'D BE WILLING
TO GIVE IT A SHOT.
GULP...
SO...
ERR...

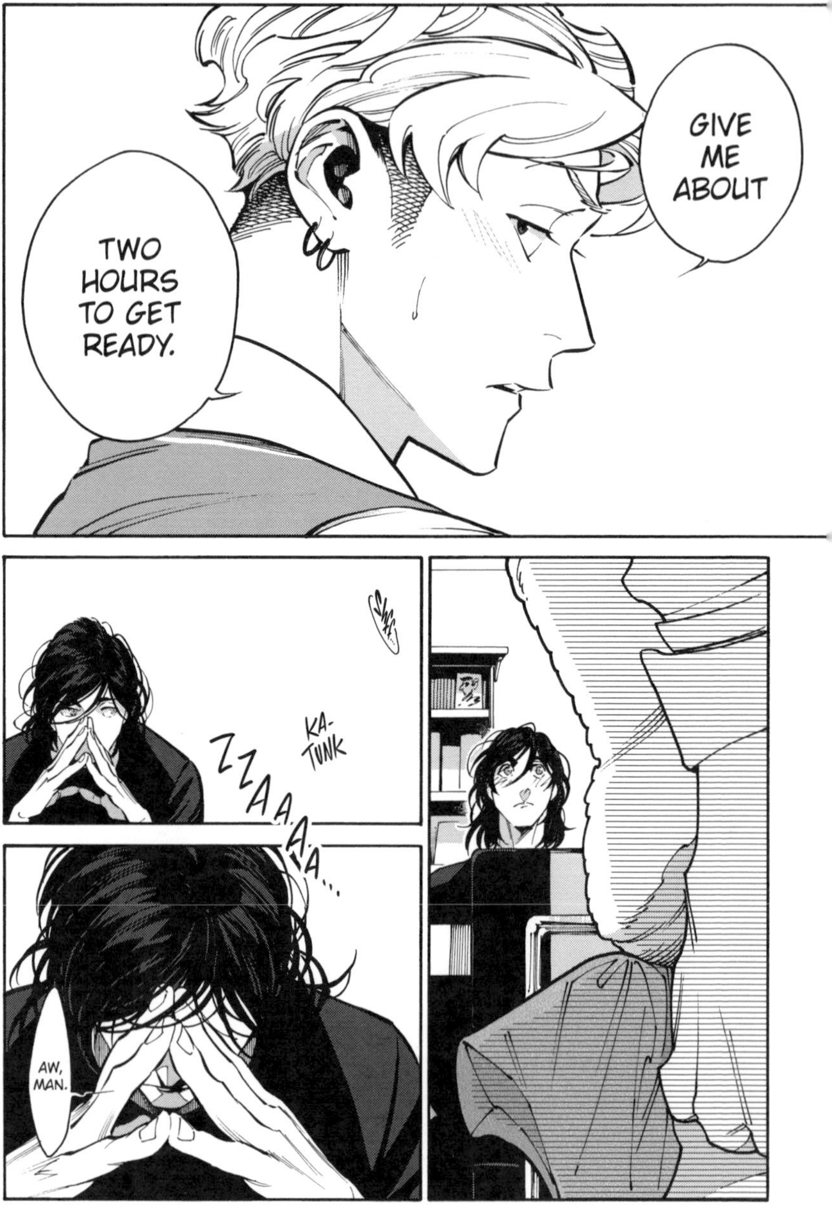
GIVE ME ABOUT
TWO HOURS TO GET READY.
KA-TUNK
ZZAAAAA...
AW, MAN.

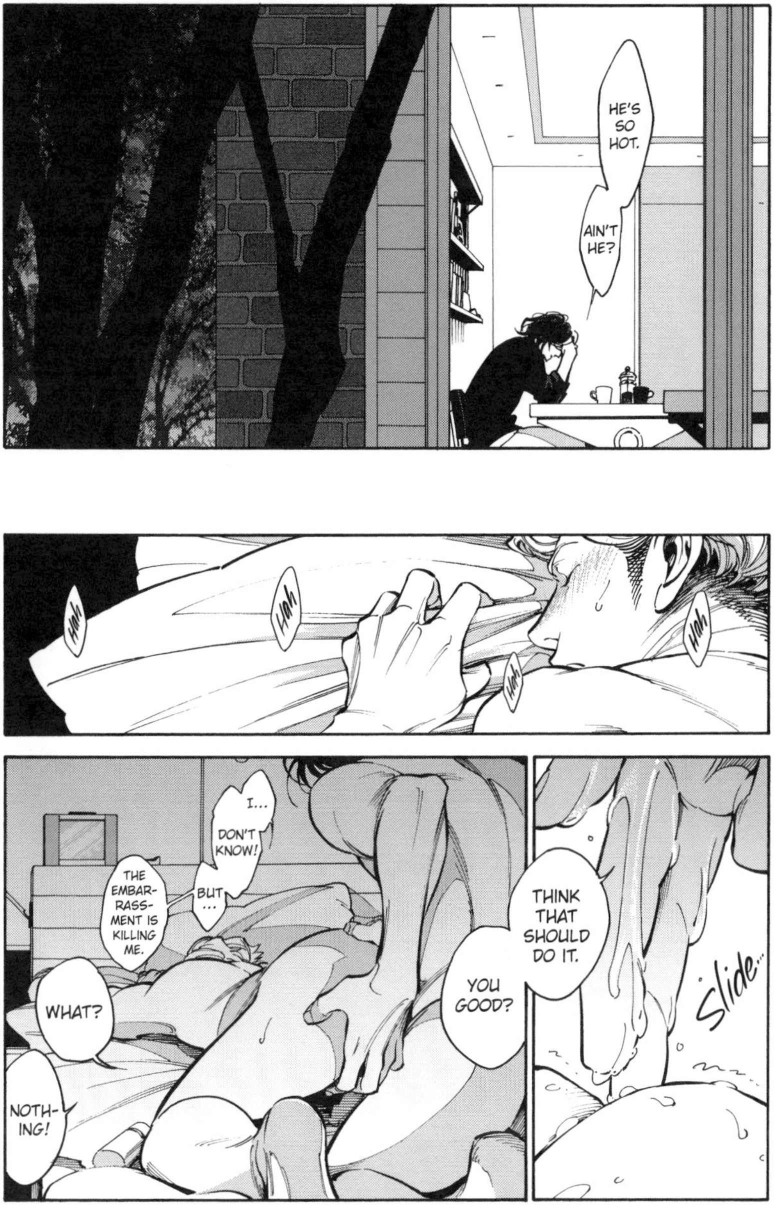
HE'S SO HOT.
AIN'T HE?
Hah
Hah
Hah
Hah
THINK THAT SHOULD DO IT.
YOU GOOD?
slide...
I... DON'T KNOW!
BUT...
THE EMBAR-RASS-MENT IS KILLING ME.
WHAT?
NOTH-ING!

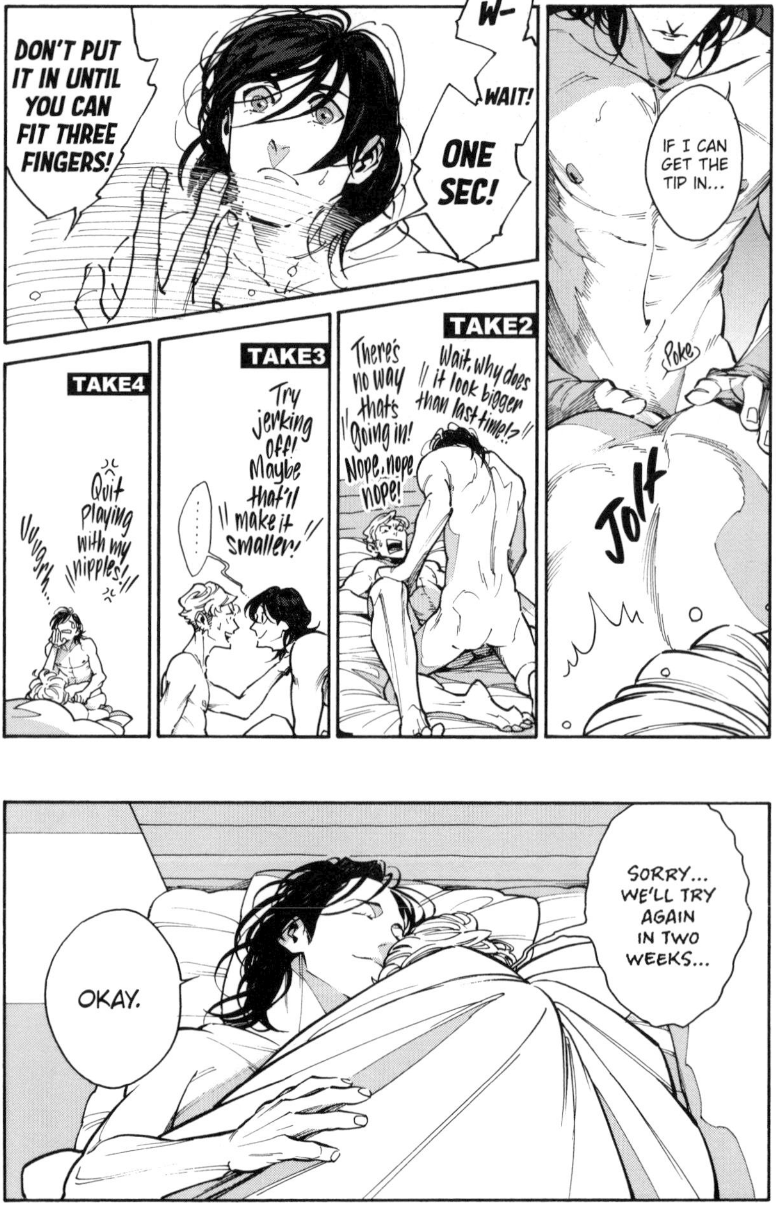
IF I CAN GET THE TIP IN...
Poke
Jolt
W-
WAIT!
ONE SEC!
DON'T PUT IT IN UNTIL YOU CAN FIT THREE FINGERS!
TAKE2
Wait, why does it look bigger than last time!?
There's no way that's going in!
Nope, nope nope!
TAKE3
Try jerking off! Maybe that'll make it smaller!
....
TAKE4
Quit playing with my nipples!!
Uuugrh...
SORRY... WE'LL TRY AGAIN IN TWO WEEKS...
OKAY.

CANIS —DEAR HATTER— EXTRA 1/END

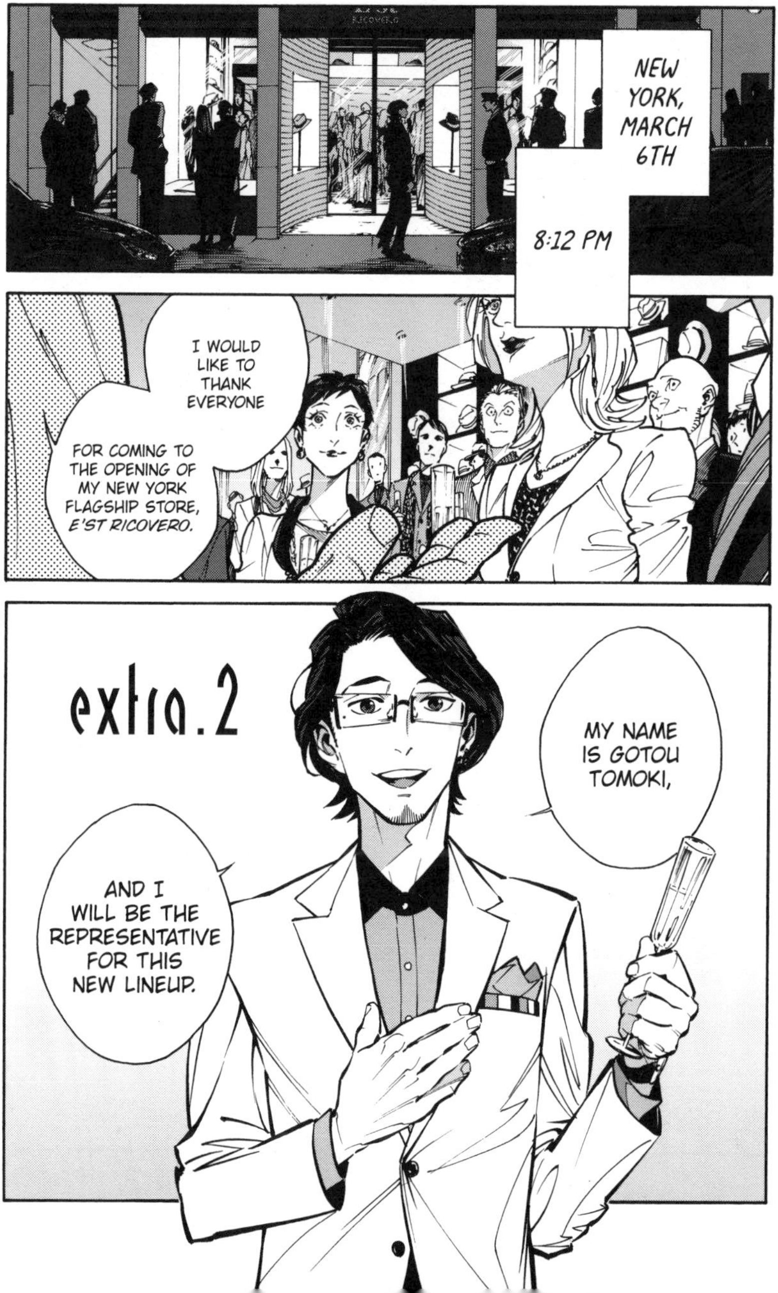
NEW YORK, MARCH 6TH
8:12 PM
I WOULD LIKE TO THANK EVERYONE
FOR COMING TO THE OPENING OF MY NEW YORK FLAGSHIP STORE, *E'ST RICOVERO.*
extra.2
MY NAME IS GOTOU TOMOKI,
AND I WILL BE THE REPRESENTATIVE FOR THIS NEW LINEUP.

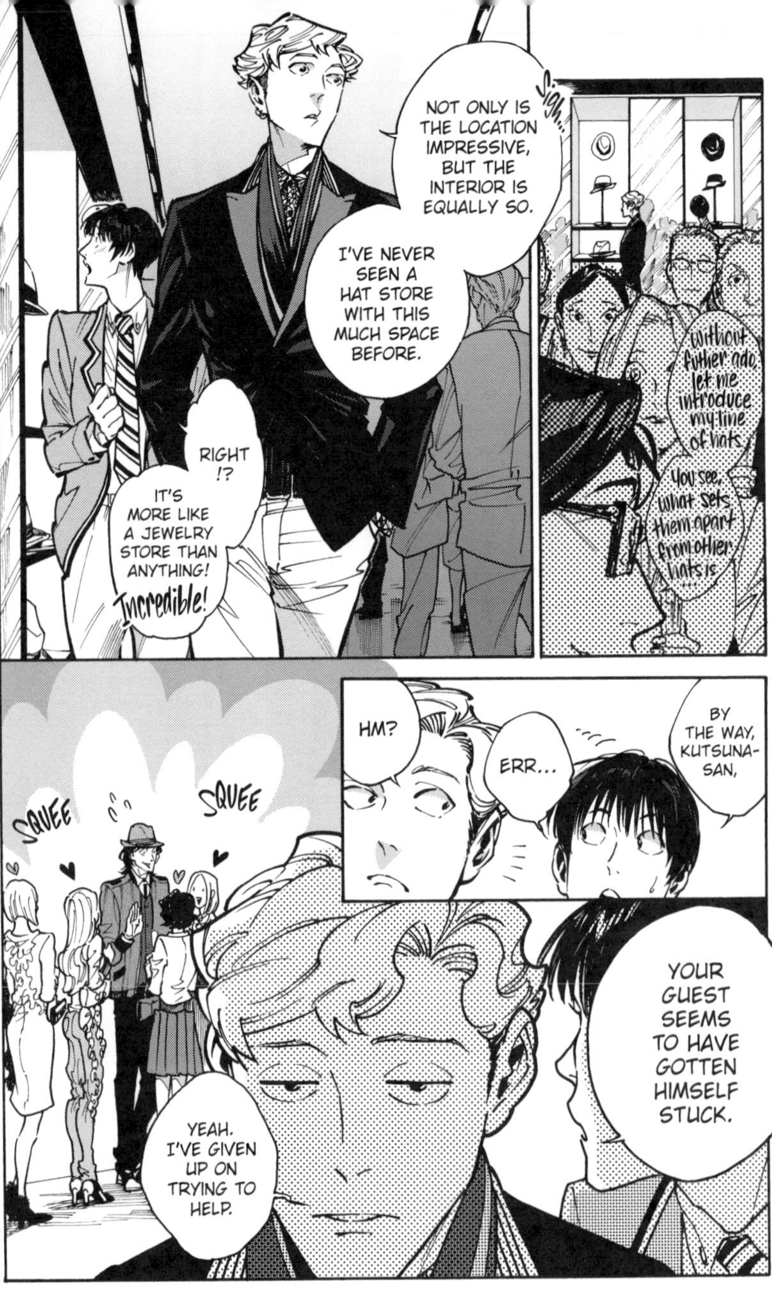
Without futher ado, let me introduce my line of hats.
You see, what sets them apart from other hats is...
Sigh...
NOT ONLY IS THE LOCATION IMPRESSIVE, BUT THE INTERIOR IS EQUALLY SO.
I'VE NEVER SEEN A HAT STORE WITH THIS MUCH SPACE BEFORE.
RIGHT!?
IT'S MORE LIKE A JEWELRY STORE THAN ANYTHING!
Incredible!
BY THE WAY, KUTSUNA-SAN,
ERR...
HM?
YOUR GUEST SEEMS TO HAVE GOTTEN HIMSELF STUCK.
SQUEE
SQUEE
YEAH. I'VE GIVEN UP ON TRYING TO HELP.

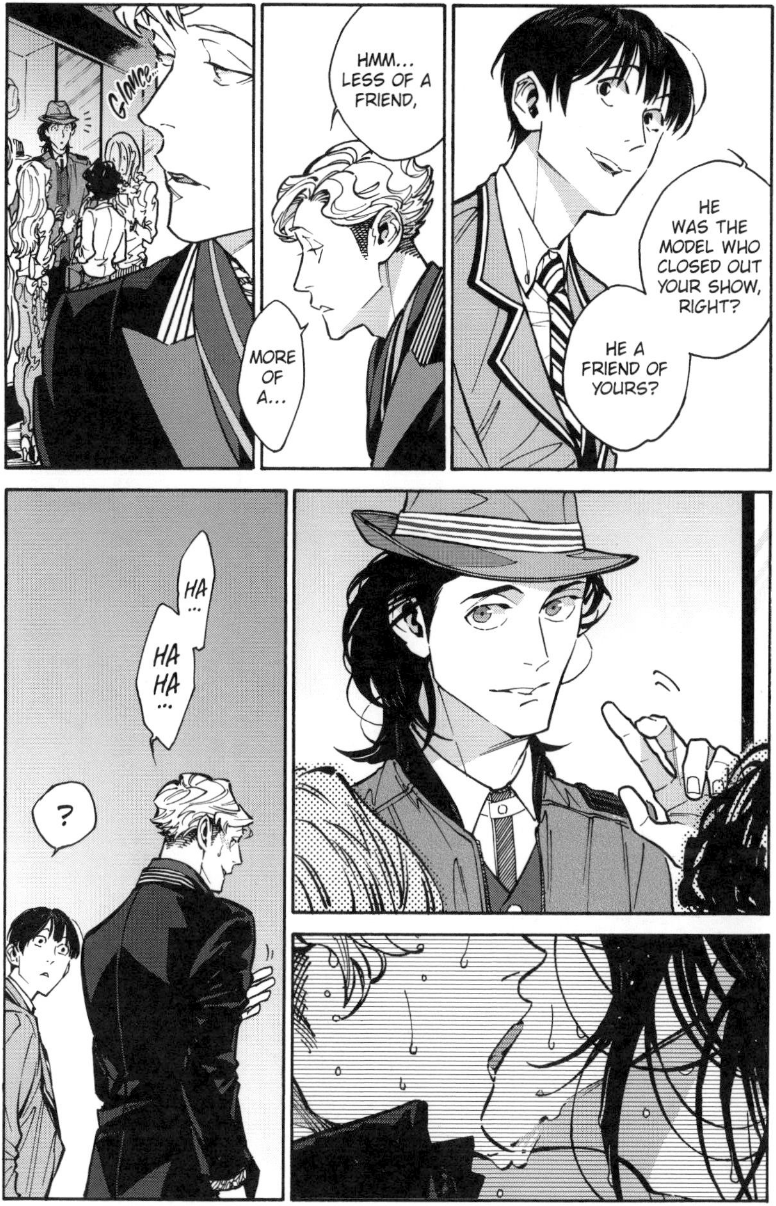
HE WAS THE MODEL WHO CLOSED OUT YOUR SHOW, RIGHT?
HE A FRIEND OF YOURS?
HMM… LESS OF A FRIEND,
MORE OF A…
Glance…
HA…
HA HA…
?

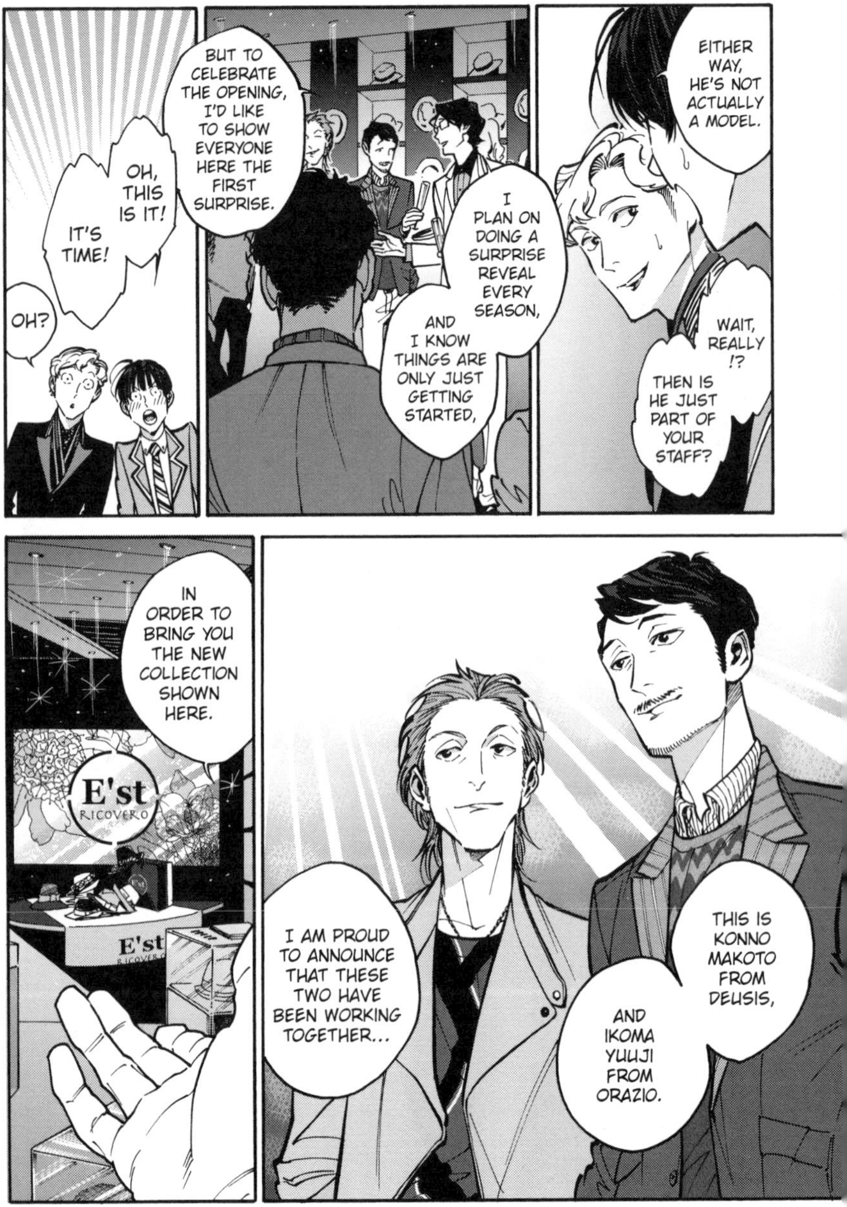
EITHER WAY, HE'S NOT ACTUALLY A MODEL.
WAIT, REALLY!?
THEN IS HE JUST PART OF YOUR STAFF?
I PLAN ON DOING A SURPRISE REVEAL EVERY SEASON,
AND I KNOW THINGS ARE ONLY JUST GETTING STARTED,
BUT TO CELEBRATE THE OPENING, I'D LIKE TO SHOW EVERYONE HERE THE FIRST SURPRISE.
OH, THIS IS IT!
IT'S TIME!
OH?
THIS IS KONNO MAKOTO FROM DEUSIS,
AND IKOMA YUUJI FROM ORAZIO.
I AM PROUD TO ANNOUNCE THAT THESE TWO HAVE BEEN WORKING TOGETHER...
IN ORDER TO BRING YOU THE NEW COLLECTION SHOWN HERE.
E'st RICOVERO
E'st RICOVERO

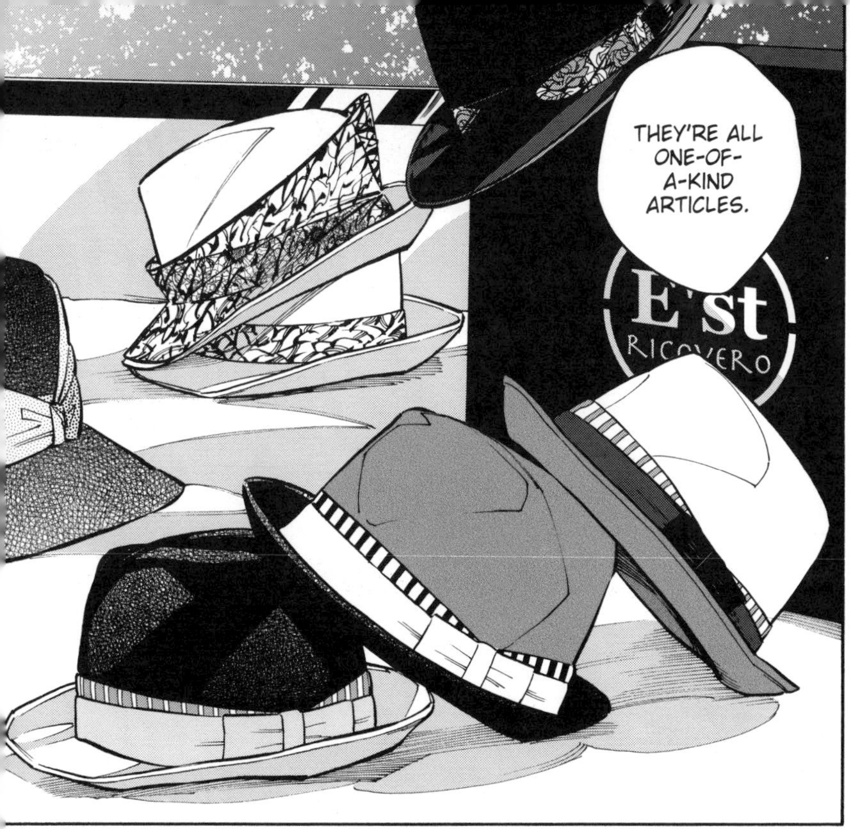
THEY'RE ALL ONE-OF-A-KIND ARTICLES.
E'st RICOVERO

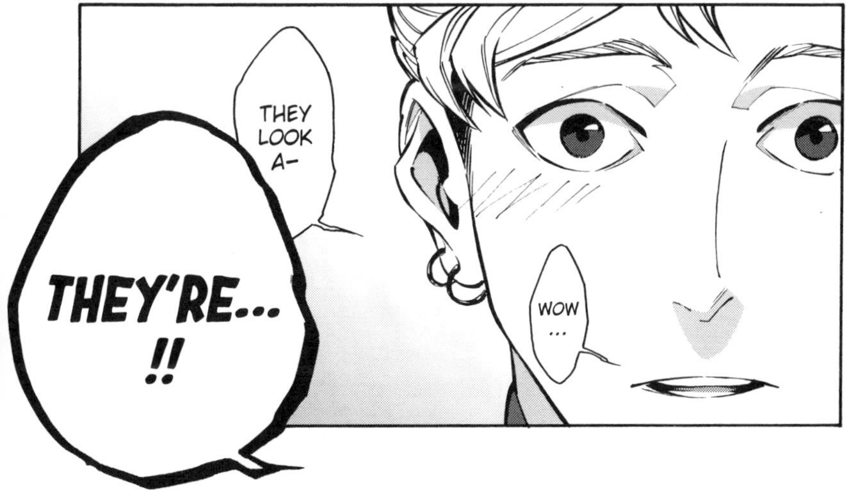
WOW...
THEY LOOK A-
THEY'RE... !!

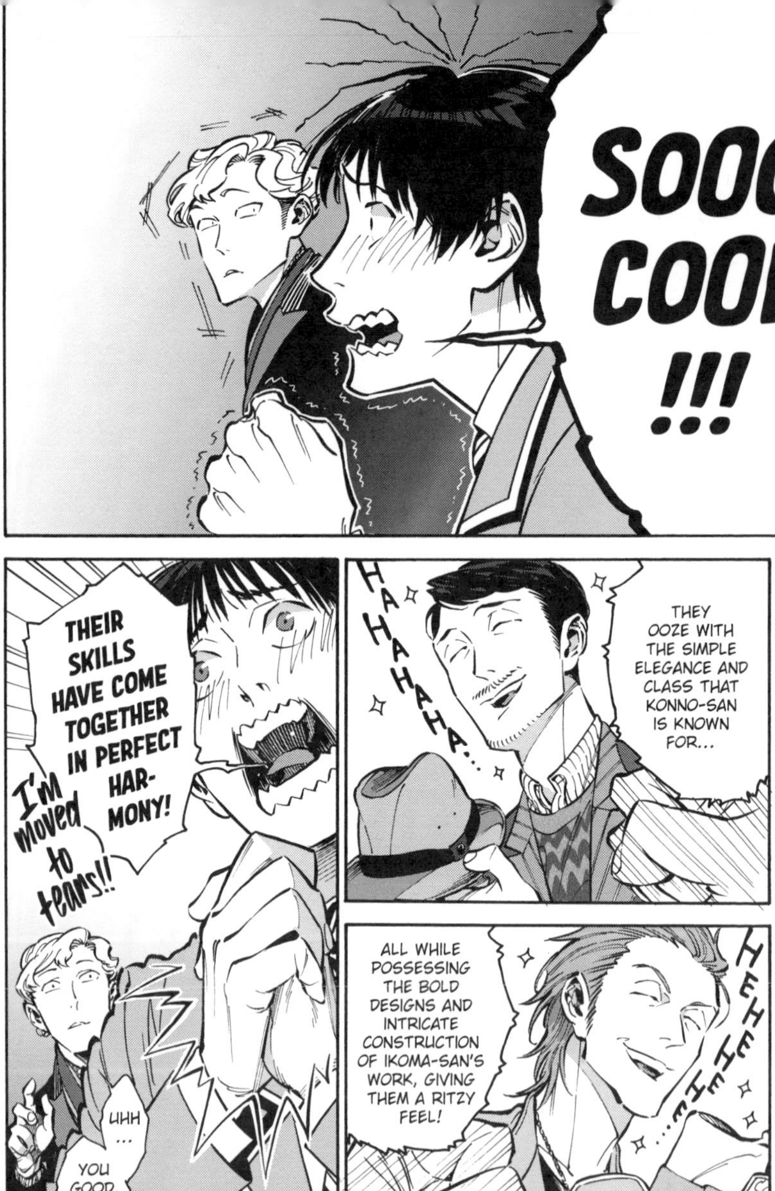
SOOO COOL!!!
HAHAHAHA...
THEY OOZE WITH THE SIMPLE ELEGANCE AND CLASS THAT KONNO-SAN IS KNOWN FOR...
ALL WHILE POSSESSING THE BOLD DESIGNS AND INTRICATE CONSTRUCTION OF IKOMA-SAN'S WORK, GIVING THEM A RITZY FEEL!
HEHEHEHE...
THEIR SKILLS HAVE COME TOGETHER IN PERFECT HAR-MONY!
I'm moved to tears!!
UHH...
YOU GOOD, HAGA-KUN?

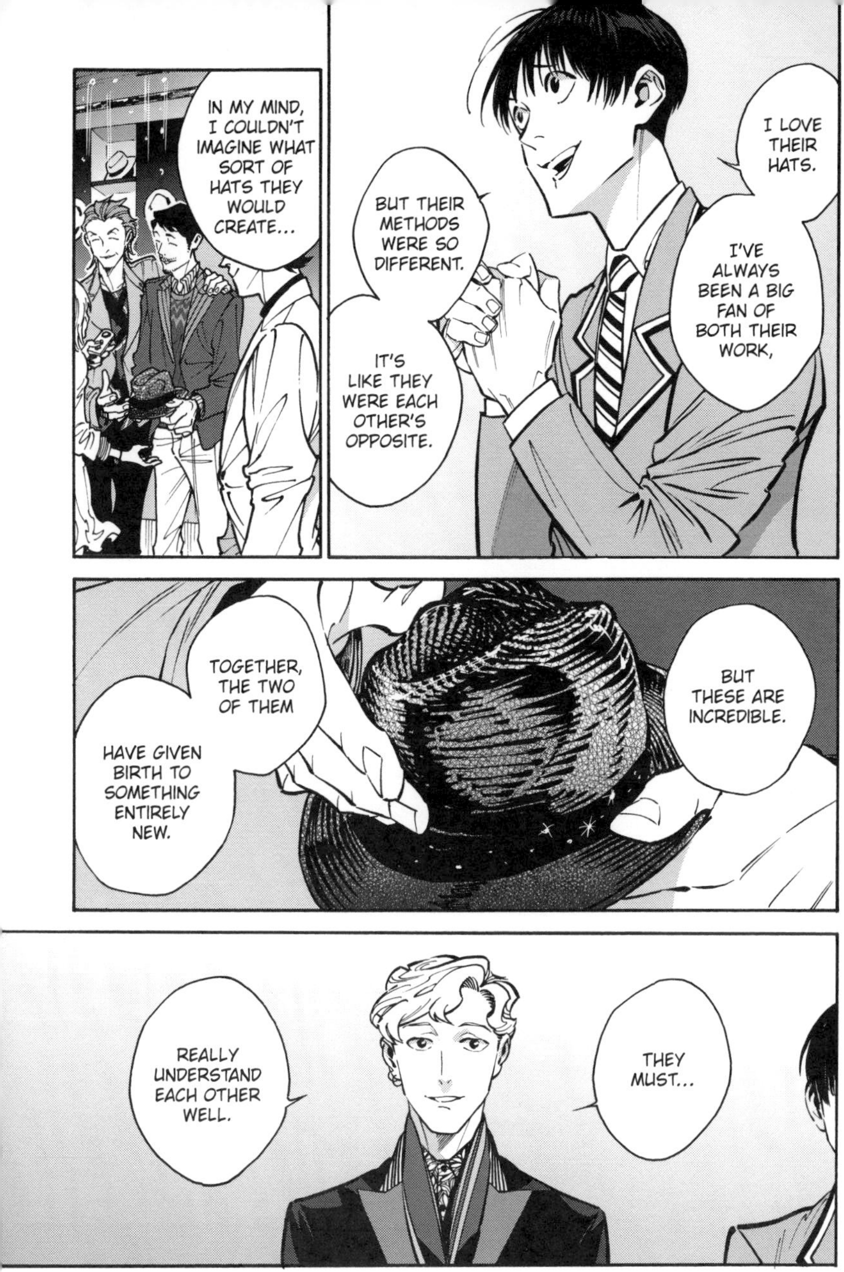
I LOVE THEIR HATS.
I'VE ALWAYS BEEN A BIG FAN OF BOTH THEIR WORK,
BUT THEIR METHODS WERE SO DIFFERENT.
IT'S LIKE THEY WERE EACH OTHER'S OPPOSITE.
IN MY MIND, I COULDN'T IMAGINE WHAT SORT OF HATS THEY WOULD CREATE...
BUT THESE ARE INCREDIBLE.
TOGETHER, THE TWO OF THEM
HAVE GIVEN BIRTH TO SOMETHING ENTIRELY NEW.
THEY MUST...
REALLY UNDERSTAND EACH OTHER WELL.

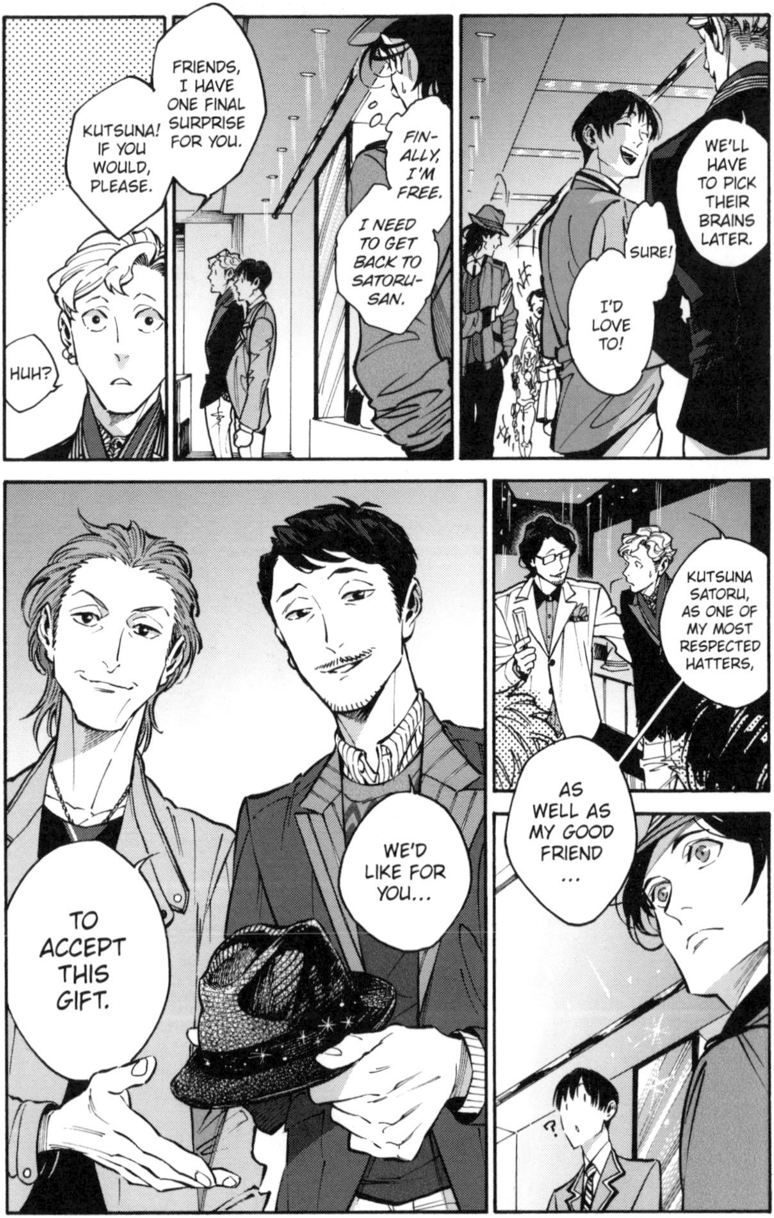
WE'LL HAVE TO PICK THEIR BRAINS LATER.
SURE!
I'D LOVE TO!
FIN-ALLY, I'M FREE.
I NEED TO GET BACK TO SATORU-SAN.
FRIENDS, I HAVE ONE FINAL SURPRISE FOR YOU.
KUTSUNA! IF YOU WOULD, PLEASE.
HUH?
KUTSUNA SATORU, AS ONE OF MY MOST RESPECTED HATTERS,
AS WELL AS MY GOOD FRIEND ...
WE'D LIKE FOR YOU...
TO ACCEPT THIS GIFT.

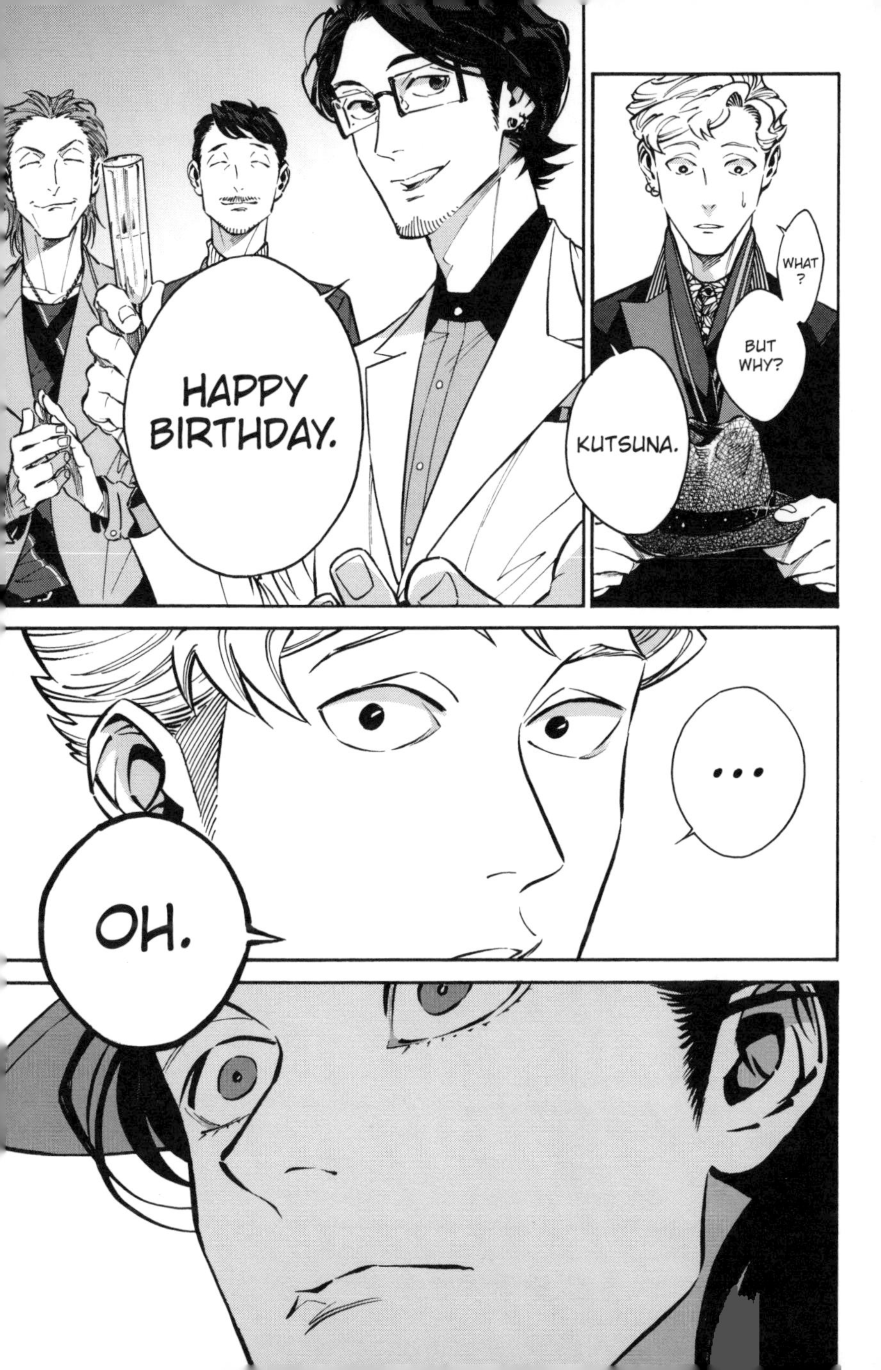
WHAT?
BUT WHY?
KUTSUNA.
HAPPY BIRTHDAY.
...
OH.

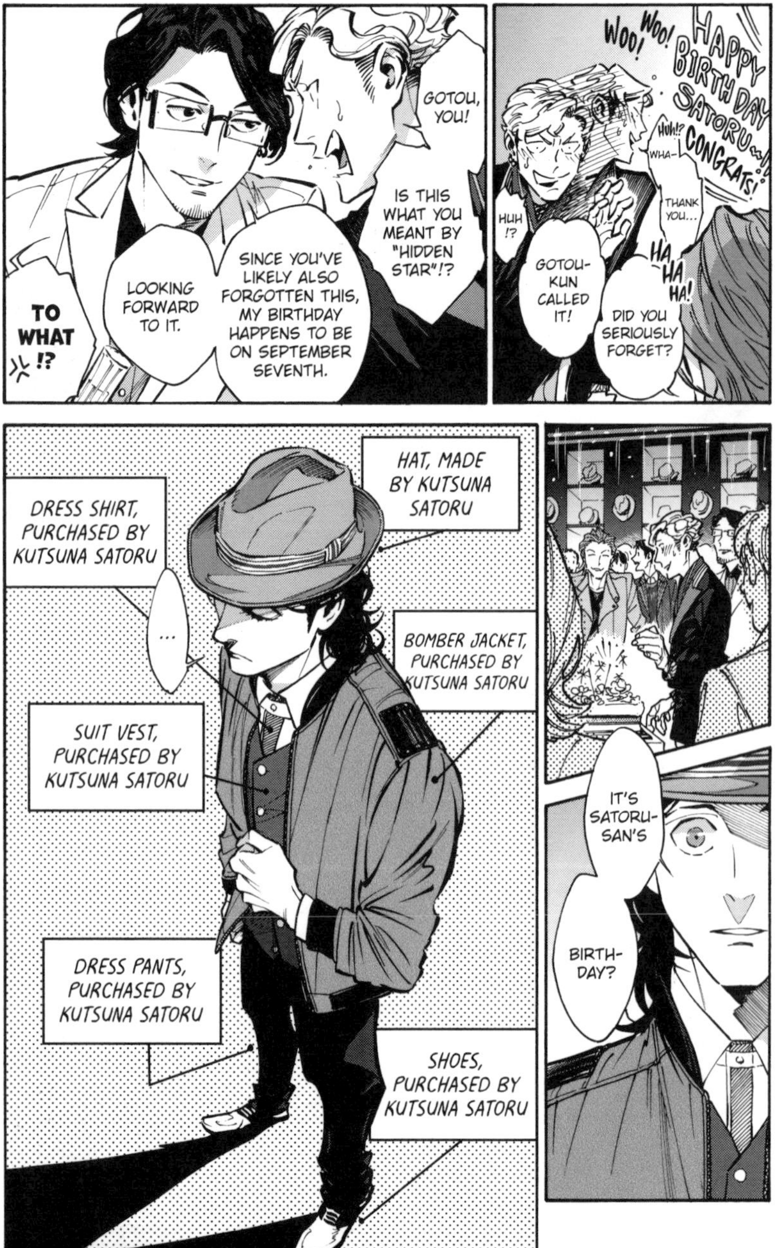
HAPPY BIRTHDAY SATORU~!!
WOO! WOO!
CONGRATS!
HUH!? WHA-
THANK YOU...
HUH!?
GOTOU-KUN CALLED IT!
HA HA HA!
DID YOU SERIOUSLY FORGET?
GOTOU, YOU!
IS THIS WHAT YOU MEANT BY "HIDDEN STAR"!?
SINCE YOU'VE LIKELY ALSO FORGOTTEN THIS, MY BIRTHDAY HAPPENS TO BE ON SEPTEMBER SEVENTH.
LOOKING FORWARD TO IT.
TO WHAT!?
IT'S SATORU-SAN'S
BIRTH-DAY?
HAT, MADE BY KUTSUNA SATORU
DRESS SHIRT, PURCHASED BY KUTSUNA SATORU
...
BOMBER JACKET, PURCHASED BY KUTSUNA SATORU
SUIT VEST, PURCHASED BY KUTSUNA SATORU
DRESS PANTS, PURCHASED BY KUTSUNA SATORU
SHOES, PURCHASED BY KUTSUNA SATORU

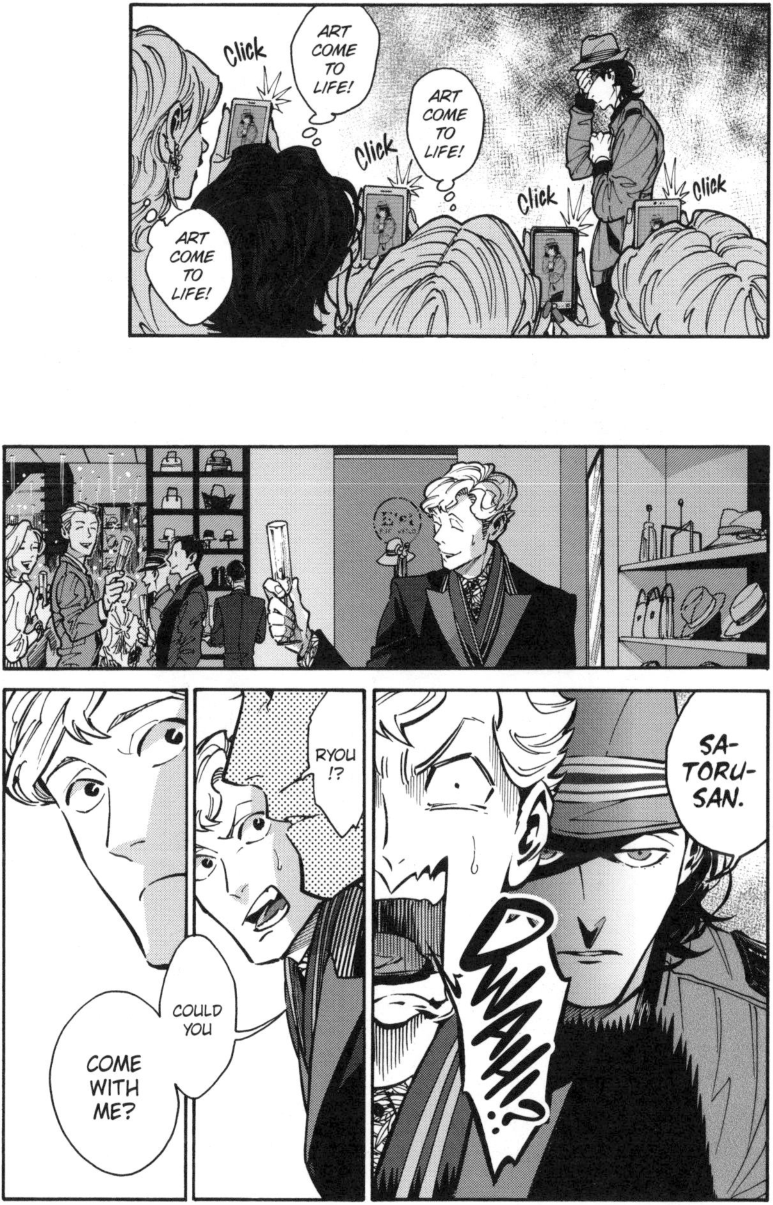
Click
Click
ART COME TO LIFE!
Click
ART COME TO LIFE!
Click
ART COME TO LIFE!
SA-TORU-SAN.
WAAH!?
RYOU !?
COULD YOU
COME WITH ME?

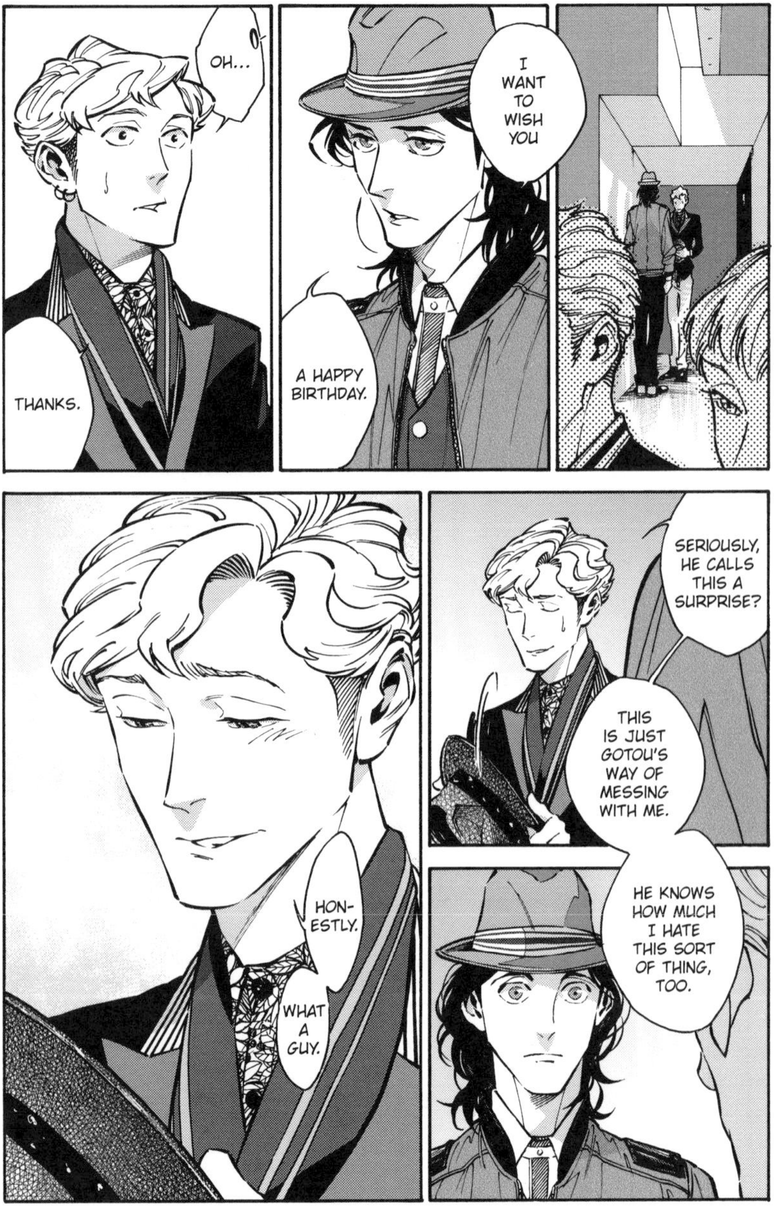
I WANT TO WISH YOU
A HAPPY BIRTHDAY.
OH...
THANKS.
SERIOUSLY, HE CALLS THIS A SURPRISE?
THIS IS JUST GOTOU'S WAY OF MESSING WITH ME.
HE KNOWS HOW MUCH I HATE THIS SORT OF THING, TOO.
HON-ESTLY.
WHAT A GUY.

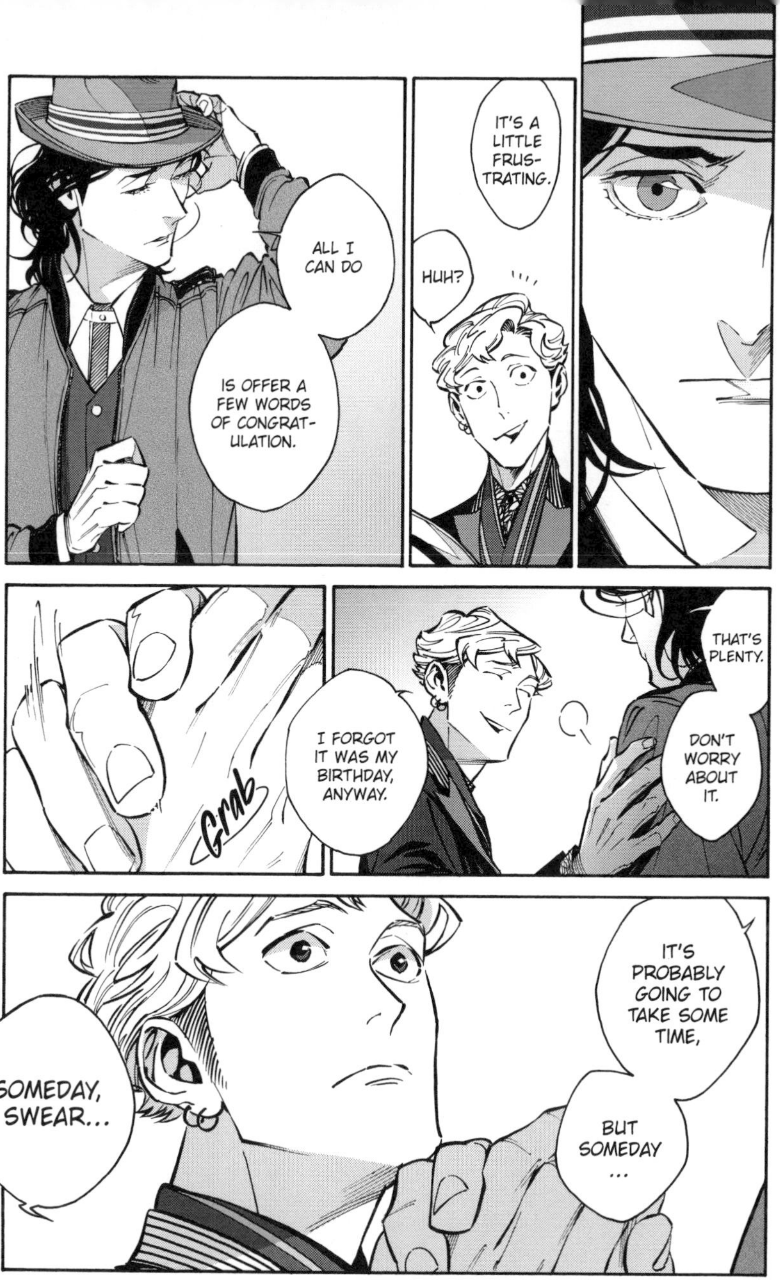

IT'S A LITTLE FRUS-TRATING.
HUH?
ALL I CAN DO
IS OFFER A FEW WORDS OF CONGRAT-ULATION.
THAT'S PLENTY.
DON'T WORRY ABOUT IT.
I FORGOT IT WAS MY BIRTHDAY, ANYWAY.
Grab
IT'S PROBABLY GOING TO TAKE SOME TIME,
BUT SOMEDAY ...
SOMEDAY, I SWEAR...

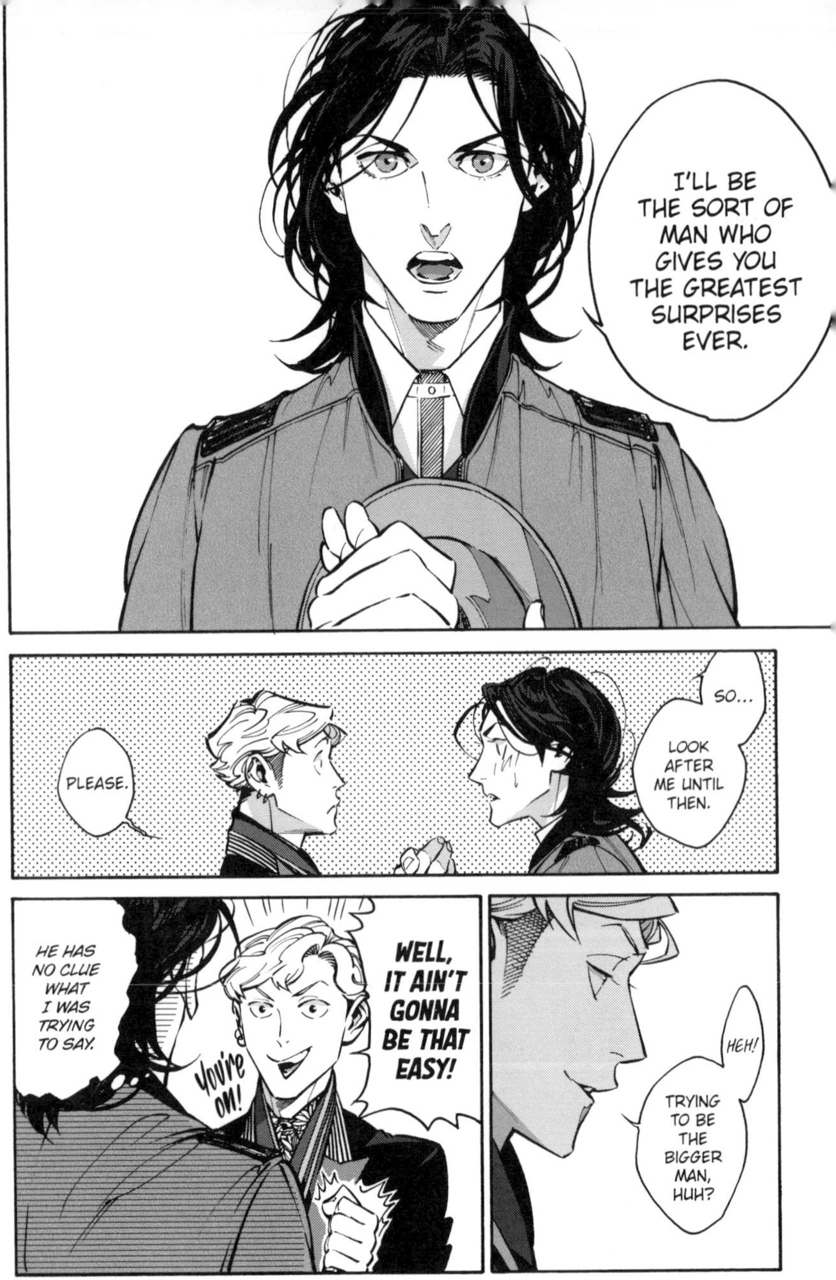
I'LL BE THE SORT OF MAN WHO GIVES YOU THE GREATEST SURPRISES EVER.
SO...
LOOK AFTER ME UNTIL THEN.
PLEASE.
HEH!
TRYING TO BE THE BIGGER MAN, HUH?
WELL, IT AIN'T GONNA BE THAT EASY!
You're on!
HE HAS NO CLUE WHAT I WAS TRYING TO SAY.

CANIS —DEAR HATTER— EXTRA 2/END

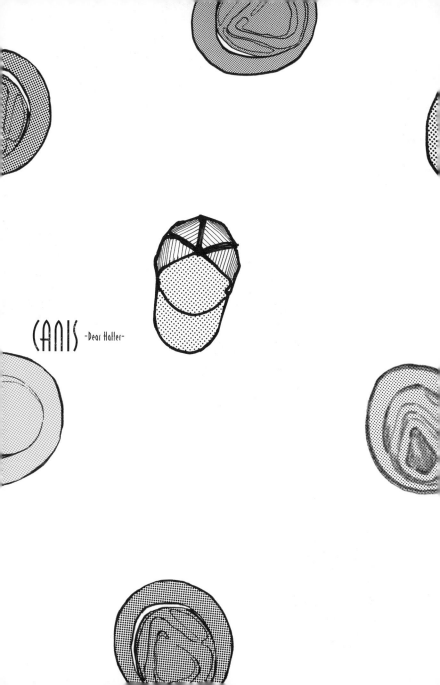

CANIS -Dear Hatter-

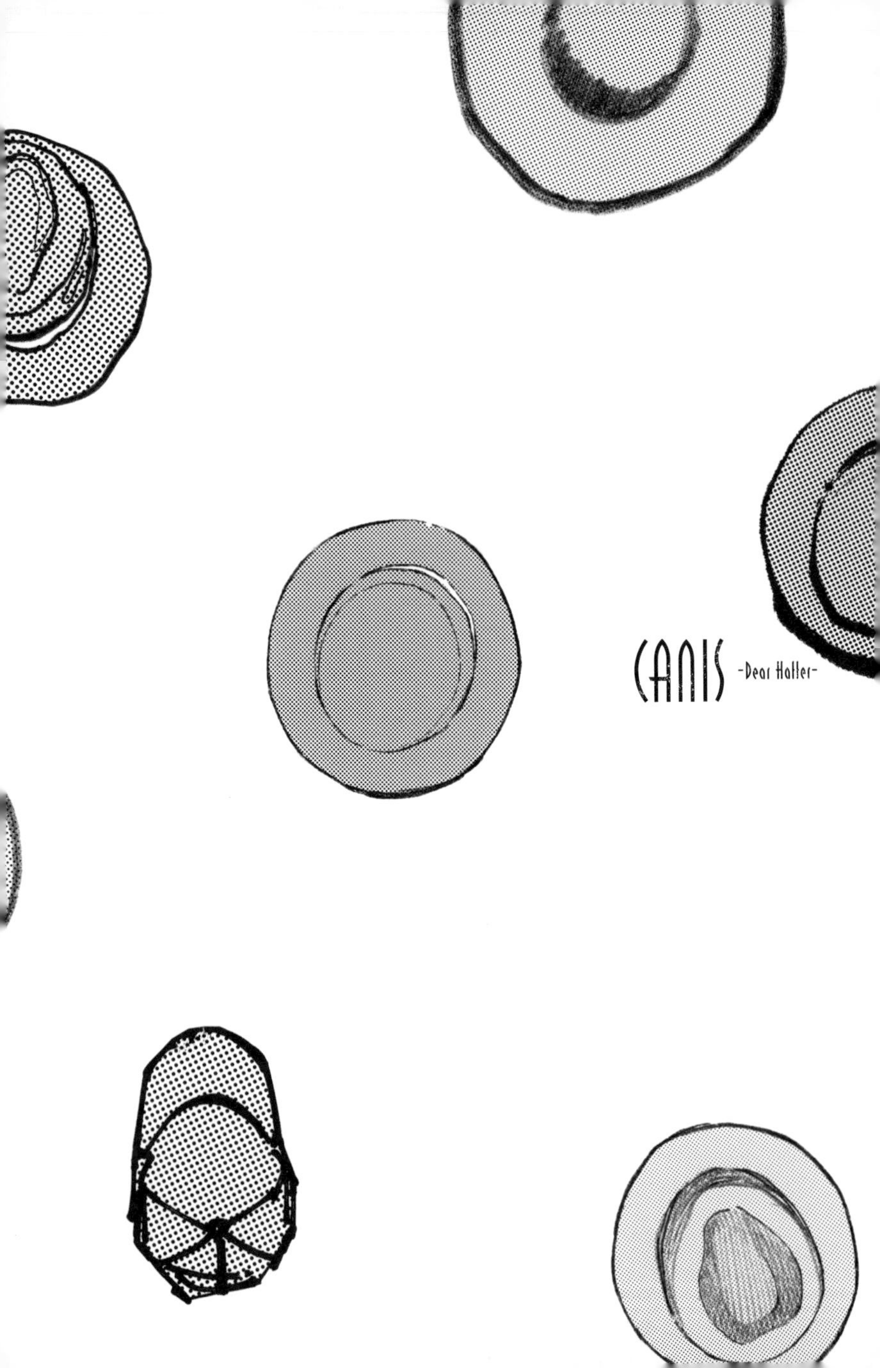
CANIS -Dear Hatter-

A Handshake Tells
a Person's Story
From A to Z

THERE
WAS ONE
TIME IN
MY LIFE

THAT I
CRIED FROM
PUTTING
ON A HAT.

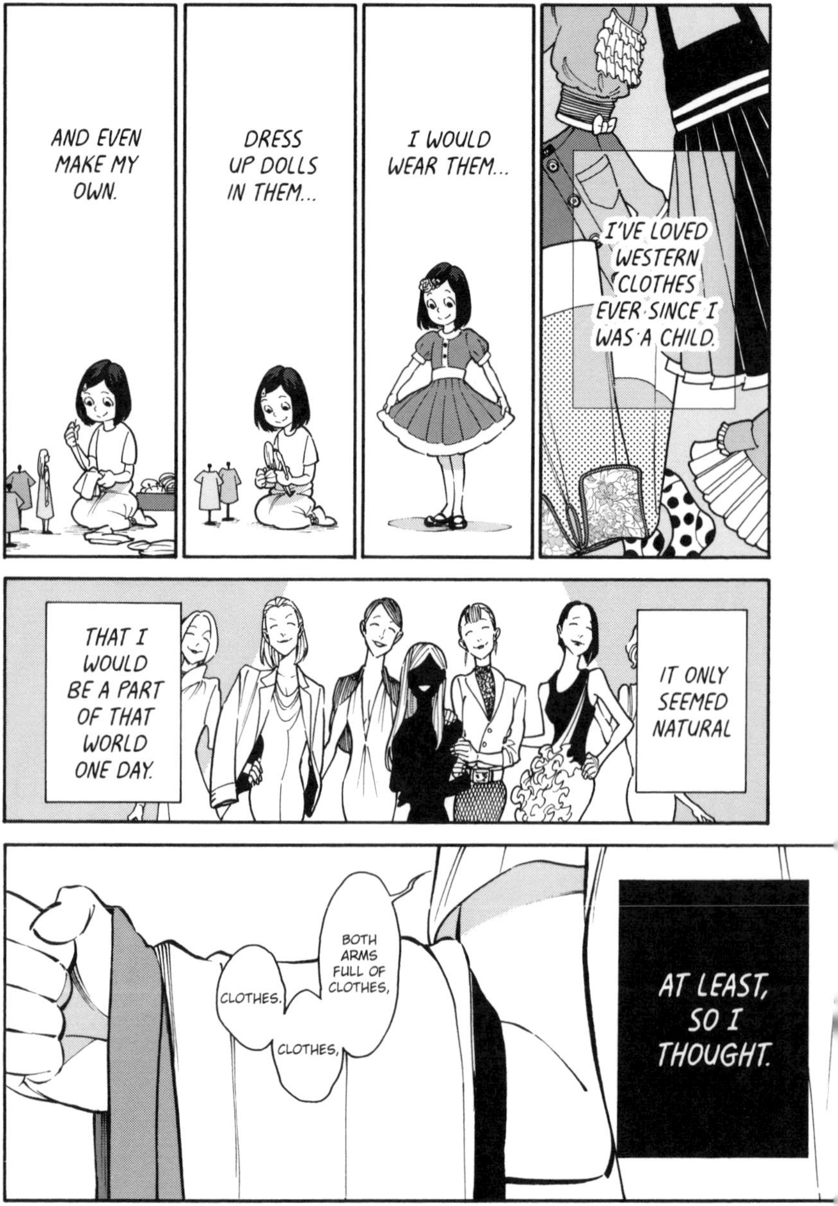
I'VE LOVED WESTERN CLOTHES EVER SINCE I WAS A CHILD.
I WOULD WEAR THEM...
DRESS UP DOLLS IN THEM...
AND EVEN MAKE MY OWN.
IT ONLY SEEMED NATURAL
THAT I WOULD BE A PART OF THAT WORLD ONE DAY.
AT LEAST, SO I THOUGHT.
BOTH ARMS FULL OF CLOTHES,
CLOTHES.
CLOTHES,

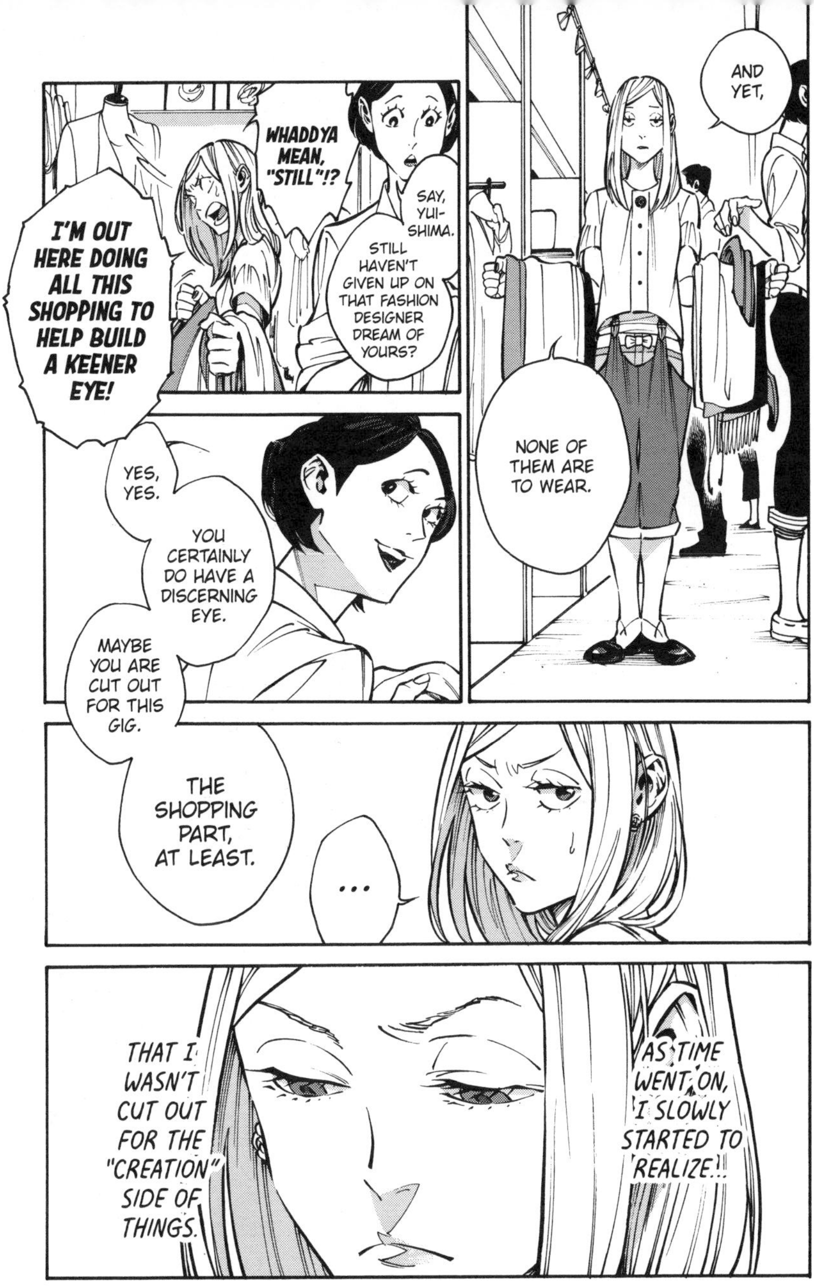
AND YET,
NONE OF THEM ARE TO WEAR.
SAY, YUI-SHIMA.
STILL HAVEN'T GIVEN UP ON THAT FASHION DESIGNER DREAM OF YOURS?
WHADDYA MEAN, "STILL"!?
I'M OUT HERE DOING ALL THIS SHOPPING TO HELP BUILD A KEENER EYE!
YES, YES.
YOU CERTAINLY DO HAVE A DISCERNING EYE.
MAYBE YOU ARE CUT OUT FOR THIS GIG.
THE SHOPPING PART, AT LEAST.
...
AS TIME WENT ON, I SLOWLY STARTED TO REALIZE...
THAT I WASN'T CUT OUT FOR THE "CREATION" SIDE OF THINGS.

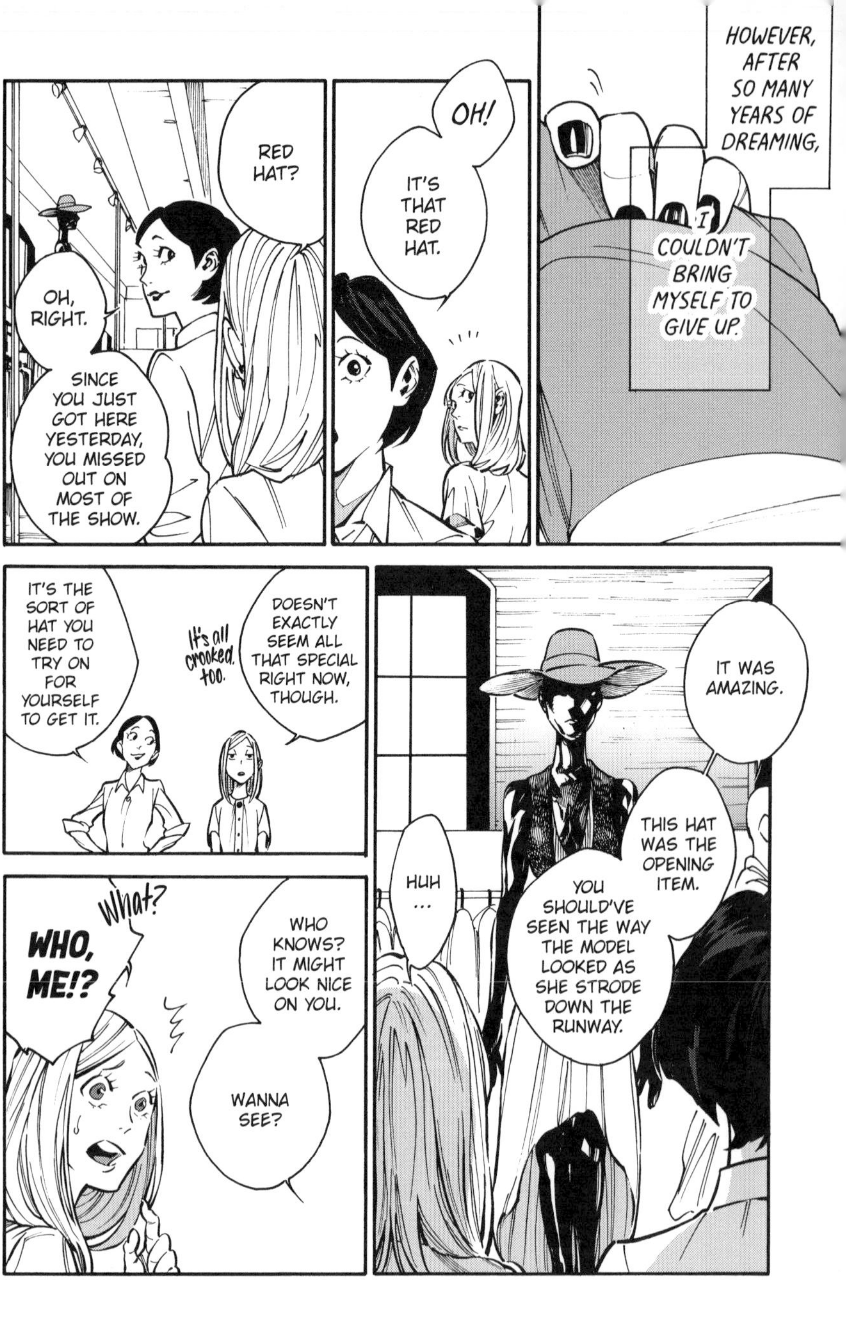
HOWEVER, AFTER SO MANY YEARS OF DREAMING,
I COULDN'T BRING MYSELF TO GIVE UP.
OH!
IT'S THAT RED HAT.
RED HAT?
OH, RIGHT.
SINCE YOU JUST GOT HERE YESTERDAY, YOU MISSED OUT ON MOST OF THE SHOW.
IT WAS AMAZING.
THIS HAT WAS THE OPENING ITEM.
YOU SHOULD'VE SEEN THE WAY THE MODEL LOOKED AS SHE STRODE DOWN THE RUNWAY.
HUH...
DOESN'T EXACTLY SEEM ALL THAT SPECIAL RIGHT NOW, THOUGH.
It's all crooked, too.
IT'S THE SORT OF HAT YOU NEED TO TRY ON FOR YOURSELF TO GET IT.
WHO KNOWS? IT MIGHT LOOK NICE ON YOU.
WANNA SEE?
What?
WHO, ME!?

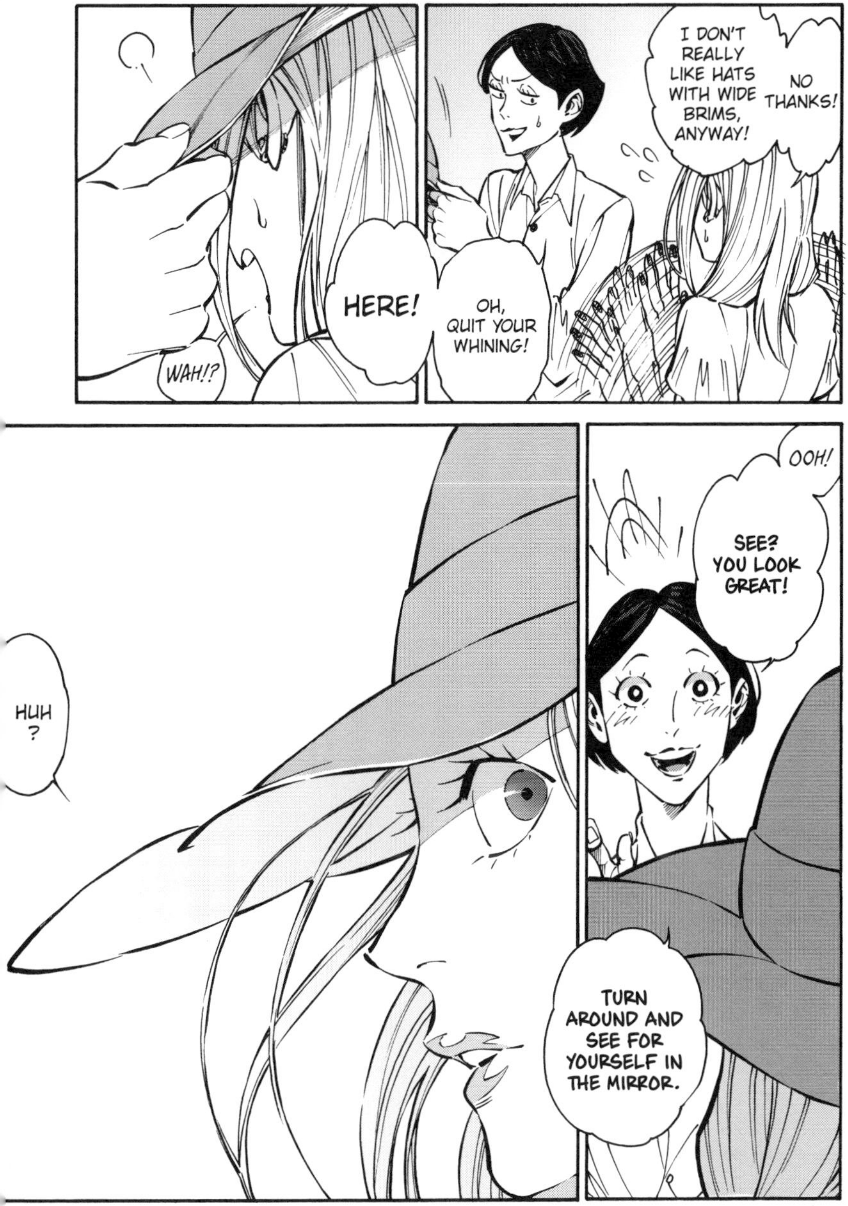
NO THANKS!
I DON'T REALLY LIKE HATS WITH WIDE BRIMS, ANYWAY!
OH, QUIT YOUR WHINING!
HERE!
WAH!?
OOH!
SEE? YOU LOOK GREAT!
TURN AROUND AND SEE FOR YOURSELF IN THE MIRROR.
HUH?

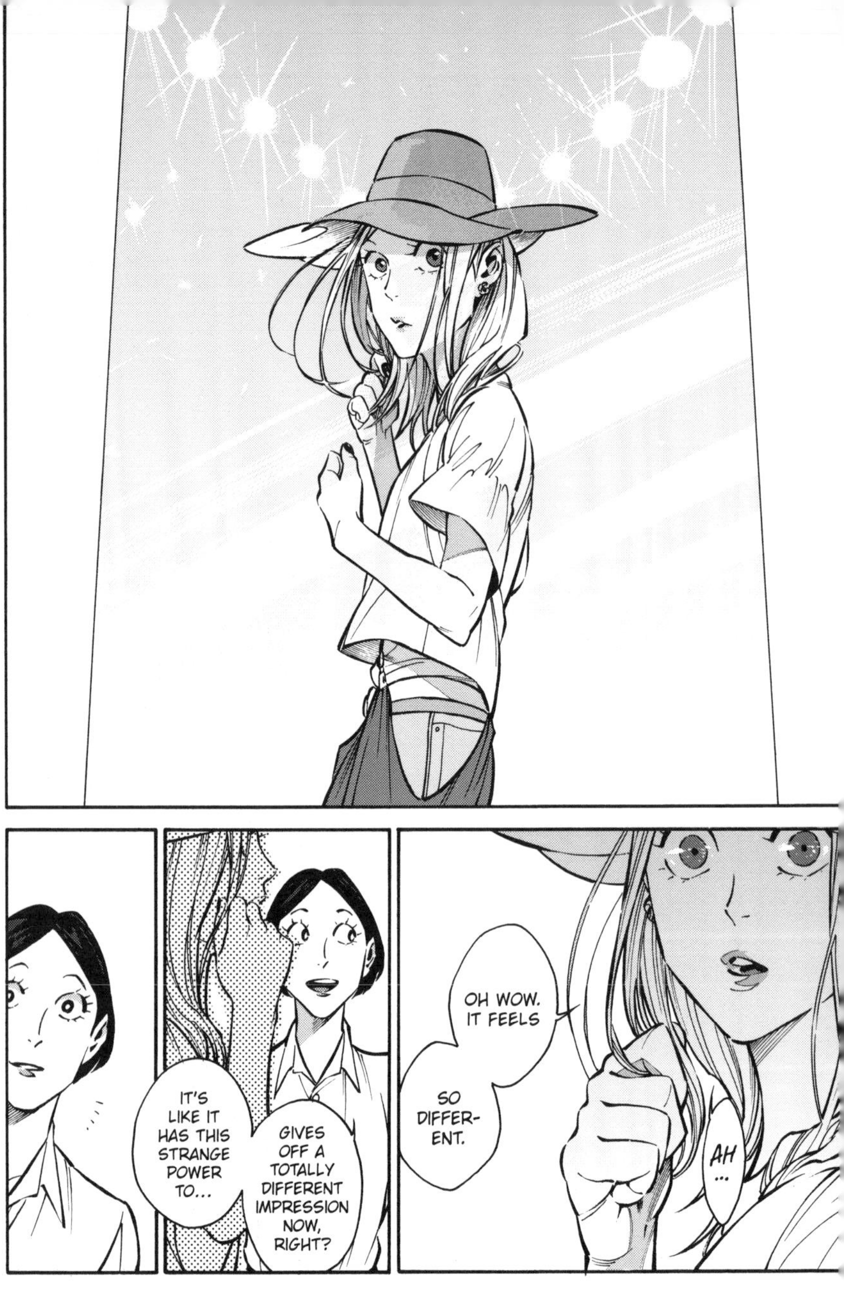
AH ...
OH WOW. IT FEELS
SO DIFFER-ENT.
IT'S LIKE IT HAS THIS STRANGE POWER TO...
GIVES OFF A TOTALLY DIFFERENT IMPRESSION NOW, RIGHT?

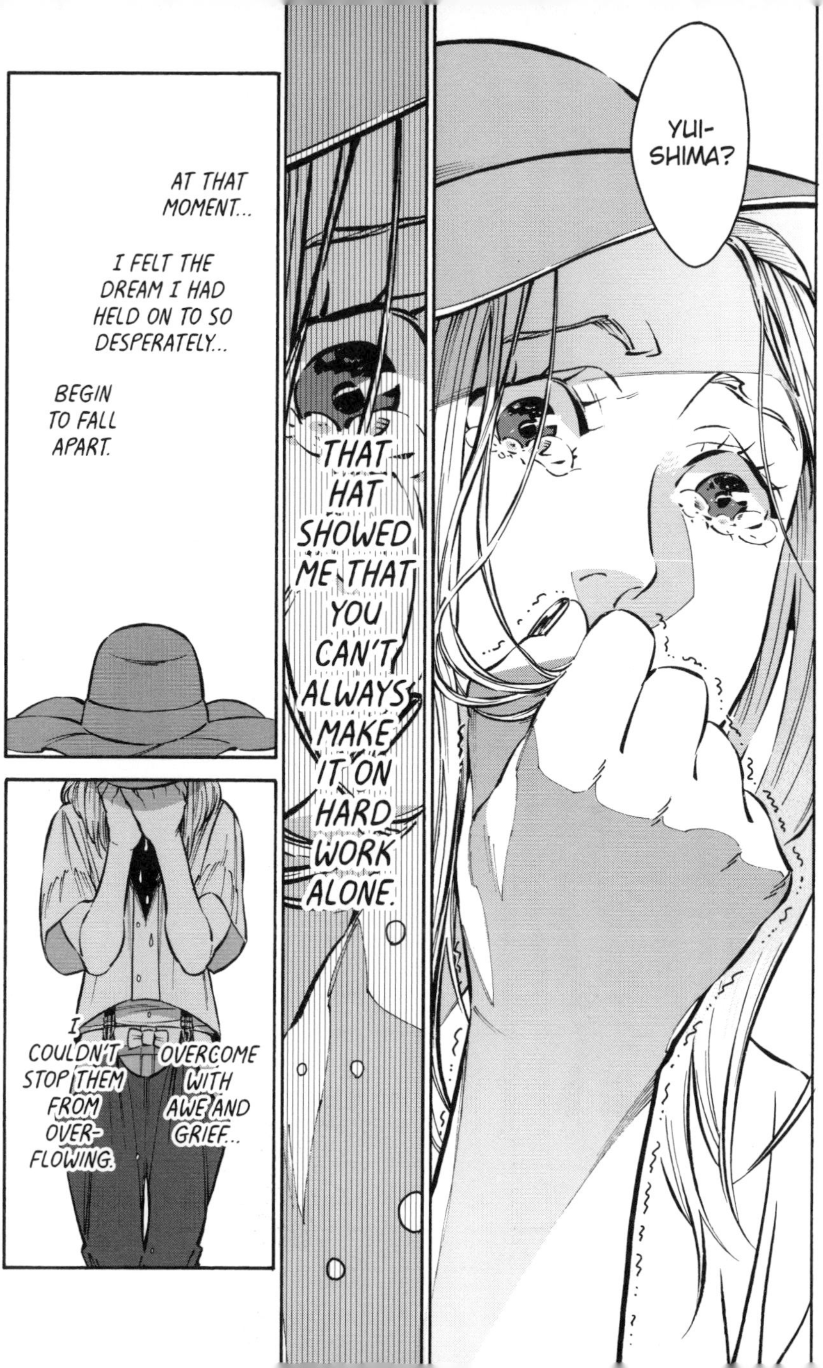
YUI-SHIMA?
THAT HAT SHOWED ME THAT YOU CAN'T ALWAYS MAKE IT ON HARD WORK ALONE.
AT THAT MOMENT...
I FELT THE DREAM I HAD HELD ON TO SO DESPERATELY...
BEGIN TO FALL APART.
OVERCOME WITH AWE AND GRIEF...
I COULDN'T STOP THEM FROM OVER-FLOWING.

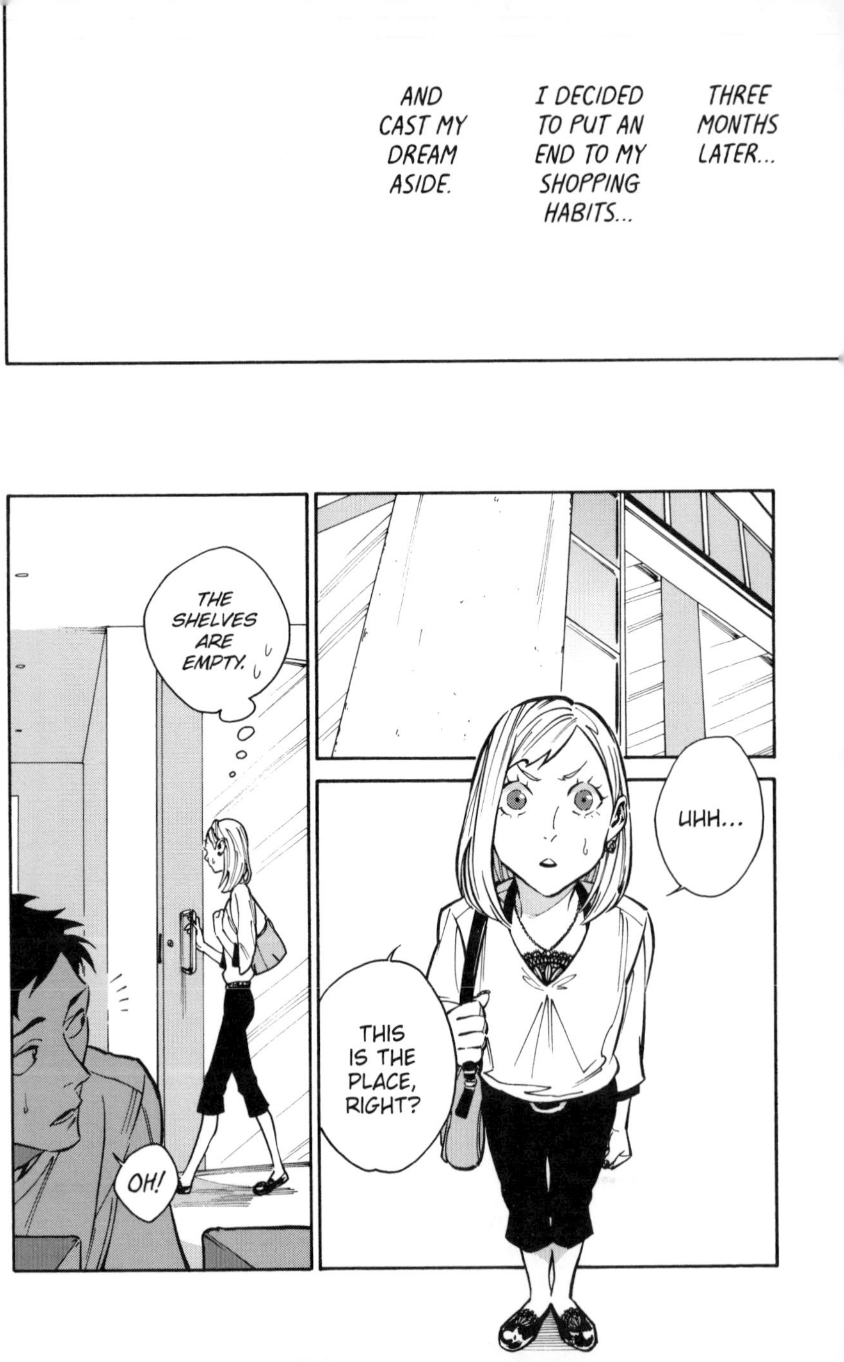
THREE MONTHS LATER...
I DECIDED TO PUT AN END TO MY SHOPPING HABITS...
AND CAST MY DREAM ASIDE.
UHH...
THIS IS THE PLACE, RIGHT?
THE SHELVES ARE EMPTY.
OH!

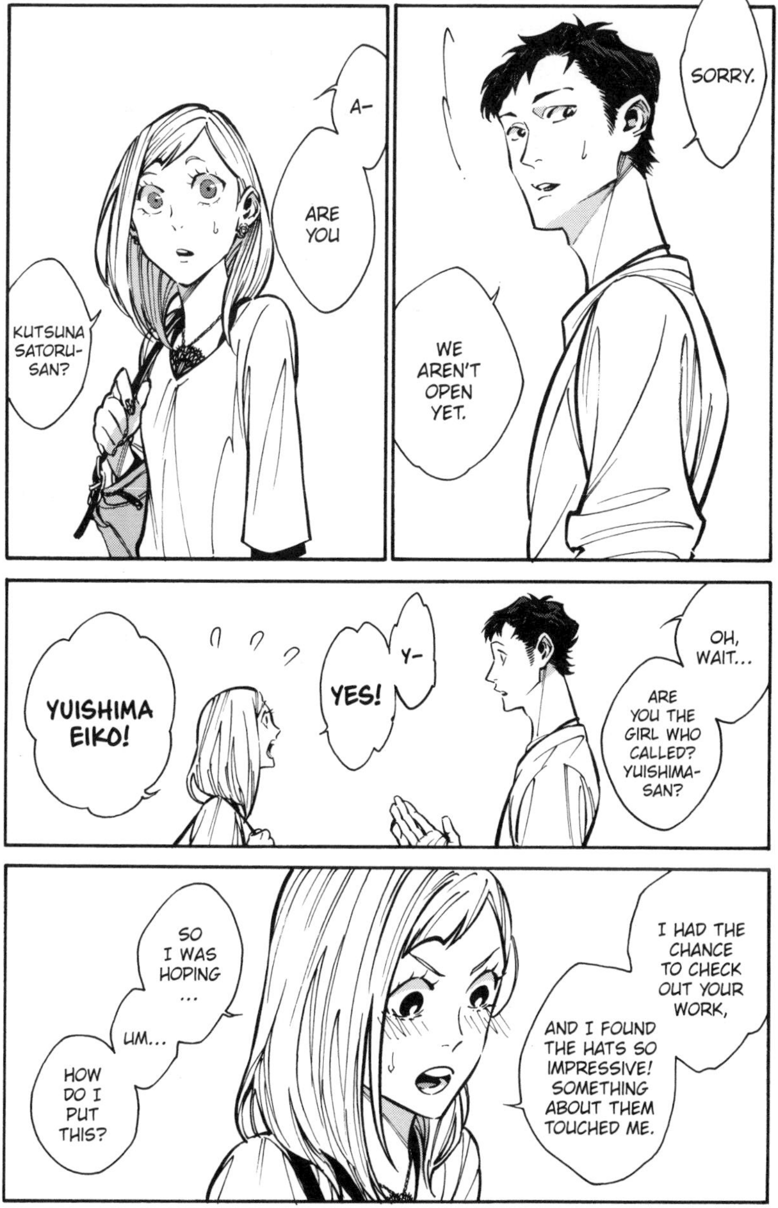
SORRY.
WE AREN'T OPEN YET.
A-
ARE YOU
KUTSUNA SATORU-SAN?
OH, WAIT...
ARE YOU THE GIRL WHO CALLED? YUISHIMA-SAN?
Y-
YES!
YUISHIMA EIKO!
I HAD THE CHANCE TO CHECK OUT YOUR WORK,
AND I FOUND THE HATS SO IMPRESSIVE! SOMETHING ABOUT THEM TOUCHED ME.
SO I WAS HOPING ...
UM...
HOW DO I PUT THIS?

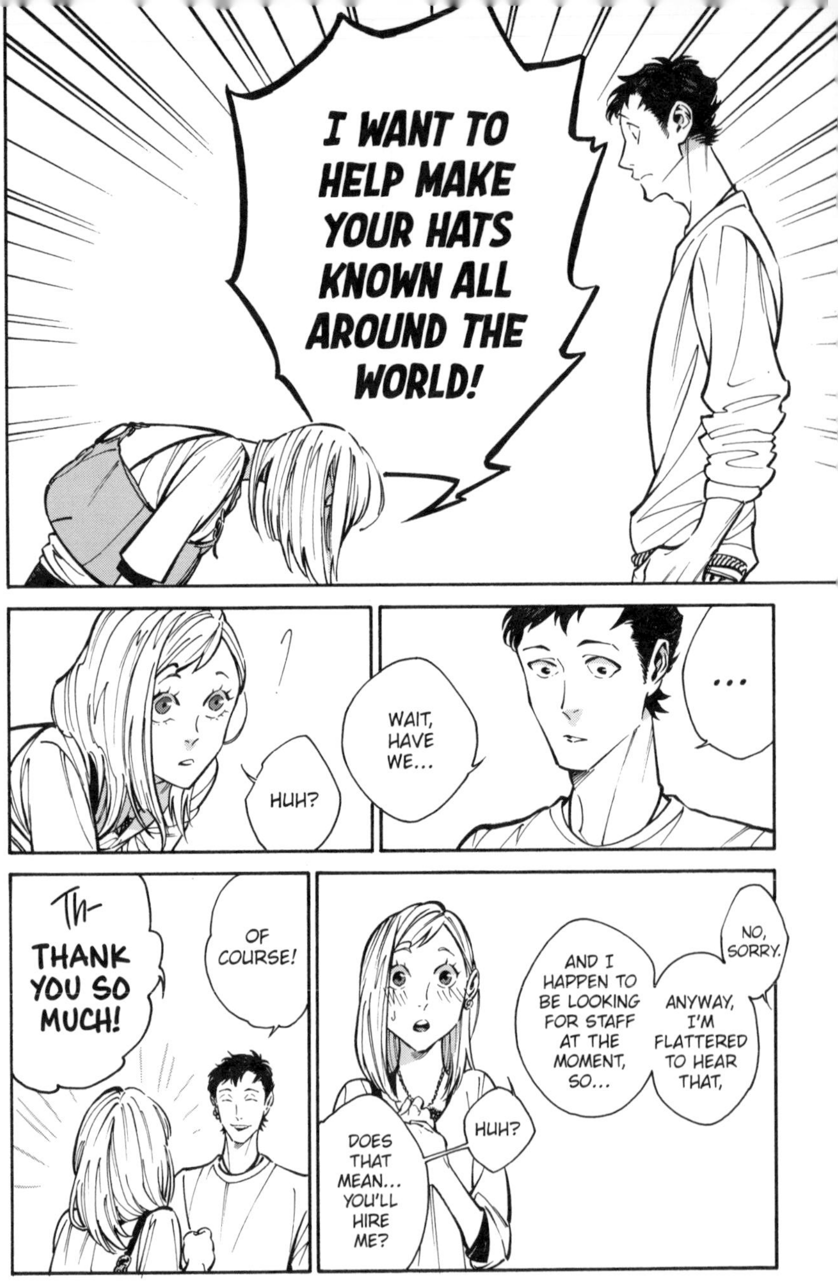
I WANT TO HELP MAKE YOUR HATS KNOWN ALL AROUND THE WORLD!
...
WAIT, HAVE WE...
HUH?
NO, SORRY.
ANYWAY, I'M FLATTERED TO HEAR THAT,
AND I HAPPEN TO BE LOOKING FOR STAFF AT THE MOMENT, SO...
HUH?
DOES THAT MEAN... YOU'LL HIRE ME?
OF COURSE!
Th- THANK YOU SO MUCH!

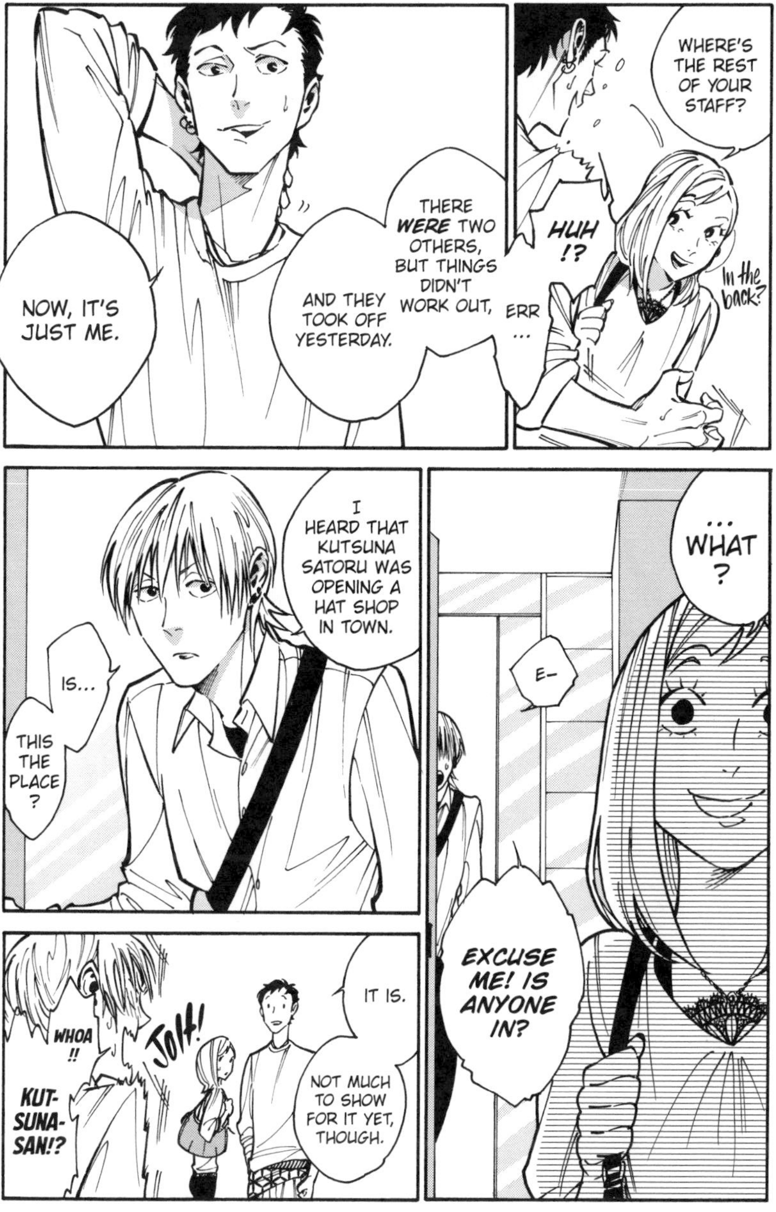
WHERE'S THE REST OF YOUR STAFF?
In the back?
HUH!?
ERR...
THERE WERE TWO OTHERS, BUT THINGS DIDN'T WORK OUT,
AND THEY TOOK OFF YESTERDAY.
NOW, IT'S JUST ME.
...WHAT?
E–
EXCUSE ME! IS ANYONE IN?
I HEARD THAT KUTSUNA SATORU WAS OPENING A HAT SHOP IN TOWN.
IS...
THIS THE PLACE?
IT IS.
NOT MUCH TO SHOW FOR IT YET, THOUGH.
JOLT!
WHOA!!
KUT-SUNA-SAN!?

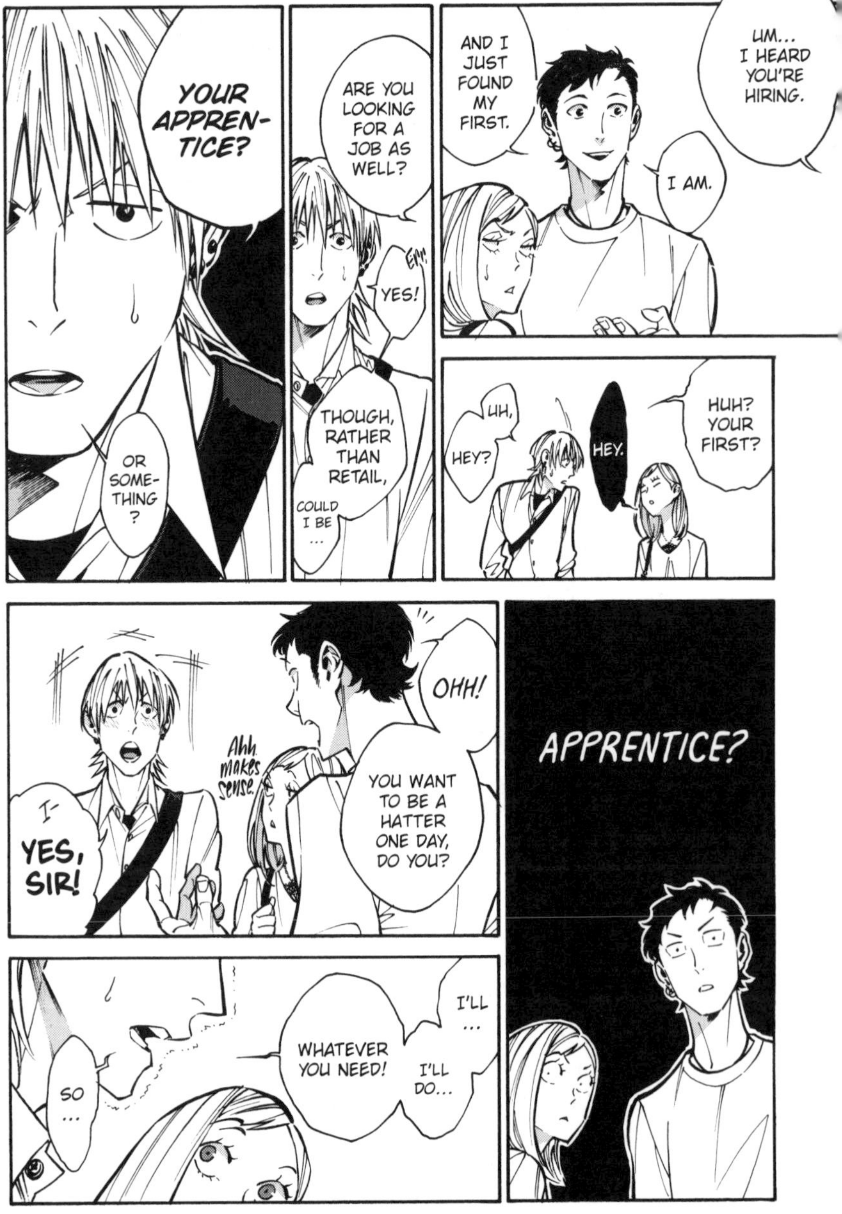
UM... I HEARD YOU'RE HIRING.
I AM.
AND I JUST FOUND MY FIRST.
HUH? YOUR FIRST?
HEY.
UH,
HEY?
ARE YOU LOOKING FOR A JOB AS WELL?
Err,
YES!
THOUGH, RATHER THAN RETAIL,
COULD I BE ...
YOUR APPRENTICE?
OR SOMETHING?
APPRENTICE?
OHH!
YOU WANT TO BE A HATTER ONE DAY, DO YOU?
Ahh. makes sense.
I-
YES, SIR!
I'LL ...
I'LL DO...
WHATEVER YOU NEED!
SO ...

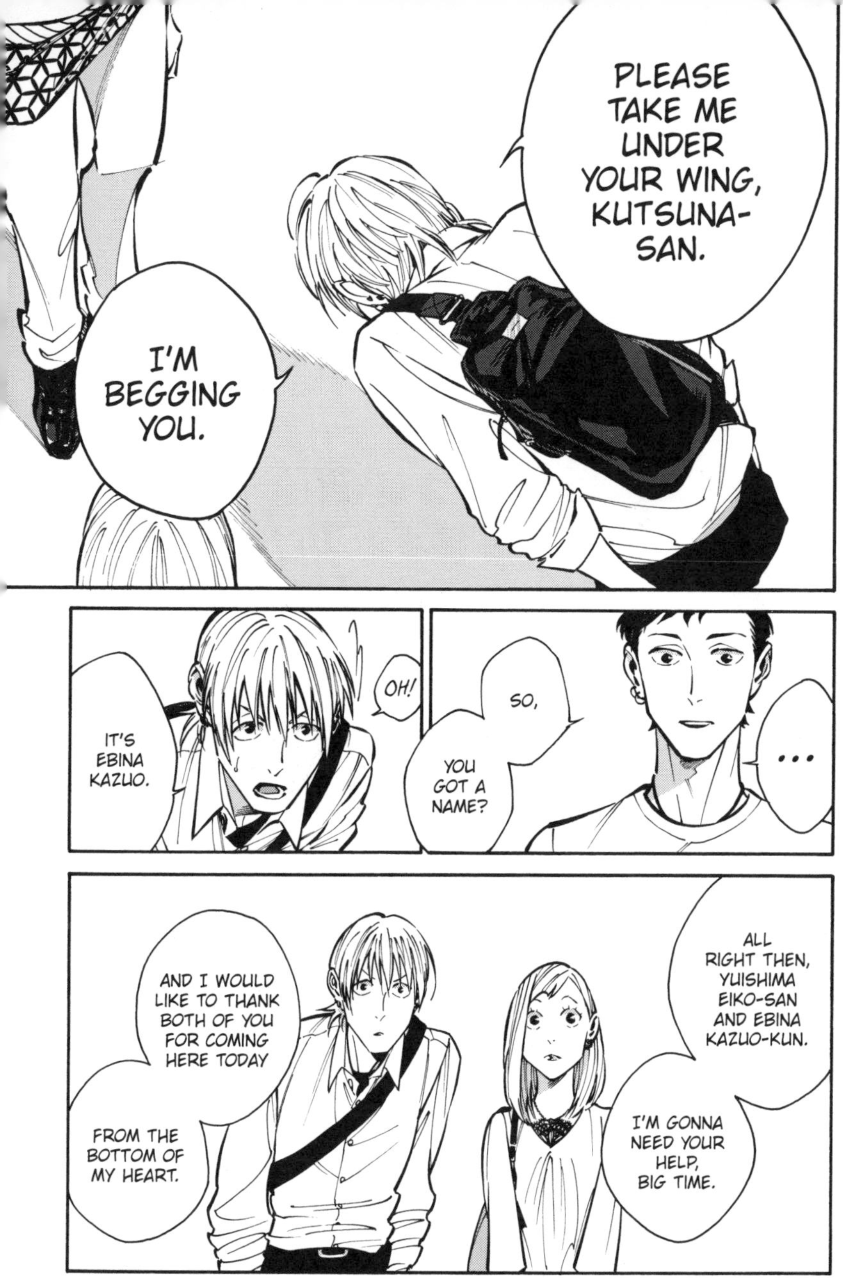
PLEASE TAKE ME UNDER YOUR WING, KUTSUNA-SAN.
I'M BEGGING YOU.
...
SO,
YOU GOT A NAME?
OH!
IT'S EBINA KAZUO.
ALL RIGHT THEN, YUISHIMA EIKO-SAN AND EBINA KAZUO-KUN.
I'M GONNA NEED YOUR HELP, BIG TIME.
AND I WOULD LIKE TO THANK BOTH OF YOU FOR COMING HERE TODAY
FROM THE BOTTOM OF MY HEART.

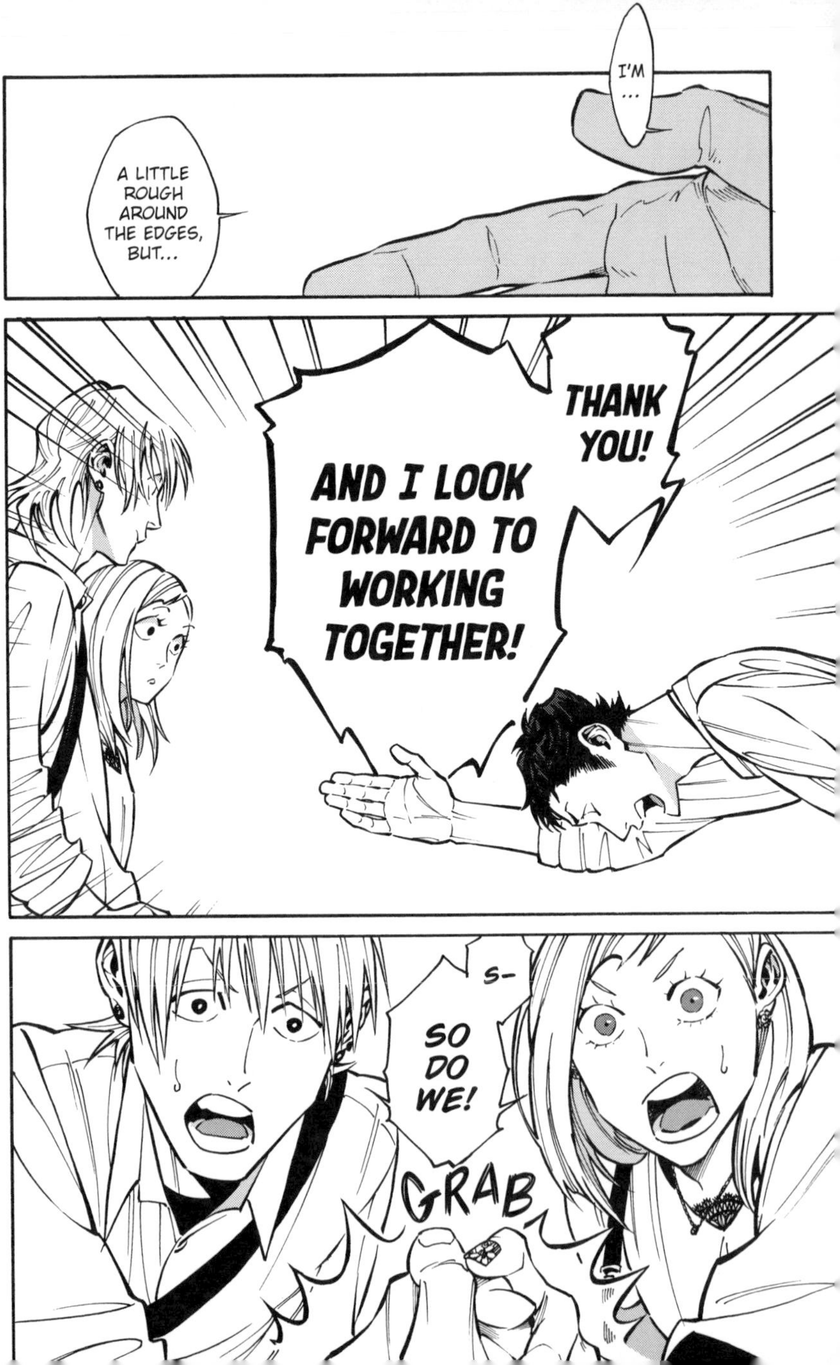
I'M...
A LITTLE ROUGH AROUND THE EDGES, BUT...
THANK YOU!
AND I LOOK FORWARD TO WORKING TOGETHER!
S-
SO DO WE!
GRAB

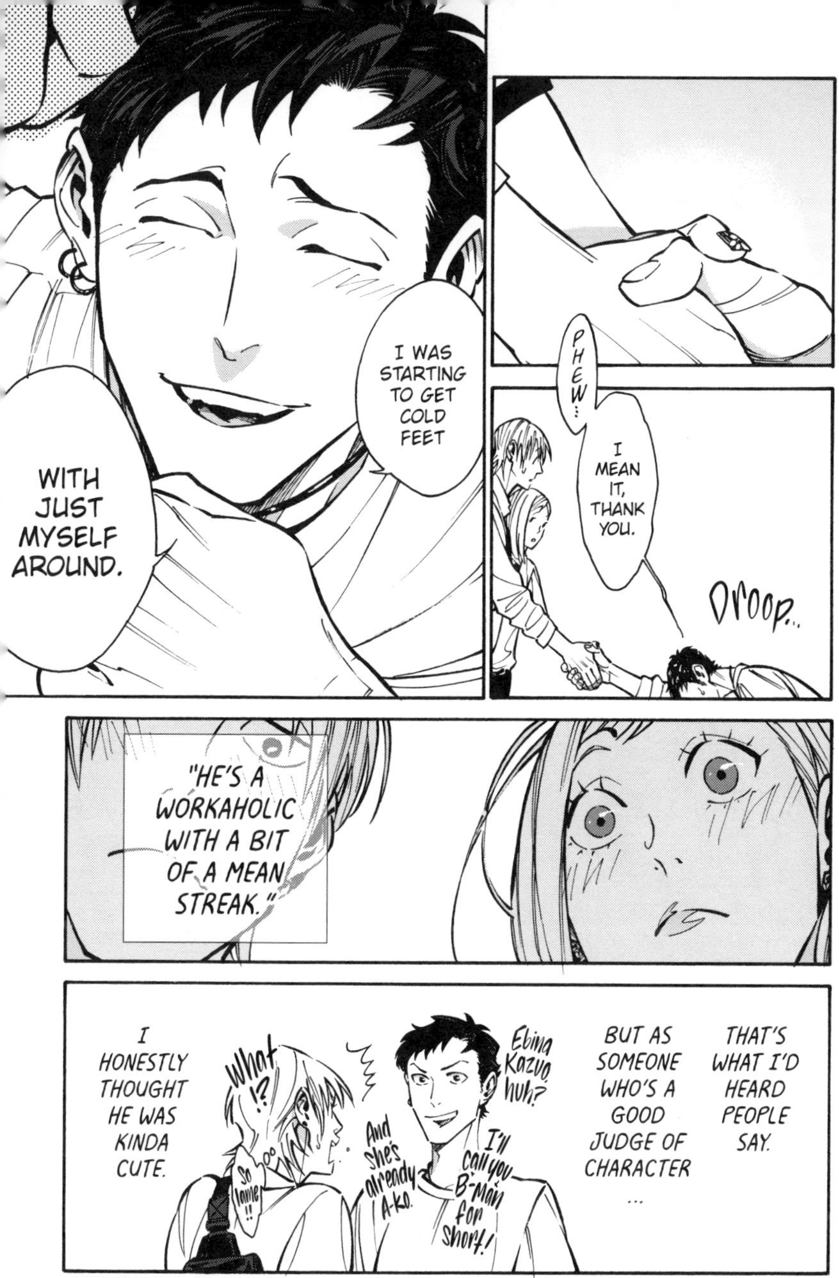
PHEW...
I MEAN IT, THANK YOU.
Droop...
I WAS STARTING TO GET COLD FEET
WITH JUST MYSELF AROUND.
"HE'S A WORKAHOLIC WITH A BIT OF A MEAN STREAK."
THAT'S WHAT I'D HEARD PEOPLE SAY.
BUT AS SOMEONE WHO'S A GOOD JUDGE OF CHARACTER ...
Ebina Kazuo huh?
I'll call you B-Man for short!
And she's already A-ko.
What!?
So lame!!
I HONESTLY THOUGHT HE WAS KINDA CUTE.

NOTE: EIKO IS PRONOUNCED A-KO.

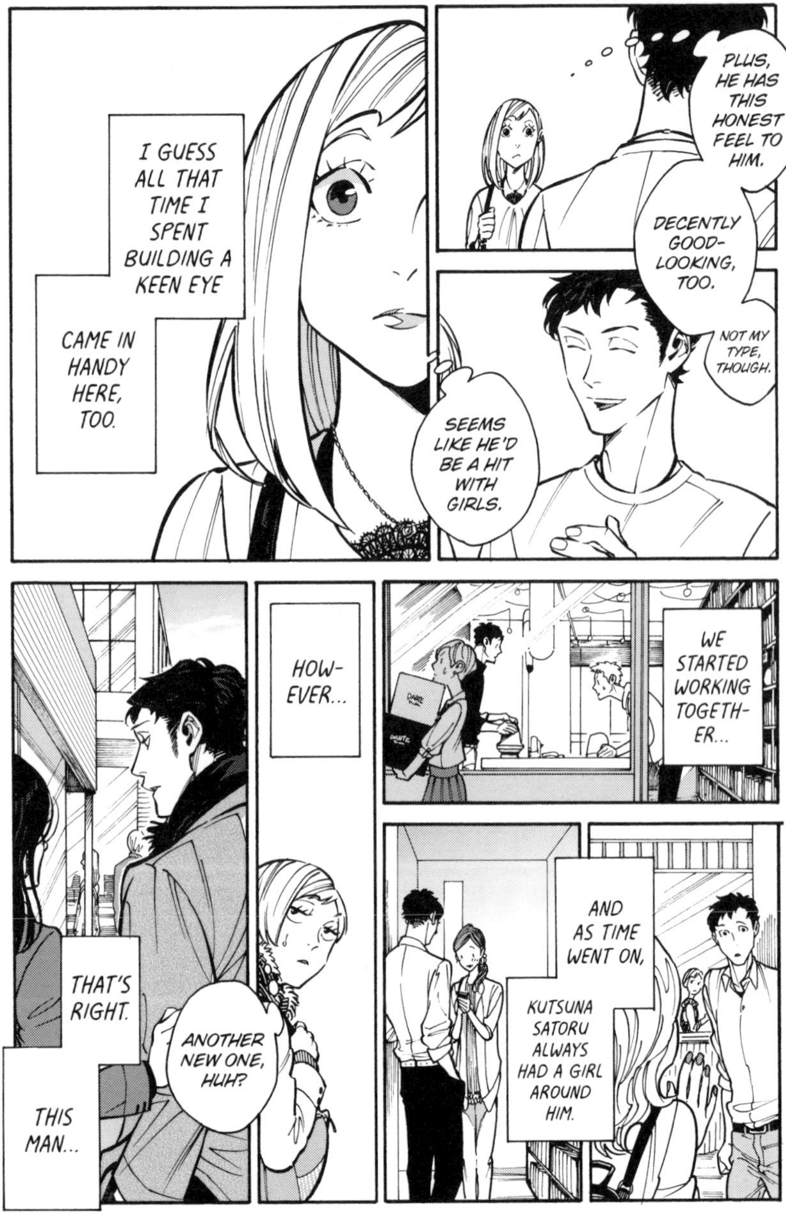
PLUS, HE HAS THIS HONEST FEEL TO HIM.
DECENTLY GOOD-LOOKING, TOO.
NOT MY TYPE, THOUGH.
SEEMS LIKE HE'D BE A HIT WITH GIRLS.
I GUESS ALL THAT TIME I SPENT BUILDING A KEEN EYE
CAME IN HANDY HERE, TOO.
WE STARTED WORKING TOGETH-ER...
AND AS TIME WENT ON,
KUTSUNA SATORU ALWAYS HAD A GIRL AROUND HIM.
HOW-EVER...
THAT'S RIGHT.
ANOTHER NEW ONE, HUH?
THIS MAN...

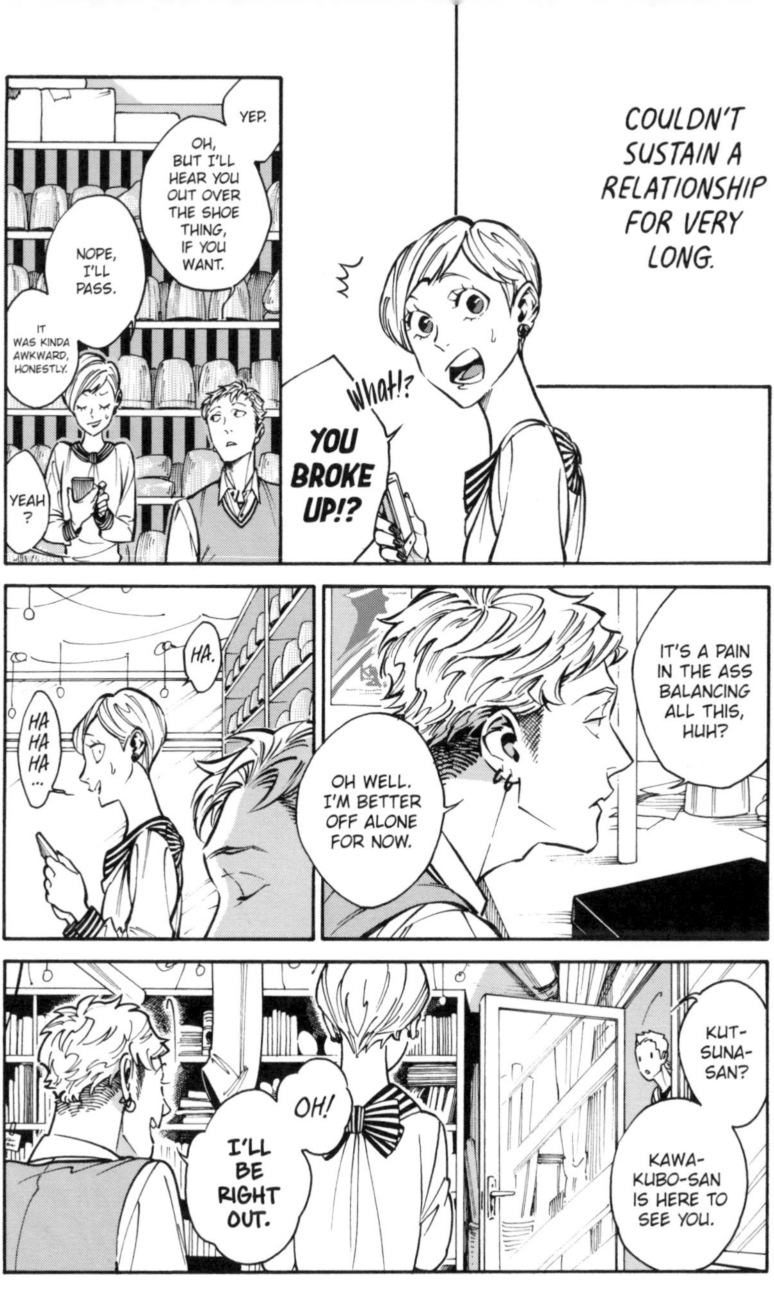
COULDN'T SUSTAIN A RELATIONSHIP FOR VERY LONG.
What!?
YOU BROKE UP!?
YEP.
OH, BUT I'LL HEAR YOU OUT OVER THE SHOE THING, IF YOU WANT.
NOPE, I'LL PASS.
IT WAS KINDA AWKWARD, HONESTLY.
YEAH?
IT'S A PAIN IN THE ASS BALANCING ALL THIS, HUH?
OH WELL. I'M BETTER OFF ALONE FOR NOW.
HA.
HA HA HA ...
KUT-SUNA-SAN?
KAWA-KUBO-SAN IS HERE TO SEE YOU.
OH!
I'LL BE RIGHT OUT.

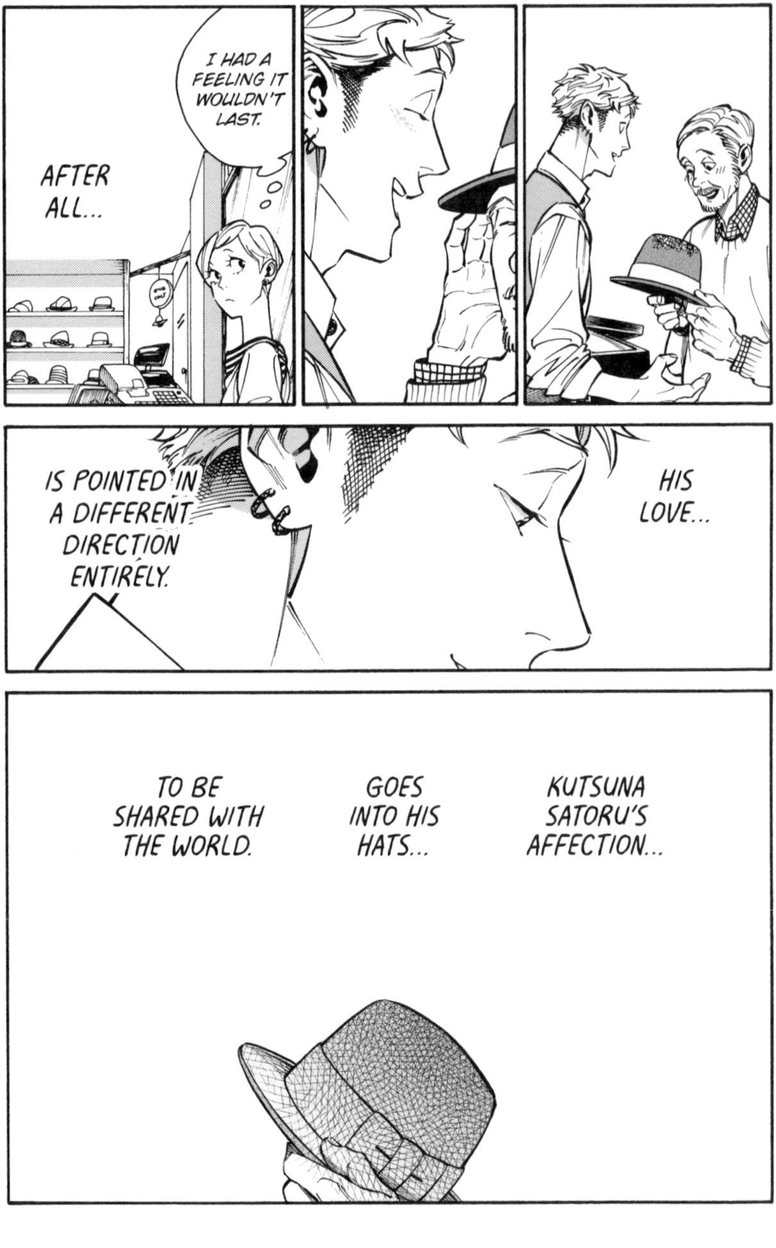
I HAD A FEELING IT WOULDN'T LAST.
AFTER ALL...
HIS LOVE...
IS POINTED IN A DIFFERENT DIRECTION ENTIRELY.
KUTSUNA SATORU'S AFFECTION...
GOES INTO HIS HATS...
TO BE SHARED WITH THE WORLD.

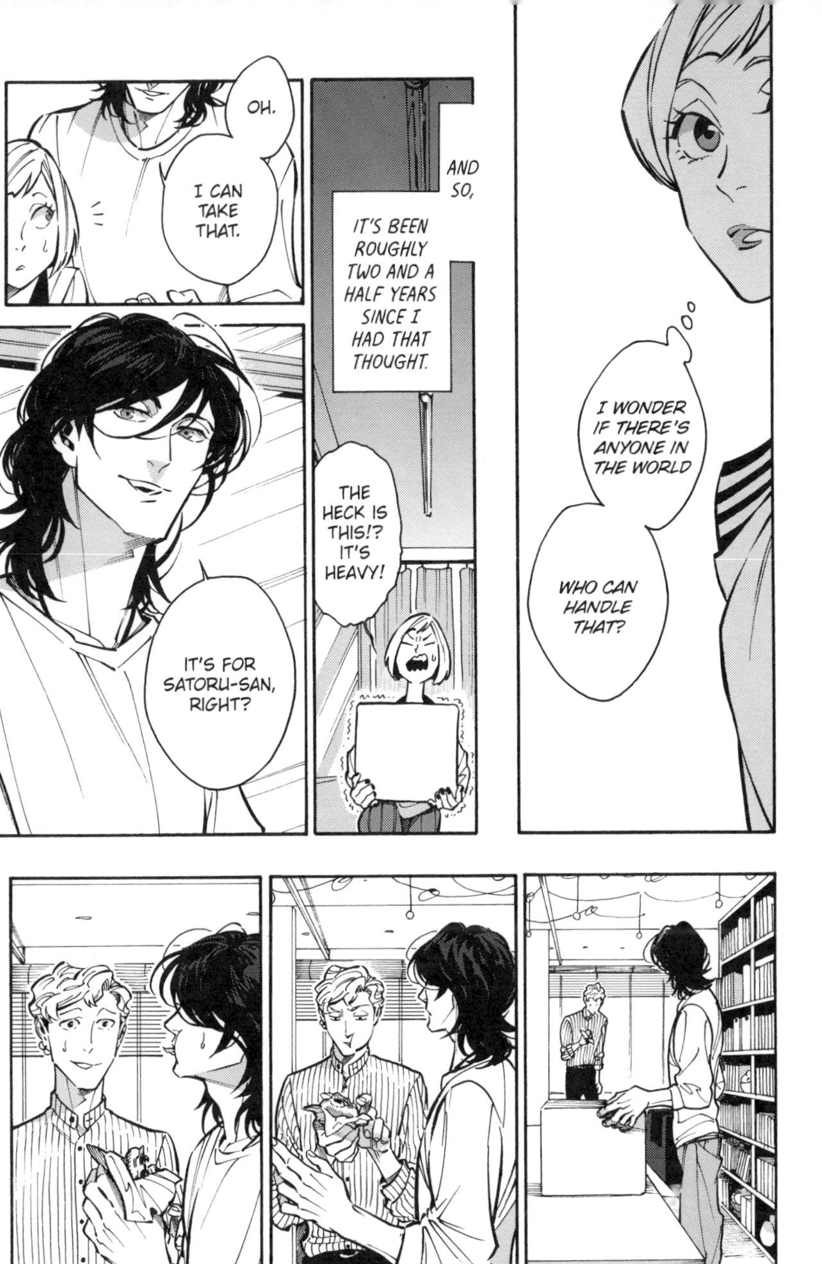
I WONDER IF THERE'S ANYONE IN THE WORLD
WHO CAN HANDLE THAT?
AND SO,
IT'S BEEN ROUGHLY TWO AND A HALF YEARS SINCE I HAD THAT THOUGHT.
THE HECK IS THIS!? IT'S HEAVY!
OH.
I CAN TAKE THAT.
IT'S FOR SATORU-SAN, RIGHT?

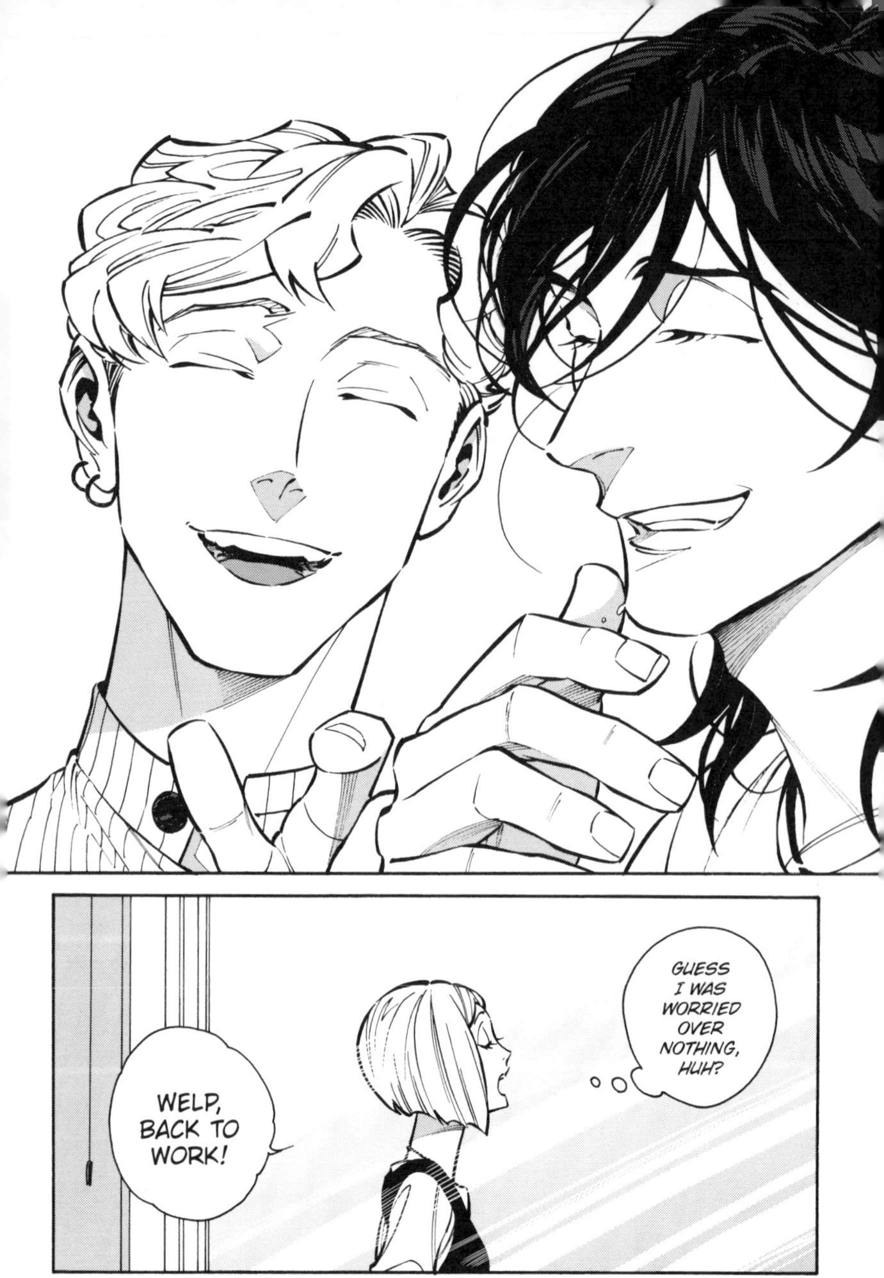
GUESS I WAS WORRIED OVER NOTHING, HUH?
WELP, BACK TO WORK!

CANIS —DEAR HATTER— EXTRA 3/END

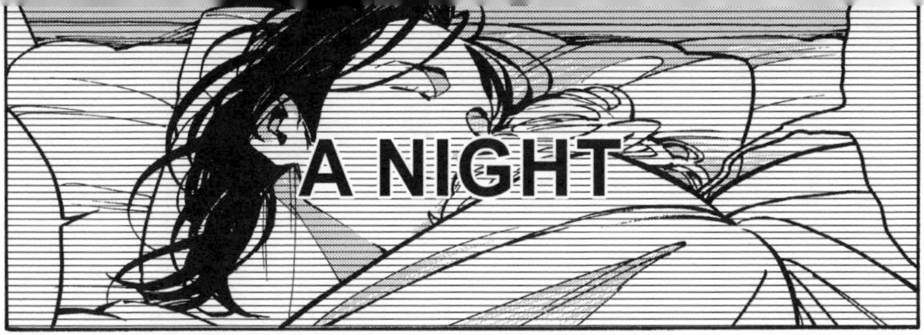
A NIGHT

Roughly One Month in the Future

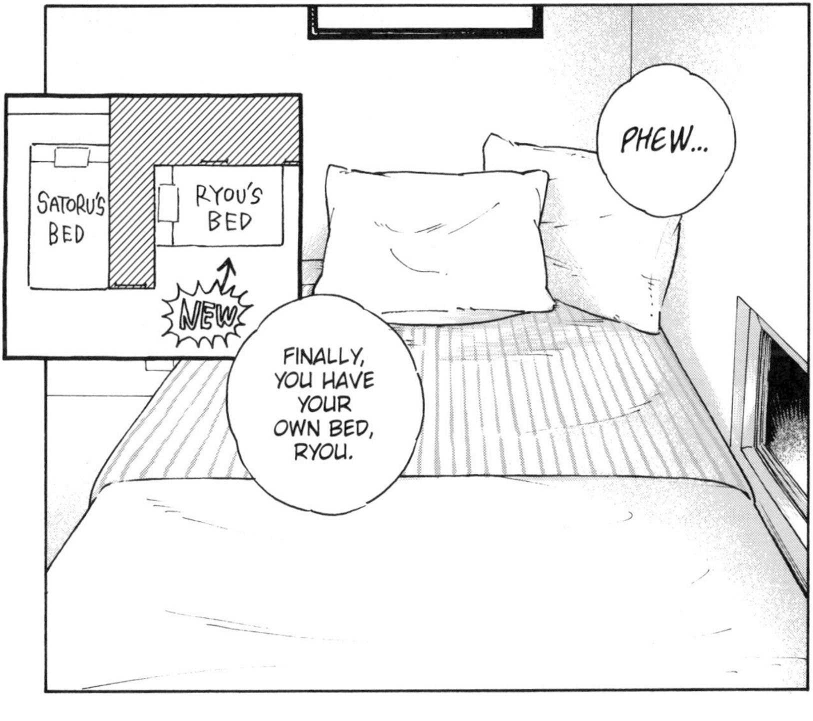
PHEW...
RYOU'S BED
NEW
SATORU'S BED
FINALLY, YOU HAVE YOUR OWN BED, RYOU.

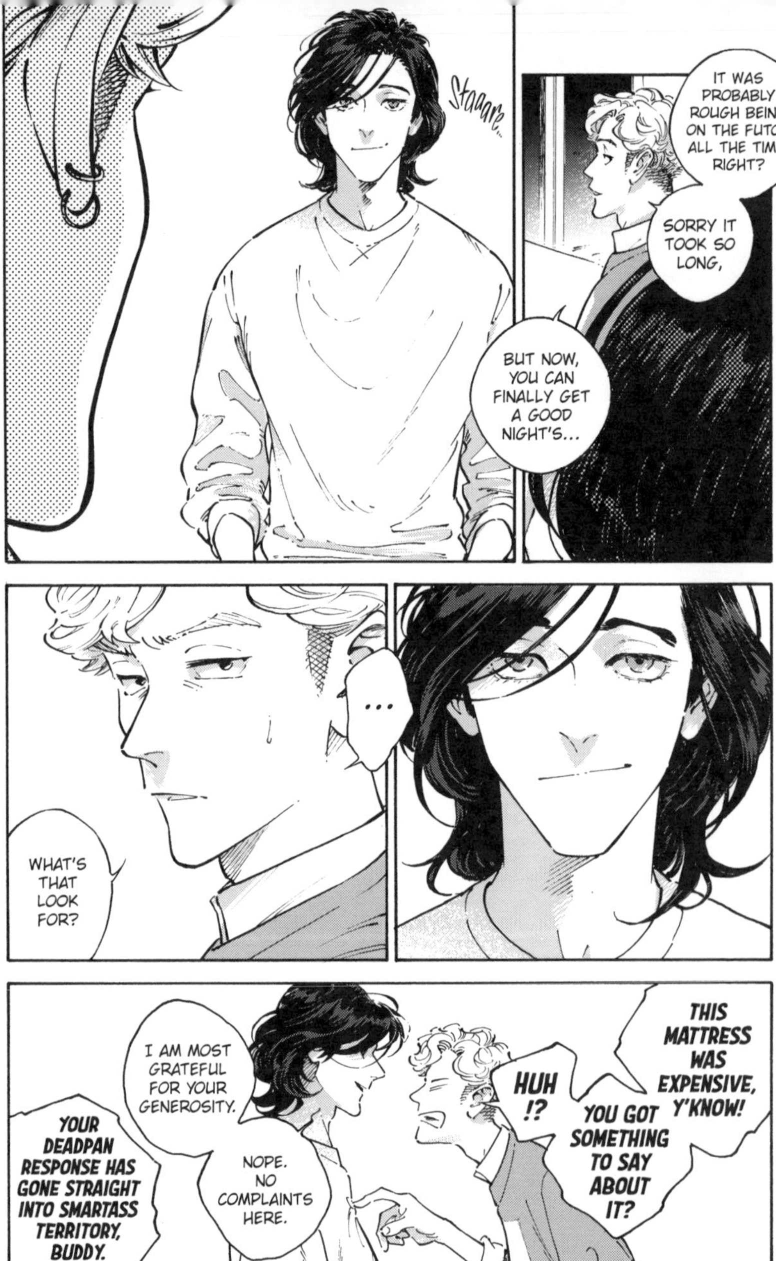
IT WAS PROBABLY ROUGH BEING ON THE FUTON ALL THE TIME, RIGHT?
SORRY IT TOOK SO LONG,
BUT NOW, YOU CAN FINALLY GET A GOOD NIGHT'S...
Staaare...
...
WHAT'S THAT LOOK FOR?
THIS MATTRESS WAS EXPENSIVE, Y'KNOW!
HUH!?
YOU GOT SOMETHING TO SAY ABOUT IT?
I AM MOST GRATEFUL FOR YOUR GENEROSITY.
NOPE. NO COMPLAINTS HERE.
YOUR DEADPAN RESPONSE HAS GONE STRAIGHT INTO SMARTASS TERRITORY, BUDDY.

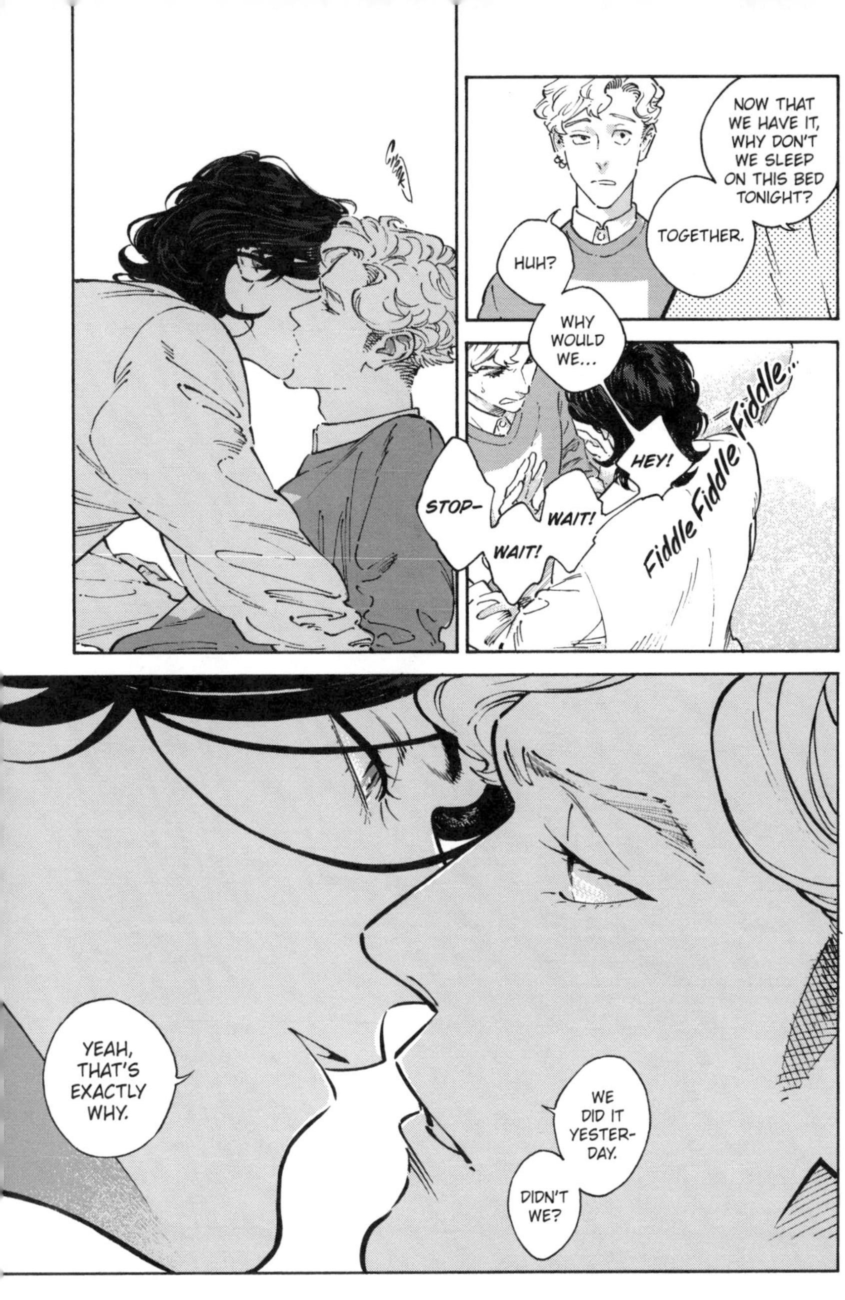
NOW THAT WE HAVE IT, WHY DON'T WE SLEEP ON THIS BED TONIGHT?
TOGETHER.
HUH?
WHY WOULD WE...
HEY!
WAIT!
STOP-
WAIT!
Fiddle Fiddle Fiddle...
CREAK
WE DID IT YESTER-DAY.
DIDN'T WE?
YEAH, THAT'S EXACTLY WHY.

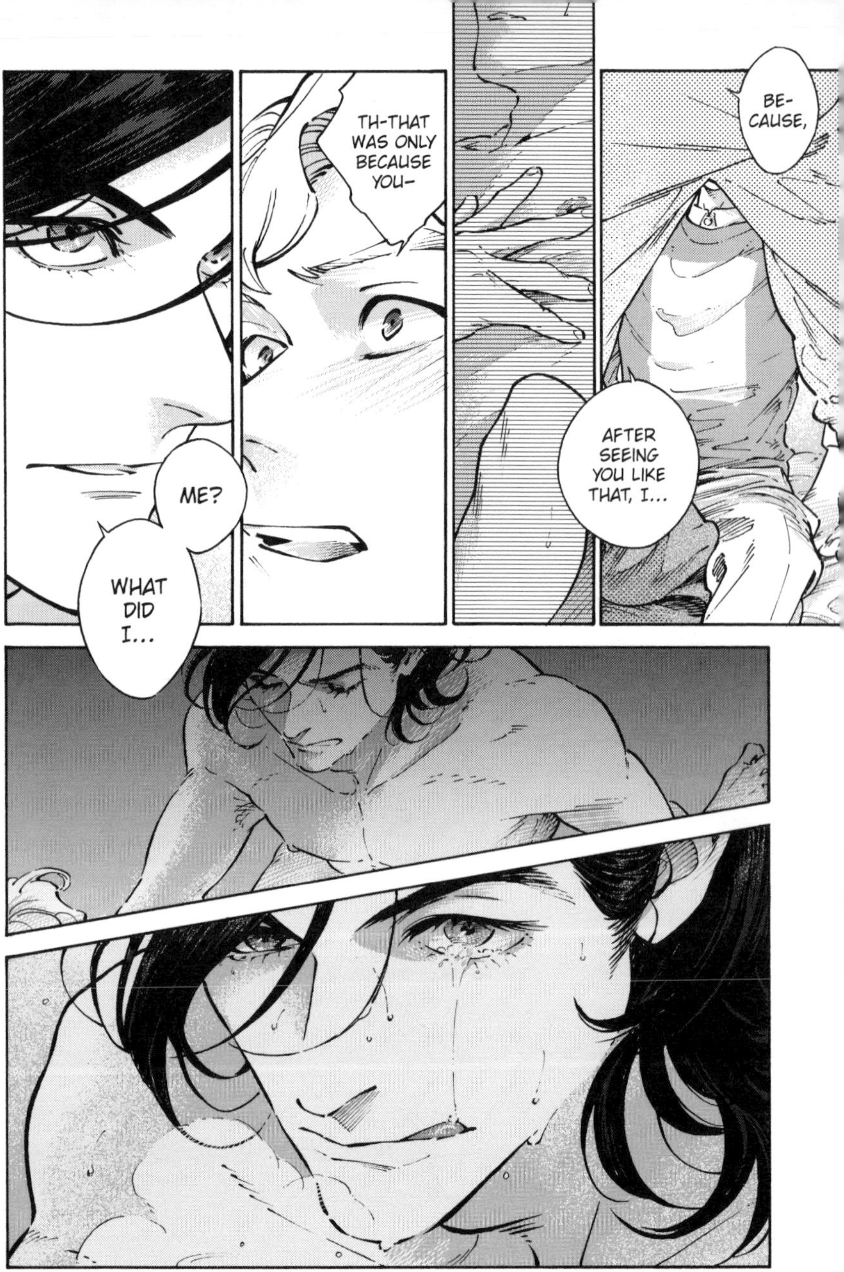
BE-CAUSE,
AFTER SEEING YOU LIKE THAT, I...
TH-THAT WAS ONLY BECAUSE YOU-
ME?
WHAT DID I...

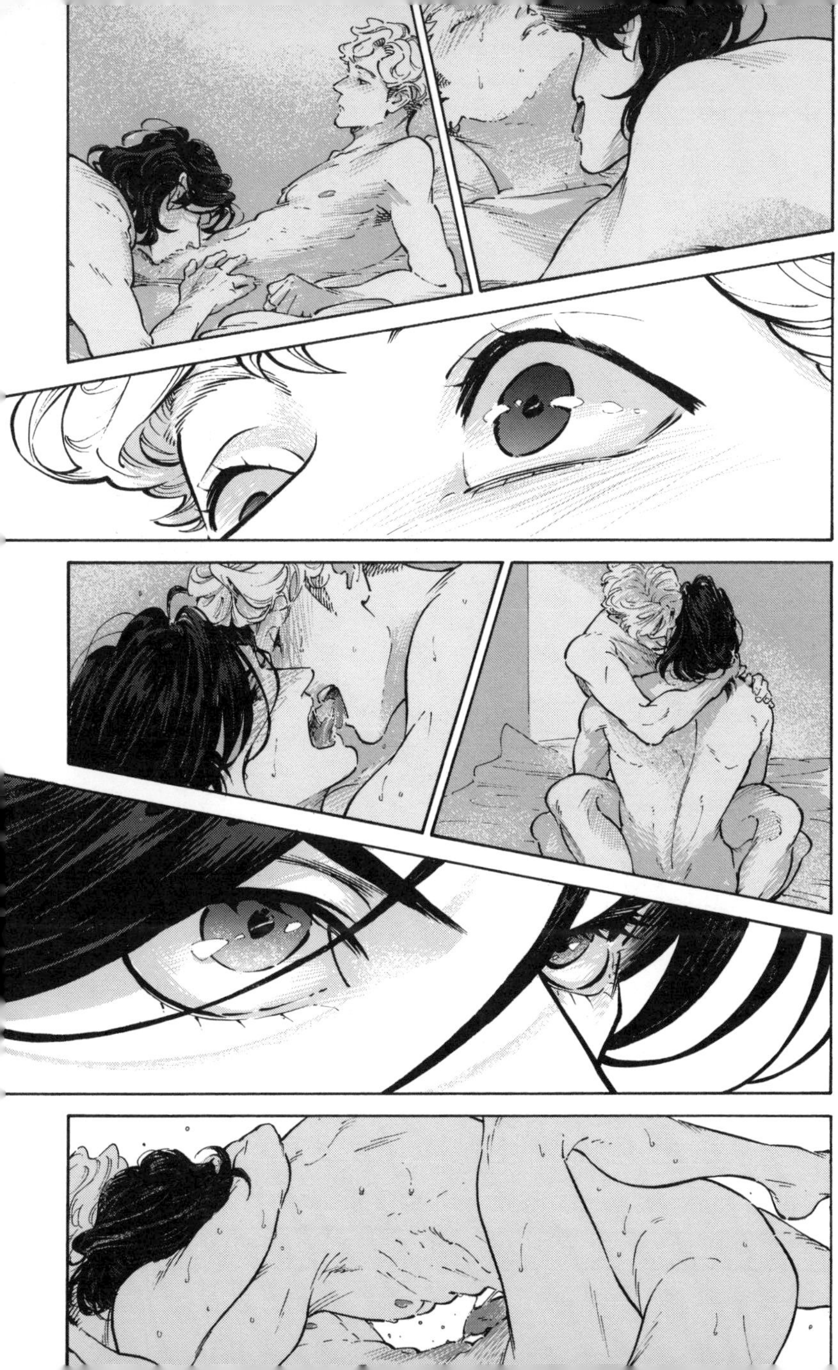

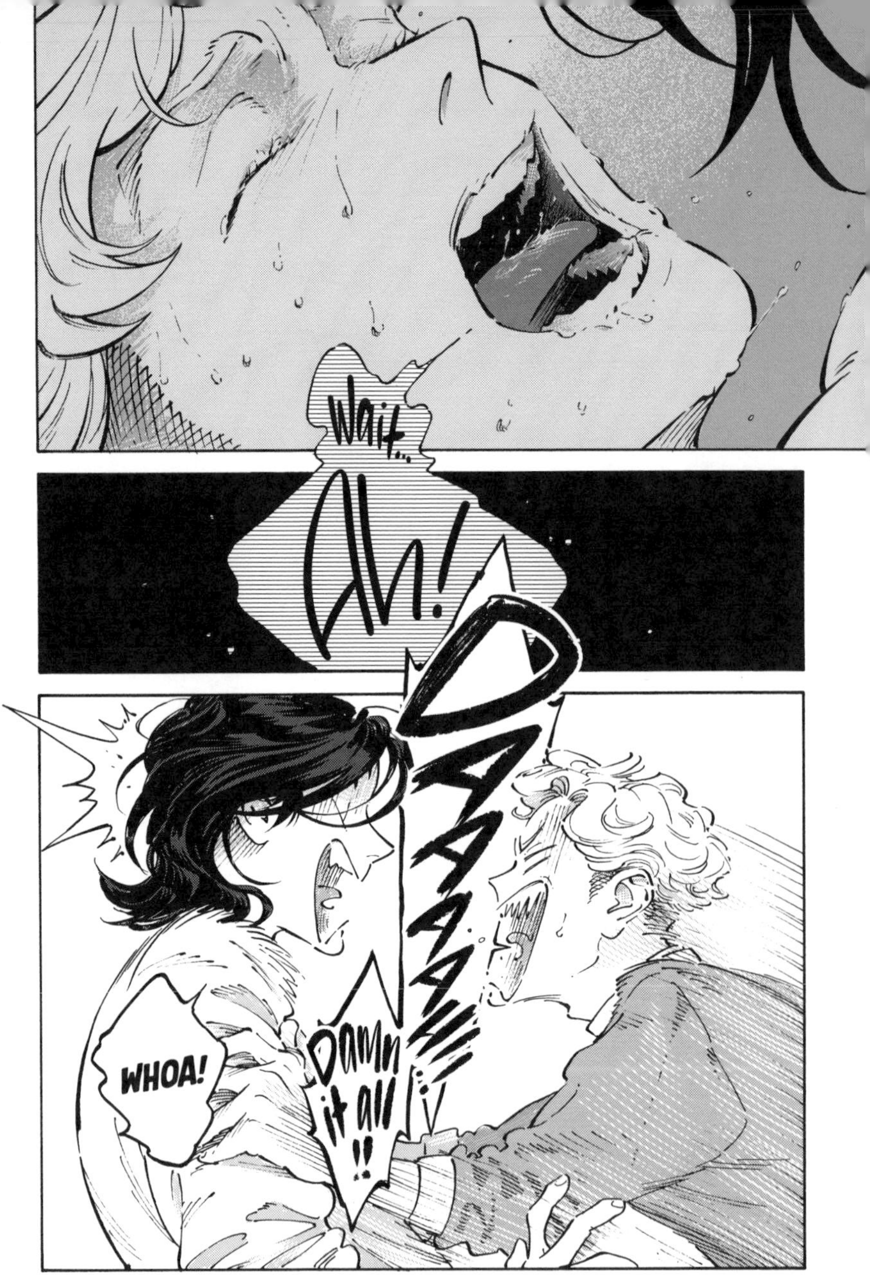

Wait... Ah!
DAAAAAH!!!
Damn it all!!
WHOA!

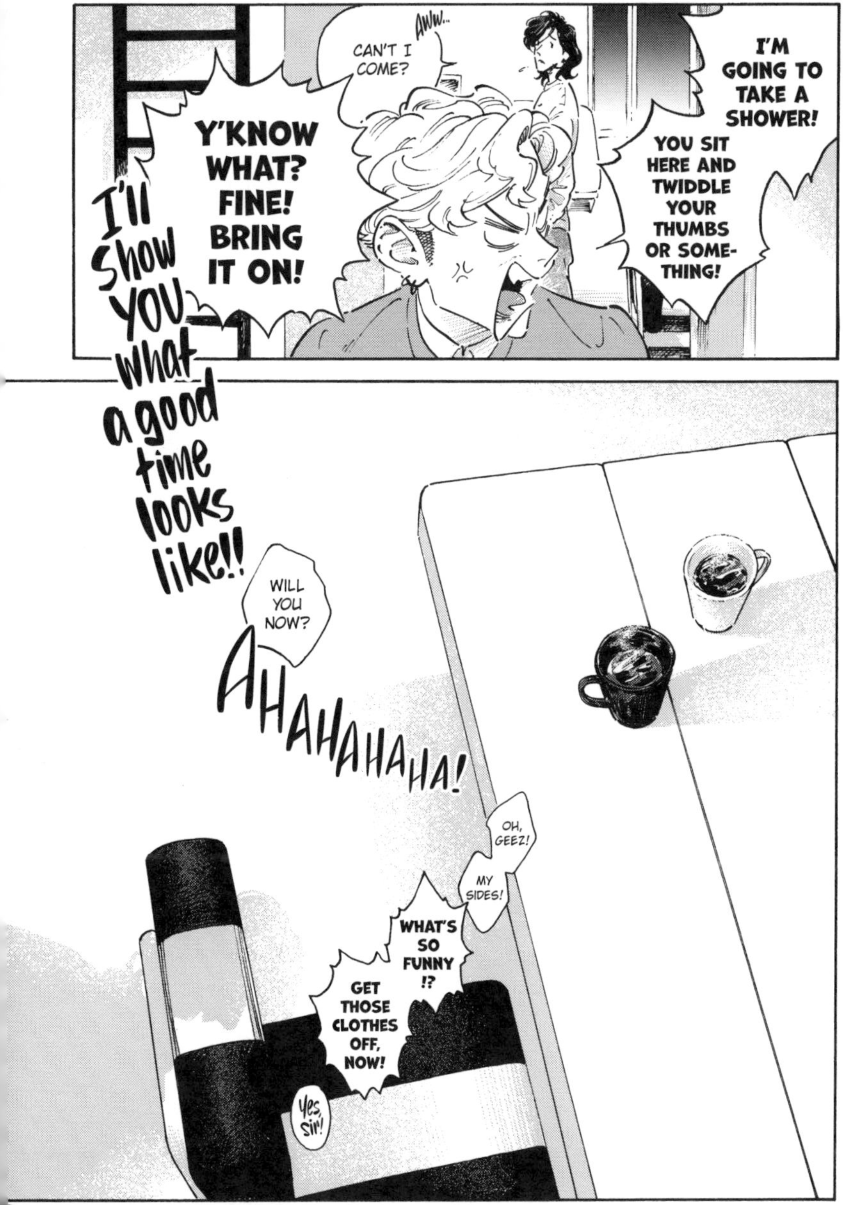
I'M GOING TO TAKE A SHOWER!
YOU SIT HERE AND TWIDDLE YOUR THUMBS OR SOME-THING!
AWW...
CAN'T I COME?
Y'KNOW WHAT? FINE! BRING IT ON!
I'll show you what a good time looks like!!
WILL YOU NOW?
AHAHAHAHAHA!
OH, GEEZ!
MY SIDES!
WHAT'S SO FUNNY!?
GET THOSE CLOTHES OFF, NOW!
Yes, sir!

END.

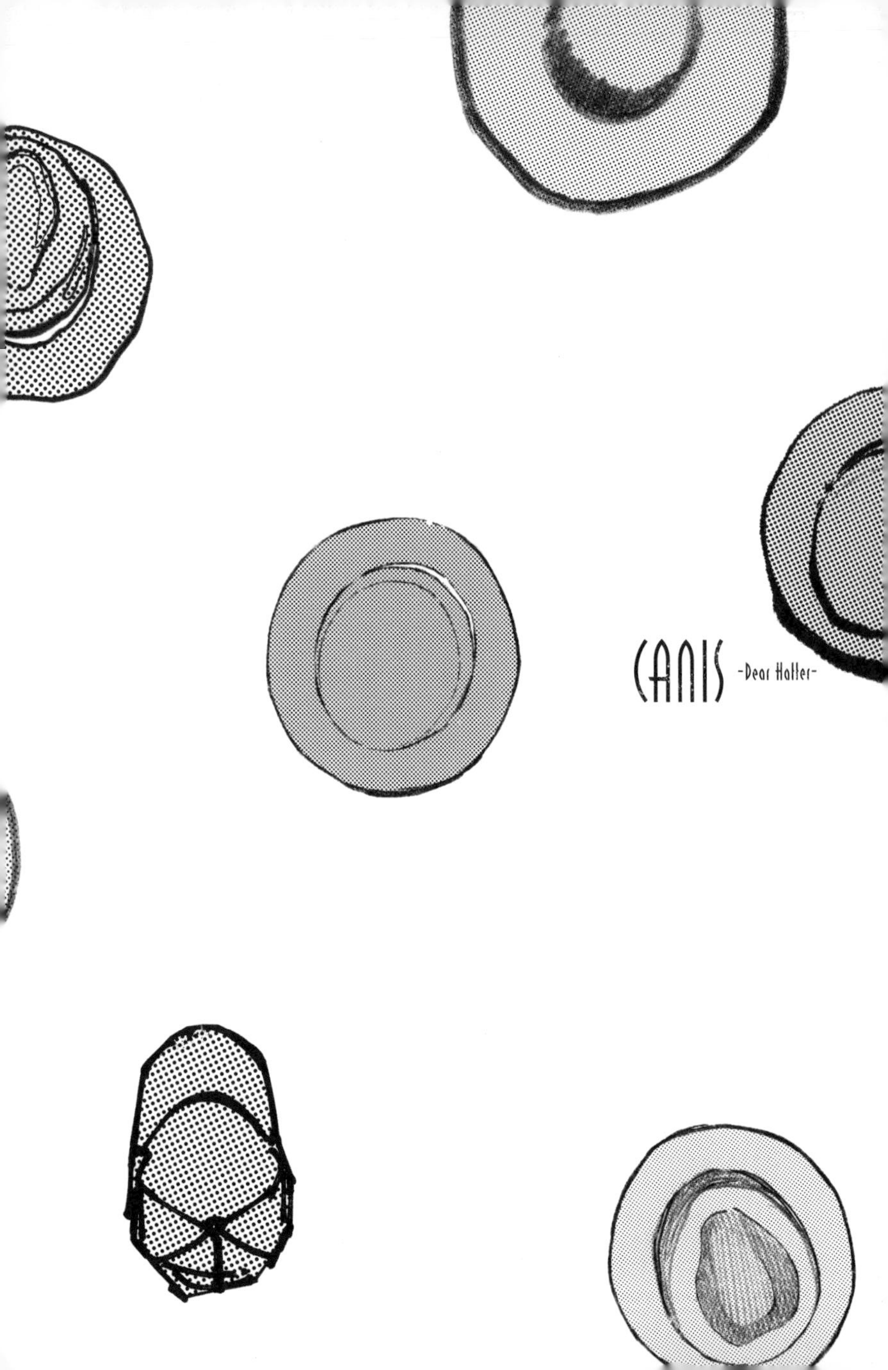
CANIS -Dear Hatter-

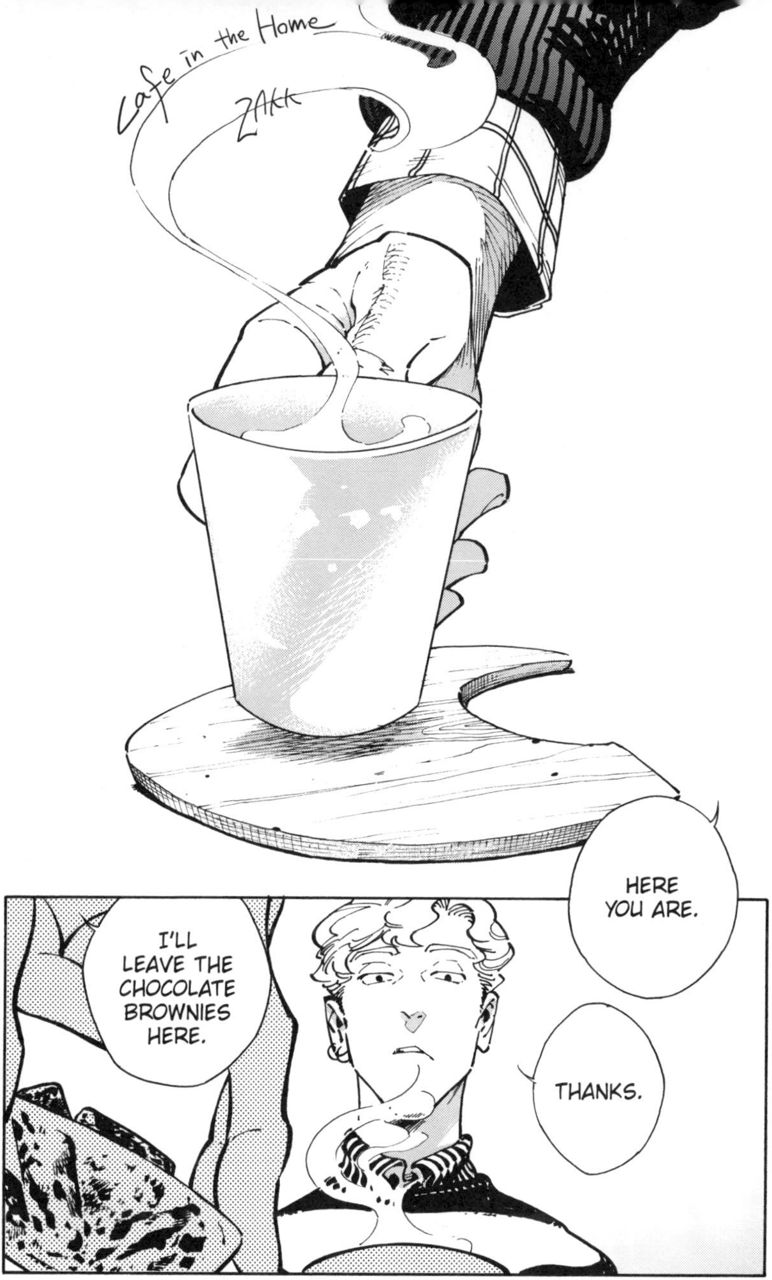
Cafe in the Home
ZAKK
HERE YOU ARE.
THANKS.
I'LL LEAVE THE CHOCOLATE BROWNIES HERE.

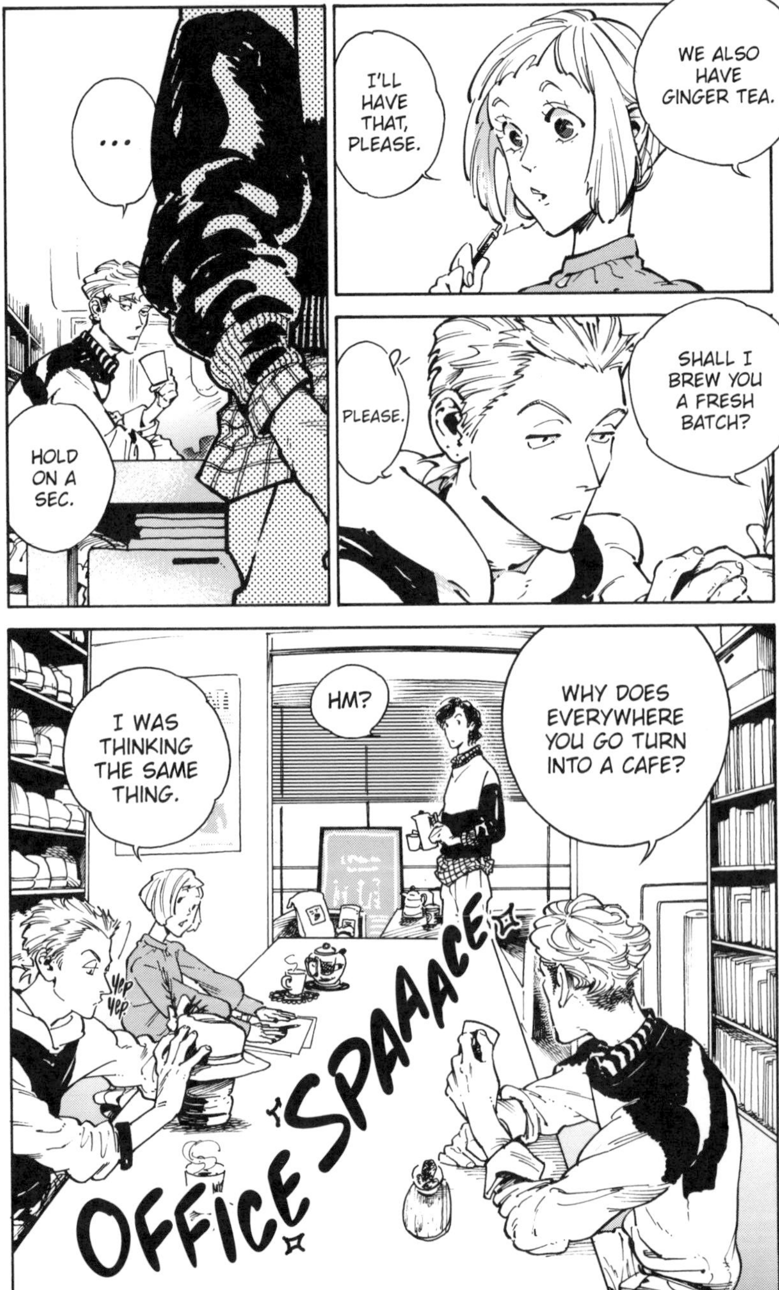
WE ALSO HAVE GINGER TEA.
I'LL HAVE THAT, PLEASE.
SHALL I BREW YOU A FRESH BATCH?
PLEASE.
...
HOLD ON A SEC.
WHY DOES EVERYWHERE YOU GO TURN INTO A CAFE?
HM?
I WAS THINKING THE SAME THING.
YEP YEP
OFFICE SPAAACE

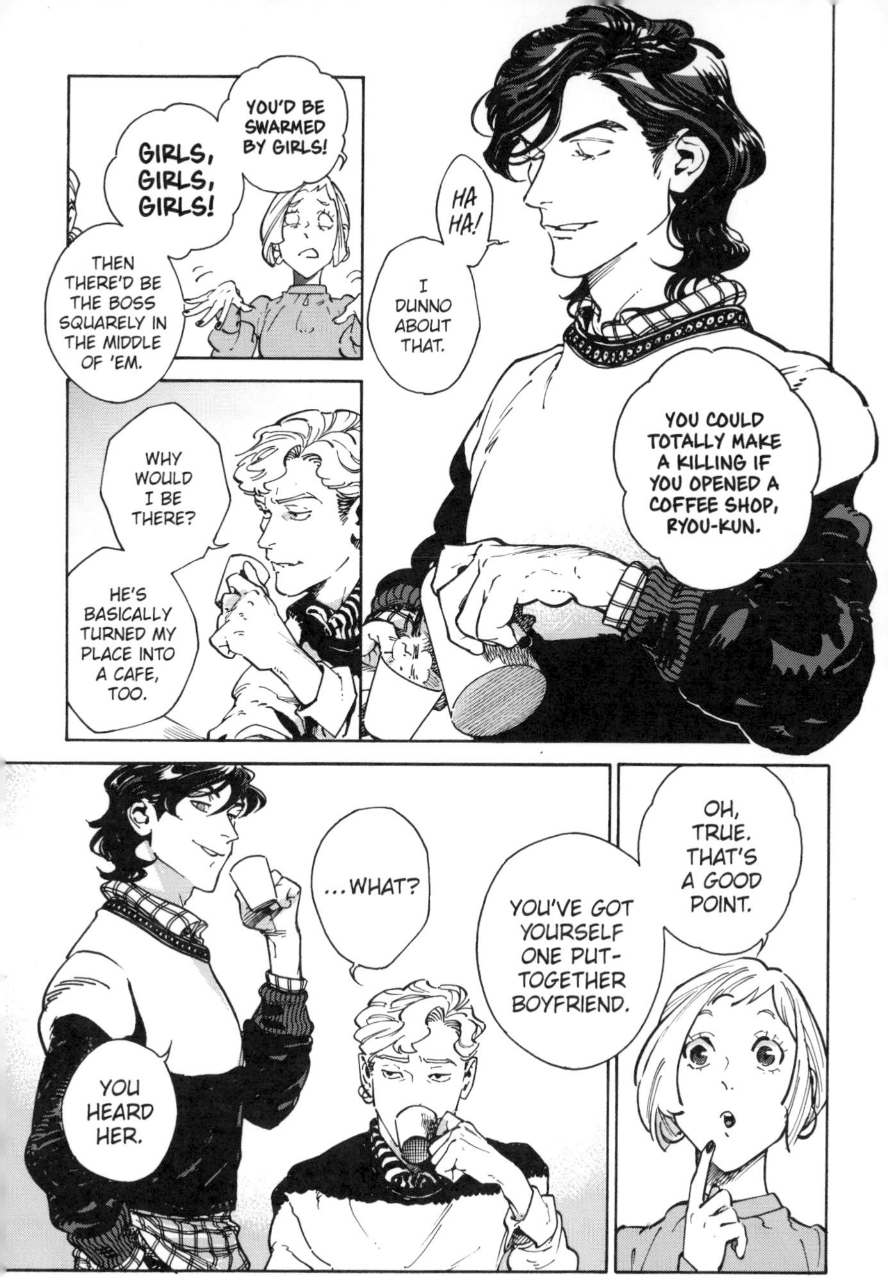
YOU COULD TOTALLY MAKE A KILLING IF YOU OPENED A COFFEE SHOP, RYOU-KUN.
HA HA!
I DUNNO ABOUT THAT.
YOU'D BE SWARMED BY GIRLS!
GIRLS, GIRLS, GIRLS!
THEN THERE'D BE THE BOSS SQUARELY IN THE MIDDLE OF 'EM.
WHY WOULD I BE THERE?
HE'S BASICALLY TURNED MY PLACE INTO A CAFE, TOO.
OH, TRUE. THAT'S A GOOD POINT.
YOU'VE GOT YOURSELF ONE PUT-TOGETHER BOYFRIEND.
...WHAT?
YOU HEARD HER.

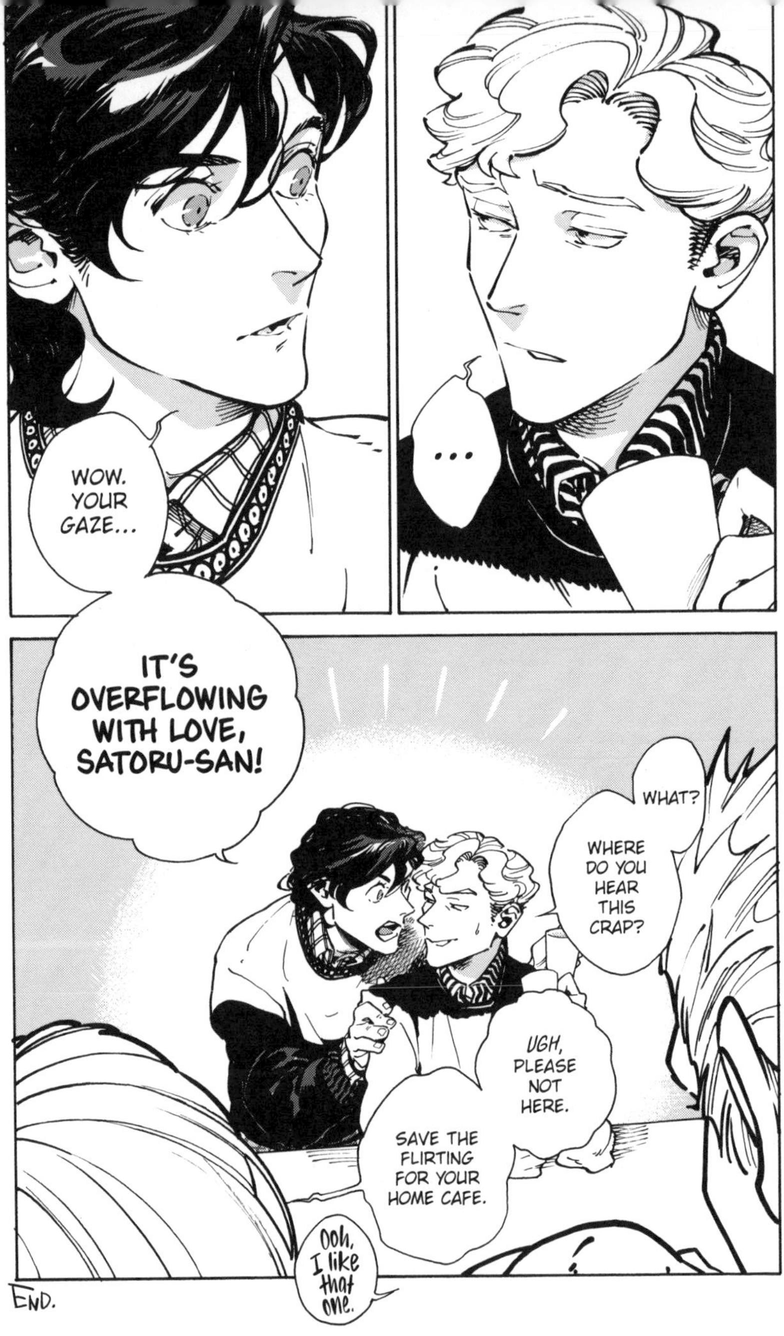
...
WOW. YOUR GAZE...
IT'S OVERFLOWING WITH LOVE, SATORU-SAN!
WHAT?
WHERE DO YOU HEAR THIS CRAP?
UGH, PLEASE NOT HERE.
SAVE THE FLIRTING FOR YOUR HOME CAFE.
Ooh, I like that one.
END.

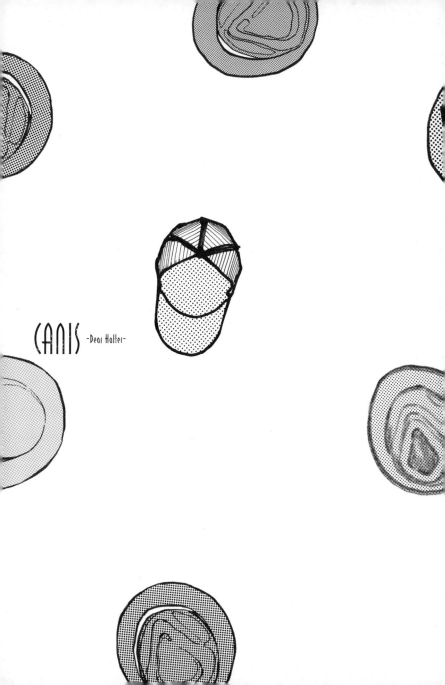

CANIS -Dear Hatter-

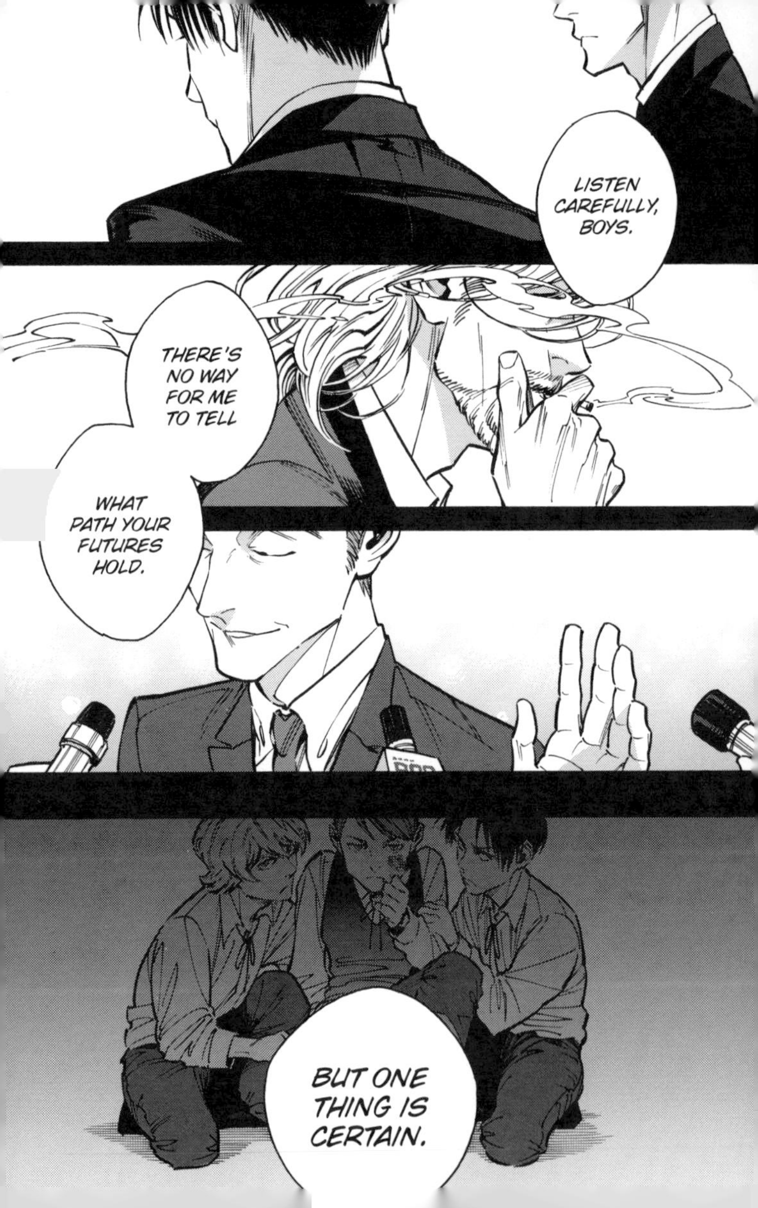
LISTEN CAREFULLY, BOYS.
THERE'S NO WAY FOR ME TO TELL
WHAT PATH YOUR FUTURES HOLD.
BUT ONE THING IS CERTAIN.

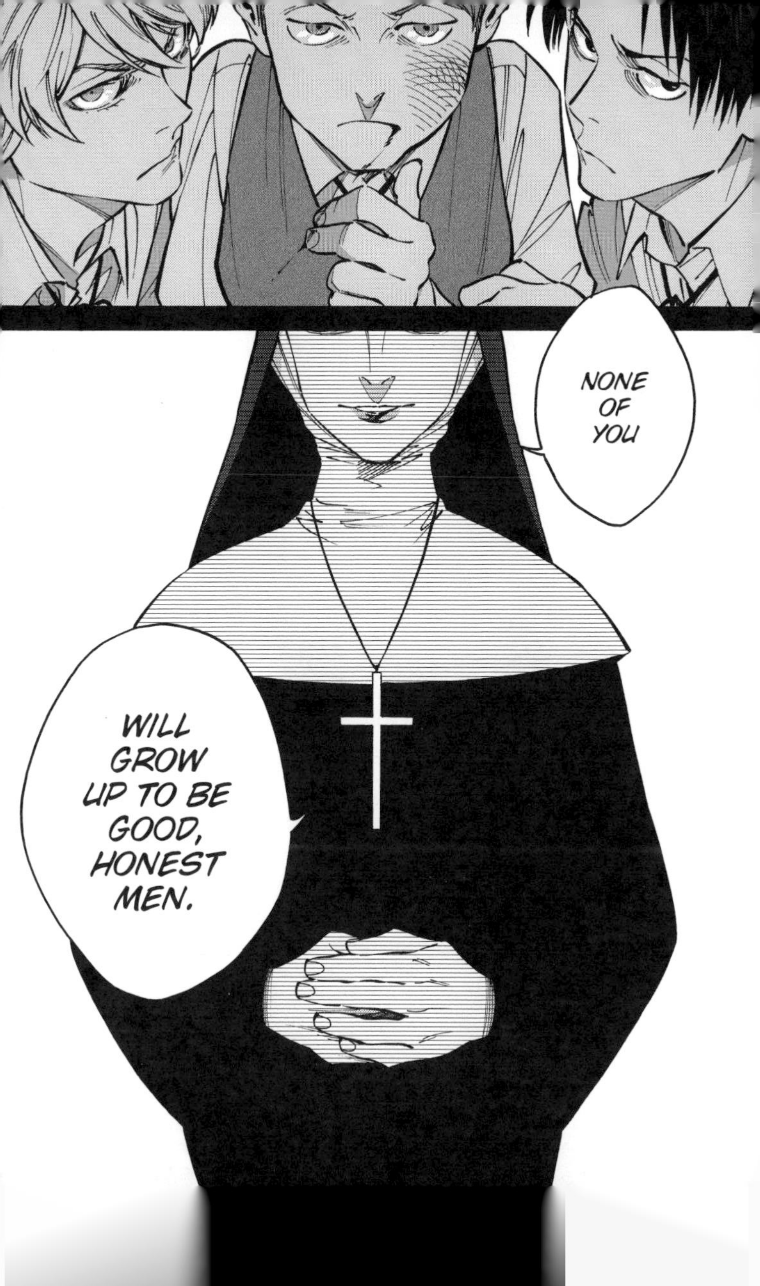
NONE OF YOU
WILL GROW UP TO BE GOOD, HONEST MEN.

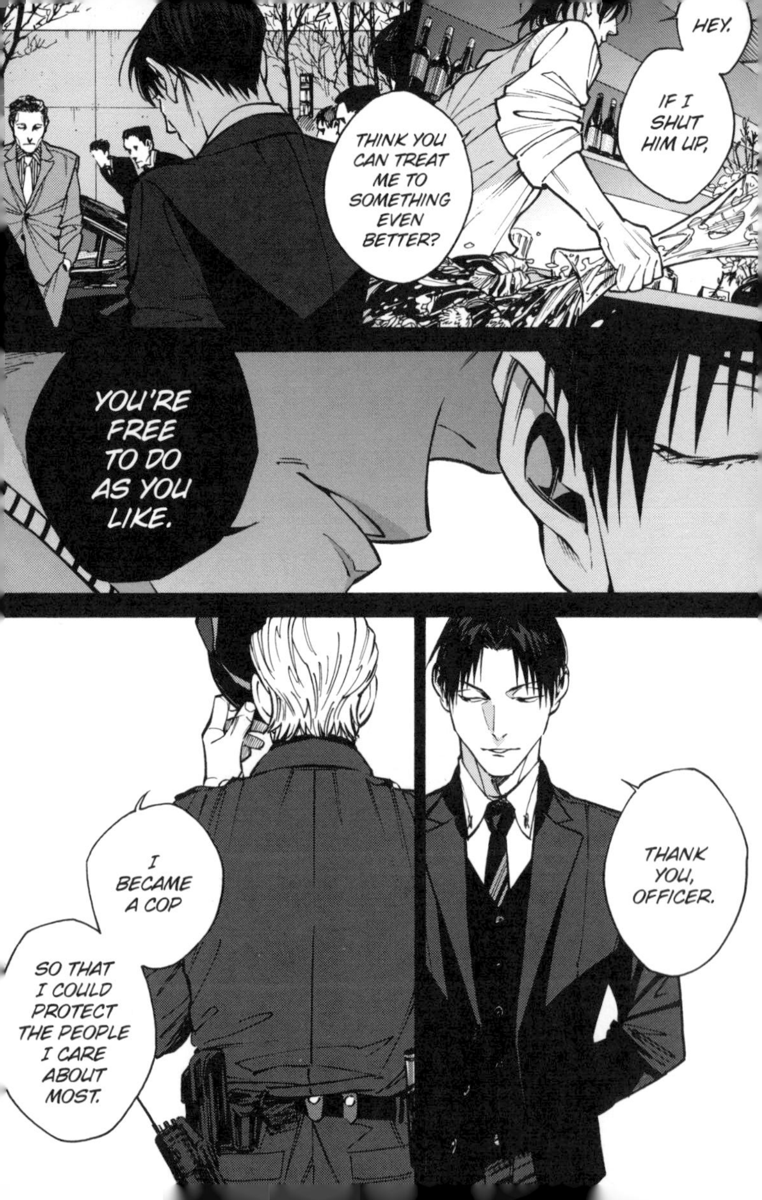
HEY.
IF I SHUT HIM UP,
THINK YOU CAN TREAT ME TO SOMETHING EVEN BETTER?
YOU'RE FREE TO DO AS YOU LIKE.
THANK YOU, OFFICER.
I BECAME A COP
SO THAT I COULD PROTECT THE PEOPLE I CARE ABOUT MOST.

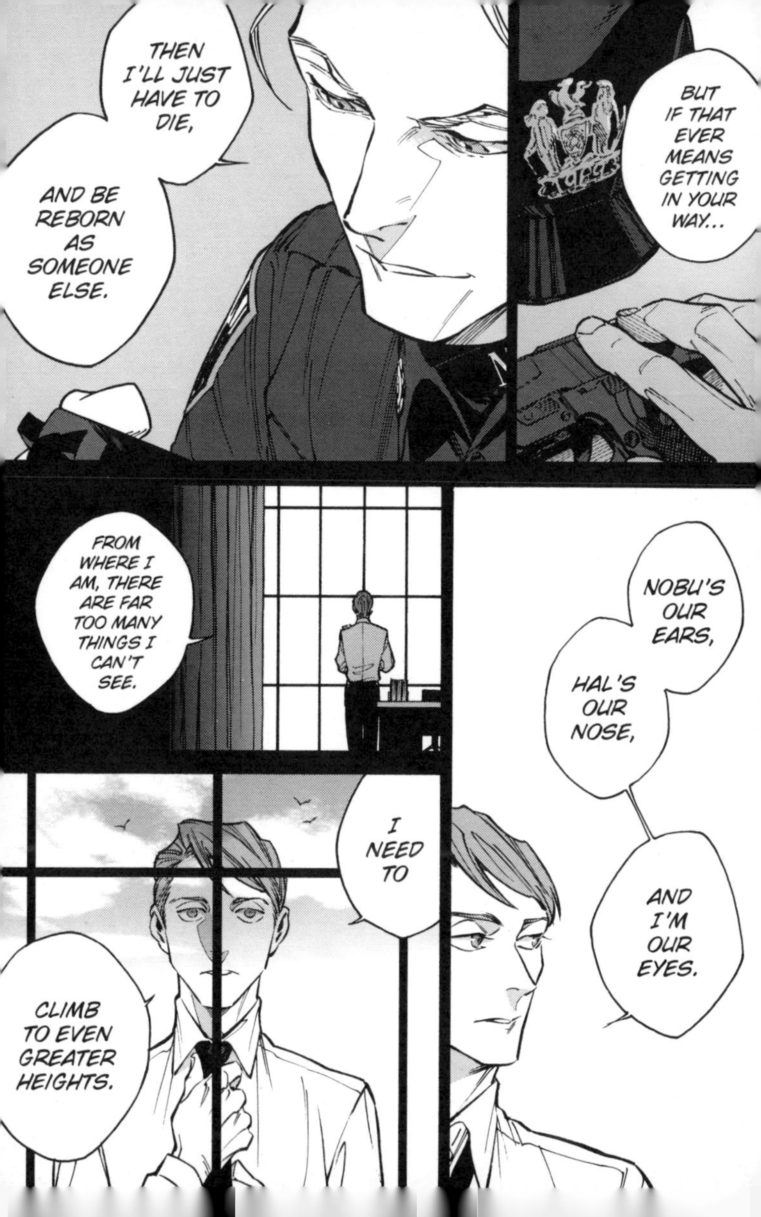
BUT IF THAT EVER MEANS GETTING IN YOUR WAY...
THEN I'LL JUST HAVE TO DIE,
AND BE REBORN AS SOMEONE ELSE.
NOBU'S OUR EARS,
HAL'S OUR NOSE,
AND I'M OUR EYES.
FROM WHERE I AM, THERE ARE FAR TOO MANY THINGS I CAN'T SEE.
I NEED TO
CLIMB TO EVEN GREATER HEIGHTS.

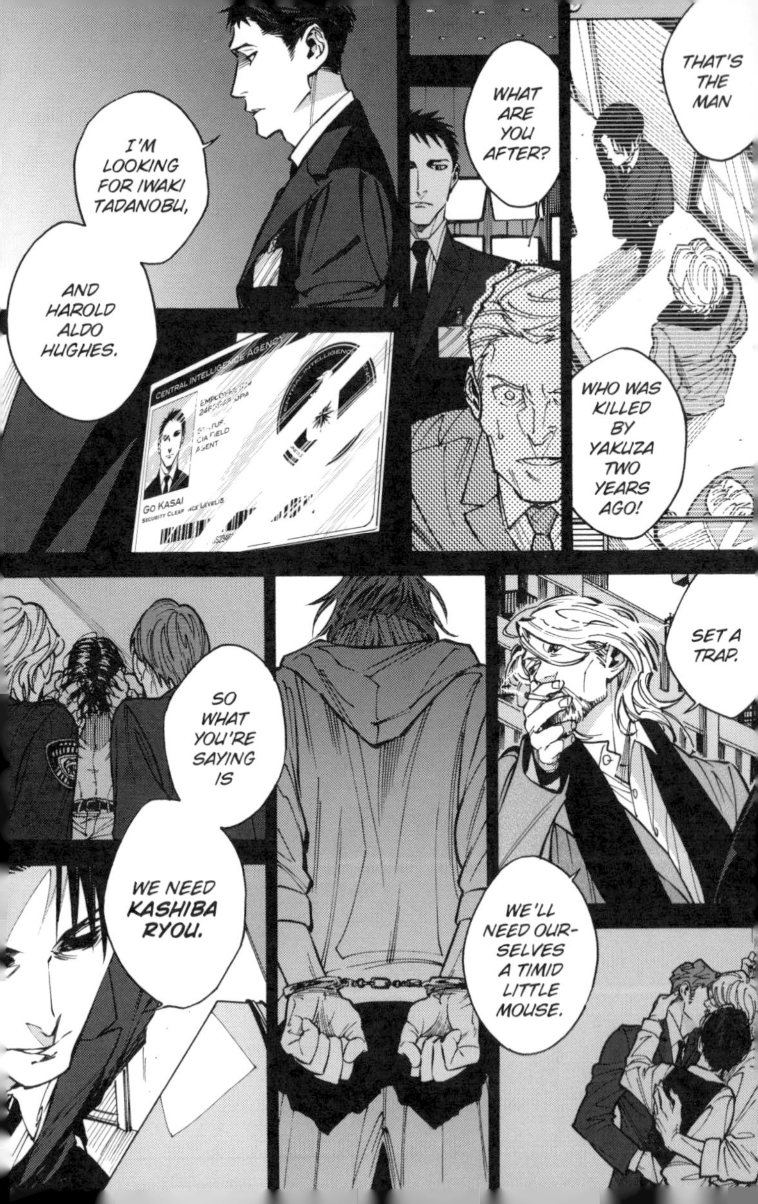
THAT'S THE MAN
WHO WAS KILLED BY YAKUZA TWO YEARS AGO!
WHAT ARE YOU AFTER?
I'M LOOKING FOR IWAKI TADANOBU,
AND HAROLD ALDO HUGHES.
CENTRAL INTELLIGENCE AGENCY
Go KASAI
SET A TRAP.
WE'LL NEED OURSELVES A TIMID LITTLE MOUSE.
SO WHAT YOU'RE SAYING IS
WE NEED **KASHIBA RYOU.**

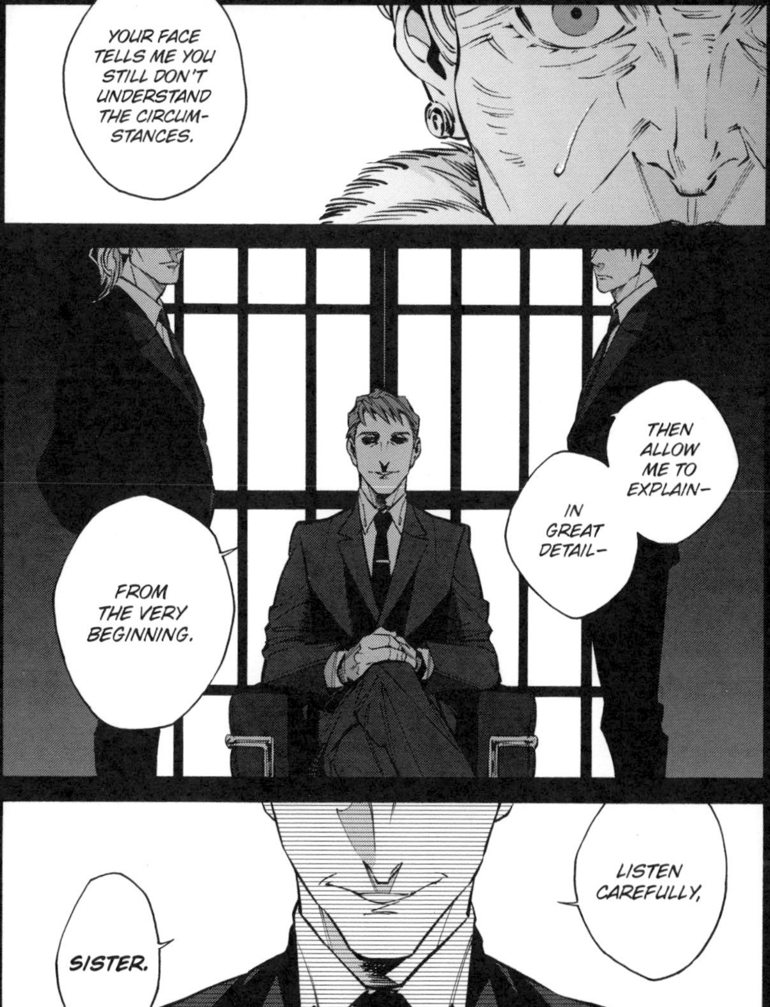
YOUR FACE TELLS ME YOU STILL DON'T UNDERSTAND THE CIRCUM-STANCES.
THEN ALLOW ME TO EXPLAIN-
IN GREAT DETAIL-
FROM THE VERY BEGINNING.
LISTEN CAREFULLY,
SISTER.

CANIS

-THE SPEAKER-

CANIS
-Dear Hatter-

Canis-Dear Hatter-#2
© ZAKK / TAKESHOBO 2021
First published in Japan in 2021
by Takeshobo Co., Ltd.
English translation rights arranged with
Takeshobo Co., Ltd. through
Tuttle-Mori Agency, Inc., Tokyo
English version published by DENPA, LLC.,
Portland, Oregon, 2022

PUBLISHING TEAM:

Translation:
Mike Wolfe

Proofreading:
Seanna Hundt

Lettering:
Andrea Donohue

Production:
Andrea Donohue,
Felix Schmid,
Eduardo Mánuel Chávez

☻KUMA

Printed in Hong Kong, China
ISBN-13: 978-1-63442-335-9